JUDGES AND JU
THE HISTORY
COMMON LAW ANL

CW01432354

In this collection of essays, leading legal historians address significant topics in the history of judges and judging, with comparisons not only between British, American and Commonwealth experience, but also with the judiciary in civil law countries. It is not the law itself, but the process of law-making in courts, that is the focus of inquiry. Contributors describe and analyse aspects of judicial activity, in the widest possible legal and social contexts, across two millennia. The essays cover English common law, continental customary law and *ius commune*, and aspects of the common law system in the British Empire. The volume is innovative in its approach to legal history. None of the essays offers straight doctrinal exegesis; none takes refuge in old-fashioned judicial biography. The volume is a selection of the best papers from the 18th British Legal History Conference.

PAUL BRAND is a Senior Research Fellow at All Souls College, Oxford and Professor of English Legal History in the Faculty of Law, University of Oxford.

JOSHUA GETZLER is a fellow and tutor at St Hugh's College, Oxford and Professor of Law in Legal History in the Faculty of Law, University of Oxford.

JUDGES AND JUDGING IN THE HISTORY OF THE COMMON LAW AND CIVIL LAW: FROM ANTIQUITY TO MODERN TIMES

Edited by

PAUL BRAND
All Souls College, Oxford

and

JOSHUA GETZLER
St Hugh's College, Oxford

CAMBRIDGE
UNIVERSITY PRESS

CAMBRIDGE
UNIVERSITY PRESS

University Printing House, Cambridge CB2 8BS, United Kingdom

Cambridge University Press is part of the University of Cambridge.

It furthers the University's mission by disseminating knowledge in the pursuit of
education, learning and research at the highest international levels of excellence.

www.cambridge.org
Information on this title: www.cambridge.org/9781107542549

© Cambridge University Press 2012

First published 2012
3rd printing 2013
First paperback edition 2015

A catalogue record for this publication is available from the British Library

Library of Congress Cataloguing in Publication data
Judges and judging in the history of the common law and civil law : from
antiquity to modern times / edited by Paul Brand and Joshua Getzler.
p.   cm.
Includes bibliographical references and index.
ISBN 978-1-107-01897-6 (hardback)
1. Judges – History   2. Judicial process – History.   3. Judicial review – History.
4. Courts – History.   I. Brand, Paul, 1946–   II. Getzler, Joshua.
K2146.J82   2012
347′.0109–dc23
2011037679

ISBN 978-1-107-018976 Hardback
ISBN 978-1-107-54254-9 Paperback

CONTENTS

PREFACE

More than 200 legal historians, from every corner of the globe, met in Oxford at the Eighteenth British Legal History Conference in early July 2007 to hear and present papers on the history of 'judges and judging'. A selection of the papers presented at the conference has now been revised and edited to form the chapters of this volume. Perhaps the theme of the conference and of this publication needs some initial explanation. The legal realists of the 1920s and 1930s rightly questioned the pre-eminence given to the study of decision-making in the courts in American legal education, and similar ideas have entered British and Commonwealth legal education in the past generation; the utterances of judges are not taken as the sum of, or even the core of, the law. But this is hardly news for legal historians. They have long been effortless, even naively unselfconscious, realists, always concerned to understand the making of the law within the context of its time, with due attention to the society in which law is embedded and the shifting mentalities of professionals and other players in the legal system. Legal historians have not tended to regard law as the process of technocratic development in courts of timeless truths. The chapters of this book bring to bear legal historical analysis of the highest order to describe aspects of judicial activity, in the widest possible legal and social contexts, across two millennia. The essays cover English common law, the Continental customary law and *ius commune*, and aspects of the common law system in the British Empire. It is noteworthy that just as none of the authors have offered traditional doctrinal exegesis, so none have taken refuge in the conventional limits of judicial biography.

The opening chapter by Paul Brand uses a variety of original sources to shed new light on the early development of the English common law judicial system. He discusses the revolutionary change which took place in later twelfth-century England: the creation of a new type of royal justice sitting as part of a group of justices in new royal courts whose authority derived from a direct relationship to the king who appointed them and to whom they gave an oath of faithful service and who granted them special authority to wield judicial power in each case where jurisdiction was exercised; who united in themselves the formerly separate roles of presiding in the court and making judgments there; and whose judgments were for the first time regularly recorded in writing. He then demonstrates, how over the course of the thirteenth century, the multiplication of available sources allows us to see in ever closer focus the ways in which judges judged in the new courts and their role in guiding the pleading of cases and in directing and questioning juries and in making judgments. He also shows how the new sources allow us to pierce the normal veil of collective judicial anonymity to glimpse the role of smaller groups of justices within courts and of the role of outsiders within the judicial process.

In his chapter David Seipp discusses the arguments about the nature of corporations made in a dozen reported cases heard between 1478 and 1482. He sees those arguments as belonging generically (in modern terms) to one of two camps: either a 'formalist' one (which sees corporations as wholly separate from the individuals who comprise them) or a 'realist' one (which pierces the veil of corporate identity to see and take account of the particular individuals who comprise them). He also looks at the possible intellectual roots of the 'formalist' position within theology and canon law and prior English politics and practice. He finds that individual serjeants and justices who participated in these cases were not, in general, consistent in the 'camp' to which they belonged from case to case, and notes that this suggests that neither group invested their own individual personalities or intellectual convictions in the performance of their professional duties.

Ian Williams's chapter looks at the development of a theory of precedent amongst English judges during the period from the sixteenth century up to the Civil War. He asks why judges by the mid seventeenth century had come to see reported case law as binding, whilst their predecessors a century earlier most emphatically did not. He suggests that the results of cases as shown on the record had long been regarded as having binding force, but not the reasoning by which judges had reached for those results. After all, reported *rationes* were often distorted or fabricated in contemporary or subsequent reporting. Matters changed as modern claims were brought in more informal guises, such as the actions on the case. Omnibus writs like these made the accompanying narrative of the claim into part of the court's reasons for giving or denying a remedy. This move to a freer narrative of facts helped the courts see the whole case as precedential, in contrast with the older law where counsel and judges were busy in debating how the pleading of stylised facts activated a particular form of action.

John Langbein writes on the slow dethronement of the jury in the civil justice procedures of the English common law. Far too slow for Langbein, who argues that the Continental procedure using a fact-finding judge with power to interrogate witnesses yielded a far more rational and accurate system of adjudication, since fact-trying lies at the core of any legal process and skilled lawyers are likely to do a better job at it than random samples of laymen. He examines the self-informing juries of the medieval common law and the lay fact-triers guided by the rules of evidence and judicial direction of later periods, and finds that the imperfections of the jury created many distortions in the giving of justice, such as arcane pleading rules and too great an emphasis on documentary evidence, notably sealed deeds. Chancery procedure was only a temporary palliative as adversarial fact-proving soon took over in that forum as well. A long battle to confine the jury with guiding laws had to be joined across the nineteenth and early twentieth centuries, until judges finally took control of fact as well as law. With newly powerful judges, a powerful appellate process was now finally installed. Langbein's puzzle is to explain why the example of Continental procedure did not provide a short-cut for the English as they slowly evolved a modern civil process.

Rebecca Probert gives the history of an important legal-historical mistake. In 1811 Sir William Scott made the confident assertion as judge of the London Consistory Court that, prior to the Clandestine Marriages Act of 1753, it had been possible for parties to marry by informal words of present consent. Probert shows that clandestine marriage historically denoted not secret marriage but a marriage cere-mony conducted before a celebrant who lacked full qualifications or who had not followed the correct canonical procedures. Probert traces the reasons for Scott's category mistake and how in later law this confusion of secrecy and validity distorted understanding of the nature of an act of marriage as a legal, a sacramental and a formal act. She also shows the crucial imperial dimensions of this mistake, as the law grappled with the application to a multi-faith empire of an antique marriage law based on the Anglican confession.

Michael Lobban paints on a broad canvas, interrogating the politics of the English judiciary in the high Victorian age, from the 1830s through to the 1880s. He shows how commercial pressures, the needs of litigants, and the Victorian yearning for rationalising reform, transformed the doc-trines and institutions of the law and gave us many of the elements of today's legal system. In a sophisticated treatment of the main judges, reformers and politicians of this era and the legal changes they worked through, Lobban suggests that politics played a role in judicial thinking, and that ideology often weighted *rationes* as much as it informed parliamentary statutes. But close attention to leading judges and their work suggests that the common law, even with statutory overlays, was becoming a technocratic exercise where strong political views were becoming largely irrelevant to the process of applying articulate legal doctrine to the facts of disputes. Lobban illustrates the complex dialectic of political values and judicial creativity by examining a wide gamut of legal problems, especially in the commercial economy.

Phil Handler's chapter suggests revisions to the view that English criminal justice moved across the nineteenth century from discretion to legal rigour. Despite the stream of modernising statutes formulated by utilitarian and humanitarian reformers, judges devoted to discretionary control of the criminal process were in fact highly successful in resisting the introduction of a rule-bound system. The application of the death penalty was successfully curbed despite strong support for this ultimate sanction amongst the judiciary, but strong discretion in prosecution, trial and sentencing continued outside the capital crimes. Handler uses evidence of how the judges engaged with Parliament and governmental commissions to show that the Victorian judiciary was a politically varied group, with Liberal and Conservative actors at both appellate and trial levels. What united them was the desire to maintain judicial freedom and power within the criminal justice system, and to that end the judges succeeded in colonising the legislative process and putting their stamp on many statutory enactments.

Chantal Stebbings peers under the Diceyan dogma of no special administrative courts in Britain, and demonstrates that in the tax field lay adjudicators appointed by the executive, whether amateur or professional, just about dominated the field. She investigates the specialist bureaucratic courts of excise and income tax appeals and the complex of appeal procedures, both legal and administrative, and shows how there was a strong impulse within government to resist full professional juridification of the tax assessment and appeal process. Partly this was to siphon off tax claims to specialist tribunals with strong expertise who could process the plethora of claims more surely and at less cost than conventional courts. Stebbings suggests that critics of administrative fiscal courts proved to be correct in their warnings that such adjudication could lack due independence from political and bureaucratic distortion, and that pragmatism sometimes triumphed over rule of law virtue.

The next group of chapters widens the geographical focus by looking at judges in classical Roman law, medieval Continental customary law and the later *ius commune*. Starting in an early period of classical Roman law, Ernest Metzger explains how the Roman procedure of trial before a lay judge endowed with fact-finding powers was regulated by quasi-delictual actions. These were claims that through incorrect use of powers something akin to a wrong had been committed which demanded a remedy. Metzger anatomises the Roman trial, showing how claimants sought a formula, joined issue, and then sought to transmogrify their claim into the remedial obligation specified in the formula. A judge who accepted a commission to test facts and decide the issue had a duty to do so properly, and if he mistook or fumbled or delayed then he was said to have 'made the cause his own', a form of bias or nullification of his role. Such a judge could be disciplined before a magistrate and sued personally to provide a surrogate remedy for the original claim. Using fresh archaeological evidence, Metzger suggests that these disciplinary actions were not a substitute process of appeal but a key means for magistrates to hold judges to their duty.

In his chapter Dirk Heirbaut looks at the makers and shapers of customary law in northern France, the Low Countries and Germany in the period from the twelfth to the early fourteenth century. He argues that in courts in these areas where there was normally a group of judges to make judgments it was the most expert member of this group who normally acted as the spokesman of the group in giving judgment but who had also normally played an important role in the prior debate which shaped the judgment agreed by the group. Evidence from the area around Lille *c*.1300 shows that these spokesmen were semi-professional legal experts, active also as legal advisers, presiding officers and as the lords in other courts; it also shows that the spokesmen kept their own brief unofficial reports of the cases in which they were involved. They were not university-educated lawyers nor were they influenced by the *ius commune*, but they were more than simply amateurs.

Ulrike Muessig's chapter provides a comparative overview of the 'superior courts' of early-modern France, England and the Holy Roman Empire, whose emergence can be viewed as part of the wider project of state-building in each of these political units. Despite the difficulties of comparison, she sees certain common themes emerging from the history of these courts: their encouragement of the development of professional lawyers and of law reporting and the tendency of some, if not all, of these courts over time to escape full monarchical control and indeed pose challenges to monarchical authority.

The functioning and jurisprudence of the eighteenth-century Supreme Court of Holland Zeeland are the concern of Boudewijn Sirks's chapter. His focus is on the unofficial notes of two leading judges of the court, Cornelis van Bijnkershoek and his son in law Willem Pauw, which were rediscovered in 1918 and published between 1923 and 2008. These cover 5,000 cases heard in the court between 1704 and 1787 and they show that judgments were reached in the court by majority vote but without members of the majority having to agree on the reasons for their decision. They also reveal that the university-educated judges of the court relied mainly on Roman law in making their judgments unless there was quite explicit local customary law to the contrary.

The final group of chapters, on legal themes from the British Empire, begins with Paul Halliday's study of the early-modern history of the writ of habeas corpus. Halliday concedes that more than most, he has to contend with a 'large presentist elephant in the room'. But his research was conceived and commenced well before the security crisis of 9/11 and the justice crisis of Guantanamo Bay. The technique of the paper is to reconstruct the intellectual parameters of the earlier habeas doctrine as 'mutual obligations binding subject to sovereign', with a strong emphasis on control of Crown powers rather than the rights of subjects. The 1679 Habeas Corpus Act is then re-characterised as no more than the codification of a vibrant practice of court control of the executive that was already in being. The chapter then examines in close detail little-known cases of prisoners of war and enemy aliens discovered in a plethora of primary sources, showing how key dimensions of the rule of law were developed by the judges during Britain's long imperial wars with its European rivals.

Martin Wiener shows how hard it could be for imperial judges to maintain the judicial rule of law in a colonial setting. He tells the story of how a Canadian barrister, Sir Henry Austin, was appointed as chief justice in the Bahamas in 1880, upsetting the local elites who wanted jobs for the boys. Austin tried to apply rule-of-law discipline to the colony, and tried two brothers for racially motivated and connected killings. The local whites angrily demanded the chief justice's recall, and the governor and law officers combined to force Austin out. When his successor as chief justice proved to be a zealous campaigner against local corruption he too was destroyed, partly through effective lobbying of influential politicians in England. Wiener wryly observes that in the law at least this was a case of the periphery controlling the centre.

Susan Priest narrates the extraordinary episode of the High Court of Australia's 'strike' of 1905, when the judges refused to hear cases in protest against the Commonwealth Attorney-General's attempts to constrain the new court's costs. The judges of the High Court saw their circuits to the far-flung states of the newly founded federation of Australia as a basic principle of the court's work, and refused to accept the dictates of the executive as to how to conceive their jurisdiction and procedure. This squall can be seen as an important step in establishing the prestige and independence of the new court as a notable forum of the common law world.

The final chapter by David Williams tells of five judges in New Zealand who grappled with the definition of native title from the middle of the nineteenth century until the Great War. He argues that native title was not the common law doctrine invented or discovered in late twentieth-century courts; rather it was a dynamic doctrine of the mid eighteenth century, born of a mixture of American constitutional creativity, international law norms and British imperial policy. This meant that extinguishment of a common law native title was unknown in an earlier period. The law was really founded on a balance of politics, as expressed in legislation and treaties, and juridification of the native rights debate came much later. Whether Williams' careful historical analysis will shift the agonised modern native title discourse into new paths will have to be seen.

The editors are grateful for the patience and co-operation of the contributors as the book wended its way to press. Material help for the success of the project was provided by Cambridge University Press, the Journal of Legal History, Oxford University Press, the Oxford Law Faculty, All Souls College, St Hugh's College and St Catherine's College where the original conference was held. Our colleague Michael Macnair helped plan the conference and advise us on elements of the book, and our colleague Boudewijn Sirks also gave us wise counsels. Tariq Baloch, Freya El Baz and Adam Turner deserve our warmest thanks for their help in planning and executing the conference, as does Eesvan Krishnan for his skilled contribution to the final editing of this book.

Joshua Getzler and
Paul Brand

CONTRIBUTORS

PAUL BRAND

Professor of English Legal History, University of Oxford and Senior Research Fellow, All Souls College, Oxford.

PAUL D. HALLIDAY

Professor, Corcoran Department of History, University of Virginia.

PHIL HANDLER

Lecturer, School of Law, University of Manchester.

DIRK HEIRBAUT

Professor, Department of Jurisprudence and Legal History, University of Ghent.

JOHN H. LANGBEIN

Sterling Professor of Law and Legal History, Yale University.

MICHAEL LOBBAN

Professor of Legal History, Queen Mary, University of London.

ERNEST METZGER

Douglas Professor of Civil Law, School of Law, University of Glasgow.

ULRIKE MUESSIG

Chair of Civil Law and German and European Legal History, Faculty of Law, University of Passau.

SUSAN PRIEST

Assistant Professor, Faculty of Law, University of Canberra.

REBECCA PROBERT
Professor, School of Law, University of Warwick.

DAVID J. SEIPP
Professor of Law and Law Alumni Scholar, School of Law, Boston University.

A. J. B. SIRKS
Regius Professor of Civil Law, Faculty of Law, University of Oxford and Fellow of All Souls College, Oxford.

CHANTAL STEBBINGS
Professor of Law and Legal History, University of Exeter.

MARTIN J. WIENER
Mary Gibbs Jones Professor of History, Rice University, Houston, Texas.

DAVID V. WILLIAMS
Professor, Faculty of Law, University of Auckland.

IAN WILLIAMS
Lecturer, Faculty of Laws, University College London.

I

Common law

1

Judges and judging 1176–1307

PAUL BRAND

I

In January 1176 King Henry II held a meeting of his great council at Northampton.[1] A decision was taken there to divide England into six judicial circuits, and the king appointed three justices to serve on each circuit. The chronicler who tells us of this then gives part of the instructions drawn up for them. Specific criminal justice responsibilities were assigned to them. They were to 'execute the assize on wicked thieves and malefactors of the land'. This meant making enquiries through local presentment juries about those reputed to have committed certain criminal offences. They were also told what to do both when those accused appeared to stand trial and also when they failed to appear. Specific responsibilities were also assigned to them in regard to civil justice. They were to enquire into complaints from heirs whose fathers had died in seisin of land but whose lords had refused to admit them to the succession and they were, if necessary, to remedy this by securing the heirs' admission. They were also to take jury verdicts on disseisins made contrary to 'the assize' (*super assisam*) since May 1175. There is no mention of the king's writ being required to provide specific authorisation for the hearing of individual cases of either of these two types. Perhaps we should envisage the justices acting without it, simply on the basis of the general authorisation and on the basis of oral complaints. A separate clause talked of the justices doing 'all justice and right' (*omnes justicias et rectitudines*) belonging to the lord king and his crown for (holdings of) half a knight's fee or less by the writ of the lord king or his representatives. This seems to refer to more general land litigation of the kind brought by the writ of right or writ *precipe* but limited their

---

[1] *Gesta Regis Henrici Secundi Benedicti abbatis*, ed. W. Stubbs, Roll Series, 2 vols. (1867), I, pp. 107–8.

jurisdiction to smaller holdings. The justices were further entrusted with making enquiries into a variety of other matters of interest to the king such as his escheats, churches and lands, women who (or whose marriages) were in his gift and (who owed) castle-guard. They were also to take fealties to the king from all the king's subjects and to arrest anyone refusing and to ensure that all unlicensed castles were properly destroyed. After their nomination, the king had each of the justices swear an oath on the gospels that they 'would keep the assizes that had been made and have them observed by all the men of the realm'. A second chronicler mentions a more general oath to 'do justice' to all.[2] The Pipe Rolls of 22 Henry II (1175–6) and 23 Henry II (1176–7) both record financial information arising out of the work of the six circuits thus established on a county-by-county basis. This confirms that the justices did indeed visit most, if not all, of the counties allotted to their circuits and also tells us something of the business they dealt with. There are also seven surviving final concords made before the same justices, recording the settlement of civil litigation heard before them. Their dates fall between mid March and late September 1176. One circuit accounts for three of the concords, a second for two, and two others for one each.[3]

It is from 1176 that we can trace the beginnings of the General Eyre as an institution within the English judicial system. Thereafter teams of justices appointed by the king brought royal civil and criminal justice to each of the counties of England within a limited period every two or three years by holding sessions in each of the counties assigned to their circuits. Later Eyre visitations, however, varied both as to the number of circuits covering the country (anywhere between two and five), and the number of justices assigned to each circuit (anywhere between three and nine).[4] It is also arguable that 1176 marks the first clear appearance of the type of royal justice characteristic of royal courts in the later Middle Ages: justices who brought to the courts in which they sat an authority derived from their own direct relationship with the king. They were appointed by the king, perhaps orally, at Northampton; they took an oath to serve the king faithfully; and they exercised only such

---

[2] *Radulphi de Diceto, Opera Historica*, ed. W. Stubbs, Roll Series, 2 vols. (1876), I, p. 404.

[3] *Pleas before the King or his Justices, 1198–1212, III*, ed. D. M. Stenton, Selden Society, vol. 83 (London, 1966), pp. lvii–lviii; The National Archives, London [TNA] PRO C 260/186, no. 1C.

[4] P. Brand, *The Making of the Common Law* (London, 1992), p. 84.

jurisdiction as they had been specifically granted by the king, either through written instructions given at the council or by royal writs. In essence, therefore, they exercised only such jurisdiction as had been delegated to them in writing by the king. Their sessions could therefore be, and were, described as sessions of the king's court (*curia regis*). The justices also united in themselves the two formerly separate, and clearly distinct, roles: of presiding officers in their court and judgment-makers of the court. Before this, sessions held by royal justices in the localities under earlier Norman kings (and perhaps in the earlier part of Henry II's reign as well) had been considered only as special sessions of the county court or courts concerned, and the usual judgment-makers of the county courts made judgments at those sessions, the royal justices only presiding.[5] In this new form of court, where the king's justice was dispensed by his appointees, the final characteristic is also a novelty, in England at least: that all of their judicial activity was recorded in writing. When the king asked for information on a variety of matters he clearly expected to receive it in written form. The *Dialogue of the Exchequer*, written c.1179, seems to presuppose the existence of a written record of other business at the Eyre, too, from which financial dues owed to the king could be extracted. It therefore seems likely that fairly complete written records of the Eyre were being made from 1176 onwards, although initially no care was taken to ensure that they were preserved in the king's Treasury and thus the earliest surviving plea rolls of itinerant justices date only from 1194.[6]

By 1176 there was also a second royal court in which civil litigation was regularly being heard. This was the 'king's court at Westminster', whose personnel seem to have been interchangeable with that of the Exchequer, the institution responsible for English financial administration. In effect, a single body exercised both financial and judicial responsibilities, the judicial ones only on an irregular basis from the mid 1160s but regularly from the mid 1170s through to the mid 1190s.[7] The main source of information on its judicial functions is the final concords made there and preserved or copied by the parties involved. These may well represent a relatively small proportion of the concords made there; nor is there any way of estimating the total volume of litigation that came to the court. In these concords the personnel are sometimes described as 'justices', sometimes as 'barons' (the later term for the main officials of the Exchequer), and the same individuals clearly exercised both judicial

[5] *Ibid.*, pp. 80-2.   [6] *Ibid.*, p. 95.   [7] *Ibid.*, pp. 86-9.

and financial roles. The references in the final concords to 'justices' or 'barons' of the lord king and to them constituting the 'king's court' also indicate that they were appointed by the king for this purpose (or these purposes).[8] The earliest specific reference to a royal writ being used to initiate litigation in the court comes only from 1178,[9] but it seems likely that specific authorisation had always been needed. The justices probably also swore an oath to the king. The king's court at Westminster, as it can be seen in the final concords, varied in size, consisting of between three and fourteen justices, with an average of around eight. The exclusion of the treasurer (the main official of the Exchequer) from a third of the concords suggests that those named in the concord owed their place to actual participation in the hearing of the specific case concerned. It is a large court by later English standards. It also seems clear that these men both presided and made judgments in the court. There are no surviving plea rolls from this court before the mid 1190s, but copies of individual entries which do survive take the compilation of plea rolls back to 1181. In 1200 it was believed that plea rolls had been compiled during the period Richard de Lucy was the king's justiciar, prior to 1178.[10] The proceedings of this court, too, were therefore probably recorded in writing from at least the mid 1170s.

II

In the mid 1190s the Common Bench separated out from the Exchequer and became a distinct institution and its justices became exclusively royal justices.[11] There is also a significant change in the surviving evidence for judicial activity. In the summer of 1195, both the Common Bench and Eyres began to make a third, official copy (the 'foot') of every final concord made in these courts and these feet were subsequently deposited in the Treasury. Most, but not all, survive.[12] From 1194 come the first surviving plea rolls recording cases heard before the royal justices of the Common Bench and the Eyre. For the next three-quarters of a century the survival rate of plea rolls remains patchy, but the rolls that do exist make it possible to see

---

[8] *Dialogus de Scaccario*, ed. C. Johnson (London, 1950), p. 70.

[9] *Bracton's Note-Book*, ed. F. W. Maitland (Cambridge, 1887), p. 1095.

[10] Brand, *Making of the Common Law*, p. 95.

[11] P. Brand, *The Origins of the English Legal Profession* (Oxford, 1992), p. 22 and n. 47.

[12] For evidence of the losses of Eyre feet of fines see D. Crook, *Records of the General Eyre*, Public Record Office, Record Handbooks (London, 1982), XX, pp. 8–9.

something of the volume and nature of the business of those courts, if only in summary form.

One other significant change took place later: the emergence of a third permanent royal court, the court of King's Bench, which travelled round England in close proximity to the king. Such a court had existed intermittently during Henry II's reign while the king was in England, and also for periods in John's reign, but as a continuously functioning institution which existed even when the king was a minor or out of the country, it dates only from the mid 1230s. It is also only from then that the court began to develop its own distinctive jurisdiction.[13]

The earliest surviving record of letters of appointment of justices in Eyre comes from 1218, when copies of the instruments appointing them to itinerate 'for the business of the king and kingdom' and notifying the relevant counties of their appointment were enrolled on the Patent and Close Rolls.[14] Thereafter such appointments were commonly, but not invariably, enrolled in this way.[15] The earliest surviving copy of any of the instruments associated with the appointment of a justice of the Common Bench comes from 1234,[16] but only seven further appointments were enrolled between 1234 and 1272.[17] Although all those appointed were described as 'justices' the formula for what they were appointed to do varied considerably and no standard form emerged. No letters of appointment are enrolled for the justices of King's Bench. It is possible that the very closeness of the relationship between the king and King's Bench rendered written appointment unnecessary.[18]

An oath to the king was probably taken by all royal justices on taking up office. There are references to a 'form of oath' (*forma sacramenti*) being given to the senior justices of each of the Eyre circuits in 1218, but no record of what it contained.[19] *Bracton* gives us an undated version of the oath taken by a justice in Eyre. This contained a threefold promise: 'to do right justice, according to his ability, in the counties where they are to hold the Eyre, to both rich and poor', to 'keep the assize in accordance with the chapters below written' and 'to perform all duties and exercise all jurisdiction

---

[13] Brand, *Making of the Common Law*, p. 24.

[14] *Patent Rolls 1216–25*, pp. 206–8; *Rotuli Litterarum Clausarum*, I, 380b.

[15] Crook, *Records of the General Eyre*, pp. 5–7.   [16] *Close Rolls 1231–4*, p. 565.

[17] *Close Rolls 1231–4*, pp. 445, 570; *Close Rolls 1234–7*, p. 348; *Close Rolls 1251–3*, p. 249; *Close Rolls 1254–6*, p. 268; *Close Rolls 1256–9*, p. 47; TNA PRO, C 66/72, m. 2 and C 66/89, m. 17.

[18] As suggested by Sayles in *Select Cases in the Court of King's Bench*, IV, Selden Society, vol. 74 (London, 1957), p. xi.

[19] *Patent Rolls 1216–25*, pp. 206–8; *Rotuli Litterarum Clausarum*, I, 380b.

belonging to the king's crown'.[20] Letters relating to the appointment of
three justices of the Common Bench in 1234 envisaged them taking an oath
in the presence of the existing justices 'to (faithfully) attend to the king's
business in the Bench' with those justices.[21] The oath may well have been
more elaborate than that. We know nothing of the oath of office taken by
the justices of King's Bench.

The justices of the king's courts continued in principle to exercise
jurisdiction only by specific delegation from the king. The Common
Bench provides the clearest and simplest case. Its justices required a written
authorisation through a royal writ for any case they heard and this had to
match exactly the claim that the demandant was trying to make or the
complaint that he wanted remedied.[22] The same seems also to be true of
King's Bench. The General Eyre is more complicated. Civil pleas business
reached the Eyre in the main via three different routes. Some civil pleas at
the Eyre were initiated by royal writs which required the sheriff to summon
the defendant (and sometimes also the requisite jurors) to appear before the
king's justices at their first session (*ad primam assisam*) when they came to
the county. Other pleas had been initiated by royal writ in the county court
but been removed into the Eyre by the writ *pone*. Both provided specific
authorisation for the Eyre justices to hear the case. The third kind of case,
however, was one pending in the Common Bench at Westminster when the
Eyre was summoned. From at least 1194 onward all cases from the county
were automatically adjourned into the Eyre by a general proclamation made
in the Common Bench.[23] For these the sole authorisation was the relevant
writ and proclamation plus the form of writ of summons for the Eyre.
Criminal pleas were brought before the Eyre mainly under a single part of
the instructions to the justices which ordered them to enquire from local
presentment juries as to 'pleas of the crown both old and new and all which
had not yet been determined before the king's justices'. There was also a
specific reference to pleas of the crown in the writ of summons to the Eyre.
The third element was the enquiries made under the articles of the Eyre. The

---

[20] *Bracton*, ed. G. E. Woodbine and tr. S.E. Thorne, 4 vols. (Cambridge: MA, 1968–77), II,
p. 309.
[21] *Close Rolls 1231–4*, pp. 445, 565, 570.
[22] Hence the relatively common form of exception to any variation between writ and
count. For two early examples see *Rotuli Curie Regis*, II, pp. 39, 95.
[23] *Chronica Rogeri de Hovedene*, ed. W. Stubbs, Roll Series, 4 vols. (1868–71), III, p. 262.

arrangements recorded in 1218 show that the articles (*capituli*) were handed over at the beginning of an Eyre circuit to the chief justices of each circuit.[24] The private treatise *Judicium Essoniorum* indicates that it was the chancellor who handed them over under seal in London. We have the set of enquiries from 1194 and a number of copies of subsequent sets. These show the list of questions put to the juries steadily growing over the period down to 1272.[25] What also becomes clear once we have a record of the Eyres themselves is that, although some of the questions were intended simply to produce information, many were intended to produce actionable information and it was for the Eyre justices themselves to take that action.

We now also begin to get glimpses of what justices actually did after their appointment. In civil pleas, a significant part of their time seems to have been spent on procedural matters: authorising the next stage of mesne process against absent defendants or the holding of a view of the land claimed, adjudging the essoins (excuses for absence) of litigants and the like. Once plea rolls begin to survive they commonly record the appearance of the plaintiff and then the court's judgment (*judicium*) that the local sheriff employ the next stage of process against the absent defendant. *Glanvill* suggests that the appearances in court on the three days preceding the day on which judgment was given on a default were also appearances 'before the justices'.[26] The justices were also responsible for issuing the judicial writs to local sheriffs ordering the next stage of process. In the first surviving set of judicial writs from the summer of 1199, which are all in the name of the justiciar, Geoffrey fitzPeter, who presided in the Common Bench, the attestations are in the names of either Richard of Herriard (regularly placed fourth in precedence out of six in final concords made in the court) or Simon of Pattishall (regularly placed fifth).[27] It seems likely that these two justices were individually responsible for checking that the writ written by one of the clerks associated with the court was indeed warranted by the record of the court's judgment as recorded on the plea roll. *Hengham Magna* of *c.*1260 tells us of the part played by the keeper of writs and rolls (*prenotarius*) in the receipt of essoins but also tells us that the

---

[24] *Patent Rolls 1216–25*, pp. 206–8.

[25] H. Cam, *Studies in the Hundred Rolls: Some aspects of thirteenth century administration*, Oxford Studies in Social and Legal History (Oxford, 1921), VI; *Crown Pleas of the Wiltshire Eyre, 1249*, ed. C. A. F. Meekings, Wiltshire Archaeological and Natural History Society, Records Branch (Devizes, 1960), XVI, pp. 27–45.

[26] *Glanvill*, ed. G. D. G. Hall (London, 1965), I, ch. 7, pp. 5–6.

[27] *Pleas before the King or his Justices, 1198–1202, I*, ed. D. M. Stenton, Selden Society, vol. 67 (London, 1953), pp. 350–418.

judgment of essoins normally required the checking of the related writs and the stage the case had reached and that 'the justices' normally did this.[28]

Of the part played by justices in the pleading of civil cases there is little evidence before the earliest law reports which come from the later years of Henry III's reign. In a 1203 case, however, we begin to see how the justices might intervene. Osbert son of Alexander claimed two hides given as a marriage portion to his mother and then held by his parents but gaged by his father after his mother's death to the current tenant, Alan.[29] Alan denied that Alexander had gaged the land to him or that he held the land in gage. He did not deny that the land had been the marriage portion of Alexander's mother. When Alan was subsequently asked (*interrogatus*) through whom he had acquired title to the land he said it had been through his own father, Philip. That question must have come from one of the court's justices. A clearer picture of judicial activity in the course of pleading emerges from the pleading manual, *Brevia Placitata*. This was compiled probably in the later 1250s, and almost certainly reflects what was happening in courtrooms in this period, and perhaps much earlier. Some of the judicial interventions were purely formal prompts. When, for example, a defendant explained why he should not have to respond in a claim for customs and services, the justice did no more than prompt the plaintiff to respond by asking him, 'John, do you know anything to be said against what he has said?'[30] But the justice's question might do more than that by pushing the party for further clarification. In a land action the tenant had pleaded that he was not obliged to answer a claim because the claimant was 'not such a one that any inheritance ought to descend to him'. The justice then pressed him by asking, 'Who is he now? You say and we will give judgment.' The tenant then explained that the claimant was a bastard who had been born before his mother's marriage.[31] We also see here examples of what are perhaps best classified as judicial rulings. In an annual rent case the defendant pleaded a quitclaim. The plaintiff noted the deed was unsealed and therefore void and asked for judgment. The defendant said it had been handed over to third parties in lieu of sealing since the plaintiff said he did not have his seal with him. The justice did not rule directly on

---

[28] *Radulphi de Hengham Summae*, ed. W. H. Dunham Jr (Cambridge, 1932), pp. 15–16.

[29] *Curia Regis Rolls*, II, 240.

[30] *Brevia Placitata*, ed. G. J. Turner and T. F. T. Plucknett, Selden Society, vol 66 (London, 1951), p. 56.

[31] *Brevia Placitata*, pp. 7–8.

the validity of the deed but warned the plaintiff that 'it is necessary that you put yourself on a jury [as to the validity of the deed] or you will lose your claim in perpetuity'.[32]

They seem also to have played at least a formal role in decisions about appropriate modes of proof and in the formal preliminaries to their acceptance by the court. In a 1220 writ of right case the claimant produced a champion, who initially offered to prove the seisin of the claimant's wife's grandfather in the reign of Henry II as of his own view. The tenant objected that the champion could hardly have witnessed the seisin he was now offering to prove. The champion then shifted his ground, saying that he was offering to prove what his father, not himself, had witnessed. The justices allowed battle to proceed, explaining that the champion could in this way claim to be a witness to the time of King Henry II.[33]

The proof stage of litigation was normally a separate stage in time in all except the petty assizes. *Bracton* has most to tell us about the latter, specifically about the assize of novel disseisin. The author did not think it proper for the presiding justice or justices to say anything much 'for the instruction of the jurors' (*ad instruccionem juratorum*) after they had been sworn, unless the defendant has said something to stay the assize on which their verdict was being sought.[34] He did, however, advocate the justice taking an active role prior to the jury being sworn in establishing the precise nature of what was being claimed, for example the plaintiff's own title to the land and the nature of his estate in it. The justice(s) ought then to ask the defendant if he knew any reason why the assize should stand over. *Bracton* also envisaged a potentially active role for the justice(s) when the jurors gave their verdict. The judge was responsible for giving a just judgment on the basis of their verdict. He therefore needed to examine the actions and words of the jurors and to compel them to elucidate any obscurities in what they said, so that he was in a position to proceed securely to judgment. The power of judgment in the assize might look as if it belonged to the jurors since judgment was in accordance with their verdict, but it was only the facts ('the truth') that were the province of the jury; justice and judgment were matters for the judge.[35] *Bracton* commented similarly on the active role that a justice should take in certain other limited circumstances in instructing jurors but only 'as much as is licit for him'.[36] When taking the verdict of an attaint jury, jurors should not be allowed to give a blank verdict affirming

---

[32] *Ibid.*, p. 112. [33] *Curia Regis Rolls*, IX, p. 120. [34] *Bracton*, III, p. 72.
[35] *Ibid.*, pp. 68–70, 72–5. [36] *Ibid.*, p. 210.

or quashing a prior verdict, but should be required to support their verdict with reasons and presumptions and to be diligently examined by the justices.[37] There is indeed some direct evidence for the justices taking an active role when receiving jury verdicts. In the 1227 Kent Eyre a grand assize jury was taken before the Archbishop of Canterbury's bailiffs but in the presence of the justices of the Eyre. The clerk carefully recorded not just the verdict for the tenant but also that the jury had shown sufficient reasons for it (*et sufficientes ostendunt raciones*).[38] The enrolment is probably recording the normal practice and expectation in all grand assize verdicts: that a justification would be given for the otherwise blank verdict, although the latter is all that normally gets recorded. Its importance is that it also provides something on which the jurors could be questioned by the justices, who could thereby help to shape that verdict. In the 1261 Northamptonshire Eyre an assize of darrein presentment was sued in the king's name as guardian of an heir. The jury gave a verdict explaining how the advowson had apparently passed to the defendants. They were then asked (evidently by the justices) if it was true that the heir's grandfather had presented as 'true patron' to the living. They not only confirmed this but explained how they knew this to be the case. They were then asked if they had ever seen a supposed charter of the heir's grandmother made after her husband's death granting the advowson. They confirmed they had not seen the charter and knew nothing of it except what they had been told. The defendants were given a chance to show the charter but refused. Judgment was then given for the king.[39] The case was recorded in detail no doubt because of the king's interest, but may well reflect general practice.

There is less we can learn about the functions of the justices in criminal business. We learn in passing from *Bracton* that the author thought it proper, when a justice received an indictment whose truth he doubted, for him to make further enquiries about how the jurors had learned about the matter, and that he even thought it possible for the justice to examine each of the jurors separately, if necessary.[40] More can be learned from a record of the 1244 London Eyre drawn up for the city itself. This shows the justices of the Eyre following up a rather blank presentment of a death with a further secret examination of two neighbours which revealed that others (not named in the presentment) had been in the house at the time of the

---

[37] *Ibid.*, p. 345.   [38] TNA PRO, JUST 1/358, m. 10.   [39] TNA PRO, JUST 1/616, m. 1.
[40] *Bracton*, II, pp. 403–4, 405–6.

death. It also shows the justices questioning the chamberlain (who acted as the city's coroner) about a child born dead after an attack on its mother. This revealed the additional information that he had seen the child with its head crushed and its left arms broken in two places and its body black from beating.[41] There is also an interesting record of the pleading in a case brought at the Eyre before the justices for crown pleas. The justices upheld the plaintiff's complaint of unlawful imprisonment against one of the sheriffs and said that equity (*equitas judicii*) required that he stay in prison for as long as he had unjustly imprisoned the complainant. The entry ends with what was evidently a single justice speaking on behalf of the court: 'For the honour of the city I concede that John [the sheriff] be now immediately imprisoned, but handed over to you on bail till I have spoken with the king.'[42]

It is during this period that we first get something looking like a clear statement of the principle that a royal court should never comprise fewer than two justices, complete with its rationale. A 1221 mandate to the justiciar of Ireland reproved him for the fact that there was only a single itinerant justice in Ireland 'which significantly departs from the custom of our realm of England, in which there are always several itinerant justices because only one justice itinerant does not customarily bear record and because there is danger in having only one roll and this is avoided by having several justices, since each has his own roll'.[43] Although stated as a rule about itinerant justices the same principle clearly also applied to the Common Bench. In England, the Eyre circuits (redrawn for each visitation) continued after 1189 to be staffed by a significantly larger number of justices than this. The average number of justices assigned to each circuit between 1189 and 1272 ranged between a minimum of four and a maximum of six.[44] In the late twelfth and early thirteenth century some Eyres (and even some circuits) still had as many as eight or nine justices assigned to them, but by the end of Henry III's reign the largest single complement of justices assigned to an Eyre was six.[45] The Common Bench also remained a multi-justice court, though with a gradual decline in the average number of justices assigned to it from seven during Richard I's reign to an average of just three for the decade 1250–60 and again for the period 1261–72. For a significant number of terms during these last two periods the nominal complement

---

[41] *London Eyre of 1244*, no. 157.   [42] *London Eyre of 1244*, no. 345.
[43] *Rot. Litt. Claus*, I, 451.   [44] Brand, *Origins of the English Legal Profession*, p. 21.
[45] Crook, *Records of the General Eyre*.

of the court was reduced further, to the minimum number of two.[46] For periods in Henry III's reign King's Bench seems to have had no more than a single full-time justice and its normal complement in Henry III's reign did not exceed two. However, it seems likely that this single justice never sat alone, for the stewards of the royal household seem also to have sat in the court as and when required.[47]

A small amount of evidence from this same period allows us to pierce the normal screen of collegial activity to see individual justices or groups of justices at work in the courts. A detailed account of litigation between the abbot of Crowland and the prior of Spalding and his superior, the abbot of St Nicholas Angers, about marshland adjacent to Crowland shows that when the abbot of Crowland was called to the Exchequer in 1192 it was Robert of Wheatfield (one of the court's more junior justices) who took the lead in asking for the four knights who had been sent to see whether his illness was such as to confine him to bed; Robert, too, who pronounced judgment that the abbot should lose seisin, but not forfeit all right in the marsh.[48] In a renewal of the case in Michaelmas term 1194 a yet more junior justice (Richard of Herriard) spoke up in the discussion between the justices that preceded judgment. He was able to reverse the judgment which the most senior of his colleagues (Archbishop Hubert Walter) had been intending to give.[49] When the case was renewed in the Common Bench in Michaelmas term 1202 it was Simon of Pattishall (again one of the more junior justices) who adjourned the case on the grounds that many of his fellow justices were absent from the court because Advent was being celebrated and this was the only case pending.[50] In Michelmas term 1266 an enrolment in the Common Bench shows that even a nominal complement of three justices might not always be relied upon. The king had ordered the justices to levy a particular final concord. Only Gilbert of Preston was present in court. Both his colleagues (William Bonquer and John de la Lynde) were overseas. Since it was hoped they would return before Hilary the business was adjourned till then.[51] Yet the surviving roll of the court's business in this same term shows that the court did continue to transact its ordinary business with only a single justice present.

---

[46] Brand, *Origins of the English Legal Profession*, p. 25. Only two justices are recorded as sitting in the court by the final concords made in T1251, T and M1255, H and E1256, E and T 1258, H1261, T1263, M1265, H1266, H, T, M1267, M1270.

[47] Brand, *Origins of the English Legal Profession*, p. 25.

[48] D. M. Stenton, *English Justice between the Norman Conquest and the Great Charter, 1066–1215* (Philadelphia, 1964), pp. 170, 172.

[49] *Ibid.*, pp. 182, 184.   [50] *Ibid.*, p. 195.   [51] TNA PRO, KB 26/176, m. 33d.

As for the Eyre, there is, as has long been known, the first evidence towards the end of this period to show the justices of the Eyre dividing into separate groups to do different types of business simultaneously. Four justices were appointed to the 1253 Rutland Eyre. An almost contemporary official reference shows that two of them heard pleas of the crown in the grange of Oakham castle while the other two heard the civil pleas of the county in the hall of the castle.[52] Rutland was the smallest English county and can have posed few problems for justices wanting to deal with all its cases in the time available. If they divided into separate groups for Rutland they must also have been doing this in other counties as well by 1253, and perhaps for long before. If there were more justices allocated to an Eyre they may well have split into more than two groups. That Eyre justices by 1272 might sometimes sit on their own is suggested by evidence from the 1271 Kent Eyre.[53] A litigant claimed he had been adjourned to Westminster by one of the four justices of the Eyre 'who then sat alone on the bench' and put himself on his 'record'. When he appeared, Hengham denied that he had been sitting alone. The claim, however, clearly shows that this was not unthinkable.

It is also in this period that we first get evidence that justices sometimes took advice from other royal officials and even had them sitting with them when making judgments. In 1202 the justices of the Common Bench went to take advice from the barons of the Exchequer (from whom they had so recently split) and other subjects of the king residing there.[54] I know of no further evidence for this before the final years of Henry III's reign. In a Common Bench case of 1269 Alexander, king of Scotland, was claiming the Nottinghamshire manor of Wheatley. One hearing of this case took place before the justices of the Common Bench as reinforced by Richard of Middleton the chancellor, Philip Basset, Robert Aguillon and master Richard of Staines.[55] Something similar seems to have happened in a difficult dower case of 1271 involving an alleged divorce where a judgment was given *de consilio curie* and is recorded as given in the presence of Richard of Middleton the chancellor, Walter of Merton and others of the king's council.[56]

The 1221 mandate to the justiciar of Ireland alerts us to the fact that there was more than one official record of what each court did.[57] In the

---

[52] TNA PRO, KB 26/168, m. 17d.   [53] TNA PRO, JUST 1/365, m. 71d.
[54] Stenton, *English Justice*, p. 194.   [55] TNA PRO, KB 26/194, m. 37.
[56] TNA PRO, KB 26/200A, m. 37d.
[57] For evidence of the survival of three different rolls compiled in Trinity term 1220 see *Curia Regis Rolls*, IX, 163.

Common Bench from at least 1219 onwards a further roll (the so-called *Rex* roll) was also being compiled for a senior clerk, the keeper of writs and rolls, who was directly appointed by the king. When the relevant part of *Bracton* was written it was this roll that was considered and treated as the 'first' or primary record of the court and its record was supposed to be followed by the rolls of all the other justices – that is, they were meant to be copied from it.[58] In 1253, however, a decision was taken that the senior justice of the court should become responsible for the court's 'first' roll, and the keeper of writs and rolls the 'second'. It seems that the other justices were also expected to continue producing identical duplicate rolls as well.[59] Something similar was evidently also true of the Eyre. There is some evidence to suggest rolls were being made for junior Eyre justices already in John's reign.[60] From Henry III's reign duplicates, and even on occasion as many as four copies of rolls, survive for some of the business heard in some Eyres.[61] In practice, therefore, serving as a royal justice seems to have meant not just having your proceedings recorded in an official record, but also being responsible, through one or more clerks, for compiling that record.

III

The reign of Edward I (1272–1307) brings a great increase in the available evidence. From 1272 the survival rate for plea rolls improves dramatically. Virtually every term of every year is represented by at least one extant plea roll in the Common Bench; surviving plea rolls (often in multiple copies) also record every aspect of the business of the itinerant justices in every county that they visited; and there is a King's Bench plea roll for almost every term of every year. From the final years of the reign of Henry III come the first surviving law reports, allowing us to hear lawyers and justices talking and arguing in the language of the courts (insular French), and within a decade also normally naming the particular lawyers and justices involved in the reported cases.[62] For its first two decades law reporting was on a relatively limited scale but a step change took place in the summer of 1291. In the case of the Common Bench, this

---

[58] *Bracton*, IV, 113.   [59] *Close Rolls 1251–3*, p. 374.
[60] Crook, *Records of the General Eyre*, pp. 13–14.
[61] Crook, *Records of the General Eyre*, pp. 14–15.
[62] P. Brand, *The Earliest English Law Reports, IV*, Selden Society, vol. 123 (London, 2007), pp. xi–xvii.

is associated with arrangements made to set aside a specific area in the courtroom for the use of the 'apprentices of the Bench', fledgling professional lawyers, for them to listen, learn the law, and take notes on what they were hearing. Thereafter, law reporting was on a much larger scale and reports begin to survive in substantial collections assigned to particular terms or individual county sessions of the Eyre.[63] There are a relatively small number of identifiable King's Bench reports, often mixed in with those of the Common Bench.

(a)

From 1278 the work of the Eyre justices changed.[64] A whole new section of *novi articuli* was added to the articles for the justices to enquire into. They were also given the task of registering claims to royal franchises in each county they visited and of hearing challenges made on behalf of the king to some of the franchises claimed, and also of hearing royal claims to land and other real property. The justices were also made responsible for hearing complaints of wrongdoing against royal and private officials and others. There was also a total reorganisation of the arrangements for holding Eyres. In place of a varying number of circuits conducting countrywide visitations within a set period of time, two groups of itinerant justices were appointed to travel round the country holding sessions, apparently on a permanent basis. Their visitations were, however, suspended on the outbreak of war with France in 1294 and thereafter there were only visitations of single counties in 1299 and 1302, though the idea of having permanent Eyre circuits had still not been abandoned by 1307.

The general principle that all royal justices were appointed by or in the name of the king was maintained after 1272. The appointment of King's Bench justices remained an oral and informal process. As before, the most fully recorded appointments were those of the Eyre justices. They were appointed to 'itinerate for common pleas' in a specific county or counties and to this was added in 1278 a responsibility to hear and determine pleas on franchises in accordance with the related provision and ordinance and to hear and determine trespasses and complaints.[65] Appointments are recorded for only nine of the twenty-eight justices

---

[63] P. Brand, *Observing and Recording the Medieval Bar and Bench at Work: The origins of law reporting in England*, Selden Society lectures (London, 1999), pp. 16–18.

[64] Brand, *Origins of the English Legal Profession*, pp. 20–1.

[65] Crook, *Records of the General Eyre*, pp. 7, 142–80.

who served in the Common Bench in Edward's reign and the precise wording of the appointments still varied.[66] It is also only after 1272 that, for the first time, we get reliable information from official sources about the wording of the judicial oaths taken by newly appointed royal justices.[67] In 1278 the Close Rolls record the oath to be taken by the justices in Eyre. It begins with a general promise to serve the king 'well and loyally in the office of justice in your Eyre', but goes on to spell out what this means. The justice is 'to do justice to rich and poor to the best of your ability' and 'not to prevent or delay justice against right or the law of the land for the great or the rich, nor out of hatred or favour, nor for the estate of anyone, nor for any benefit, gift or promise given or to be given or in any other way, but loyally to do right to all according to law and custom and in particular not to receive anything from anyone'. The wording is substantially revised from that included in *Bracton*, but much of the revision may have taken place prior to 1278. In 1290 the two Exchequer Memoranda Rolls also record the form of oath taken by the justices of the Common Bench as revised after the disgrace of Weyland CJ and most of his colleagues. The oath is closely related to that taken by the justices in Eyre in 1278, though the initial promise is for service to the king 'in the office of justice'. The promise to take nothing from anyone has been modified to allow this with the king's permission and the entries record an oral concession by the king allowing the justices to receive food and drink for a day. There is also a new clause promising not to agree to any wrongdoing on the part of the justice's colleagues, but to attempt to prevent it if possible, and to report it, if necessary, to the king's council or to the king himself.

(b)

The general principle that the jurisdiction of the king's justices was delegated and that for each piece of business there should be either some general or specific warrant also continued to be applicable. It is, moreover, in this period that we first begin to see in much more detail and much more frequently what it was that justices were actually doing. We do not know for certain how the order in which cases were heard was determined. In the case of the Common Bench and King's Bench the

---

[66] TNA PRO, C 66/104, m. 3; C 66/108, m. 6d; C 66/109, m. 43; C 54/109, m. 9; C 66/111, m. 4; C 66/113, m. 12d; C 66/117, m. 5d; C 66/121, m. 7; C 66/127, m. 27.

[67] Brand, *Making of the Common Law*, pp. 149–51.

court's business was normally allocated to 'return days' within each term, generally at intervals of about a week, both by the process writs which required the defendant to be constrained to appear on one of these days and by the terms of the most recent adjournment given to the plaintiff. Thus there was always a sizeable number of litigants (some ready to plead, some not) with cases put down for hearing on the same return day but with no obvious way of determining relative priority between them. The problem is even greater in the case of the Eyre, where all civil cases in theory came on for hearing at the same time. The evidence, such as it is, seems to indicate that priority was determined by the discretion of the justices. This is suggested by a number of complaints made in 1289–93 alleging that a particular justice or justices had prevented a case being heard out of favour or in order to secure a bribe.[68]

When they did hear pleading in cases, the justices evidently took their responsibilities seriously. In a 1294 case a serjeant challenged a defective count and asked for the court's judgment. Mettingham CJ admitted that he and his colleagues had not been paying proper attention and refused to do so. The reason he gave was that the justices rendered judgment 'on peril of their souls', which was probably a reference to their judicial oath and the perils of breaking it. Counsel was therefore requested to count afresh.[69] The justices were active participants in the pleading stage, joining in the argument, making substantive points and giving their opinions on points at issue. An action of escheat was brought by the king in the 1285 Northamptonshire Eyre, claiming that a manor had been forfeited by its former Norman tenants (Pain and Hugh de Saint Philibert) when they left England to live within the allegiance of the king of France.[70] Counsel tried to argue that one of them had died in the king's allegiance and had an heir who was also in the king's allegiance. Saham J said that this response was available only to that heir himself and suggested reasons why he too would be barred. But at the end of his argument he was careful to say 'But we do not say this by way of judgment.'

Of particular importance was the role of the justices in asking factual questions of individual parties or their counsel. Take the action of waste brought by John de Neufmarche against his mother in 1301 for various

---

[68] P. Brand, 'Ethical standards for royal justices in England, c.1175–1307' (2001) 8 *U. Chi. L. Sch. Roundtable* 257–60, 263–5.

[69] LI MS. Miscellaneous 738, f. 121v.

[70] *Earliest English Law Reports, III*, Selden Society, vol. 122 (London, 2005), pp. 286–8 (85 Northants. 22).

actions which had lessened the longer-term value of two manors and other property in Yorkshire which she held in dower and would revert to John after her death. This case is reported in seven different versions.[71] One of the buildings which John said had been 'knocked down and sold' by Joan was a grange allegedly worth £40. The plea roll enrolment simply records Joan's defence. The house of Eustace Kirkeman close to the grange had been accidentally set on fire. The fire had spread to the grange. She was not responsible for an accident like this. John's response claimed it had not been an accident caused by outsiders, but that the grange had been burned by the negligence of Joan and her servants.[72] Only the reports reveal the part Bereford J's questioning had played in the formulation of this issue.[73] Counsel initially said simply that the grange had been burned by accident. Some reports suggest that he also said it was full of the lady's own corn at the time;[74] and some that she was also ready to rebuild the grange.[75] Two suggest that counsel also asked for the judgment of the justices as to whether any kind of accident did not constitute a legally valid excuse for the admitted damage.[76] Bereford's questioning indicates that he did not agree, for he pressed counsel to specify what kind of accident was involved.[77] He persevered in

---

[71] TNA PRO, CP 40/135, m. 268d. This case is reported in (i) BL MS. Additional 37657, ff. 145v–146r; (ii) BL MS. Stowe 386, f. 117r; (iii) BL MS. Hargrave 375, f. 86v; (iv) BL MS. Additional 31826, ff. 125r–v; (v) BL MS. Harley 673, ff. 45v–46v; (vi) BL MS. Harley 493B, ff. 46r–47r; (vii) BL MS. Harley 2183, ff. 86r, 87r.

[72] 'Et eadem Johanna quo ad predictam grangiam quam predictus Johannes asserit fuisse precii quadraginta librarum etc., dicit quod ipsa nullum vastum fecit etc. Dicit revera quod quedam domus cujusdam Eustachii Kyrkeman igne incensa fuit per infortunium etc., que quidem domus prope predictam grangiam fuit, ita quod per ignem predictam illuminatam predicta grangia combusta fuit etc., quod quidem infortunium eidem Johanni imputari non debet etc. ... et quo ad predictam grangiam combustam etc. dicit quod grangia illa non fuit combusta per infortunium sicut predicta Johanna dicit, immo per defectum ipsius Johanne et serviencium suorum etc., qui custodiam adhibere debuissent in hac parte etc.'

[73] The questioning is specifically ascribed to Hengham CJ in (iii) and to an unnamed justice in (ii), but in all the other reports it is ascribed to Bereford.

[74] (ii), (iv). In (vii) the fact that it was full of corn worth £20 is adduced as a reason for not further specifying what kind of accident it was.

[75] (i). In (iv) the possibility of rebuilding is mentioned later and it is Bereford J who says that it is now too late to do this.

[76] (ii), (v).

[77] In (ii) it is the unnamed justice who says that if the fire took place because of the negligence of the lady through a candle not being properly guarded or other negligence then she would be liable. Bereford says something similar in (vii). In (i) and (vi) it is counsel for the plaintiff (Herle) who suggests that under these circumstances the lady will be liable.

doing so despite the argument of counsel (recorded in only two of the reports) that, if the fire had taken place against Joan's wishes, it could not be accounted waste since negligence alone was not enough to render her liable; and the argument of a second counsel that this was for the jury to discover, not a matter to be established by the questioning of parties by the justices.[78] Eventually, counsel specified that the accident was caused by a fire spreading from the house of a neighbour. Again it was Bereford J who forced the defendant to name the neighbour as well.[79] The questioning did not decide the case, but it narrowed down the issue on which the jury was to give its verdict and in a way that ensured that the jury's verdict was in accordance with the law on responsibility for accidental damage, as understood by the court. Asking leading factual questions was for the justices of this period evidently a normal and well-accepted part of the judicial function. Counsel could resist answering them, but only for cause. If they did resist, there was some danger that they would be taken by the court as tacitly conceding a response unfavourable to their client. Positive answers to these questions, as well as tacit admissions, might form the factual basis for judgments given by the court or might help to shape the issue put to the jury.

A further function performed by royal justices gave them a direct role in the control of the system of 'tentative pleading' as it functioned in this period, more specifically in the rejection of exceptions of law advanced 'tentatively' by defendants. There seems to have been some uncertainty or perhaps ambiguity about the nature of this function since some of our evidence indicates that this constituted giving 'judgment', but other evidence suggests it is not. The distinction between an indicative 'ruling' by the court (merely an implied ruling in this case) and a judgment proper on a formal demurrer is clearly being made in a short piece of dialogue in a case from the 1299 Cambridgeshire Eyre. The unnamed justice asks 'Do you wish to say anything else?' Counsel for the defendant answered 'if you adjudge that we should say something else we will respond sufficiently'. The justice responded: 'That is not for us to do, to adjudge your response; but if you demur for our judgment you will see what will happen.' Another counsel for the defendant took the hint and answered.[80]

---

[78] In (i), (vi). [79] He is recorded as doing this in (i), (iv), (vi), (vii).

[80] '*Justice.* Volez autre chose dire? *Scotere.* Si ws agardez ke nus diom autre, nus responom assez. *Justice.* Ceo nest pas a nus de agarder vostre response, mes si ws demorez en nos agarz ws verrez ke envendra': BL MS. Stowe 386, ff. 107r–v. The overruled exception is not mentioned in the plea roll enrolment of this case: TNA PRO, JUST 1/96, m. 22 (*Eve widow of Robert Tibetot v. Warin son of Edmund of Bassingbourn*).

They might also rule on the forms of issue appropriate for jury trial. In a 1297 action of mesne, counsel for the defendant pleaded that his client was not obliged to acquit the plaintiff of a rent being demanded by the king. After the making of a final concord the initial grantee of the land had charged the land with the rent by agreeing to pay it without contesting the demand or seeking acquittance. His brother (the plaintiff's father) had done the same thing when he had taken possession of the land under the terms of the settlement, as had the plaintiff himself. Counsel for the plaintiff pressed him to specify only one of these, but counsel wanted to be allowed to prove all three. Bereford J's issued clear directions on this: '[Hold] to one, if you wish, for if the inquest was joined on the three it might be that the inquest spoke for you in respect of one and against you in respect of another. How could judgment be made in that case? So hold to one.' Counsel for the defendant took his advice.[81] The offer of proof (in the amended form) is recorded in the enrolment, but nothing is said of the ruling that had led to this.

Only a relatively small number of law reports tell us anything about the workings of jury trial, though individual plea roll enrolments also provide some information about this. There is, however, no reason to suppose that the glimpses these give us of what happened are misleading. They suggest that justices also played an active role during and after jury trial itself. When justices 'charged' juries at the beginning of the jury trial stage they did not just tell the jury about the issue the parties had reached and which they were to try. Sometimes, the justices significantly broadened out the issue on which they expected a verdict; sometimes they specifically instructed the jurors on the law they were to apply in doing so. In an assize *utrum* (the special action available only to the rectors of parish churches for the recovery of land lost or alienated by their predecessors) heard in 1300, for example, the rector of a parish church had counted, as the action required him to do, on the seisin of a particular predecessor as his title to the property. Mettingham CJ, however, expressly charged the jury to say not just whether that predecessor had actually been seised but also whether any of his predecessors had been seised and whether the messuage being

---

[81] '*Ber*' [Tenez vous] al un, si vous volez, qe si lenquest joinisit sur les iij poet estre qe lenqueste dirreit pur vous endreit de un e encontre vous endroit de un altre. Coment se freit jugement en ceo cas? Pur ceo tenez vous al un. *Inge*. Richard le chargea, prest etc.': BL MS. Additional 35116, f. 198v.

claimed was or was not the right of the church.[82] Any such seisin would be enough to entitle the plaintiff to recovery, if the messuage was the right of his church.

The justices seem also to have played an active role once juries began giving their verdicts by requiring them to clarify those verdicts. In an assize of mort d'ancestor brought before Gilbert of Rothbury sometime in the early 1290s the issue before the jury was whether the plaintiff was the next heir of the deceased ancestor or if his next heir was the William who had entered the land after the ancestor's death and then alienated the land to the current tenants.[83] The jury said that William had indeed entered as his son and next heir. Rothbury then asked them to explain how he was his next heir. They answered that 'he was born and engendered of the same mother and father and his father on his death bed had acknowledged that he was his son and heir'. This was not acceptable. The common law did not recognise death-bed acknowledgements as capable of turning illegitimate children into legitimate ones. Rothbury warned the jury that they would need to give him another and better reason for accepting William as next heir or they would be locked up without food or drink till the following day. They then said that he had been born before the marriage ceremony but after the betrothal of his parents. This gave Rothbury the information he wanted. He went on to ask them about the appropriate damages, if any were to be awarded, before adjourning the assize for judgment. The question of William's legitimacy was one for the justices, not the jury, to decide but on the basis of the facts Rothbury had managed to elicit.

In other cases the justices seem to have taken the initiative in examining the jury to build up the factual picture on which the justices would subsequently give their judgment. Take, for example, the plea roll record of the jury stage of an action brought by writ of entry *ad terminum qui preteriit* which took place in 1291.[84] The defendants had claimed that the tenant through whom they had gained title to the land (Joan, then wife of

---

[82] BL MS. Additional 31826, f. 166v: '*Met*' charga lenqueste e dist: vus nus dirrez si J. fut seisi e pur ceo qe la persone nad autre bref de dreit si nus dirreit si nul de ses predecessors fut seisi e le quel cest mes seit le dreit de son eglise ou nun.' The case is *John of Dalton, parson of the church of St Michael by the Ouse bridge of York* v. *Richard de Lisle*, enrolled on TNA PRO, CP 40/133, m. 1.

[83] *YB 21 & 22 Edward I*, pp. 269–73. It appears with a section of Common Bench reports of Trinity term 1293. It may indeed belong to that term but is evidently not from the Common Bench.

[84] TNA PRO, CP 40/80, m. 154d.

Henry fitzRalph) was the tenant in fee of this land and thus in a position to convey a good title to it and not, as the plaintiff had claimed, simply a tenant for life by his grant. At the beginning of their verdict the jury stated that the tenements had originally belonged to Joan but that she and her husband Henry had sold them to the plaintiff, who was Joan's son by her first husband. The plaintiff had then granted them back to Joan for her lifetime. They were then asked a series of questions about the first crucial transfer to discover whether it had been validly executed. Had the vendors' chattels remained on the land after the sale? Had the sub-tenants attorned to the purchaser? Had the purchaser worked the land? How long had elapsed between the sale and the subsequent grant back? Had any specific time been fixed for the regrant? It was on the basis of the answers that the court, and not the jury, concluded that title had indeed been validly transferred to the purchaser and thus that the tenant really had been only a tenant for life and so incapable of making a further grant in fee to the defendants.

One plea roll enrolment suggests how much judicial questioning and decision-making may lie behind some of the numerous relatively simple enrolled records of jury verdicts. This is a case found on a 1296 plea roll but in which the jury verdict was given in 1298.[85] The plaintiff's complaint was that he had been distrained by animals taken from his plough contrary to statute; the defendant's answer that he had never so distrained him. The verdict, as enrolled, said simply that the defendant had not taken or impounded any animals belonging to the plaintiff on the day in question. We get to see behind this blank verdict because the plaintiff's attorney protested at the judgment. This led to Beckingham J (before whom the jury had given its verdict) giving a verbal report on what the jury had said. The jurors had given a much more detailed verdict. They had said that a complaint had been made against the plaintiff and others to the defendant as bailiff of the local hundred court. He had sent his under-bailiff to the plaintiff's manor, where he had taken eight horses from the plaintiff's plough on the day alleged. He had kept them until the following Tuesday, when the plaintiff's steward had found sureties for the appearance of the plaintiff's men in court, though not for the appearance of the plaintiff himself. The jurors had been asked if the under-bailiff could have found other distresses. They replied that he could. They were also asked if the defendant had ratified his under-bailiff's action and they answered yes. They then

[85] TNA PRO, CP 40/115, m. 70.

explained that, once the defendant had realised that he should not have retained the animals, he had returned them. On the basis of this final action alone, it seems, Beckingham J had ruled that the verdict amounted to an acquittal of the defendant, as recorded in the enrolment. It is, however, easy to see that another justice, on the same facts, might well have held the allegation proved. This must have been why the plaintiff protested. The court quashed the judgment and the last thing that appears in the record is the court's order for the defendant to be summoned back to court for further proceedings.

There is also some evidence to suggest that the awarding of judgment after a jury verdict might require the justices to consider the rights of the case, and might even involve some legal argument. In an action brought by writ of entry *ad terminum qui preteriit* the defendant claimed that 4 acres of land had been given to his father by the mother of the claimant, and not leased to him for a term of years.[86] In its 1297 verdict the jury found that the land had been mortgaged to the defendant's father for 100 shillings on condition that the mortgagors or their heirs might re-enter on payment. The money had not, however, been paid. Howard J gave judgment in 1300 but only after further consideration by the court. The defendant had failed to prove his assertion that the land had been granted in fee. Because he had claimed a higher estate than the one he actually possessed, he had acted to the plaintiff's disinheritance. He had thereby forfeited such interest as he did have. Howard bolstered this with a second argument. The land had been mortgaged by a husband, who had no right to do this for any period longer than his own life. He was now dead and so the arrangement had lapsed. The plaintiff recovered.

(c)

It seems to have been relatively common for judgments to be given by the justices applying or making procedural rules or substantive legal rules but without any prior fact-finding by juries. Firm figures are provided by my unpublished study of cases of replevin heard in the Common Bench during the reign. The plea rolls record 2,278 cases where there was an exchange of pleadings between the two sides. In 1,995 cases an issue of fact was joined and the record shows a jury being summoned to decide that issue. There is a recorded outcome, however, in only 267 cases,

---

[86] BL MS. Additional 31826, f. 164r. The eventual judgment is enrolled separately from the original record of the case in Hilary term 1300: TNA PRO, CP 40/132, m. 213d.

around 12 per cent of the total number pleaded to issue. In the remainder the case disappears without any recorded verdict. Verdicts may just not have been recorded on the rolls for some cases. In most it must be assumed that the parties agreed out of court or that the plaintiff failed to pursue process until he secured a verdict. In 223 cases, around 10 per cent of those for which there are recorded pleadings, judgment was given solely on the basis of what had been said in court. Thus 45 per cent of replevin cases decided in the courts were decided without jury trial. Around a quarter of these (fifty-six cases) were determined on the basis of a defect in the writ originating proceedings or authorising their removal out of the county court into the Common Bench. A further thirty cases were dismissed on the basis of a challenge to a defective count. Most commonly, the problem was that the count was inconsistent with one of the plaintiff's writs. It might be, for example, because the original writ had been acquired before the date of the distraint whose legality was being challenged.[87] In the remaining cases the court was applying or creating rules of substantive law in reaching its judgment. In seventy-two cases (just over 40 per cent) judgment was given after an avowry (a justification by the defendant of the distraint): in thirty-five the defendant was successful and in thirty-seven the plaintiff. In twenty-five cases judgment was given for the plaintiff after an avowry had been followed by a disavowal by the tenant, denying that he held of the lord who had made the avowry. It is probably also safe to add to the number those twenty cases recording the defendant making an avowry and which then simply add that the plaintiff was unable to deny that this was justified. Certainly, in at least one case where we have such a formal record and parallel reports the latter indicate that there had indeed been legal argument about substantive legal issues before the judgment in the defendant's favour.[88] It seems reasonable to conclude that it was the justices alone, applying rules of substantive law, who decided as many as 117 replevin cases. This is no more than about 5 per cent of the total number

---

[87] For examples see *Richard de Loveny* v. *Ralph d'Aubeny and ors*: TNA PRO, CP 40/27, m. 183d (Michaelmas 1278); *Peter of Possbury* v. *Mauger de St Aubyn*: CP 40/31, m. 78 (Michaelmas 1279); *Robert de Camville* v. *Giles de la Garderobe*: CP 40/31, m. 8d (Michaelmas 1279); *Thomas del Heved* v. *Hugh de Heryz*: CP 40/51, m. 57 (Michaelmas 1283); *Robert Towy of Ashton* v. *Thomas de Berkeley and ors*: CP 40/60, m. 95d (Michaelmas 1285); *William of Kirkby* v. *Richard of Chigwell and anor*: CP 40/91, m. 221d (Michaelmas 1291); *Hamon atte Grene* v. *Richer of Cawston*: CP 40/101, m. 71d (Trinity 1293).

[88] TNA PRO, CP 40/134, m. 78: *William Revenyng* v. *Edmund Jale*: reported in BL MSS. Additional 37657, f. 26v, Additional 31826, f. 95v, Harley 25, f. 7r (=Additional 35116, ff. 151v–152r).

of cases pleaded to issue, but it is just under a quarter of all cases known to have been determined directly by the courts. The action of replevin worked rather differently from most other legal actions, but it was not wholly exceptional in the extent to which decisions in this action were made by the justices alone. The law reports of the reign show the courts regularly making judgments deciding cases without the assistance of juries and on the basis not just of technical points of procedure but also by the application of rules of substantive law and on some occasions by the deliberate creation of new rules.

We have already encountered one significant reason why the judicial disposition of cases may have been more common in this period than seems to have been true later. This was the power exercised by the justices of asking leading questions, which allowed them to form their judgments on the basis of those answers. The relative frequency of the disposition of litigation by justices without the need for jury trial in this period was also due to the use made of written evidence. Strong presumptions attached to certain kinds of written evidence which might be produced in court in the course of pleading and also to the failure to produce such evidence. The rules about written bonds attesting debts provide one well-known example. By the later thirteenth century it had come to be the rule that the only defence which could be pleaded to a claim backed up by such a bond was a written acknowledgement of payment of the debt or accord and satisfaction in written form; the only exception was to challenge the genuineness of the bond itself. The rule was evidently felt to be a harsh one where, for example, the defendant claimed his written acknowledgement of payment had been accidentally destroyed, but the courts in 1294 definitively rejected the use of jury trial to prove the existence and terms of such lost documents.[89] Thus the normal outcome of any case where the plaintiff claimed a debt on the basis of a bond was a judgment of the court awarding recovery.

It also seems to have been relatively common for the justices simply to give judgment on the basis of the arguments made before them without apparently needing to question the parties or even rely on written evidence. A good example is a 1301 case in which a widow claimed dower against her

---

[89] See the discussion of these matters in P. Brand, 'Aspects of the law of debt, 1189–1307' in P. R. Schofield and N. J. Mayhew (eds.), *Credit and Debt in Medieval England, c.1180–c.1350* (Oxford, 2001), pp. 19–41, 25–7.

son.[90] The son pleaded that his mother was not entitled to dower because she had held on to all her late husband's land and he had needed to bring an assize of mort d'ancestor before the assize justices in 1298 before he could recover it. She had claimed the lands had been jointly acquired by her late husband and herself in fee tail. He asked whether she was now entitled to claim dower from the same holding since she had previously claimed the whole of the holding to his disinheritance. He was appealing to the well-established rule of land law that any action by a widow to the heir's disinheritance forfeited her right to dower in the land concerned. She denied that there was any potential disinheritance. He was the couple's heir and the land would revert to him after her dower in the same way as it would have descended to him after her death under the entail. The case was adjourned for judgment. Eventually the court gave its judgment. The claim of a higher estate was to the heir's disinheritance and so she was barred from claiming dower.

(d)

The main royal courts remained collegiate courts throughout Edward I's reign. The number of justices serving in the Common Bench never fell below four. The maximum number was seven, and the average had risen from five to six by the final years of the reign.[91] For the four Eyre sessions held between 1273 and 1278 the number of justices varied between three and five. For the 'northern' circuit Eyres of 1278–88 the standard complement of justices was four; the 'southern' Eyre circuit of 1278–89 oscillated between four and six justices. The Eyre circuits of 1292–4 both had a standard complement of five justices, and this was also true of the isolated Eyre sessions of 1299 in Cambridgeshire and 1302 in Cornwall.[92] The court of King's Bench presents the greatest problems. There are no records of appointments to the court and only a few final concords survive for the court for the reign. All we have is the record of the biennial payment of its justices and occasional incidental references to them elsewhere. From these it seems clear that the court remained the smallest of these regular royal courts. However, there were now never

---

[90] TNA PRO, CP 40/136, m. 166. The case is reported in BL MS. Additional 31826, f. 170r and there is a copy of the plea roll enrolment with only the judgment in French in the same MS. at f. 127r.

[91] Brand, *Origins of the English Legal Profession*, p. 25.

[92] Crook, *Records of the General Eyre*, pp. 142–80.

fewer than two full-time justices and the 'normal' complement was three.[93] For a few terms four or even five justices sat in the court.[94]

The more plentiful evidence of Edward I's reign gives us a much better chance of seeing individual justices or small groups of justices at work dealing with particular business in these courts. In the Common Bench one junior justice, Roger of Leicester, sat on his own in Trinity term 1276 and again in 1278 to adjudge and adjourn essoins, and in Michaelmas term 1287 he and another junior justice (Beckingham) sat separately to render judgment on a default.[95] All this might be compatible with a picture of particular justices sitting apart from their colleagues only when there was a particular press of business in the court. The evidence of the surviving pre-1290 law reports, however, suggests that it was a more regular arrangement. Leicester does not make an appearance in any of the pre-1290 reports, suggesting that he may have regularly sat apart from his colleagues (perhaps after 1285 in association with Beckingham) to deal with more routine, and therefore unreported, business. And the reports suggest that most of the court's more significant cases were in fact heard by just two of its justices, Thomas Weyland CJ and his junior colleague, William of Brunton. Brunton and Weyland appear together without recorded colleagues in twenty cases; in twenty-two reported cases Brunton alone appears in the report; in twenty-seven Weyland alone.[96]

The post-1290 Common Bench evidence tells us more. Beckingham, who continued to sit in the court down to the end of 1306, makes only a single appearance in the law reports before 1302.[97] The plea rolls reveal why. There are references in 1291, 1292 and 1298 to judgments being made by him alone.[98] In Easter term 1291 the repleading of a case before him is said to have taken place *extra bancum*, apparently meaning away from the main place of session of the court.[99] Probably the same thing was described in Michaelmas term 1294 as 'the other part of this bench' (*ex alia parte istius banci*).[100] Beckingham therefore probably sat on his own in the court on a regular basis prior to 1302. Peter Mallore sat as a justice of the court from

---

[93] *Select Cases in the Court of King's Bench*, I, ed. G. O. Sayles, Selden Society, vol. 55 (London, 1936), pp. cxxix–cxxxiii. For incidental references see TNA PRO, JUST 1/1246, m. 4d; KB 27/101, m. 8d; KB 27/121, m. 13; CP 25/1/249/5, no. 15.

[94] Five justices were paid at Easter 1273; four from Michaelmas 1285 to Michaelmas 1287 and at Michaelmas 1289 and Easter 1294.

[95] *Earliest English Law Reports*, I, p. cxlix.   [96] *Ibid.*, pp. cxlix–cliii.

[97] This conclusion is based on a survey of both the edited and unedited reports of this period.

[98] TNA PRO, CP 40/87, m. 46d; CP 40/95, m. 122d; CP 40/115, m. 70.

[99] TNA PRO, CP 40/89, m. 112.   [100] TNA PRO, CP 40/108, m. 6d.

Michaelmas term 1292. He does make occasional appearances in law reports prior to 1302 but these are infrequent and he is often the only justice named. The plea roll evidence shows him sitting on his own in 1293 and 1298.[101] Arrangements were made by the justices of the court in Easter term 1300 for Beckingham and Mallore to sit at the north end of the hall of pleas in York castle separately from their colleagues to deal with defaults sued at the quindene of Easter.[102] There are references to a 'second bench' in the headings to certain membranes of plea rolls recording some of the business of the court in 1305, 1306 and 1307 but these relate only to the appointment of attorneys and adjournments made by the consent of the parties.[103] Overall the evidence falls short of demonstrating that there was any long-term division of the court's business between the justices, merely a common practice of dividing it so that certain justices were entrusted with hearing cases on their own or with only one other colleague. The law reports show that between 1290 and 1307 most cases were heard by one or two justices. None were heard by more than three prior to 1301. Thereafter in a few cases four out of the six justices are mentioned, but never more.[104] This evidence could be misleading. Silent justices and those who said nothing worth recording might simply have been ignored by the reporters. But the evidence of the law reports tends to confirm what the plea rolls have already suggested. This does not mean that the justices of the court never acted collectively as a whole. They clearly did. In 1298, for example, a judgment rendered by Beckingham alone was quashed after reconsideration and it was agreed 'by all the colleagues, justices of the Bench' that the parties should appear in court for a rehearing.[105] In Trinity term 1303 a disgruntled litigant made disparaging remarks about Hengham, who had delivered the court's judgment, but we are told that the court had reached that judgment 'by unanimous consent' (*unanimi consensu*).[106] It seems clear nonetheless that such collective action by the court as a whole was very much the exception, not the rule.

---

[101] TNA PRO, CP 40/101, m. 97d; CP 40/123, m. 149.

[102] TNA PRO, CP 40/134, m. 178d.

[103] TNA PRO, CP 40/155, mm. 238, 239, 240, 254, 255, 264; CP 40/158, mm. 299, 318; CP 40/161, mm. 512, 513, 515, 517, 520, 525, 539, 541, 542, 545, 547, 548, 558, 559, 561, 562, 564, 566, 567, 570 (and note reference to the *primo banco* on m. 544); CP 40/162, mm. 350, 352, 369, 375; CP 40/163, m. 286.

[104] This conclusion is based on my survey of both the edited and unedited reports of this period.

[105] TNA PRO, CP 40/115, m. 70.

[106] TNA PRO, CP 40/148, m. 209d. And note the emendation of an entry made in the same term *communi assensu justiciariorum*: CP 40/148, m. 13d.

The records of general Eyre sessions divide up the business into a number of separate sections: civil pleas from the county, civil pleas from other counties ('foreign pleas'), crown pleas and the closely connected gaol delivery, *quo warranto* and other king's pleas, and plaints. Each of these kinds of business seems to have been handled separately and at the same time by different individual justices or groups of justices, though there was some flexibility, with justices who had been assigned a certain type of business joining others when their colleagues needed advice or if they had finished the business assigned to them. In the 'northern' Eyre circuit of 1278–88 for which many reports survive, William of Saham, who was debarred by his clerical orders from hearing crown pleas, heard civil pleas, but was joined in a minority of cases by up to two other colleagues. There is evidence of something similar happening on the contemporary southern circuit.[107] In 1292–4 civil pleas on the northern circuit were fairly consistently held by Cressingham and Mortimer and on the southern circuit by Berwick and Cave (and sometimes Bereford).[108] Mettingham is known to have sat on his own or with an associate who was not one of the justices named to the general commission for *quo warranto* pleas in three Eyres of the 1278–89 northern circuit,[109] and chronicle evidence shows Hopton and Siddington being assigned to hear such pleas in the 1286 Norfolk Eyre.[110] Occasionally we hear of common action by all the justices. A grand assize in the 1286–7 Suffolk Eyre was heard by all the justices of the Eyre,[111] and in the following Eyre of Hertfordshire all six justices met together to discuss the taxation of damages in a case after a verdict had been given and judgment rendered by three of their number.[112]

In general principle, however, even where the justices divided up the business between themselves they seem normally to have remained collectively responsible for everything done in the court while they were sitting in it. In 1290 all the justices sitting in the Common Bench in Trinity term 1288 (plus the court's chief clerk, the keeper of rolls and writs) were held responsible for the chief justice's erasure of his roll and substitution of a judgment by default for the joining of jury issue, though only Weyland had heard the case and it seems unlikely that they were all

---

[107] *Earliest English Law Reports*, III, pp. xc, xciii–xciv.
[108] This conclusion is based on a survey of the edited and unedited law reports for these Eyres.
[109] *Earliest English Law Reports*, III, pp. lxxii–lxxxiii.   [110] *Ibid.*, p. lx.
[111] *State Trials of the Reign of Edward the First, 1289–93*, ed. T. F. Tout and H. Johnstone, Camden Society, 3rd series (1906), IX, pp. 67–70.
[112] TNA PRO, JUST 1/541B, m. 30.

were implicated in his misconduct.[113] Something similar happened in
1290 to the justices and chief clerk of the crown in the 1286 Norfolk Eyre,
though it seems likely that only two of them had been directly responsible.[114] This theory of joint responsibility was also applied in various
proceedings in 1289–93 where a complaint was made of misconduct
against a justice of the Common Bench or the Eyre or King's Bench.
Their immediate response was that they were not obliged to answer for
this without their colleagues who had then been sitting in the same court.
However, when a complaint was made against William of Saham in 1290
relating to his conduct as a justice of the 1286 Huntingdonshire Eyre he
pointed out that John of Mettingham (recently appointed chief justice
of the Common Bench) had been associated with him. The auditors
of complaints did not automatically assume Mettingham's responsibility
but asked him if he was present at the plea with Saham. Mettingham
was able to say that he had then been hearing pleas of *quo warranto*
in a separate building and so should not be held liable. They also
elicited from the complainant that he had no wish to proceed against
Mettingham since he had not been present when the misconduct had
taken place.[115] In two other cases from the same circuit Mettingham was
similarly exempted from any responsibility on his 'recording' that he had
not been sitting with Saham at the time.[116] There is also at least one other
instance where the general rule of collective responsibility seems not to
have been applied.[117]

(e)

There is much more evidence for the period after 1272 of 'outside'
justices and others who had not been appointed as permanent members
of courts playing a significant role in assisting and reinforcing the
justices of particular royal courts in making their decisions and judgments. Sometimes this was done on specific instruction from the king. In
1283 the Common Bench was to hear a case brought by its chief justice,
Thomas Weyland, claiming the right to present to the living of Chipping
Sodbury. The king gave written orders for the association of outsiders
(here the treasurer and barons of the Exchequer) in the hearing of this
particular case.[118] Something similar happened in cases heard in 1284

---

[113] Brand, 'Ethical standards for royal justices', p. 266.   [114] *Ibid.*, p. 269.
[115] *State Trials*, p. 76.   [116] TNA PRO, JUST 1/541B, mm. 9d, 11d.
[117] *State Trials*, p. 6.   [118] TNA PRO, SC 8/308, no. 15374.

and 1307.[119] The justices might also take the initiative themselves. In answer to another complaint of 1290 Hengham denied responsibility for a judgment made in the Common Bench even though he had been present for the pleading of the case. He said that it often happened that he sat in on the court at the request of its justices when they had difficult cases to decide to provide them with advice and assistance.[120] The pre-1290 Common Bench reports show Hengham sitting with the justices of the court on a number of occasions, and there are also mentions of Mettingham, Siddington and Saham doing the same thing.[121] The plea rolls mention the discussion of cases with the justices of King's Bench after 1290 as well,[122] and the reports reveal the presence of Thornton, Brabazon, Rothbury and Spigurnel while justices of King's Bench at the hearing of Common Bench cases.[123] In one of the proceedings on complaints made in 1290, we see John of Mettingham (at the time simply a regular Eyre justice) sitting in on the jury stage of a case in another royal court because he was a 'well-wisher' to one of the parties.[124] The evidence for outside justices sitting in on Eyre cases is less extensive but it certainly did happen.[125] It could also occur in King's Bench. Judgment in a contentious and difficult 1279 assize of novel disseisin was noted on the roll as given in the presence of the Common Bench justices Weyland and Brunton as well as that of Hengham and Wimborne.[126]

'Outsiders' also include men sitting as temporary justices apparently without any kind of formal appointment. Henry of Guildford acted as a temporary justice of the Common Bench in both Trinity and Michaelmas terms of 1305 even before his formal appointment as a temporary justice in late November;[127] and Nicholas of Warwick, the king's serjeant, sat as a justice in Hilary and Trinity terms of 1307 without any formal appointment.[128] After 1272 we also get much clearer evidence of senior clerks playing a quasi-judicial role in the pleading of cases, with the reports recording the arguments or decisions of successive chief clerks of the chief justice of the Common Bench (Anger of Ripon and Henry of Hales), the

---

[119] TNA PRO, CP 40/54, m. 30; CP 40/164, m. 210d .
[120] TNA PRO, KB 138/4, no. 81.   [121] *Earliest English Law Reports*, I, pp. cxxi–cxxii.
[122] TNA PRO, CP 40/96, m. 19; CP 40/103, m. 77.
[123] This draws on a survey of edited and unedited reports of the period.
[124] TNA PRO, JUST 1/541B, m. 36d.
[125] *Earliest English Law Reports*, III, pp. lviii–lxi.   [126] TNA PRO, KB 27/45, m. 6.
[127] TNA PRO, CP 40/156, m. 136; CP 40/153, m. 141; *YB 33–35 Edward I*, pp. 63–7, 73–7.
[128] TNA PRO, CP 40/162, m. 367; *YB 33–35 Edward I*, pp. 461–3, 565.

keeper of rolls and writs (John Bacon) and the future Common Bench justice, Hervey of Stanton.[129] The phenomenon is also attested in the Eyre, though not on the same scale.[130] The evidence also suggests that senior clerks were playing a significant role in dealing with process, but subject to the ultimate oversight and control of the justices. In 1306 a writ of right was removed into the Common Bench by a defective writ. It was Henry of Hales (the chief clerk of John of Mettingham and of his successor Ralph de Hengham as chief justices of the Common Bench) who looked at the writ when the essoin was made and made the initial judgment that 'we do not have power to hold this plea'. But he was not acting on his own. The reporter notes that Hengham CJ was also present in court and agreed with him.[131] From an unidentified early fourteenth century report we learn of a writ of *sicut alias* that came to Henry of Hales for sealing. Bereford advised him not to do so.[132]

(f)

The general practice seems to have been observed throughout the period down to at least 1290, and perhaps as late as 1307, that a separate plea roll was compiled for each of the justices of the major royal courts and also for the keeper of writs and rolls in each. When in 1290 Walter of Hopton petitioned to escape his share of responsibility for the collective failure of the justices of the 1286 Norfolk Eyre to take action on two presentments, he said that he did not then possess a sufficient warrant to sit and 'could not be at their council nor have a clerk nor a roll' (*ne il ne pout estre a lur consail ne clerk aver ne roule*).[133] Most of the surviving Common Bench rolls are those made for successive chief justices, but a substantial number of *Rex* rolls made for the keeper of rolls and writs also survive,[134] and three made for the junior justice, John de Lovetot.[135] From a list of the rolls he handed over in 1290 we know there were once more.[136] It is relatively common down to 1290 for rolls to survive for many, and sometimes for all, of the justices sitting in an Eyre plus the keeper of rolls and writs. This only ceases in 1290, after which only the rolls made for the chief justice and the keeper of rolls and writs survive. A rare

---

[129] Brand, *Making of the Common Law*, pp. 176–8.   [130] *Ibid.*, pp. 181–2.
[131] *YB 33–35 Edward I*, pp. 153–5.   [132] BL MS. Hargrave 375, f. 118r.
[133] TNA PRO, SC 8/263, no. 13125.
[134] TNA PRO, CP 40/1B, 2B, 6, 7, 16, 22, 26, 35, 37, 43, 55, 71, 77, 84, 88, 94, 97, 99, 114, 120, 128, 137, 140, 165, 166, 167.
[135] TNA PRO, CP 40/12, 65, 74. There is also a single surviving roll made for master Robert of Thorpe: CP 40/85.
[136] TNA PRO, E 159/63, m. 7.

glimpse of enrolment practice given by the record of proceedings on a complaint made in 1290 shows that the practice followed in the 1287 Hertfordshire Eyre was for an enrolment of the case to be made 'in the presence of the justices' and first in the 'chief roll' (evidently the roll of the chief justice), then in the 'rolls of the lord king' (evidently the *Rex* roll made for the keeper of writs and rolls) and only then of the other justices.[137] This had been the procedure laid down in 1253 for the rolls of the Common Bench, but was evidently of wider application. These rolls were not handed in to the king's treasury immediately and there seems to have been a sense that only then were the rolls accepted as a formal record. The justices were evidently meant to check their rolls before doing so or had often been given the opportunity to do so. In 1279 master Roger of Seaton responded to a letter from the keeper of the rolls asking him to hand in his writs and rolls by saying that he was willing to hand them over but was not willing to 'avow' them since 'perhaps one thing was done and another has been written in the rolls by the clerks, because they are not always able to understand correctly pleaders and litigants'.[138] It was perhaps only at this stage that the justice's own memory of what had been decided in a case was allowed to trump what was written in the rolls. The special status of the rolls once handed in to the treasury is alluded to in proceedings on a complaint against two of the clerks of Solomon of Rochester at the 1287 Hertfordshire Eyre. The clerks' eventual position in this case was that the rolls had been delivered into the treasury and these rolls (therefore) 'bear full and perfect record and they ought not to answer in any respect for those things contained in those rolls since nothing could be added or removed from them'. [139]

IV

The history of royal justices and of the functions they exercised in England begins in the reign of Henry II with the creation of the Eyre and the addition of a judicial function to the existing financial functions of the Exchequer. In this reign we see for the first time justices appointed by the king and taking an oath of faithful service to him exercising only such jurisdiction as was delegated to them in writing, uniting in themselves the hitherto separate functions of presiding officer and judgment-makers, and creating a permanent written record of their activities. Over the next century or so, the historian of the English judiciary benefits from a steady increase in the range

[137] TNA PRO, JUST 1/541B, m. 30.
[138] *Select Cases in the Court of King's Bench*, I, p. clxviii.
[139] TNA PRO, JUST 1/541B, m. 30.

of relevant information available: plea rolls (the earliest coming from 1194 and the survival rate becoming much better after 1272), feet of fines (surviving in large quantity from 1195), some evidence of the forms of appointment and the oaths justices took from 1218 onwards, and from the later 1260s onwards the earliest surviving unofficial law reports. This increase in quantity also means an increase in quality. Its main drawback is that it sometimes makes it difficult to be sure whether what we can see is really something new or merely something we have simply not been able to see beforehand but has a longer, invisible, history. What is visible from early on is the part played by royal justices in handling and determining procedural matters. What comes into better focus only in the second half of the thirteenth century is the active role they took in pleading in civil litigation, especially through making rulings and questioning litigants, and in determining appropriate methods of proof and also their role at the proof stage in instructing and questioning the jury and making judgments on the basis of the jury's verdict. What also comes into better focus, though clearly it also existed earlier as well, is their role in determining the outcome of certain cases by judgment even without the need for a prior jury verdict. Royal justices in England in this period, as later, were all members of multi-member courts whose records tend to give the impression that everything done in or by the court was done by all the justices of the court as a group. Our better sources of information from the mid thirteenth century onwards, however, show not just that not all justices were present in court for all the court's business but also that the Eyre and the Common Bench in practice operated some, if not most, of the time in two or more separate divisions. In general principle, however, all the justices remained responsible, and might be held responsible, for everything done in any of the court's divisions, whether or not they had participated in the action or judgment concerned. And our picture of the way that 'judging' operated also needs to bear in mind one further complicating factor, visible on at least an occasional basis from the early years of the thirteenth century onwards; this is that justices from other royal courts and other royal officials as well as clerks of the court could also participate in the court's work and help it in reaching its decisions. Royal justices were central to the making of the English medieval common law. This chapter has attempted to show what we can know about what they did and how they operated. This should help us to understand better an important part of the context within which the common law itself was created.

2

Formalism and realism in fifteenth-century English law: Bodies corporate and bodies natural

DAVID J. SEIPP

Thomas Reed Powell, a US law professor, said seventy years ago or more, 'if you think you can think about a thing, inextricably attached to something else, without thinking of the thing it is attached to, then you have a legal mind'.[1] Though many lawyers claim they have this legal mind as a matter of pride, Professor Powell, I am sure, did not mean this as a compliment. The Legal Realism movement that swept through US law schools in the 1920s and 1930s taught, among other things, that lawyers must see the real attachments between things, attachments that Legal Formalism had been so good at ignoring.

I was reminded of things inextricably attached to each other and of the legal mind that could so completely separate them as I worked my way through the Year Book reports of the end of the reign of Edward IV. In about a dozen reports from 1478 to 1482, many of them extending over several folios, English lawyers and judges made arguments that reminded me of formalist and realist positions. Let me say at once that I am not trying to claim that American Legal Realism was invented in 1478 in Westminster Hall. All Year Book discourse took place within a decidedly formalist framework. But in cases about what late fifteenth-century English lawyers and judges called corporations and bodies politic, some of these lawyers and judges argued that these collective entities were entirely separate from the real human beings who composed them, arguments that I will label formalist here, and others broke down that separation and argued that the legal positions of the

---

[1] Thomas Reed Powell, quoted in T. W. Arnold, *The Symbols of Government* (New Haven, CT, 1935), p. 101.

individuals inside these collective entities could affect the collective entities themselves, arguments that I will label realist.[2]

Frederic William Maitland took up many of these same cases in his classic *History of English Law* in 1898 and found one of them at least to be among 'the most interesting cases in all the Year Books'.[3] Maitland had asked whether the theoretical basis of medieval English corporations was a canonist legal fiction idea or a more Germanic organic unity of groups. Here is a passage from his discussion of these late-fifteenth-century cases:

> The corporation is invisible, incorporeal, immortal; it can not be assaulted, or beaten or imprisoned; it can not commit treason; a doubt has occurred as to whether it can commit a trespass, but this doubt (though it will give trouble so late as the year 1842) has been rejected by practice, if not removed by any consistent theory. We even find it said that the corporation is but a name. On the other hand, it is a person. It is at once a person and yet but a name; in short it is *persona ficta*.[4]

After Maitland set the topic in 1893, Cecil Carr, Frederick Pollock, Harold Laski, William Holdsworth, H. Ke Chin Wang and Heinz Lubasz rang the changes on Maitland's thesis down through 1964.[5] I will review some of

---

[2] For a similar application of this twentieth-century terminology to medieval legal materials, see M. T. Clanchy, 'A medieval realist: Interpreting the rules at Barnewell Priory, Cambridge' in E. A. G. Attwool (ed.), *Perspectives in Jurisprudence* (Glasgow, 1977), pp. 176–94. The notion of 'realism' as a pragmatic approach to law sceptical of formal legal distinctions has a contested modern history familiar to American lawyers, reviewed in William Twining, *Karl Llewellyn and the Realist Movement* (London, 1985), pp. 70–83.

[3] F. Pollock and F. W. Maitland, *A History of English Law*, 2nd edn, 2 vols. (Cambridge, 1898), I, p. 491. Maitland took Otto von Gierke's *Das Deutsche Genossenschaftsrecht* (Berlin, 1873) with him on his first winter spent in the Canary Islands. He was strangely attracted to Gierke's idea of the organic reality of groups in German law. H. A. L. Fisher, *Frederick William Maitland: A biographical sketch* (Cambridge, 1910), pp. 157–9. The German influence on English and American corporation law is well examined in R. Harris, 'The transplantation of the legal discourse on corporate personality theories' (2006) 63 *Wash. & Lee L. Rev.* 1421–78.

[4] Pollock and Maitland, *History of English Law*, pp. 490–1. Maitland based this passage on a lecture he delivered to Liverpool law students on 25 May 1893. F. W. Maitland, *The Corporation Aggregate: The history of a legal idea* (Liverpool, 1893), p. 6.

[5] C. T. Carr, *The General Principles of the Law of Corporations* (Cambridge, 1905), pp. 150–3 ('Anthropomorphism'); F. Pollock, 'Has the common law received the fiction theory of corporations?' (1911) 27 *L.Q.R.* 219–35; H. J. Laski, 'The early history of the corporation in England' (1917) 30 *Harv. L. Rev.* 561–88; W. S. Holdsworth, 'English corporation law in the 16th and 17th centuries' (1922) 31 *Yale L. J.* 382–407; W. S. Holdsworth, *A History of English Law*, 3rd edn, 9 vols. (London, 1923–1931), III, pp. 482–7; J. Dewey, 'The historical background of corporate legal personality' (1926) 35 *Yale L. J.* 655–73; H. K. C. Wang, 'The corporate entity concept (or fiction theory) in the Year Book period' (1942) 58 *L.Q.R.* 498–511, and (1943) 59 *L.Q.R.* 72–86; H. Lubasz, 'The corporate borough in the common law of

these same arguments from the corporation cases, but with a different question in mind.

What I expected to find when I worked on each of these cases in isolation, as they came up in Year Book order, was that arguments that a corporate entity was entirely separate from the real individuals who comprised it and opposing arguments that the court should see through the corporate entity to consider the people inside of it would be made by two opposing groups of lawyers and judges. I wanted to find formalist serjeants and justices regularly making the first type of argument in opposition to realist serjeants and justices regularly making the second type of argument. If lawyers as advocates couldn't differentiate themselves in this way, because they had to take their clients and their clients' best arguments as they found them, I expected that then at least judges would be consistent along this formalist–realist divide. What I found instead was that these lawyers and judges switched sides regularly, making arguments that seemed to me not only inconsistent, but having entirely different theoretical orientations.

First, a few words about terminology. The term 'body politic' (*corps politique*) was introduced in the Year Books in Michaelmas 1478, when Serjeant Starkey said that there was a distinction between bodies politic and natural bodies.[6] Ten more reports used the term in the next four years, and a steady stream thereafter. Body politic did not mean the whole realm of England, but meant a mayor and commonalty of a city or town, a dean and chapter of a cathedral, a master and scholars of a college, or an abbot and convent of an abbey. Two abridgers of Year Book reports interpolated the term body politic into entries for cases from 1429 and 1388 but these are later additions to the original text.[7] I did not find a Parliament roll referring to a body politic until 1484, though then it was to 'the body politic of

---

the late Year-Book period' (1964) 80 *L.Q.R.* 228–43. And see now J. H. Baker, *The Oxford History of the Laws of England* (Oxford, 2003), VI, pp. 622–7, and S. Reynolds, 'The history of the idea of incorporation or legal personality: A case of fallacious teleology' in S. Reynolds, *Ideas and Solidarities of the Medieval Laity* (Aldershot, 1995), sec. VI, pp. 12–14.

[6] Mich. 18 Edw. 4, pl. 17, ff. 15b–16a (1478.088). Parenthetical references in Year Book citations are to the author's index and paraphrase of printed Year Book reports, www.bu.edu/law/seipp.

[7] R. Brooke, *La Graunde Abridgement* (London, 1573), tit. Corporations, pl. 24, f. 188v (London, 1573), excerpting Mich. 8 Hen. 6, pl. 2, ff. 1a–1b (1429.086) and adding words, 'to wit, a body politic and a natural body'; D. Jenkins, *Eight Centuries* (London, 1661), p. 64 (2nd century, case 21), 145 E.R. 46, a version of Trin. 12 Ric. 2, pl. 10, Ames 19–20 (1388.058am).

England',[8] and a statute first used the term in 1523.[9] *The Oxford English Dictionary* has no earlier references to a body politic.

The term corporation is older than body politic in the Year Books, appearing from 1429, the word corporate from 1408, incorporate from 1439, and the rather redundant 'body corporate' (*corps corporate*) in a 1481 report[10] as well as in a statute of 1461, which has also the first occurrence of the word corporation in any statute.[11] When distinguished from these collective bodies, we ordinary human beings were called bodies natural, private persons, singular persons, sole persons, natural persons, single persons, common persons, natural men and material men.[12]

Now, to start with, two earlier cases led into the sort of disputes that raised these arguments around 1480. In 1372, a plaintiff prosecuted a nuisance action against the Dean and Chapter of St Peter of Exeter and against a clerk named John Weliot. Counsel for the defendants pleaded that the named clerk was also a member of the chapter, and was thus sued twice. We have two reports of the case, but both just say that this plea 'was not allowed'.[13]

The same issue came up again in 1429, and the reports show a much more interesting argument. (Maitland liked this case too.) The mayor, bailiffs and commonalty of Ipswich were sued for trespass, along with one J. Jabe as an individual defendant. Serjeant Rolf for the defendants pleaded that the individual defendant was one of the commonalty, and so was sued twice as a defendant. Martin J agreed with Rolf that if this writ were allowed the individual defendant could be charged twice for the same wrong or there could be inconsistent verdicts, and so the writ should be thrown out. Babington CJ and Paston J disagreed with Martin. Martin had argued that if judgments were given against both

---

[8] A roll of Parliament referred to 'the body politic of England' in 1484, 6 Rot. Parl. 237a (23 Jan. 1484). A Year Book report of 1522 had the statement that the King, Lords, and Commons in Parliament were a corporation. Mich. 14 Hen. 8, pl. 2, 119 SS 98, 101 (Fyneux CJ (KB)) (1522.011ss).

[9] 14 & 15 Hen. 8, ch. 6, sec. 5 (1523).

[10] Mich. 8 Hen. 6, pl. 2, ff. 1a–1b (1429.086) (corporation); Mich. 10 Hen. 4, pl. 5, f. 3b (1408.005) (corporate); Mich. 18 Hen. 6, pl. 6, ff. 21a–22a (1439.006) (incorporate); Pasch. 21 Edw. 4, pl. 21, ff. 7a–7b (1481.029) (body corporate).

[11] 1 Edw. 4, ch. 1 (1461).

[12] Most of these terms can be found in the *Lincoln* and *Norwich* cases cited below; natural body in Mich. 18 Edw. 4, pl. 17, ff. 15b–16a (1478.088); material man in Hil. 21 Edw. 4, pl. 9, ff. 16a–16b (1482.009) (Sjt Sulyard); and common person in Hil. 10 Hen. 7, pl. 15, ff. 16a–6b (1495.015) (Sjt Wode).

[13] Mich. 46 Edw. 3, pl. 7, ff. 23b–24a (1372.075); 46 Edw. 3, Lib. Ass. 9, ff. 306b–307a (1372.123ass).

the collective entity and the individual defendant then that individual's goods could be put in execution twice. Babington and Paston insisted that when judgment is given against a collective entity, damages are only collected from goods that were collectively owned. Martin pointed out that when the king fined or amerced a collective entity, the king levied the fine on goods of the individual members, not just collectively owned goods. The reports differ on whether Babington conceded this point about fines to the king, as he should have, because Martin was right, but if there was one sure rule of the early common law it was, as Babington remarked in one of these reports, that there was a big difference between the king and everybody else. Maitland saw here the first stirrings of limited liability, the separation of corporate assets from individual assets for some purposes. Strangeways J joined with Babington and Paston on the formalist side saying that 'no individual person is the commonalty', calling it an aggregate and at the same time a body. Like so many Year Book cases, this one has no judgment reported, but the weight of judicial authority seems to line up with the 1372 case on the formalist side.[14]

In 1478, an abbot and convent of an abbey brought a writ of trespass for trees cut down in the time of the abbot's predecessor. The defendant pleaded the legal maxim that personal actions die with the person, so it was too late to sue about what happened in the time of the previous abbot. Before the case went off on the application of the Statute of Marlborough (1267) as to standing trees, Serjeant Humfrey Starkey explained that the abbot and convent as a corporation, a body politic, unlike a natural body, could not die, could not be dead, and so its personal actions would always survive.[15] This point that corporations could not die had been made in 1465, and would be made again in four different cases in 1481 and 1482.[16]

The two principal cases that best contrast formalist and realist arguments, one with five reports from 1478 to 1482 and the other with four reports all from 1481, were about a jury challenge and a duress defence.

---

[14] Mich. 8 Hen. 6, pl. 2, ff. 1a–1b (1429.086); Mich. 8 Hen. 6, pl. 34, ff. 14b–15a (1429.118); Mich. 9 Hen. 6, pl. 9, f. 36b (1430.056).

[15] Mich. 18 Edw. 4, pl. 17, ff. 15b–16a (1478.088).

[16] Mich. 21 Edw. 4, pl. 3, f. [38]b (1481.071) (per Fairfax J (KB)); Mich. 21 Edw. 4, pl. 4, ff. 12b–15a (1481.068) (per Sjt Townshend); Hil. 21 Edw. 4, pl. 3, ff. 15a–15b (1482.003) (per Catesby J (CP)); Hil. 21 Edw. 4, pl. 9, ff. 75b–77b (1482.038) (per Sjt Pygot, 'a crabbish case'). The practical difficulty that these religious entities did not die had been realised at least as early as the mortmain legislation in 1279.

Both were 'serjeants' cases' in which every one of the serjeants spoke. The jury challenge case can be called the 'Dean and Chapter of Lincoln v. Prat'. A party, presumably Prat, challenged one of the prospective jurors on the grounds that the juror was a brother of one of the canons or prebendaries of Lincoln Cathedral, thus a brother of one member of the chapter.[17]

In the Lincoln case, the formalist position, argued by four serjeants, one apprentice, and one justice, said that the canon's brother should not be struck off the jury. Some of the arguments were that the dean and chapter together as a collective entity could not have a brother or any other relative; that the canon himself was a stranger to the action and not a party or privy to it; that the canon's death or excommunication or a release from the canon would not affect the lawsuit; that if the collective body lost a judgment the canon's own goods would not be executed upon, as was said in 1429; and finally that the canon had no advantage or individual benefit or interest if the collective body won. The collective entity of dean and chapter was completely separate, completely estranged from the canons who made up the chapter.

The realist position in this Lincoln case, argued by four serjeants, four justices, and one serjeant who became a justice while argument continued, was that the challenge was good and the canon's brother should be struck from the jury for presumed bias. Some of the arguments were that the canon was a party or privy to the action and not a stranger; that he had advantage by the collective body's recovery to their common use; and that the canon's brother would be permitted to appear in court and give evidence (if he had any), as a family member not barred by the law of maintenance, so that as to the dean and chapter he was family. Most often, those arguing the realist position said simply that the brother of one of the canons could be presumed to be biased when the dean and chapter were a party.

Though the justices said during argument that this question was evenly poised, *aequedubium*, all but one of the justices whose speeches were recorded argued the realist position, and it prevailed, striking the canon's brother from the jury. Older Year Book cases struck from juries brothers or other relatives of monks or nuns when the abbot and convent were on trial,[18] but the formalist position tried to distinguish these cases because

---

[17] *Dean and Chapter of Lincoln v. Prat* (1478–1482) was reported in Hil. 17 Edw. 4, pl. 1, f. 7a (1478.001); Pasch. 21 Edw. 4, pl. 28, ff. 31a–33b (1481.059); Mich. 21 Edw. 4, pl. 3, ff. 11b–12b (1481.067); Mich. 21 Edw. 4, pl. 33, ff. 63a–63b (1481.101); and Hil. 21 Edw. 4, pl. 29, ff. 20b–21a (1482.029).

[18] e.g. Trin. 28 Hen. 6, pl. 17, f. 10a (1450.007); 34 Edw. 3, Lib. Ass. pl. 6, ff. 203b–204b (1360.006ass).

monks, unlike cathedral canons, were dead in law, had no separate possessions, and depended for their entire sustenance on the abbot's gain or
loss. In the same way, a wife's brother could not be a juror when the
husband was on trial, because husband and wife were one person in law.

What I find so exasperatingly unrealistic about the losing arguments,
the formalist arguments in this Lincoln case, is the premise that just
because the lawyers could completely separate the collective entity from
its members, that the members themselves and their relatives should be
presumed to make the same separation and to feel also no interest, no
benefit, no advantage from the collective entity's victory. If my brother's
corporation were on trial, I would want it to win.

The second case, the duress defence, arose in Norwich. The abbot of
St Benet of Hulme sued the mayor, sheriffs, and commonalty of
Norwich on a sealed obligation, a bond stating that Norwich owed
the abbey £100. The Norwich defendants pleaded that when the
obligation was made the mayor of Norwich had been in prison, so the
bond was void for duress.[19] Local historians recount that a Norwich
mayor actually was imprisoned in the Fleet prison by a group including
the abbot of Hulme and the earl of Suffolk in 1442, thirty-nine years
before this case was argued, and that a bond for that amount was sealed
by the city's common seal during the mayor's imprisonment.[20] If you

---

[19] *Abbot of St. Benet (Benedict) of Hulme v. Mayor and Commonalty of Norwich* (1481)
Pasch. 21 Edw. 4, pl. 21, ff. 7a–7b (1481.029); Pasch. 21 Edw. 4, pl. 22, ff. 27a–28b
(1481.053); Mich. 21 Edw. 4, pl. 4, ff. 12b–15a (1481.068); and Mich. 21 Edw. 4, pl. 53, ff.
67b–70b (1481.121).

[20] After a disputed mayoral election in 1433, former mayor Thomas Wetherby feuded with
a succession of mayors, aldermen, and commons. Wetherby enlisted the earl of Suffolk
and the abbot of Hulme on his side. Norwich enlisted the duke of Gloucester on their
side. In 1441, Wetherby instigated the abbot to prosecute Norwich for erecting new mills
on the river Wensum. A commission under the earl of Suffolk awarded that Norwich
destroy their mills and enter into a bond for £100 with the abbot to be forfeited if they
ever erected the mills again. When the parties were ordered to appear before the king's
council, the mayor was committed to Fleet Prison from 13 Feb. to 26 Mar. 1443. On
10 Mar. 1443, while the mayor was in the Fleet, Wetherby took the Norwich common
seal and, according to the earl's award, sealed the bond for £100 to the abbot of Hulme.
W. Hudson and J. C. Tingey, *The Records of the City of Norwich*, 2 vols. (Norwich, 1906),
I, pp. lxxxiiii–xciii, 348–55 (I thank Ben McRee for this reference); F. Blomefield, *An
Essay Towards a Topographical History of the County of Norfolk*, 5 vols. (London, 1806),
III, pp. 144–9. Blomefield recorded that a successor abbot's lawsuit in 1481 to recover on
the bond was unsuccessful, as was a commission subsequently brought to destroy the
new mills. *Ibid.*, p. 149, n. 7. See also J. R. Green, *Town Life in the Fifteenth Century*,
2 vols. (London, 1907), I, pp. 387 at n. 1, 391–3; H. A. Doubleday, *The Victoria History of
the County of Norfolk*, ed. W. Page, 6 vols. (London, 1906), II, p. 334.

doubt that abbots went around imprisoning others in order to enter into bond obligations, six earlier Year Book reports show pleadings that abbots had imprisoned priors, imprisoned monks, threatened imprisonment, or had been imprisoned themselves.[21]

The formalist position, argued by five serjeants and one justice, took the abbot's side and contended that imprisoning the mayor was not duress, so the city had to pay the abbot on the bond. Some of the arguments were that it was impossible to imprison a collective entity, just as it could not be beaten or wounded; that a collective entity likewise could not commit treason or felony or any corporal wrong for which it could be imprisoned; that the mayor was a stranger to the collective body; that the mayor was not imprisoned 'as mayor'; that if the mayor had been insane, an infant, excommunicated, outlawed, or a villein, or had given a release, none of these would have voided the collective entity's bond; and that the collective body had no cause of action for its mayor's imprisonment. As with the jury challenge case, there were earlier Year Book cases on the duress defense establishing that imprisonment of an abbot would invalidate the abbot and convent's deed. The formalist position again distinguished these old cases in the same way, arguing that the monks of the abbot's convent were dead in law, while all of the commonalty were fully capable at law.

The realist position, argued by five serjeants and two justices, took the Norwich side and argued that the city's bond was void for duress. Some of the arguments were that without the mayor's free and willing personal agreement the collective entity's bond was void; that thus not all of the collective body had made the bond and it was not their bond; that the mayor was imprisoned as mayor; that the mayor was not a stranger to the collective body, but was its principal member and head; that if the head be imprisoned the rest of the body can do nothing; and that the collective entity could sue a writ of false imprisonment when their mayor was imprisoned. No judgment is reported in this case. Two justices of Common Pleas, including the chief justice, favoured the realist side and the defendant city. One justice and a serjeant who was appointed justice in the same term the case was reported favoured the formalist side.

Again I find the formalist arguments odd and unpersuasive. The extreme formalist position seemed to be that every single member of

---

[21] Trin. 28 Hen. 6, pl. 7, f. 8b (1450.017); Mich. 35 Hen. 6, pl. 26, ff. 17b–18a (1456.080); Pasch. 38 Hen. 6, pl. 7, f. 27a (1460.015); Mich. 39 Hen. 6, pl. 48, ff. 35b–36a (1460.076); Hil. 39 Hen. 6, pl. 16, ff. 50b–51b (1461.016); Mich. 15 Edw. 4, pl. 2, ff. 1b–2a (1475.034).

the collective body could be imprisoned, and yet the collective body itself was somehow distinct from and a stranger to all of them, could not be imprisoned and thus could never have a duress defence. The same chief justice who took the realist side in this case made that very formalist argument in 1475.[22] This again supposes that real human beings experience their role in a collective entity as entirely disconnected from their individual personal situations. I doubt the mayor of Norwich in Fleet prison would have had much consolation if he had known that half the serjeants and justices of England thought that he was not imprisoned 'as mayor'. If my dean were imprisoned to force us as a dean and faculty to enter into a promissory note, I think we should have a duress defence.

In both cases, those arguing the realist position tended to concede many of the narrow points made by the formalists but then disputed that those points did not lead to the formalist result. Those arguing the formalist position, perhaps ironically, made the most pragmatic arguments. Thus, no jury could ever be sworn when the mayor and commonalty of London were on trial, if relatives of every Londoner were excluded, to which Huse CJ on the opposing realist side said that such a particular point would not change the law.[23] And if imprisonment of any one member of the commonalty would void an obligation for duress, then the mayor and commonalty of no city could ever make a valid bond when any of the commonalty was in prison. Bryan CJ, to refute this argument, announced that to enter into a bond or to take any other action a commonalty required only majority agreement, not unanimous consent.[24] His is a rare judicial endorsement of majority rule in the Year Books.[25]

The form of most Year Book argument from the thirteenth century onward was argument by analogy. Serjeants and justices would put hypothetical cases that were meant to seem obvious to both sides or would assert what had often been adjudged, and then the similarity of the hypothetical

---

[22] Mich. 15 Edw. 4, pl. 2, ff. 1b–2a (1475.034).

[23] Pasch. 21 Edw. 4, pl. 28, ff. 31a–33b (1481.059) (Fairfax J (KB) and Huse CJ (KB)).

[24] If the greater part of the commonalty agrees, it is as if all agree (Bryan CJ (CP)), in Mich. 21 Edw. 4, pl. 4, ff. 12b–15a (1481.068). In the greater part their body resides (Choke J (CP)) and if the greater part agree, it is good; perhaps they will never all agree, and where the majority are, there are all (Bryan CJ (CP)), in Mich. 21 Edw. 4, pl. 53, ff. 67b–70b (1481.121).

[25] Notable earlier examples are 1281–1284 Lincolnshire Eyre pl. 2, 122 SS 89–92 (1282.003) (Saham J or Spigurnel J); Mich. 9 Hen. 6, pl. 3, ff. 32b–34b (1430.050); Pasch. 19 Hen. 6, pl. 1, ff. 62a–65a (1441.028) (Hody CJ (KB)); Mich. 20 Hen. 6, pl. 25, ff. 12b–13b (1441.080) (Fray CB (Ex.)). I thank Dr Paul Brand for the earliest citation.

case to the actual litigated case was supposed to persuade the rest of the court and bar. These analogies tended to be far broader, far more distant than we would use today. Many of the formalist and realist arguments in these cases followed this form, reasoning from dean and chapter to mayor and commonalty to husband and wife to one's hand and one's head. But what seem new to me in these corporation cases from the early 1480s are the arguments that pursue and extend this concept, the collective entity, its separate existence, and thereby its estrangement from the real people who made it up. So I suppose what I am calling formalism here could more precisely be called conceptualism.

When Serjeant Humfrey Starkey first said, in 1478, that there was a distinction between a natural body and a body politic, which is ordained by the policy of a man (or of one man), this suggests that the body politic and the arguments associated with it were consciously invented.[26] Many of the arguments pursue and elaborate the metaphor of a disembodied incorporeal yet corporate body composed of many natural bodies. The most obvious and proximate source of this talk in Westminster Hall about bodies politic, their heads and their members was the 'conciliarist' writing earlier in the fifteenth century by theologians and canonist lawyers, mostly in Paris, about the 'mystical body' (*corpus mysticum*) of the church, based on 1 Corinthians chapter 12, and the church's *corpus politicum*.[27] These church reformers had an immediate, practical need to differentiate the church as an ideal entity from the individual popes and prelates who led it at the time. Their writings clearly influenced English constitutional writers of later centuries.

Fairfax J, in a case in 1481 about charging a successor abbot for his predecessor's act, actually called an abbacy a 'mystical body' that never died.[28] There are hints as well of other religious models for these arguments. Bryan CJ and two serjeants all said in various ways that in the body politic of Norwich there were 'three separate persons' – mayor, sheriffs and commonalty – 'this body is in three parts', three 'distinct

---

[26] 'il [est] diversity enter un corps natural & un corps politick, le quel est ordeine per le policy d' un home' (Sjt Starkey), in Mich. 18 Edw. 4, pl. 17, ff. 15b–16a (1478.088).

[27] F. Oakley, 'Natural law, the *corpus mysticum*, and consent in conciliar thought from John of Paris to Matthias Ugonius' (1981) 56 *Speculum* 786, 794–5, 800–6, citing particularly Pierre d' Ailly and Jean Gerson. See also H. de Lubac, *Corpus Mysticum: The Eucharist and the Church in the Middle Ages*, tr. G. Simmonds (London, 2006), pp. 101–19 (pp. 116–35 of Paris, 1949 edn).

[28] 'cest mystical corps del Abbe ne unques morust', in Mich. 21 Edw. 4, pl. 3, f. [38]b (1481.071).

members'. This recalls the theologians' mystery of the Trinity preached every Trinity Sunday. Serjeant Pygot, whose formalist arguments were the most detailed, said that 'the corporation … is only a name that cannot be seen and does not have substance'.[29] Choke J said that a body politic is made up of natural men and yet when it is made it is a dead person in law, which could not be arrested, a body dead in law.[30]

Ernst Kantorowicz in his masterful *The King's Two Bodies* of 1957 joined other scholars in attempting to show that these Year Book lawyers in 1478 and afterwards were transplanting Pope Alexander III's late twelfth-century decretal *Quoniam abbas*,[31] and its accompanying glosses and elaborations from Innocent IV in the mid thirteenth century, translating the canonist *dignitas* now for some reason as body politic and corporation in the late fifteenth century.[32] Some of the arguments these lawyers made, that the body politic never died and that a legal act taken in one's personal name had completely different consequences from the same act taken in the name of one's role in a collective entity, do support that link. In many other contexts, Year Book lawyers stated much more clearly that they were drawing on the law of holy church or were talking to doctors of the canon-law side.[33] I'm not convinced.

Kantorowicz and others have also suggested an origin for these arguments in the high politics of the realm, linked to the decision supposed to have been made by Edward IV's legal counsellors changing the Duchy of Lancaster from a personal possession of the Lancastrian kings to a corporation held by the House of York.[34] Successors of these Year Book lawyers were to build upon these body politic arguments eighty years later in 1561 in Plowden's report of the case of the Duchy of Lancaster, a great matter of state, in which it was resolved that the nine-year-old Edward VI had in him two bodies, to wit a body natural and a body politic.[35] It is hard to imagine that these 1481 arguments about the canon's brother's jury duty or the mayor's imprisonment were dictated by crown policy or eight decades' foresight. King's serjeants

---

[29] All in Mich. 21 Edw. 4, pl. 4, ff. 12b–15a (1481.068).
[30] Mich. 21 Edw. 4, pl. 53, ff. 67b–70b (1481.121).
[31] X. 1.29.14 (Decretals of Gregory IX), in E. Friedberg, *Corpus Juris Canonici*, 2 vols. (Graz, 1879), II, col. 162.
[32] E. H. Kantorowicz, *The King's Two Bodies: A study in medieval political theology* (Princeton, 1957), pp. 385–401.
[33] D. J. Seipp, 'The reception of canon law and civil law in the common law courts before 1600' (1993) 13 *O.J.L.S.* 388–420.
[34] Kantorowicz, *The King's Two Bodies*, pp. 7–20, 403–9.
[35] *Dutchy of Lancaster Case* (1561) 1 Plowden 212, 213; 75 E.R. 325, 326.

were about as likely to make realist arguments as formalist ones, as was
Humfrey Starkey, former Recorder of London.

I suspect that in a broader sense the appeal of these formalist arguments was simply the lawyers' love of the counterintuitive result. For
legal reasoning to be different from and better than ordinary common
sense, there seems to be a need for legal reasoning to reach unlikely,
surprising, tricky, paradoxical outcomes. So we have lawyers' loopholes,
technicalities and traps for the unwary. Guilty defendants go free.
Bequests to grandchildren at their christening are void as perpetuities.
And we have collective entities that have nothing to do with the people
collected within them. We have brothers who are not brothers, mayors
who are not mayors and imprisonment that is not imprisonment.

As I said already, I did not find a consistent group of formalists to
deplore nor a consistent group of realists to admire among the bench and
bar of 1481. In Michaelmas 1481, there were nine serjeants at law, four
justices of Common Pleas, and three justices of King's Bench. Between
the two cases that I have studied most closely, the Lincoln jury challenge
and the Norwich duress defence, two serjeants (Catesby and Pygot)
stayed formalist, two (Tremayle and Townshend) switched from formalist to realist, two (Starkey and Bridges) switched from realist to formalist,
and one (Vavasour) stayed realist. Both serjeants who remained formalist in these two cases (across nine different reports), Catesby and Pygot,
took the realist position against Starkey in 1478, refusing to find a body
politic separate from the dead abbot.[36] The one consistent realist in the
Lincoln and Norwich cases, Vavasour, took formalist positions in cases
involving interpretation of a jury exemption in 1481 and disseisin of rent
from a dean and chapter in 1483.[37] I found no consistently formalist nor
consistently realist serjeants.

These serjeants were advocates, of course, who pleaded for the clients
they had, so their inconsistency is perhaps to be expected. But my two
principal cases were so-called serjeants' cases, in which every serjeant at
the bar took part, and it seems unlikely that the two parties would have
paid counsel fees to all of the serjeants who spoke, when in one case the
dispute was merely a challenge of one juror in an assize. There has
sometimes been an assumption that in civil cases every lawyer who
spoke in support of one side's position or another's was paid a fee by

---

[36] Mich. 18 Edw. 4, pl. 17, ff. 15b–16a (1478.088).
[37] Mich. 21 Edw. 4, pl. 28, ff. 55b–59b (1481.096); Trin. 1 Edw. 5, pl. 10, ff. 4b–5b
   (1483.028).

the litigant, and an opposite assumption in criminal cases. The truth probably lies somewhere in between. I still find it puzzling that the serjeants who might be expected to argue their own opinions as if they were judges showed so little consistency in this regard.

We can and should expect more consistency from the judges. Justices of Common Pleas spoke in both cases. Two of them, Nele and Bryan CJ, stayed on the realist side, and one, Choke, switched from realist to formalist. Bryan, a consistent realist in the Lincoln and Norwich cases, made some very formalist arguments in cases before and since. Bryan argued in 1475 that it was impossible to imprison an abbot and convent even if the abbot and all the monks were imprisoned, and in 1488 he argued that a collective entity could not hire or command a servant without writing, though he did not use quite as formalist an argument as Serjeant Wode employed in 1492 on the same issue, that a corporate body had no mouth, so it was reduced to writing, although somehow then it did have hands.[38] The other consistent realist, Nele J, was not reported in any other case raising these issues.

All these serjeants and justices, so renowned for finding distinctions between seemingly identical situations, did not make a distinction between the Lincoln jury-challenge dispute and the Norwich duress defence. They did not distinguish between the corporate identity of the dean and chapter as a religious group and that of the mayor and commonalty as civic group. The jury challenge and duress defence situations are analytically similar as instances of sworn obligations overcome by presumed human frailties: a juror's oath to give a true and impartial verdict overcome by family loyalty (presumed bias), and a contractual obligation to pay money overcome by imprisonment (presumed lack of consent). Consistency of approach across these two and other similar cases is not too much to expect.

So I find distinct, persistent patterns of two types of opposing arguments, but not two distinct, consistent groups of lawyers or judges who make these opposing arguments. I find formalism and realism, but no formalists, no realists. Year Book reports carefully name the speakers in almost every case, but the content of the named lawyers' and judges' speeches does not differentiate them well at all. Any judge's speech could have been made by any other judge, and any serjeant's speech by any other serjeant. I have not found any speaker in the late fifteenth century Year Books as distinctive as Thomas Rolf, who in the 1420s and 1430s barked animal noises, sang snatches of

---

[38] Mich. 15 Edw. 4, pl. 2, ff. 1b–2a (1475.034); Mich. 4 Hen. 7, pl. 7, ff. 17b–18a (1488.042); Hil. 7 Hen. 7, pl. 2, ff. 9a–10a (1492.002).

ballads, reported a seven-year pregnancy, introduced Latin grammar and logic terminology, and made arguments from etymology.[39]

Thomas Littleton, the author of the famous treatise on tenures, stands out in the years before his death in August 1481 because his pronouncements often seem didactic. Littleton conveniently died just months before these arguments took place about bodies politic and their separation from the people inside them, but when he did speak in prior cases raising similar issues he tended to split the difference between formalist and realist positions in oddly modern-sounding ways.[40]

In this examination of formalist and realist arguments I intended to find heroes and villains, but in failing to find them, I find another lesson about fifteenth-century English judges and lawyers. They did not seem to invest their personalities in the performance of their professional duties. They seemed to appreciate that the full range of the legal profession's stockpile of arguments needed to be preserved, and a serjeant or judge would take up an argument in one case, inconsistent with what he had just said in another case, simply because no one else was making that argument, or no one else was making that argument well enough. I suspect that these judges and lawyers were not interested in driving one or another type of argument out of existence, but were consciously preserving modes of argument because the next generation's clients might need them. These fifteenth-century judges did not view the opposing arguments the way I read them (and Maitland read them), as so fundamentally opposed to one another that no single person could seriously make both sorts of arguments in different cases. Each side did not think the other side's arguments were silly or not worth making, though Maitland would say that Edward Coke and Robert Brooke made an awful nonsense of those arguments in later centuries.

Looking for distinctive, consistent individual judicial philosophies, what I find instead is a consistent collective judicial commitment to preservation of conflicting philosophies and conflicting approaches. What I find is a corporate, collective personality separable from the individuals who comprised the judiciary and bar of fifteenth-century England.

---

[39] e.g. 'bawwaw for thy reason', in Hil. 8 Hen. 6, pl. 7, ff. 21b–23a (1430.007); Robin Hode en Barnesdale stode, in Pasch. 7 Hen. 6, pl. 45, f. 37b (1429.051); seven-year pregnancy, in Mich. 1 Hen. 6, pl. 8, ff. 3a–3b (1422.042).

[40] e.g. in some respects the abbot and convent are one person in law and in other respects not (Littleton J (CP)), in Mich. 15 Edw. 4, pl. 2, ff. 1b–2a (1475.034).

3

Early-modern judges and the practice of precedent

IAN WILLIAMS*

The history of ideas of precedent is understandably important; it is the history of the logic of authority, which Maitland saw as the divide between historians and lawyers when using materials from the past.[1] The importance of prior cases and the doctrine of precedent as distinguishing features of the English common law means that any ideas of precedent, or its practice, are important for the history of the common law and when considering the place of the common law in a European context.[2] Ideas of precedent are remarked upon by the majority of writers dealing with legal theory in the time of the Year Books and the first nominate reports. However, investigations through the materials usually come to little: an acknowledgement that judges did, on occasion, describe what they were doing as making a 'precedent', followed by an admission that 'precedent' had a different meaning to that we have now,

---

* My thanks to Professor David Ibbetson for reading an earlier draft of this chapter and to the editors for their helpful suggestions. Spelling has been modernised except in titles. Translations are the author's own, although often based on published translations where available. Original punctuation has generally been retained unless alteration was required for comprehension.

[1] F. W. Maitland, 'Why the history of English law is not written' in H. A. L. Fisher (ed.), *The Collected Papers of Frederic William Maitland* (Cambridge, 1911), p. 491. To investigate the history of precedent skirts perilously close to the vexed question as to the historical sense of early-modern lawyers raised in J. G. A. Pocock, *The Ancient Constitution and the Feudal Law: Reissue with a retrospect* (Cambridge, 1987), but that shall not be considered here.

[2] Although an increasingly casuistic focus has been discerned in both English and European legal systems in the early-modern period, see J. H. Baker, 'English law and the Renaissance' [1985] *C.L.J.* 44, 54–6 and 59 and D. J. Ibbetson, 'Common law and *ius commune*', 2001 Selden Society Lecture, in *The Selden Society Lectures 1952–2001* (Buffalo, NY, 2003), pp. 679–81.

being associated with the record rather than reports.[3] This linguistic approach does not work. Early-modern judges did pay considerable attention to their predecessors, as the plethora of case citations in printed and manuscript law reports of the time shows.[4] Such citations are not necessarily precedent. What will be examined here is 'precedent' in the modern sense, that of previous decisions binding a judge in a case to a particular conclusion on a point of law, whatever the language used.[5] It must be acknowledged that the evidence is relatively sparse, as even in a system with a functioning doctrine of *stare decisis*, cases where judges are entirely constrained by previous cases are relatively rare: given the opportunity, lawyers can (and lawyers did) distinguish cases not congenial to their argument rather than submit to an unwelcome earlier decision.[6]

This chapter concludes that there was a notion of the binding force of previous cases by the time of the Civil War, although it is only seen rarely. Such a notion developed principally through the use of the court record, rather than law reports. The special probative power of the record as evidence of a past decision gave it especial authority – for early-modern common lawyers the lawyer's 'logic of authority' was consequently not distinct from the historian's 'logic of evidence'.[7] The reliance on court record links early-modern law directly with medieval use of 'precedents', but the practice was changing. Crucially, early-modern lawyers began to conceive of the record in a different way to

---

[3] N. Doe, *Fundamental Authority in Late Medieval English Law* (Cambridge, 1990), pp. 22–4 addressing both 'legislative' expressions in the Year Books and express references to the creation of 'precedent'.

[4] J. W. Tubbs, *The Common Law Mind* (Baltimore, MA, 2000), pp. 181–2.

[5] D. J. Ibbetson, 'Case-law and doctrine: A historical perspective on the English common law' in R. Schulze and U. Seif (eds.), *Richterrecht und Rechtsfortbildung in der Europäischen Rechtsgemeinschaft* (Tübingen, 2003), pp. 28–9. I have attempted to avoid the word 'authoritative' with regard to prior cases. Tubbs in *The Common Law Mind*, p. 182, comments that '[b]y the time of Coke and Bacon in the early-seventeenth century, prior decisions unquestionably became authoritative'. The ambiguity here is important. Close reading of Tubbs would suggest that he did not mean to suggest prior cases were binding at this point, as he states on the previous page that cases were not binding until later.

[6] Simpson makes precisely this point with regard to the decision of the House of Lords to be bound by its own authority in *London Tramways Co.* v. *London County Council* [1898] A.C. 375 (H.L.): A. W. B. Simpson, 'The ratio decidendi of a case and the doctrine of binding precedent' in A. G. Guest (ed.), *Oxford Essays in Jurisprudence* (Oxford, 1961), p. 155.

[7] The language is that of Maitland, 'Why the history of English law is not written', p. 491.

their predecessors and derive different conclusions from it. At the same time, there was a theoretical movement conflating record and report, claiming the authority of the record for law reports. These developments suggest a decline in importance for the record with an accompanying elevation of the role of (printed) law reports.

The binding nature of the record

In the late sixteenth century it is apparent that law reports cannot be binding precedents. Judges, but much less frequently counsel, are seen disagreeing with cases put to them, simply as they disagree with the conclusion. *Dighton* v. *Bartholmew* (1602) provides a good example. In that case:

> it was agreed by all [the Judges of the King's Bench] that a villein may not maintain an appeal of mayhem against his lord, and yet Fenner cited that it was agreed in the reports of Keilway newly put in print by Mr. Recorder, that if the villein sue an appeal of mayhem against his lord, this well lies, and that if he obtains judgment in this he shall be enfranchised. But they all agreed that the law is not so.[8]

This disagreement, and others like it, is not with the accuracy of the report but with the conclusion, the point of law.[9] Any system which has such a power in the judges cannot be considered to have a true notion of binding precedent if precedents can be undermined at will.

However, we also see judges disagreeing with the conclusion in law reports, but admitting that they will change their mind if the record, in the language of the time 'precedents', supports the conclusion seen in the reports. An example can be found in *Stucley* v. *Thynne*, where Browne J of the Common Pleas rejected a Year Book case showing that a writ of distress had been issued in similar circumstances to that under discussion, but once it had been vouched by officials that there were precedents for such an issue, he said he would change his mind if he could be shown them.[10] This seems to be a a purely procedural issue, that of whether or

---

[8] *Dighton* v. *Bartholmew* (1602) British Library Additional Manuscript [BL MS Add.] 25203 ff. 488–9.

[9] For concern about the accuracy of material see nn. 28–35, below, and, more generally, I. Williams, '"He creditted more the printed booke": Common lawyers' receptivity to print, *c.*1550–1640' (2010) 28 *Law and Hist. Rev.* 40, 55–59.

[10] *Stucley* v. *Thynne* (1567) in J. H. Baker, *Reports from the Lost Notebooks of Sir James Dyer*, Selden Society, vol. 109 (London, 1994), pp. 127, 128. Coke's report of *Manser's Case* (1584) 2 Co. Rep. 1, 3v; 76 E.R. 387, 394, might be an example of binding precedent; certainly the use of the record seems to have been important in changing the views of the judges. However, the report is not entirely clear, and Coke's description

not a writ should issue. To a modern legal historian there is clearly a substantive issue concealed behind the discussion: to refuse a writ would be to deny a remedy and thereby limit the ambit of the substantive law of distress. There is no evidence of Browne J approaching the matter from such a perspective. As such, whilst law reports, and decisions, could be rejected, it seems that precedents from the record were regarded as conclusive. From a modern perspective we would therefore regard the record, where capable of being cited, as having more authority than a report.

This approach continues; in Easter Term 1629 we see a judge consciously admitting that he will change his mind if a particular case put in argument is confirmed by the record. The judge therefore considered himself constrained to act in a particular way. In *Browne* v. *Strode* in the King's Bench, Jones J said that 'if the case of 8. James 1 [previously put by Hyde J] is as my Lord has vouched it, I will no more doubt in this matter and so he spoke to Noy to search the roll for it'.[11] The case does not seem to be reported in Trinity term, but by Michaelmas of 1629, on the same question, Jones J is reported as saying that it 'is not necessary to be argued' and his view was now that of the others.[12] The point at issue, as in *Stucley* v. *Thynne*, seems to be a purely procedural one: it is whether joint covenantees are entitled to sue in the same action and if both joint covenantees must be joined in the action. So far this is not that dissimilar to earlier references to the record. However, the report makes it clear that whilst the point appears to be procedural, participants were well aware that there was a substantive issue here, it was noted that only one of the joint covenantees had assured the covenant and was burdened by it to pay money.[13] Other cases put make it clear that the issue was seen as if 'he shall have the action[,] to whom the benefit of a promise is made'; in effect, the issue was one of privity of contract mixed with consideration.[14] Furthermore, argument was made showing the differences between parol promises and covenants.[15] As such, there was a clear underlying tendency to see these issues as related to the general question of enforceability of contracts, not merely covenants, despite the fact that

---

of the case cited is different to that reported by Dyer (*Wotton* v. *Cooke* (1574) 3 Dyer 337v; 73 E.R. 761) making interpretation difficult.

[11] *Browne* v. *Strode* (1629) Cambridge University Library Manuscript [CUL MS] Gg.ii.19, ff. 2–4. The case is reported much more briefly at BL MS Add. 35965, f. 2.

[12] CUL MS Gg.ii.19, f. 110.   [13] CUL MS Gg.ii.19, ff.2–2v.

[14] CUL MS Gg.ii.19, ff. 2–3.   [15] *Ibid.*

some of the contracts would have been unenforceable through the writ of covenant under discussion, as the contracts wanted writing. This case brings out an important trend in early-modern legal thought which needs to be understood.

The traditional categories of the forms of action were breaking down in the late sixteenth century. This point has been made before,[16] but it is important to realise that it did not necessarily constitute a problem and the importance it has for the emergence of ideas that prior cases are binding on a point of law. Some lawyers were happy to admit that the learning from the forms of action could be applied in new contexts, such as John Stone in the introduction to his 1612 reading in the Inner Temple, who considered that 'all real actions learnings' were applied in trespass and ejectment, rather than in the medieval real actions themselves.[17] Edward Coke provides another example. Coke's commonplace book does not feature separate sections for covenant, debt and assumpsit, but does include a section entitled 'Contract Bargain &c'.[18] Coke seems to have separated notions of contract from the particular forms of action involved. The examples of Stone and Coke are very important, as their approach meant that learning associated with particular forms of action (whether in the Year Books, common learning, or found from the record) was no longer tied to a procedural context, but was instead a freestanding source of general ideas and treated as such. Such an approach was not only novel, but seems to have been so recognised, at least by Stone. Lawyers were extracting substantive legal ideas from earlier materials based around the availability (or not) of remedies in the form of writs. Seventeenth-century lawyers were, therefore, acting just as a modern legal historian using the Year Books does: they saw where the remedies stopped and from that could discern substantive law applicable in a wider variety of contexts. For the lawyers, rather than the legal historians, this was necessary to resolve disputes in the different procedural context of the seventeenth century. It is the paradigm example of Edward Coke's new corn coming from old fields.[19] Debate that would once have seemed to be procedural became substantive – more accurately was procedural and substantive simultaneously.

---

[16] Ibbetson, 'Common law and *ius commune*', pp. 696–8.
[17] Library of Congress Law Manuscript 94109274, f. 112.
[18] British Library Harleian Manuscript 6687, ff. 67–67v (f. 106 also has a heading of 'contract').
[19] *Calvin's Case* (1608) 7 Co. Rep. 1, 3v; 77 E.R. 377, 381.

An important example of the change is in actions on the case. In the context of defamation, many actions concerned the substantive question whether or not particular words could constitute defamation in particular circumstances. However, defamation was an action on the case and as such the words used, and their attendant circumstances, would all be included in the writ on the record. The question of whether words constituted defamation was both substantive and procedural, in that if words did not constitute defamation (the substantive question) then the writ did not lie, a classic procedural issue. In defamation cases at the end of the sixteenth century we can therefore see Anderson CJ (C.P.) saying that precedents from the record should be followed and wanting to see them.[20] Thirty years later Crooke J was unwilling to accept counsel's argument (against a judgment in the Exchequer Chamber) unless precedents could be shown.[21]

As such, although the record had previously been used to resolve procedural questions,[22] by the seventeenth century any answers would no longer be purely procedural; they would, in effect, have been decisions on points of law. This change has massive repercussions: instead of the record serving simply to determine a point of procedure, typically before trial, it could instead be used to resolve questions of substantive law raised after trial.[23] The citation of a case from the record could, in itself, determine the outcome of a case. At this point, 'precedents' in the early-modern or medieval sense can be seen as a binding force on later judges on points of law.

There are some important clarifications and qualifications to be made to the evidence put forward to this point. The first is that the record was not always treated as an essential part of legal argument. In

---

[20] *Holwood v. Hopkins* (1600) in R. H. Helmholz, *Select Cases on Defamation to 1600*, Selden Society, vol. 101 (London, 1985), p. 91.

[21] *George v. Harvey* (1633) CUL MS Gg.ii.19, ff. 332v–334. Evidently this gives a considerable role for prior cases without the record, but also shows that the record could override known, decided cases.

[22] The earliest example where the record is used in this manner seems to be a case in *Kaynes v. Kaynes* (1285) in P. Brand (ed.), *Earliest English Law Reports, II*, Selden Society, vol. 112 (London, 1996), pp. 185, 186, where the justices of the Common Bench justified giving judgment despite the absence of one of the parties, as had been done in the reign of Henry III 'as will be found in the roll of Trinity term in the fifty-fifth regnal year'. Such procedural uses of the record still occurred, for example in *Andrewes v. Lord Cromwell* (1602) BL MS Add. 25203, ff. 493, 493v–494v.

[23] On these changes in the nature of disputes see J. H. Baker, *The Oxford History of the Laws of England, 1483–1558* (Oxford, 2003), VI, pp. 385–407.

Dighton v. *Bartholmew* Yelverton J referred to his 'consideration of all the books' but not the record cited by counsel for the plaintiff.[24] However, this is probably because Yelverton's judgment accepted the argument of the plaintiff, so recourse to the record was unnecessary. More important are the unusual cases where the record was rejected. Perhaps the simplest is *Bright* v. *Forte* (1595), where counsel, Drewe, sought to have the record rejected for being wholly inaccurate as evidence of the past. According to Drewe, 'this judgment was secretly entered without the order of the court and I have spoken with Ewens Baron of the Exchequer who was of counsel in the case who said to me that after the judgment he brought a writ of error to reverse this for the opinion of all the justices was against the judgment'.[25] Where the record was inaccurate, then it would not be followed in argument. This is perhaps unsurprising as the accuracy of the record seems to have been the principal explanation for both its role and authority in argument. Such a concern with accuracy might be associated with humanist textual awareness and the increased focus on memory found in the early-modern common law.[26]

Many references to the record were simply for the purpose of verifying a report and ensuring accuracy. If the record were inaccurate it could not perform this function. *Dighton* v. *Bartholmew* provides a good example of this concern for accuracy. Counsel produced a copy of the record of a case from the reign of Henry VI which had been 'certified' by the second prothonotary of the King's Bench, Zachary Scott, at the time of *Dighton* itself.[27] The use of a 'certified' copy of the record would suggest a concern for accuracy. This procedure has not been found replicated elsewhere and is probably a consequence of the fact that here counsel produced the record independently, rather than having the justices direct him to search for it.

This role of the record as verification is twinned with (and perhaps explains) an absence of conceptual discussion of that role. Lawyers instead relied upon the presumed accuracy of the record. This presumption is reflected in both contemporary legal literature and in curial discussion. At its most general level, some common lawyers drew

---

[24] *Dighton* v. *Bartholmew*, BL MS Add. 25203, ff. 488–488v.
[25] *Bright* v. *Forte* (1595) BL MS Add. 25211, ff. 121v–122.
[26] R. J. Ross, 'The memorial culture of early modern English lawyers: Memory as keyword, shelter, and identity, 1560–1640' (1998) 10 *Yale J. L. & Human.* 229–326.
[27] *Dighton* v. *Bartholmew* (1602) BL MS Add. 25203, f. 488. A list of prothonotaries can be found in J. H. Baker, *The Reports of Sir John Spelman, II*, Selden Society, vol. 94 (London, 1977), p. 377.

conclusions from an etymological association between 'record' and the Latin *recordor*.[28] Most of the lawyers who made this link stressed that the record was of particular 'credit' in verifying the truth of a particular assertion.[29] Authors of law reports also relied upon the accuracy of the record: in his report of *Pinchon's Case* (1611) Coke justified his decision to quote at length from the record in his report, explaining that 'I have reported out of the record itself at length, to the intent the reader may be assured of the truth of the said case.'[30] Similar ideas are found earlier, in *The Case of Mines* (1568) reported by Plowden, where it is argued that 'the reports of our law are made for the greater part of the words and sayings of the judges, and that to which they assent is taken to be the law, a fortiori their judgments and affairs entered in the record of courts must be taken to be of as great or much greater effect than their words or sayings'.[31] In Plowden's report Onslow and Gerrard assert that 'the records of any court are the most effectual proofs of the law'.[32] These statements all suggest that the record was the most accurate information that could be procured about cases, and was therefore of especial authority, but there is no explanation as to why it is right to rely upon prior cases.[33] The only hint found in discussion of the record is by William Lambarde who suggested 'to keep in mind' as a translation of *recordor*, implying that it was correct to take account of the prior decision on the record, but such an implication is not drawn out or sustained by Lambarde.[34] Theoretical discussion which did consider the authority of the record did not distinguish between the record and reports, an important point to be considered below.[35]

Nevertheless, there are cases where the record is rejected without any such challenge to its accuracy. Gawdy J seems to suggest in *Lowen*

---

[28] Ross, 'The memorial culture of early modern English lawyers', pp. 302–3.

[29] The first was W. Lambarde (*Eirenarcha: or of the Office of the Iustices of Peace* (London, 1581), p. 70), whose language was repeated by Fraunce (A. Fraunce, *The Lawiers Logike, exemplifying the Precepts of Logike by the Practise of the Common Lawe* (London, 1588), f. 64v). See also E. Coke, *The Third Part of the Institutes of the Laws of England* (London, 1644), p. 71. John Doderidge was unusual in not referring to the 'credit' of the record (*The English Lawyer* (London, 1631), pp. 72–3).

[30] *Pinchon's Case* (1611) 9 Co. Rep. 86v, 89v; 77 E.R. 859, 865.

[31] *The Case of Mines* (1568) 1 Plowden 310, 321v; 75 E.R. 472, 489.

[32] *The Case of Mines* (1568) 1 Plowden 320v; 75 E.R. 487.

[33] For discussion as to the often-incoherent ideas underpinning casuistic argument in the early-modern common law, see I. S. Williams, 'English legal reasoning and legal culture, c.1528–c.1642', unpublished PhD Thesis, University of Cambridge (2008), pp. 66–106.

[34] Lambarde, *Eirenarcha*, p. 70.   [35] See nn. 44–59 and text, below.

v. *Cocks* (1599) that 'perhaps' he would change his mind if counsel, Tanfield, could show a case to be adjudged as he claimed.[36] This case might reflect Gawdy's somewhat combative nature on the bench, but in *Jenkin* v. *Griffith* (1630) Jones J noted that there was a judgment against his conclusion and 'many precedents agreeing with that', but persisted in his views.[37] Jones argued that it had been agreed many times to the contrary in the King's Bench and that the precedents 'come too late'. Given Jones was also the judge who seems to have acknowledged that he was bound by a prior case in *Browne* v. *Strode*, this is a problematic case. Whilst it could be dismissed, as there is no recourse to the record visible in the report, despite Jones' language of 'precedent', it is a salutary reminder that notions of authority were flexible and that a judge could, if he so desired, express sentiments seemingly contrary to them. A reference to the record as binding was one of a number of responses open to judges, depending on their attitude to the case in hand, albeit a reference that counsel seems to have expected the judges to accept and, indeed, comply with. In *Bright* v. *Forte* (1595), once it seemed possible that the judges might decide against their client, Williams and Harris exclaimed 'but you have the record of a judgment in the King's Bench in the very point'.[38] To them, it was evidently wholly unanticipated that the judges might decide contrary to a decision found in the records of the court.

The record's principal role was to show what judgment (if any) had been reached in a case, but the importance of judgment is taken for granted. Lawyers using the record were not concerned with whether or not a particular judgment was in some sense right, but merely that it was a judgment. This was the essence of the complaint about the record in *Bright* v. *Forte*, that there was no judgment despite the evidence to the contrary on the record. Jones J, in *Browne* v. *Strode*, made it clear that he would 'no more doubt in this matter' if the record of a judged case against him could be shown,[39] whilst Browne J admitted that he would 'subdue' his 'reason' to such precedents.[40] These judges did consider themselves to be constrained by an earlier case – in modern terms, bound by an authority. Caution should still be exercised; the role of record as the 'ultimate authority' is not a 'strict doctrine of precedent such as is

---

[36] BL MS Add. 25203, ff. 64–64v.   [37] CUL MS Gg.ii.19, ff. 131–2.
[38] *Bright* v. *Forte* (1595) BL MS Add. 25211, ff. 141v, 122.
[39] *Browne* v. *Strode* (1629) CUL MS. Gg.ii.19, ff. 2–4.   [40] *Stucley* v. *Thynne*, 128.

found in the later Common Law'.[41] There is not a clear 'doctrine' of precedent; rather we can see an occasional, but powerful, practice of precedent, albeit a practice without clear rules or much of an underlying theory. This absence of theory was a vulnerability in the status of the record.

The decline of the record

In the longer term the record of the court ceased to be of major importance in legal argument. Its moment in the spotlight was brief. By the time of the publication of his *Commentary on Littleton*, even Coke was reducing its significance. Although the record is included in Coke's list of arguments from 'authority' (together with reports), when Coke described argument from authority as the 'strongest' form of argument, he referred only to 'book cases'.[42] Whilst the record clearly was still of use in legal argument, as demonstrated by *Browne* v. *Strode* in 1629, the reduced role of the record and the enhanced strength of reported cases, as described by Coke, is both indicative of changes in legal argument and perhaps formative of the attitudes of later generations. The declining role of the record can be explained by two broad factors: the conflation of reports and the record in practice and theory, and deliberate attempts at exclusion of the record from legal argument.[43]

Law reports and the record came to be closely intertwined due to developments in the practice of reporting. Printed reports acknowledged as of high quality (Plowden and subsequently Coke) provided both the record and report, and the same occurred with regard to some volumes of manuscript reports.[44] By the end of the 1590s, references to printed reports far outnumbered references to manuscripts, so this change in the format of the printed reports in particular would have altered perceptions of what was normal in a law report.[45] The style of printed reports

---

[41] D. J. Ibbetson, 'Report and record in early-modern common law' in A. Wijffels (ed.), *Case Law in the Making: The techniques and methods of judicial records and law reports,* 2 vols. (Berlin, 1997), I, pp. 63, 66. Ibbetson does not discuss the cases considered here.

[42] E. Coke, *The First Part of the Institutes of the Lawes of England. Or, A Commentarie upon Littleton* (London, 1628), ff. 11, 254.

[43] Practical difficulties in using the record (much like those confronting modern legal historians) were always an obstacle, but as lawyers did use the record these difficulties cannot have been insurmountable. The practical problems explain only the relative rarity of references to the record in all periods.

[44] Ibbetson, 'Report and record', pp. 65–6.

[45] On this change, see Williams, '"He creditted more the printed booke"', nn. 35–6 and text.

developed by Plowden and Coke meant that by the second decade of the seventeenth century a lawyer referring to a report would also have access to the record. The record and report of a case were therefore not fully separate sources. Although not a theoretical development in itself, such a presentation in the literature must have contributed to ideas that reports and records were not essentially different.

This essential similarity in both function and appearance of record and report can also be seen in the actions on the case. Legal historians generally acknowledge the difficulties in using the record to show the state of the law at any given time due to the typically bland, stereotyped, assertions found on it.[46] Such entries on the record were consequently difficult for lawyers to use. Actions on the case were unusual in present- ing the facts of the case on the writ itself and any judgment (at least any judgment where the plaintiff was successful) would indicate that a writ on such facts was acceptable. Given the relatively brief nature of many early-modern law reports, such as those by Dyer, this would often be as much information as a reader would obtain from the reports too.

These practical changes had the potential to intertwine the record and reports, their literary similarity joined to functional equivalence. If that were so, then it was only a small conceptual step to assume they would have similar authority. The conflation of the record and report would not simply be practical, but also theoretical. Precisely such a theoretical equivalence did emerge. William Fulbeck described the Year Books as the 'record' of the common law,[47] whilst the preface to Coke's *Third Reports* makes it clear that the record was to be seen as consisting of 'reports' of 'equal authority but less perspicuity' compared to the printed reports.[48] This is interesting, as Coke clearly regarded the record as being capable of use in legal argument as a report. In functional terms, Coke therefore equated the record with reports. This is accurate as a description of early-modern legal argument, distinct from legal reasoning, in that reports were clearly the principal mode of legal argument by the time of Coke. Comparing the record to reports could be seen as paving the way for an increased use of the record in legal argument. Edward Coke the evangelist seems unlikely, however; much

---

[46] Ibbetson, 'Report and record', p. 55 and J. H. Baker, 'Why the history of English law has not been finished' [2000] *C.L.J.* 59, 70–3.

[47] W. Fulbeck, *The Pandectes of the law of Nations: contayning severall Discourses of the Questions, Points, and Matters of Law, wherein the Nations of the World doe Consent and Accord* (London, 1602), f. 27v.

[48] E. Coke, *Le Tierce Part des Reportes del Edward Coke* (London, 1610), sig. Cii(v).

more probable is that Coke was simply reflecting existing practice by counsel in argument, that the record was used like reports, but less frequently due to the difficulties in comprehension. Coke himself certainly did use the record in a similar manner to reported cases, as did later lawyers.[49]

The incongruity in Coke's remarks comes with the comment that the record has 'equal authority' with reports. The other evidence does suggest that if we conceive of authority in something like the modern manner, the record was more authoritative than law reports, being capable of overriding them and the only material seen in the sources binding judges. It may be that Coke was writing as the advocate he still was in 1602. Certainly his advice that a lawyer should set down 'all authorities, precedents, reasons, arguments, and inferences whatsoever that may be probably applied to the case in question; For some will be persuaded, or drawn by one, and some by an other' is the attitude of an advocate (perhaps more accurately, a rhetorician) rather than someone handling binding material.[50] It is the judges who were bound by the record, seemingly willingly, and counsel may not have addressed argument to the judges in terms of being 'bound' by the record simply because such arguments may not have been politic. Nevertheless, the theoretical equation of report and record remains.

Walmesley J went further. In the defamation case of *Holwood* v. *Hopkins* from which Anderson CJ's earlier remarks came, Walmesley J made a presumably deliberate statement that '[o]ur books are good precedents to guide us'.[51] This was in response to Anderson CJ's view in the case that the Common Pleas ought to follow the precedents of the King's Bench. Walmesley was clearly trying to argue that there was, at least, no difference between printed reports and the record. This was unorthodox at the time and did not work. However, note that Walmesley was expressly trying to claim the authority of the record, through the use of the language of 'precedent', for printed law reports. This is an early version of the modern language of 'precedent' and is a deliberate piece of verbal disingenuity attempting to subvert the force of references to the record and transfer that to reports.[52] As Walmesley disagreed with the position supported by

---

[49] For Coke, see *Hallyocke* v. *White* (1599) BL MS Add. 25203, ff. 53–4. For later lawyers see *Anon* (1633) CUL MS Gg.ii.19, ff. 393v–395 and *Russell* v. *Ligorne* (1637) CUL MS Gg.ii.20, ff. 1023v–1024. All of these cases were initiated using trespass on the case writs (ejectment, trover and defamation respectively) and all the record references were to relatively recent cases (within the preceding fifteen years).

[50] *Ibid.*, sig. Cii(v).   [51] *Holwood* v. *Hopkins*, 91.

[52] *Skymer's Case* (1561) CUL MS Ll.3.14, ff. 59–62v contains Catlyn CJ (K.B.) apparently stating a view 'contrary to the precedent'. However, the record is not reported as having

the records of the King's Bench, his remark is good evidence of the perceived strength of the record. Walmesley's position would also seem to undermine Coke's suggestion that the record enjoyed 'equal authority' to reports, as he tried to claim reports had authority equal to the record. In this regard, Walmesley's argument, and attempted subversion, is actually more accurate and revealing as to the position of the record in argument, at least from the perspective of a judge.

Coke's discussion of the role and nature of citations from the record did not end or begin with his comments in the *Third Reports*. Coke's argument in, and report of, *Slade* v. *Morley* also discusses the role of the record.[53] In *Slade's Case*, Coke explained that precedents are to be followed and that this is due to following the judges, who are held in high regard. In itself this may not be especially important: it is Coke providing a justification for an existing form of legal argument. The conceptual development is the separation of judicial and non-judicial 'precedents', although Coke does not use that language until later in his career.[54] Coke regarded 'precedents' in the sense of arguments from the record based on writs issued as more powerful where the judges have debated them. The notion of debate leading to authority can also be seen with regard to reports of cases.[55] As such, Coke's justification for the authority of the record shows a further clear tendency to conflate the record with reports, this time through a common theoretical justification for their place in argument.

Whilst Coke's views on 'silent' precedents may not have been original (a similar argument had been used against Coke by Tanfield in *Ognel* v.

---

been put in argument, although Whiddon J had referenced an 'adjudged' case in the Common Pleas. Given the record is not referenced, the reporter (at least) was able to equate a verbal report of a case with a 'precedent', suggesting that there might have been a stronger tradition of equating report and record, albeit one that is not readily visible in the sources. If so, this would be evidence of legal theory (as outlined here) running to a great extent behind practice.

[53] *Slade* v. *Morley* (1601) 4 Co. Rep. 91, 93v; 76 E.R. 1072, 1076, printed in 1604. Coke's manuscript report contains the same idea, British Library Harleian Manuscript 6686, ff. 526, 527–8. Coke's manuscript report does not include a reference to Coke being shown precedents by a prothonotary, and includes a legible deletion unsurprisingly not included in the printed version. The manuscript report is otherwise largely identical to the printed version. Coventry's report of Coke's argument also includes the point, BL MS Add. 25203, ff. 391, 393v–394.

[54] The language of 'judicial' precedents is not in *Slade's Case* itself, but is used in the preface to E. Coke, *A Booke of Entries* (London, 1614), sig. Ai, relying on one of the same cases (M.39.H.6.pl.43, f. 30, per Prisot C.J.) as cited in *Slade's Case*.

[55] It is already present in E. Plowden, *Les Comentaries* (London, 1571), sig. qiii(v).

Paston),[56] it was Coke's printed report of *Slade's Case* which popularised the distinction, and carried with it the shared theoretical basis for the use of material from both report and record. Francis Bacon relied on *Slade's Case* for the same distinction between precedents in the Star Chamber in 1614, and whilst this may have been a deliberate goad to Coke (who was sitting as one of the judges), presumably Bacon would not have made the argument unless he considered it had some weight.[57] In Caroline England the distinction between judged and unjudged precedents, and the concern about a lack of judicial discussion, was an important part of argument in *Lord Mountjoy* v. *Sir Henry Mildmay*[58] and the notorious case of ship money, both of which referenced *Slade's Case* on the point.[59]

As such, we can see that the record could be a binding authority and at the same time at least some lawyers began to regard the record and reports as equivalent. This had the potential to create a situation where reports could be viewed with the same authority as the record, although Walmesley's approach in *Holwood* v. *Hopkins* is the only express attempt at this yet found in curial discussions.

The authority of the record had one other impact on the practice of precedent. Given the power of references to the record, lawyers developed strategies to overcome it. Walmesley J's remark in *Holwood* v. *Hopkins* is the first example of this found, but there were others. In the dispute over the jurisdiction of the Common Pleas to grant writs of prohibition in the late sixteenth and early seventeenth centuries, arguments against the Common Pleas' jurisdiction had to contend with the fact that the Common Pleas clearly had 'precedents', albeit recent ones, supporting its claims.[60] The dispute casts light on a number of issues, particularly the relationship between print and manuscript in the early

---

[56] *Ognel* v. *Paston* (1587) 2 Leonard 84, 87; 74 E.R. 377, 380. When Coke cited precedents for the issuing of the relevant form of writ, Tanfield criticised such precedents for being 'silent' (although the court ultimately decided for Coke's client, the plaintiff).

[57] T. G. Barnes, 'A Cheshire seductress, precedent, and a "sore blow" to Star Chamber' in M. S. Arnold *et al.* (eds.), *On the Laws and Customs of England: Essays in honor of Samuel E. Thorne* (Chapel Hill, NC, 1981), p. 370, citing Folger Library Manuscript V.a.133, f. 35.

[58] (1632) CUL MS Gg.ii.19, ff. 293–5.

[59] *R* v. *Hampden*, III State Trials col. 825, col. 1229, per Finch CJ (C.P.). Finch's remarks at cols. 1227–9 make it clear that he has a very different understanding to that of Coke as to the position of the record and indeed the nature of the common law.

[60] Several examples are referenced in British Library Cottonian Manuscript Cleopatra F.1, ff. 207v–208. On the dispute generally see R. G. Usher, *The Rise and Fall of the High Commission* (Oxford, 1963), pp. 149–235.

seventeenth-century common law, but for present purposes, opponents of the Common Pleas made a number of attempts to undermine the jurisdiction of the court to issue writs of prohibition. The doctrinally innovative position was to question the judges as to whether the jurisdiction of the Common Pleas could be justified by reference to printed material, thereby entirely excluding the record as there were no relevant reports containing the record in print.[61]

Whilst this attempt to exclude the record was not entirely successful in the prohibitions dispute, it seems to have had a longer-term impact. In 1616, when James I listed the materials of which judges should take account when performing their function, references to the record (or at least to recent entries) were as conspicuously absent as Coke's Reports. James expounded that the judges were to follow precedents but 'not every snatched precedent, carped now here, now there, as it were running by the way; but such as have never been controverted, but by the contrary, approved by common usage, in times of best Kings, and by most learned Judges'. More precisely, he instructed them to '[l]ook to Plowdens Cases, and your old *Responsa prudentum*: if you find it not there then (*ab initio non fuit si*) I must say with Christ, Away with the new polygamy, and maintain the ancient Law pure and undefiled'.[62] Similarly, when Lord Keeper Thomas Coventry instructed new judges as to their duties in the 1630s, he told them to judge according to reported cases. Coventry advised Robert Heath 'not to stand upon novelties or new inventions of wit, but *upon the authority of books*' [emphasis added] and a year later instructed Francis Crawley 'to judge according to the precedents and cases *before times reported* and judged' [emphasis added],[63] omitting the record once again. If judges were discouraged from relying upon the record, prudent lawyers would avoid founding their arguments upon it. This may not have been unwelcome; given the need to descend into 'Hell' to view the record,[64] it is perhaps unsurprising that few lawyers fancied themselves an Orpheus and instead relied on more readily available (increasingly, printed) texts.

---

[61] Williams, "'He creditted more the printed booke'", nn. 52–60 and text.

[62] James I, 'A speech in the Starre-Chamber, the XX. of June. Anno 1616' in King James VI and I, *Political Writings*, ed. J. P. Somerville (Cambridge, 1994), pp. 216–17. James's speech was included in the printed collection of *The Workes of the Most High and Mightie Prince, James* (London, 1616).

[63] W. R. Prest, *The Diary of Sir Richard Hutton 1614–1639*, Selden Society Supplementary Series, vol. 9 (London, 1991), pp. 89, 93 (Michaelmas terms 1631 and 1632).

[64] See Baker, 'Why the history of English Law has not been finished', p. 70.

Conclusion

By the Civil War, there were sea-changes in ideas of legal argument and the manner of citation of earlier cases, especially from the record. Some of these developments suggest that the earliest experience of binding case law in a modern sense was to be found through the use of the record and that the unusual, but powerful, arguments using it were increasingly conflated with the more familiar arguments using reports. An awareness of the rise of the reports fills in a gap in the history of case law and gives a suggestion as to why lawyers may have come to see law reports as having particular authority.

4

Bifurcation and the bench: The influence of the jury on English conceptions of the judiciary

JOHN H. LANGBEIN

The jury system, in which local laypersons decided civil and criminal cases, was the defining institution of the English common law. Organising the legal system in this way profoundly affected the other institutions of the legal system, in particular the judiciary. My theme is that the jury system severely impaired the development of the judicial function in English law. My focus is on civil justice, although there were many points of overlap with the administration of criminal justice.

Adjudication, the work of determining the rights of the parties to a dispute, is the central activity of a civil justice system. *Most of what adjudication is about is fact-finding.* Blackstone underscored this point in a notable passage, remarking that 'experience will abundantly show that above a hundred of our lawsuits arise from disputed facts, for one where the law is doubted of'.[1] Was the traffic light red or green? Was the signature on the document forged or genuine? Was the claimant in the celebrated Tichborne affair really the lost heir, Roger Tichborne, or was he the imposter, Arthur Orton?[2] Decide the facts in such cases, and the law is usually easy.

The jury system divided adjudicative responsibility between judge and jury. The judges decided questions of law, juries decided matters of fact.[3] In the jargon of comparative law, this division of function in the Anglo-American

---

[1] W. Blackstone, *Commentaries on the Laws of England*, 4 vols. (Oxford, 1765–69), III, p. 330 (spelling modernised).

[2] See J. B. Atlay, *The Tichborne Trial* (London, 1899); R. Annear, *The Man Who Lost Himself: The unbelievable story of the Tichborne claimant* (Melbourne, 2002).

[3] 'Ad questionem facti non respondent judices ... ad questionem juris non respondent juratores'. E. Coke, *The First Part of the Institutes of the Laws of England*, 1st edn (London, 1628); ed. F. Hargrave and C. Butler, 16th edn (London, 1823), bk 2, ch. 12, §234 at 155(b). Of course, Coke's formula oversimplifies the division of function, by omitting the jurors' role in law applying, that is, fitting the facts to the law as stated to them.

tradition is known as the bifurcation of the trial court.[4] By isolating the judge from the work of fact-finding, the English common law emerged with a stunted or impoverished concept of the judicial function. A judge who is kept away from fact-finding is so remote from the core function of adjudication that he is only peripherally responsible for the court's decision.

I begin this account with a comparative glance at European civil justice, which, from the Middle Ages onward, made judges responsible for adjudication. I then contrast the English development and discusses some of the ways in which the medieval jury system, by impairing the judicial function, undermined the substantive law. I explain why Chancery procedure, although rooted in the European adjudicative tradition, failed to become the path of judicial empowerment in England. Rather, English judges acquired adjudicative authority incrementally across early modern times, by developing techniques of jury control that slowly transferred effective decision-making power to the bench. This process of reallocating power within the bifurcated court led ultimately to the suppression of civil jury trial in the twentieth century.

Roman-canon procedure

For purposes of comparison, it will be instructive to begin on the European Continent. Roman-canon civil procedure was developed in the church courts in the twelfth and thirteenth centuries and then spread to the secular courts.[5] Roman-canon procedure was jury-free;[6] it placed on legally trained judges full responsibility for adjudication on matters both of fact and of law.

In a case involving disputed facts, it was the judge's responsibility to examine the witnesses whom the parties nominated,[7] collect any documentary evidence, hear the parties and their lawyers and render a written

---

[4] See e.g. M. R. Damaska, *Evidence Law Adrift* (New Haven, 1997), pp. 46–7.

[5] For a succinct overview in English, see R. C. van Caenegem, 'History of European civil procedure' in *Int'l Encyc. Comp. Law* (Tübingen, 1973), VI, §§2–13/16, at pp. 16–19; see also J. A. Brundage, *The Medieval Origins of the Legal Profession* (Chicago, 2008). Regarding the procedure in the English church courts, see R. H. Helmholz, *The Oxford History of the Laws of England: The canon law and ecclesiastical jurisdiction from 597 to the 1640s* (Oxford, 2004), pp. 311–53.

[6] Regarding the elimination of lay judges in France and Germany, see J. P. Dawson, *A History of Lay Judges* (1960), pp. 35–115.

[7] Regarding the practice in medieval English ecclesiastical courts, see C. Donahue Jr, 'Proof by witnesses in the church courts of medieval England: An imperfect reception of the learned law' in M. Arnold *et al.* (eds.), *On the Laws and Customs of England: Essays in honor of Samuel E. Thorne* (Chapel Hill, NC, 1981), p. 127.

judgment. The aspiration that the judgment should contain a statement of reasons for the decision (*jugement motivé, Begründung*) was not, however, always realised.[8]

Because court-conducted investigation and adjudication concentrated power in the hands of the judge, careful provision was made to protect against abuse of discretion or other error. The main safeguard[9] was liberal appellate review. A dissatisfied litigant was entitled to have a higher court re-examine the case under a *de novo* standard of review – that is, with no presumption of correctness attaching to the first-instance decision.[10]

The three core attributes of this system continue to this day in refined form to characterise European civil justice systems: (1) judge-conducted evidence-gathering and adjudication; (2) the written, reasoned opinion; (3) and liberal appellate review.[11]

Adjudication in the medieval common law

I turn now to the medieval English common law. The pretrial pleading process, in which the judges decided issues of law, was jury-free, but in matters that required fact-finding, jury trial was the mode of trial in virtually all[12] cases. Within the bifurcated court, the judge presided, but adjudicative power rested with the jury.

---

[8] Regarding the pressures that restrained the giving of reasoned judgments in French practice until the Revolution, see T. Sauvel, 'Histoire du jugement motivé' (1955) 61 *Revue du Droit Public et de la Science Politique en France et à l'Étranger* 5; regarding the distortions in the style of French judicial opinions that resulted from revolutionary ideology, see J. P. Dawson, *The Oracles of the Law* (Ann Arbor, MI, 1968), pp. 375–86.

[9] Another was the complex law of proof that was meant to guide and restrain the judge's discretion, remarked by van Caenegem, 'History of European civil procedure', §2–17, at p. 20. I have discussed this topic in connection with criminal procedure in J. H. Langbein, *Torture and the Law of Proof: Europe and England in the Ancien Régime* (Chicago, 1977), pp. 3–17.

[10] *De novo* review was feasible because the evidentiary record assembled in the dossier at first instance was sent up to the reviewing court. Retrial for the most part entailed only a re-reading of the file.

[11] I have discussed the German system in J. H. Langbein, 'The German advantage in civil procedure' (1985) 52 *U. Chi. L. Rev.* 823; see generally P. L. Murray and R. Stürner, *German Civil Justice* (Durham, NC, 2004); H. Koch and F. Diedrich, *Civil Procedure in Germany* (The Hague, 1998).

[12] See Blackstone's chapter on 'the several species of trial' (Blackstone, *Commentaries*, III, p. 325), concluding that trial by jury was 'the principal criterion of truth in the law of England', *ibid.*, p. 348. Regarding wager of law (compurgation), which was the mode of proof under the writ of debt, see T. F. T. Plucknett, *A Concise History of the Common Law*, 5th edn (London, 1956), pp. 115–16, 363–4.

In the formative years of English civil procedure, the jury was largely self-informing. As Thayer put it, medieval jurors were persons 'chosen as being likely to be already informed'.[13] The vicinage requirement, that jurors be drawn from the immediate neighbourhood of the events in dispute, was meant to produce jurors who already knew what had happened, or whose communal relations would enable them to find out on their own.[14] Medieval jurors came to court mostly to speak rather than to listen. (The question of just how self-informing the medieval jury actually was is a question that has been subjected to reconsideration in the legal historical literature of the past generation. I follow Daniel Klerman in reading that scholarship as having left intact the basic account from Thayer and Maitland that the juries of the twelfth and thirteenth centuries were prevailingly self-informing, while showing us a good deal about how and why the system of self-informing juries unwound in later centuries.[15])

The trial judge was ordinarily not privy either to the evidence or to the rationale for the jury's verdict. A verdict so opaque (in Plucknett's apt term, 'inscrutable'[16]) was effectively unreviewable. Accordingly, the early common law not only isolated the trial judge from any significant role in fact-finding, it also precluded the development of any effective system of appellate review of first-instance adjudication.[17]

---

[13] J. B. Thayer, *A Preliminary Treatise on Evidence at the Common Law* (Boston, MA, 1898), p. 90.

[14] *Ibid.*, p. 91. It was the duty of the jurors, in Maitland's words, 'so soon as they have been summoned, to make inquiries about the facts of which they will have to speak when they come before the court. They must collect testimony; they must weigh it and state the net result in a verdict.' F. Pollock and F. W. Maitland, *The History of English Law before the Time of Edward I*, 2nd edn, 2 vols. (Cambridge, 1898), II, pp. 624–5.

[15] D. Klerman, 'Was the jury ever self-informing?' (2003) 77 *S. Cal. L. Rev.* 123, 146–8; another version appears in M. Mulholland and B. Pullan (eds.), *Judicial Tribunals in England and Europe, 1200–1700: The trial in history*, 2 vols. (2003), I; regarding the vicinage requirement, see M. Macnair, 'Vicinage and the antecedents of the jury' (1999) 17 *Law and Hist. Rev.* 537.

[16] Plucknett, *Concise History*, p. 125.

[17] The medieval common law developed two largely ineffective remedies to challenge first-instance outcomes, the writs of attaint and of error. The writ of attaint would quash a verdict as perjured, visiting savage consequences on the trial jurors for their false oaths. Regarding the shortcomings of attaint, see Blackstone, *Commentaries*, III, pp. 402–4. Under the writ of error, review was limited to matters of record, which included neither the evidence nor the judge's direction. Accordingly, 'the grossest errors of fact or of law may occur without being in any way brought upon the record'. J. F. Stephen, *A History of the Criminal Law of England*, 3 vols. (London, 1883), I, p. 309, emphasised in B. L. Berger, 'Criminal appeals as jury control: An Anglo-Canadian historical perspective on the rise of criminal appeals' (2005) 10 *Can. Crim. L. Rev.* 1, 6.

The main work of English judges was to process cases for decision by juries. In the pleading process, much of what judges did was to supervise the process of framing cases for jury trial. At trial, the judges took verdicts about which they commonly knew little or nothing. So long as the juries were largely self-informing, the role of the judge at trial was essentially administrative as opposed to adjudicative. It is in this sense that I speak of the judicial role in England as stunted or impoverished.

Adjudication by laypersons acting on unknown evidence poses a serious risk of error,[18] a risk that helps explain many of the limitations on adjudication that the judges developed, above all the requirement of single-issue pleading.[19] Single-issue pleading allowed only one contested issue of fact to reach the jury for decision, no matter how complex the facts of the case. Single-issue pleading was a way to restrict and simplify the jury's task, but often at the heavy cost of oversimplifying and distorting the case.

Another example of the judges' distrust of jury fact-finding was the exalted status that the medieval common law gave to sealed instruments. The judges insistently refused to allow fact-based defences such as prior payment to be pleaded against sealed instruments. Seal precluded adjudication.[20] The message that these judge-made rules sent to transacting parties was, seal your deal. Use a sealed instrument and you will not be subjected to jury trial.

Concern about the shortcomings of jury trial also underlies the various judge-made rules that hobbled the early contract writs of debt and covenant. I have in mind the *quid pro quo* and sum-certain requirements

---

[18] Regarding the concept of error-risk in the modern law of evidence, see A. Stein, *Foundations of Evidence Law* (Oxford, 2005), pp. 111–40.

[19] Regarding single-issue pleading, see J. H. Baker, *An Introduction to English Legal History*, 4th edn (London, 2002), pp. 76–8. 'The logic of medieval pleading was directed to the possible misleading of juries.' S. F. C. Milsom, *Historical Foundations of the Common Law*, 2nd edn (London, 1981), p. 79.

[20] See C. H. S. Fifoot, *History and Sources of the Common Law* (London, 1949), pp. 232–3. Bacon put the point as a maxim: 'the law will not couple and mingle matter of specialty, which is of the higher account, with matter of averment, which is of inferior account in law, for that were to make all deeds hollow'. F Bacon, *The Elements of the Common Lawes of England*, *Regula* 23, at 91 (1630), cited by A. W. B. Simpson, 'The penal bond with conditional defeasance' (1966) 82 *L.Q.R.* 399. Defences such as 'failure of consideration, impossibility of performance, or fraud in the underlying transaction were quite irrelevant'. E. G. Henderson, 'Relief from bonds in the English Chancery: Mid-sixteenth century' (1974) 18 *Am. J. Legal Hist.* 298, 300. The common law did leave to the determination of a jury a claim that a sealed instrument was a forgery, or that the maker had been coerced to execute it. D. J. Ibbetson, 'Words and deeds: The action of covenant in the reign of Edward I' (1986) 4 *Law and Hist. Rev.* 71.

for debt, and the seal requirement and the elimination of specific relief in covenant.[21] If your civil justice system does not allow you to compel witnesses' testimony and documentary evidence, and if it does not provide you with an experienced and legally skilled decision-maker to evaluate the evidence and to apply the law, then the system is simply not able to explore the issues of intent and performance that arise in contractual relations. Instead, medieval English law channelled commercial business, especially lending, into the penal bond and the confessed judgment, which were modes of obligation that effectively dispensed with adjudication.[22]

The limitations of jury-based adjudication also underlie the failure of the common law to develop specific remedies such as injunction and specific performance. Tailoring and supervising specific relief requires continuing factual investigation of a sort that was beyond the capability of a jury of laypersons convened for a one-time sitting at an itinerant *nisi prius* trial court.

These examples underscore that the impoverishment of the judicial role in English civil procedure had the consequence of retarding the substantive law. Bifurcation so impaired adjudicative capacity at common law that in many cases neither judge nor jury could do a proper job of rendering civil justice.[23] The medieval common law was rooted in a failed system of adjudication.

Chancery

Into this breach stepped the Lord Chancellor, with his jury-free, bifurcation-free Court of Chancery. In the late fourteenth and fifteenth centuries, when Chancery procedure took shape, the Chancellor was usually a bishop or an archbishop,[24] steeped in the Roman-canon

---

[21] Discussed in Fifoot, *History and Sources*, pp. 228–9, 257–8.

[22] See especially Simpson, 'Penal bond'. On the origins, see J. Biancalana, 'The development of the penal bond with conditional defeasance' (2005) 26 *J. Legal. Hist.* 103. Regarding the prevalence of defeasible bonds and contracts of record in sixteenth-century commercial transactions, see S. E. Thorne, 'Tudor social transformation and legal change' (1951) 26 *N.Y.U.L. Rev.* 1, 19–21.

[23] See W. T. Barbour, *The History of Contract in Early English Equity* (Oxford, 1914), pp. 54–8 (summarising gaps in contract law).

[24] Of the eighteen Chancellors from Edmund Stafford in 1396 until Thomas More in 1532, 'almost all were bishops or archbishops and several were cardinals. Thus they were well versed in ecclesiastical administration.' T. S. Haskett, 'The medieval English Court of Chancery' (1996) 14 *Law and Hist. Rev.* 245, 260; biographical detail on each is collected, *ibid.*, pp. 311–13.

procedure that he or his officials were applying in the ecclesiastical courts. The ecclesiastical Chancellors based Chancery's procedure on the Roman-canon model.[25] The early Chancellors themselves took witness testimony[26] and documentary evidence, and they adjudicated based on what they learned.

Because the Chancellor could obtain and evaluate witness testimony, he could ventilate types of transactional legal relations such as contract and trust that turned on evidence of the intention of the parties. In a study published nearly a century ago, Willard Barbour showed how close Chancery came to capturing the law of contract in the fifteenth century.[27] Chancery's investigative capacity also made possible its incursion into the common law's jurisdiction over freehold land. Chancery's enforcement of the use (trust) and the mortgage rested on Chancery's ability to require the production of relevant documents; and to put the parties and other witnesses on oath, in order to examine them about the purpose of the conveyance or transaction in question. Chancery's procedure also enabled the court to develop an appellate function of sorts, by enjoining enforcement of a common law decree and then employing Chancery's superior procedures of investigation to examine or re-examine the merits of the case.[28]

Because Chancery procedure was based upon a workable concept of the adjudicative function, Chancery had the potential to supplant much

---

[25] Macnair presents authority for the view that the English 'courts of equity [were] fundamentally civilian in their proof procedure and concepts'. M. Macnair, *The Law of Proof in Early Modern Equity* (Berlin, 1999), p. 14.

[26] 'In one case in 1438 the Chancellor examined the defendant orally at the Chancellor's own manor in the country and secured a confession that a particular feoffment had been made in trust.' Dawson, *Lay Judges*, p. 149. In a commercial dispute heard in the 1460s, which involved conflicting evidence about the circumstances in which a sealed instrument had been created, the surviving depositions indicate that the Chancellor (and in one instance his principal deputy, the Master of the Rolls) conducted examinations of parties and witnesses. Barbour, *Contract*, pp. 148–9, 218–19.

[27] Barbour, *Contract*, p. 23.

[28] Mansfield remarked that before the new trial remedy became available (in the mid seventeenth century) to correct mistaken verdicts, the situation was 'so intolerable, that it drove the parties into a Court of Equity, to have in effect, a new trial at law, of a mere legal question, because the verdict, in justice, under all the circumstances, ought not to conclude [the case]. And many bills [in equity] have been retained upon this ground, and the question tried over again at law, under the direction of a Court of Equity.' *Bright* v. *Enyon* (1757) 1 Burr 390, 394–95; 97 E.R. 365, 367 (K.B.). Rainsford CJ had voiced a similar concern a century before, observing in 1674 that 'denying a new trial [in King's Bench] will but send the parties into the Chancery'. *Martyn* v. *Jackson* (1674) 3 Keble 398; 84 E.R. 787, 788 (K.B.).

or even all of the common law, as happened in several places in Northern Europe in the roughly contemporaneous movement known as the reception of Roman law.[29] But no such thing happened in England. Instead, Chancery procedure became so dysfunctional that by the nineteenth century, Dickens was advising the prospective litigant to '[s]uffer any wrong that can be done you, rather than sue in Chancery'.[30]

What kept Chancery from fulfilling its adjudicative promise is that Chancery never came to grips with the staffing implications of the Roman-canon procedures it was employing. Gathering and evaluating witness testimony and documentary evidence is time-consuming work. If you are going to have such a system, you need a large bench. In a famous passage in his *History of Lay Judges*, John Dawson calculated that France, with four times the population of England, had about 5,000 judges at a time when the English royal courts had about a dozen. Population adjusted, therefore, the ratio was about a hundred to one.[31] Yet Chancery, using procedures of the sort then found in France, was a one-judge court – indeed, less than a one-judge court, because the Chancellor was a high officer of state who had to devote time to many other duties. The result of Chancery's under-staffing was that, although the court had the power to adjudicate, it failed to develop the resources to adjudicate effectively.

As Chancery's subject-matter jurisdiction grew, Chancery responded by delegating ever more of its workload, especially evidence-gathering. The pattern that emerged was to allow private lawyers acting on behalf of the litigants to control the investigation, by drafting interrogatories to be put to witnesses. This departure from the Roman-canon model of court-conducted evidence-gathering effectively privatised the investigative phase of the adjudicative process.

---

[29] For English-language accounts of the reception in Germany, see F. Wieacker, *A History of Private Law in Europe with Particular Reference to Germany*, tr. T. Weir (Oxford, 1995), pp. 71–142; Dawson, *Oracles*, pp. 176–213.

[30] C. Dickens, *Bleak House* (London, 1853), ch. 1, 'In Chancery'.

[31] Dawson estimated that by the eighteenth century, '[t]he total number of royal judges [in France] ... must certainly have exceeded 5,000', whereas 'from 1300 to 1800 the judges of the English central courts of common law and Chancery rarely exceeded fifteen'. Dawson, *Lay Judges*, p. 71. Dawson's figure for England omits the lay Justices of the Peace, some of whose functions, such as the exercise of summary jurisdiction over lesser offenses, would in France have fallen to the royal bench. Dawson also did not take account of the masters in Chancery, whose work resembled that of the examiners in French practice.

Outside London, Chancery used country gentlemen – parsons and Justices of the Peace and such – to administer the interrogatories – that is, to read the questions to the witnesses, to summarise the responses, and to return the resulting depositions to the court.[32] The lawyers for the parties were forbidden to attend the examination of witnesses. Accordingly, there was no opportunity for cross-examination, in the sense that there was no opportunity to formulate follow-up questions in light of the responses that a witness gave during the examination. Every line of potential questioning had to be fully anticipated in advance, a daunting and fundamentally impossible task. Only after all the examinations had been taken were the depositions disclosed to the parties.[33] If the case did not settle or go to arbitration, it was commonly sent to a master to formulate recommendations for the court. If the case turned on a fact dispute, the Chancellor was, in Blackstone's phrase, 'so sensible of the deficiency' of the court's procedures for investigating fact that he sometimes sent the disputed question to a common law court for trial by jury on a feigned issue.[34]

In an eerie way, therefore, adjudication in Chancery wound up replicating the fundamental failing of common law procedure: Chancery procedure isolated the judge from the facts. Delegation of functions by an overburdened Chancellor came to have much the same effect that bifurcation had produced in the medieval common law. Both were systems of adjudication in which the judge was unable to adjudicate fact. Like common law, Chancery became a failed system of adjudication.

I should say in passing that I regard the failure to staff Chancery properly as one of the great puzzles of English legal history. Why did Chancery remain a one-judge court until the nineteenth century? One way to understand the fusion of law and equity that got underway in the 1850s and that culminated in the Judicature Acts of the 1870s is that

---

[32] Dawson, *Lay Judges*, pp. 151–62.

[33] '[T]he cross-examination of witnesses, both friendly and hostile, had to be undertaken before their testimony had been heard'. *Ibid.*, p. 157. Because '[a]ll the lines of testimony that might develop had to be anticipated' in the initial interrogatories, the procedure invited 'prolixity'. *Ibid.*

[34] Blackstone, *Commentaries*, III, pp. 452–3. Chancery's reluctance to exercising its fact-finding powers has been misread as indicating that Chancery lacked the power to find facts. H. Chesnin and G. C. Hazard Jr, 'Chancery procedure and the Seventh Amendment: Jury trial of issues in equity cases before 1791' (1974) 83 *Yale L.J.* 999. The Chancellor did have the power to find facts, but as a practical matter he lacked the resources to exercise that power in most cases. See J. H. Langbein, 'Fact-finding in the English Court of Chancery: A rebuttal' (1974) 83 *Yale L.J.* 1620, 1629.

fusion turned every High Court judge into a mini Chancellor. What needs explaining is why it took English law so long to escape the convention that there could be only one judge with Chancery powers of discovery and remedy.

The law of jury control

How, then, did English civil justice overcome the stunted conception of the judicial role that was its legacy from the Middle Ages? The path of reform did not lie through Chancery, although Chancery did contribute important tools of discovery and remedy in the final phase of fusion. Rather, what occurred was a three-centuries-long process of incremental adjustment inside the bifurcated common law trial court. The judges steadily diminished the jurors' adjudicative power, by developing techniques of jury control. This process got underway in earnest in the seventeenth century, although there are some earlier antecedents.[35] By the twentieth century, the web of controls had become so extensive that the judges had effectively captured the jury's decisional role. Control of the jury ultimately led to its suppression.

The decline of the self-informing jury was an essential precondition. What had kept the judges so isolated from fact-finding in the formative period of the common law was that the jurors alone knew the facts. By the end of the Middle Ages, however, the structure and composition of trial courts[36] and juries[37] had undergone significant change. As more and more jurors came to court largely ignorant of the events in dispute, trial became an instructional proceeding, at which evidence was presented to inform the jurors' verdict.[38]

The great consequence was that the jury lost its monopoly over the facts. The judge who presided over the instructional trial would now know the evidence as well as the jurors. That change gave the common law bench its

---

[35] See n. 55, below.

[36] Regarding the emergence of the assize system, see J. S. Cockburn, *A History of English Assizes 1558–1714* (Cambridge, 1972), pp. 15–22.

[37] Fortescue, writing about 1470, voices the expectation that jurors would routinely hear witness testimony at trial. J. Fortescue, *On the Laws and Governance of England*, ed. and tr. S. B. Chrimes (Cambridge, 1942); ed. S. Lockwood (Cambridge, 1997), ch. 26, pp. 38–40.

[38] For early glimpses of the trend to informing jurors in court, see Thayer, *Evidence*, at pp. 97–124; A. Musson, *Public Order and Law Enforcement: The local administration of criminal justice, 1294–1350* (Woodbridge, 1996), pp. 201–5.

opening, its opportunity to fashion rules of jury control that steadily diminished, and finally eliminated, the adjudicative role of the jury.

The practice of jury control took three main forms: judicial comment regarding the evidence, judicial instruction regarding the law, and judicial review of verdicts by means of the motion for new trial. A fourth device, mandating that jurors disclose their thinking and reconsider their verdict before the court accepted it, was also employed, although this practice fell out of favour in later times.

Judicial comment

The trial judges developed, and exercised extensively, a power to advise the jury about the merits of the evidence. Especially in civil cases, jurors welcomed the views of these experienced and learned officers of the law. Matthew Hale, the most prominent judge of the middle decades of the seventeenth century, praised what he called the 'Excellency' of this practice. '[I]n Matters of Fact', Hale said, the judge gives the jury 'great Light and Assistance by his weighing the Evidence before them, and observing where the Question and Knot of the Business lies, and by showing them his Opinion even in Matter of Fact, which is a great Advantage and Light to Lay Men'.[39]

Jurors routinely followed the judge's guidance. When Boswell asked Lord Mansfield in 1773 whether juries always took his direction, Mansfield answered: 'Yes, except in political causes'[40] (which were mostly criminal cases, notably in Mansfield's time prosecutions for seditious libel). I have elsewhere pointed to examples of detailed comment on the merits in civil cases recorded in the judicial trial notebooks of Sir Dudley Ryder, chief justice of King's Bench in the years 1754-6.[41] Instances of judicial comment on the merits in criminal cases abound in the pamphlet accounts of Old Bailey trials that commence in the later seventeenth century.[42]

---

[39] M. Hale, *The History of the Common Law of England*, 1st edn (London, 1713); ed. C. M. Gray (Chicago, 1971), pp. 164–5 (a posthumous publication; Hale died in 1676).

[40] J. Oldham, *The Mansfield Manuscripts and the Growth of English Law in the Eighteenth Century*, 2 vols. (Chapel Hill: NC, 1992), I, p. 206, n. 44, quoting G. Scott and F.A. Pottle (eds.), *The Private Papers of James Boswell from Malahide Castle*, 18 vols. (Mt Vernon, NY, 1928–34), VI, p. 109.

[41] See J. H. Langbein, 'Historical foundations of the law of evidence: A view from the Ryder sources' (1996) 96 *Colum. L. Rev.* 1168, 1191–93.

[42] Examples are discussed in J. H. Langbein, 'The criminal trial before the lawyers' (1978) 45 *U. Chi. L. Rev.* 263, 285–87.

Judicial comment left undisturbed the nominal division of adjudicative function within the trial court. The jurors still decided the facts and
applied the law. But the functional reality was that judicial comment
allowed the judge to shape the jury's verdict when he thought it important to do so.[43] By the nineteenth century, contemporary legal observers
were saying as much. Chitty, for example, wrote in a practice manual in
the 1830s that jurors 'in general . . . follow the advice of the judge, and
therefore in substance, the verdict is found . . . by the judge's direction'.[44]
A Middle Temple barrister writing in 1859 contended that jurors
'generally do little more than find a verdict which [the trial judge]
has already suggested to them . . . [W]hen they do take it upon themselves to find contrary to his opinion, the court will most commonly
set aside the verdict, and order a new trial', except in cases of small
value.[45]

---

[43] In the nineteenth-century United States, a movement to forbid judicial comment on the
evidence took hold in state constitutions and statutes. See R. L. Lerner, 'The transformation of the American civil trial: The silent judge' (2000) 42 *Wm. & Mary L. Rev.*
195, 213; K. A. Krasity, 'The role of the judge in jury trials: The elimination of judicial
evaluation of fact in American state courts from 1795 to 1913' (1985) 62 *U. Det. L. Rev.*
595. Reacting to this development, Thayer wrote that it was 'impossible to conceive of
trial by jury [in England] as existing in a form which would withhold from the jury the
assistance of the Court in dealing with the facts. Trial by jury, in such a form as that, is
not a trial by jury in any historic sense of the words. It is not the venerated institution
which attracted the praise of Blackstone and of our ancestors, but something novel,
modern, and much less to be respected.' Thayer, *Evidence*, p. 188, n. 2. In a similar vein,
Wigmore thought that this 'unfortunate [American] departure from the orthodox
common law rule has done more than any other one thing to impair the general
efficiency of jury trial as an instrument of justice'. J. H. Wigmore, *A Treatise on the
Anglo-American System of Evidence in Trials at Common Law*, 3rd edn, 10 vols. (Boston,
MA, 1940), IX, §2551, pp. 504–5. Ironically, this American departure played a significant role in the ultimate survival of civil jury in the United States. By silencing the judge,
the Americans enhanced the ability of the trial lawyers to affect the outcome of the trial,
and thus gave the trial bar a vested interest in preserving jury trial. To be sure, other
factors also played a role in the survival of civil jury trial, especially the entrenchment of
the right to civil jury trial in the federal and state constitutions.

[44] J. Chitty, *The Practice of Law in All Its Departments*, 2nd American edn, 4 vols.
(Philadelphia, PA, 1836), III, p. 913. I owe this reference to Renée Lerner.

[45] J. Brown, *The Dark Side of Trial by Jury* (London, 1859), p. 14. Because the jury's verdict
will be overturned 'the moment they presume to differ with him', what 'is the use of
troubling the jury for their opinion?' *Ibid.* Michael Lobban directed attention to this tract
in his chapter 'The strange life of the English civil jury, 1837–1914' in J. Cairns and
G. McLeod (eds.), *'The Dearest Birth Right of the People of England': The jury in the
history of the common law* (Oxford, 2002), pp. 173, 175 and n. 10.

Judicial instruction on the law

Closely connected to judicial comment on the evidence was the power that the judges developed to instruct jurors on the law.[46] Across the eighteenth and especially the nineteenth centuries, the judges devised ever more detailed jury instructions, whose effect was to treat as questions of law matters that had previously been regarded as fact. As yet this phenomenon has not been well studied, although its importance has been widely noticed. Both Brian Simpson and John Baker have remarked on what Simpson calls the 'progressive dethronement of the jury'[47] in nineteenth-century contract law. Many questions that came to be treated as law were matters that had previously been 'left to juries as questions of fact'.[48] The celebrated case of *Hadley* v. *Baxendale* (1854),[49] which established the standard for remoteness of damages in contract law, exemplifies this process.[50] Until that case, it had been 'entirely the province of the jury to assess the amount [of damages], with reference to all the circumstances of the case'.[51]

The development of the law of evidence in the eighteenth and especially the nineteenth centuries was another chapter in this process of recasting questions of fact as questions of law.[52]

---

[46] Indeed, there was not much demarcation at trial between the judge's summation of the evidence and his instruction regarding the law. Speaking of the practice in criminal cases, Green has observed that '[t]here was no real separation between the judge's comments upon the evidence and his charge to the jury'. T. A. Green, *Verdict According to Conscience: Perspectives on the English criminal trial jury, 1200–1800* (Chicago, 1985), p. 139.

[47] A. W. B. Simpson, 'The Horwitz thesis and the history of contracts' (1979) 46 *U. Chi. L. Rev.* 533, 600. The courts produced law 'where before there was little or none'. *Ibid.*

[48] J. H. Baker, 'Book review of Patrick Atiyah, *The Rise and Fall of Freedom of Contract* (1979)' (1980) 43 *M.L.R.* 467, 469, discussed in Oldham, *Mansfield*, I, pp. 222–3. Baker has made a similar point about criminal jury practice: 'by enlarging the scope of the substantive law the judges were able to tell the jurors what conclusions followed if they found certain facts to be true.' J. H. Baker, 'The refinement of English criminal jurisprudence' in L. A. Knafla (ed.), *Crime and Criminal Justice in Europe and Canada* (Waterloo, ON, 1981), pp. 17, 19.

[49] (1854) 9 Ex 341, 156 E.R. 145 (1854).

[50] See R. Danzig, '*Hadley* v. *Baxendale*: A study in the industrialization of the law' (1975) 4 *J.L.S.* 249, 252–7; see also F. Faust, '*Hadley* v. *Baxendale*: An understandable miscarriage of justice' (1994) 15 *J. Legal Hist.* 41, 54–65.

[51] J. Chitty, *A Practical Treatise on the Law of Contracts*, 4th edn (London, 1850), p. 768, cited by Danzig, '*Hadley* v. *Baxendale*', at p. 255 and n. 21.

[52] Regarding the timing and character of the law of civil evidence, see Langbein, *Historical Foundations*, p. 41; T. P. Gallanis, 'The rise of modern evidence law' (1999) 84 *Iowa L. Rev.* 499; regarding the development of the law of criminal evidence, see J. H. Langbein, *The Origins of Adversary Criminal Trial* (Oxford, 2003), pp. 178–251.

An important contributor to this reworking of the law/fact line was
the growth and refinement of the law reports, both *en banc* and at *nisi
prius*.[53] Another background factor of deep importance was the growing
confidence in the integrity of the judiciary, which was connected to the
development of judicial independence across the eighteenth century.[54]

New trial

The third main component of the law of jury control, in addition to
judicial comment and instruction, was the development of judicial
review of jury verdicts, which took place under the rubric of new trial.
The judges' power to order new trial had originated in late medieval
times as a means of remedying jury wrongdoing in exceptional cases
such as bribery or jury tampering.[55] In the second half of the seventeenth
century the judges began extending their power to grant new trial to
cases in which they regarded the verdict as contrary to instruction or
contrary to the weight of the evidence,[56] and by the later eighteenth
century, the law of new trial had acquired immense range.[57]

[53] The five volumes of Burrow's *King's Bench Reports*, which became the gold standard for
law reporting, cover the years 1756–72, and were published from 1766 to 1780. See
generally W. P. Courtney, rev. D. Ibbetson, 'Burrow, Sir James (1701–1782)' in *Oxford
Dictionary of National Biography* (Jan. 2008 (online ed.)), www.oxforddnb.com.

[54] See C. Hanly, 'The decline of civil jury trial in nineteenth-century England' (2005) 26 *J.
Legal Hist.* 253, 255–9; D. Lemmings, 'The independence of the judiciary in eighteenth-
century England' in P. Birks (ed.), *The Life of the Law: Proceedings of the Tenth British
Legal History Conference, Oxford, 1991* (London, 1993), pp. 125, 127–8.

[55] Regarding the practice of quashing verdicts (and disciplining jurors) for misbehaviour in
late medieval times, see D. J. Seipp, 'Jurors, evidences and the tempest of 1499' in Cairns
and McLeod, *Birth Right*, pp. 75, 86; see also J. H. Baker, 'Introduction' in *The Reports of
Sir John Spelman, II*, Selden Society, vol. 94 (London, 1978), pp. 112–3 (discussing early
sixteenth-century sources).

[56] The landmark case was *Wood* v. *Gunston* (1655) Style 466; 82 E.R. 867 (Upper Bench), on
which see Thayer, *Evidence*, pp. 170–1. For an overview of the history of new trial in
England, see R. B. Lettow [Lerner], 'New trial for verdict against law: Judge-jury relations
in early nineteenth-century America' (1996) 71 *Notre Dame L. Rev.* 505, 510–15 (reviewing English case law); regarding the American practice, see *ibid.* at pp. 515–53. The subject
gave rise to a treatise, D. Graham, *An Essay on New Trials* (New York, 1834) (cited by
Lerner); the second edition took up three volumes: D. Graham, *An Essay on the Law of
New Trials in Cases Civil and Criminal*, ed. T.W. Waterman, 2nd edn, 3 vols. (New York,
1855).

[57] For Mansfield's expansive view of the 'numberless causes of false verdicts' that merit
correction by means of new trial, see *Bright* v. *Enyon* (1757) 1 Burr 390, 393; 97 E.R 365,
366 (K.B.). For the law of new trial immediately post-Mansfield, see W. Tidd, *The
Practice of the Court of King's Bench in Personal Actions*, 2 vols. (London, 1790–94),

Requiring jurors to disclose their rationale

Reinforcing the judges' power to grant new trial was the authority that they claimed to probe the basis for a proffered verdict before accepting it. In *Ash* v. *Ash*,[58] decided in 1697, Holt CJ explained that jurors were expected to disclose their thinking to the court in order that the court could assist them to amend their verdict. In that case he reversed what he deemed to be a grossly excessive award of damages (£2,000 for an incident of false imprisonment involving the detention of a youth for a couple of hours), saying: 'The jury were very shy of giving a reason for their verdict, thinking that they have an absolute, despotic power, but I did rectify that mistake, for the jury are to try cases with the assistance of the judge, and ought to give reasons when required, that, if they go upon any mistake, they may be set right.'[59]

Having learned the basis for a proffered verdict, the trial judge could – if he thought the verdict mistaken – reinstruct the jurors and require them to redeliberate. We have a particularly detailed example of this practice in the pamphlet account of a criminal case tried at the Old Bailey in 1678. The defendant was accused of statutory rape. The jurors twice deliberated and proffered a verdict of acquittal; the trial judge rejected the verdict both times, reinstructed the jurors twice and succeeded on their third deliberation in obtaining from them the conviction that the judge thought appropriate to the facts.[60] This practice of requiring redeliberation endured into the nineteenth century,[61] although signs of unease about it appeared earlier, at least in criminal cases.[62]

II, pp. 605–10. Regarding the mechanics of obtaining new trial, see Oldham, *Mansfield*, I, pp. 131–3.

[58] (1697) Comb 357; 90 E.R. 526 (K.B.).

[59] (1657) Comb 357, 357–8; 90 E.R. 526, at 526.

[60] *Arrowsmith's Case*, in *Exact Account of the Trials of the Several Persons Arraigned at the Sessions-House in the Old Bailey for London & Middlesex* (London, 1678), pp. 14–16 (concerning statutory rape). The case is reprinted in Langbein, *Lawyers*, pp. 291–3.

[61] The principle was restated judicially as late as 1862: 'A judge has a right, and in some cases it is his bounden duty, whether in a civil or in a criminal cause, to tell the jury to reconsider their verdict.' *R.* v. *Meaney* (1862) Le & Ca 213, 216; 169 E.R. 1368, 1370 (Crown Cas. Res. per Pollock C.B.). However, the report continues, the trial judge is 'bound to receive [the jury's] verdict [if the jury] insist[s] upon his doing so'. *Ibid*. I owe the references in this and the next note to S. Lilley, 'The decline of jury control: 1690–1860', unpublished, on file at the Yale Law Library (Jun. 2006), pp. 8–11.

[62] Hawkins wrote in his influential treatise in 1721 that requiring redeliberation 'is by many thought hard, and seems not of late years to have been so frequently practiced as formerly'. W. Hawkins, *A Treatise of the Pleas of the Crown*, 2 vols. (London, 1716–21), II, p. 442.

Across time, the application of the three main techniques of jury control – comment, instruction and new trial – transferred ever more of the adjudicative role from jury to judge. By relabelling law as fact, the judges used instruction as a means of diminishing the scope of the jury's authority. Within the sphere that nominally remained for the jury, the judges used their powers of comment to dominate jury fact-finding. In cases in which the judges thought that the jury had resisted their direction or their view of the merits, they used their power to order new trial to make their views prevail.

In the end, it came to be understood that the jury's role had become so confined that the jury had ceased to affect outcomes. The work of abolishing civil jury trial took about a century, roughly from the mid nineteenth to the mid twentieth. Conor Hanly's important article has traced out that development.[63] He emphasises that the benign experience with jury-less adjudication for petty matters under the County Courts Act of 1846 helped legitimate jury-less adjudication in the superior courts.[64]

The breakthrough came in the Common Law Procedure Act of 1854,[65] which, for the first time, authorised judges to decide questions of fact in common law cases. The Act applied only to cases in which the parties were willing to waive jury trial, but in later decades as bench trial became familiar, further legislation whittled away the parties' right to demand jury trial, transferring to the judges the power to decide whether or not to permit a jury.[66] By the middle of the twentieth century, civil jury trial had been abolished, except for a handful of marginal cases such as slander, seduction, malicious prosecution and fraud.

The final collapse of civil jury trial in England was astonishingly rapid. Not until 1854 did an English common law judge ever make a finding of fact, yet a century or so later the work of finding fact in traditionally common law matters had become the exclusive province of the bench. In this way, English judges finally became judges in function as well as in name, adjudicators as opposed to jury minders.

---

[63] Hanly, 'Decline'.   [64] Ibid., pp. 266–74.   [65] 17 & 18 Vict., c. 125 (1854).
[66] Hanly, 'Decline', p. 278 and nn. 186, 189.

5

Sir William Scott and the law of marriage

REBECCA PROBERT

Introduction

Sir William Scott, who presided over the London Consistory Court from 1788 to 1820, had a considerable influence on the law of marriage, both during his tenure and since. During his tenure of this post he was required to resolve many issues relating to disputed marriages, and was often called upon to determine whether the parties had complied with the requirements of what was then the governing legislation, the Clandestine Marriages Act 1753. But it is the enduring effect of his rewriting of the history of marriage that will be under consideration in this chapter – specifically his claim in *Dalrymple* v. *Dalrymple*,[1] decided in 1811, that prior to the Clandestine Marriages Act it had been possible to celebrate a marriage in England and Wales by a simple exchange of consent in words of the present tense, without any further formalities. On this view, all the parties would have had to have done was to state 'I take you as my wife' and 'I take you as my husband' in order for a valid marriage to come into existence.

The reason why this particular claim deserves such scrutiny is the impact that it had, both in practical terms and on the way that subsequent generations approached the history of marriage. The Clandestine Marriages Act, which required that marriages be celebrated after the calling of banns or the obtaining of a licence and in the church of the parish where at least one of the parties was resident, only applied to marriages in England and Wales (and even then those of Jews, Quakers, and members of the Royal Family were exempt).[2] Marriages celebrated

---

[1] (1811) 2 Hag. Con. 54; 161 E.R. 665.

[2] For a full account of the formal requirements, see R. Probert, *Marriage Law and Practice in the Long Eighteenth Century: A reassessment* (Cambridge, 2009), ch. 6. On the law applicable to members of the Royal Family, see R. Probert, *The Rights and Wrongs of Royal Marriage: How the law has led to heartbreak, farce and confusion, and why it must be changed* (Kenilworth, 2011).

in British territories overseas were governed by the law as it had stood in 1753, save where explicit legislation had intervened.[3] And so the decision in *Dalrymple* had an immediate and practical impact on the resolution of disputes about marriages that had been celebrated across the burgeoning British Empire. Prior to *Dalrymple*, the governing assumption of the courts had been that the presence of an episcopally ordained priest was necessary to ensure the validity of the marriage; after *Dalrymple*, the qualifications of the celebrant were deemed irrelevant. That a single case can overturn previous beliefs in this way also raises questions about the process of 'judging' itself, and whether individual judges regard themselves as free to exercise their judgment.

Turning to the impact of the case on the history of marriage, it is common to find *Dalrymple* being cited as an authority for the state of the law before the Clandestine Marriages Act, to the exclusion of other authorities.[4] This is unsurprising, given that Scott's judgment provided a clear-cut statement of the law not to be found in earlier authorities. More subtly, the judgment also provided a prism through which earlier cases were read. Like judges, we all too often tend to read history backwards, interpreting earlier precedents through the filter of subsequent cases. *Dalrymple* held that a contract *per verba de praesenti* ('by words of present intention') created a valid, if clandestine, marriage, and earlier cases and documents were interpreted accordingly, with any evidence that did not fit being ascribing to contemporary confusion.[5]

The blurring of the distinction between the clandestine marriage and a contract *per verba de praesenti* in Scott's judgment in *Dalrymple* was to be particularly problematic for subsequent interpretations of the history of marriage. It was a result of the way in which the case was argued before him: counsel had argued that the marriage was clandestine – using that word in the more popular sense of private, surreptitious or nefarious. But in early eighteenth-century usage a clandestine marriage had been one that was celebrated before an Anglican clergyman but without

---

[3] A brief note on terminology is necessary here. Prior to the Clandestine Marriages Act coming into force in 1754, marriage in England and Wales was governed by the canon law, and even after 1754 the ecclesiastical courts retained jurisdiction over the determination of the validity of marriages. By the nineteenth century one finds the pre-1754 regime being described as 'the common law of marriage' in order to distinguish the canon law from the statutory scheme.

[4] The case is cited by, among others, R. B. Outhwaite, *Clandestine Marriage in England, 1500–1850* (London, 1995), p. 2; R. H. Helmholz, *Marriage Litigation in Medieval England* (Cambridge, 1975), p. 26.

[5] See Probert, *Marriage Law and Practice*, p. 59.

observing all of the requirements of the canon law. A contract *per verba de praesenti* had not been a sub-species of clandestine marriage: it was, rather, an entirely separate entity, a binding contract rather than a valid marriage. But when, in the wake of *Dalrymple*, a contract *per verba de praesenti* came to be regarded as a type of clandestine marriage, any earlier references to the validity of clandestine marriages were taken to apply equally to such contracts.

I have argued elsewhere that Scott's claim in *Dalrymple* was based on a misunderstanding of the law prior to the Clandestine Marriages Act.[6] Put briefly, the case law, commentaries and practices of the time are utterly inconsistent with the idea that it was possible to marry by a simple exchange of consent. If it had been possible so to marry, there would have been no need to debate the status of the celebrant who had conducted the marriage, as occurred in so many of the early cases.[7] There would have been no question as to the validity of the marriages of Quakers, whose marriage ceremonies consisted only of a simple exchange of consent. And if a couple could acquire the status of married persons simply by exchanging vows in private, why did so many flock to the Fleet prison to secure the services of an Anglican clergyman, sometimes at an exorbitant price?

But so deeply has *Dalrymple* permeated case law and scholarship in this area that anyone setting out to dispel its authority faces a difficult task, a fact which a most eminent reviewer of my interpretation in *Marriage Law and Practice* recognises:

> Professor Probert believes that the judgment of Sir William Scott (Lord Stowell) in *Dalrymple* (1811) 2 Hag. Con. 54 is responsible for the (in her view erroneous) belief that 'a contract *per verba de praesenti* [amounts] to a full marriage'. She believes that Scott had simply 'misunderstood the law' . . . Yet it must be said that if Stowell was wrong he was only the first of many.[8]

Cretney's review illustrates how *Dalrymple* bears the weight of authority not only of Scott as a judge but of those who followed in his wake. This chapter will subject Scott's analysis to a closer scrutiny and show that the

---

[6] *Ibid.*, ch. 2.

[7] See e.g. *Weld* v. *Chamberlaine* (1684) 2 Shower K.B. 301; 89 E.R. 952, in which allusion was made to the fact that the celebrant was in orders, and *R* v. *The Inhabitants of Luffington* (1744) Burr. Sett. Cas. 232, No. 79, in which the crucial issue was deemed to be whether the celebrant was in orders or not.

[8] S. Cretney (2010) 6 *Int. J. L. C.* 193, 194.

cases he relied upon do not bear the construction that he put on them. But of course to contend that Scott was wrong, as Cretney points out, does raise the question as to why the mistake was not corrected at the time. So a further theme explored in this chapter will be why certain legal ideas win acceptance, a story that relates to the very process of judging.

Yet it is important to bear in mind that the actual facts of *Dalrymple* did not require any comment on the law of England and Wales, before or after 1753. The disputed marriage in the case had taken place in Scotland, and the issue of its validity was accordingly determined by Scottish law. Scott, however, steeped in the learning of the civilians, chose to present the canon law of marriage as a seamless whole, consistent in its application across different jurisdictions, and therefore the same in England and Wales prior to legislative intervention as it was in early nineteenth-century Scotland. The story of *Dalrymple*, therefore, also illustrates the perils of a certain type of judgment that attempts to range across centuries and jurisdictions. A copious display of learning may be a dangerous thing, in that the deference it inspires in readers may turn out to be misplaced.

Since the case has for so long been regarded as authoritative, it is necessary to proceed by small steps in demonstrating that it was, in this respect at least, wrong. The first section accordingly advances a number of reasons for exercising caution in accepting *Dalrymple* as an authority on the law of England and Wales prior to the 1753 Act. The second then examines the authorities on which Scott relied: it is shown that they are capable of a different interpretation, and do not support his central claim. The third shows that *Dalrymple* was responsible for bringing about a change in the way in which simple exchanges of consent were regarded in English law. The final part considers *why* Scott asserted that an exchange of consent constituted a marriage in this particular case, and why his version was accepted by his peers so uncritically, even with enthusiasm.

Scott's (lack of) qualifications to decide the case

The very circumstances in which *Dalrymple* was decided should make us wary of relying on it as an authority as to the law of England and Wales prior to 1754. The case originated in a suit for restitution of conjugal rights brought by Johanna Gordon, a Scotswoman, in the London Consistory Court. She claimed to have married John Dalrymple, an Englishman, when he was quartered in Scotland with his regiment a few years earlier, in 1804. Young Dalrymple – only nineteen when he ventured north of the border – had subsequently been required to leave Scotland. Initially he wrote passionate letters to the woman he termed his 'wife', but his affections waned and then became fastened on a new object. It was when he went through a ceremony of marriage with Miss Laura Manners that the spurned Johanna brought her claim.

So the question for the court was whether the declarations made by John and Johanna constituted a valid marriage according to the law of Scotland, where the relevant events took place. Sir William spoke frankly of his 'inferior qualifications'[9] to decide the matter, but then took the view that the Scottish law of marriage was the same as the canon law of marriage that had been applied across Europe until the Council of Trent in the mid sixteenth century unless the contrary could be proved, remarking airily that '[i]t is not for me to attempt to trace the descent of the matrimonial law of Scotland since the time of the Reformation'.[10] Indeed, he made no attempt to do so. But had the law of Scotland been as clear as this heritage might suggest, one would expect unanimity among the experts examined by the court, and consistency in the case law. The very length of Scott's judgment in *Dalrymple*, in which he sifted the relevant texts, considered the case law and evaluated the evidence given by contemporary experts, illustrates that this was far from being the case.

Scott's modesty did not extend to admitting that his qualifications to pronounce on the law of England and Wales as it stood prior to 1754 were also open to question. A later judge, supporting the authority of Scott's judgment, alluded to the fact that the Clandestine Marriages Act had been passed in his lifetime. Since Scott was born in 1745, this argument was, to say the least, somewhat specious. Even the most precocious of students would have been unlikely to have gleaned much understanding of law and practice before their tenth year. Of course, one does not need to have experienced events in order to understand them, else historians would be out of business. But the fact that Scott had no personal practical experience of the law as it stood in 1753 means that his understanding of it has to be assessed as that of a historian would be, with no first-hand knowledge being assumed.

These facts should immediately alert us to the need for caution in relying on *Dalrymple* as a precedent in the English context. It may be true that, as Sir William pointed out, there are very few cases 'upon acknowledged and settled rules'.[11] But if the most oft-cited authority for the

---

[9] At p. 59.   [10] At p. 70.   [11] At p. 93.

proposition that English law once regarded an exchange of consent as an
actual marriage is a Scottish case decided sixty years after the issue ceased
to be of immediate practical relevance for those marrying in England and
Wales, by a judge who had no direct experience of the law he was
pronouncing on and who drew his ideas from the canon law of Europe
as it stood in the sixteenth century, one does begin to wonder about the
absence of other authorities.

Scott's authorities

Indeed, when one reads the judgment in *Dalrymple* it is startling just how
little support was available for Scott's claim. His judgment does contain
detailed discussion of the law of Scotland: there is a lengthy analysis of
case law, evidence from experts and consideration of key legal texts.
All this was to be expected given that the case was to be decided by
Scottish law. Scott's discussion of English law as it stood prior to 1754
was rather more perfunctory: a mere four cases were cited. Even more
importantly, all were more ambiguous than Scott's interpretation of
them would suggest.

First was the sixteenth-century case of *Bunting* v. *Lepingwell*.[12] The
key facts were relatively straightforward. Agnes Adenshall had been
contracted to Bunting by an exchange of vows in words of the present
tense. She then married Twede, and Bunting sought to enforce the
contract. The court upheld it and ordered the contracted couple to
marry, which they did before the birth of the child whose legitimacy
was in question. This, however, is perfectly consistent with the view that
an exchange of consent was no more than a binding contract: it was
sufficient to invalidate the marriage to Twede, but Agnes and Bunting
were required to solemnise their union in church before they lived
together.[13]

Secondly, Scott cited the statement of Holt CJ in the early eighteenth-
century case of *Collins* v. *Jessot* to the effect that 'if a contract be *per verba
de praesenti*, it amounts to an actual marriage, which the very parties
themselves cannot dissolve or release by mutual agreement; for it is as
much a marriage in the sight of God as if it had been *in facie ecclesiae*
['within the church' or 'in the presence of the congregation']'.[14] This

---

[12] (1585) 4 Co. Rep. 29a; 76 E.R. 950.
[13] See further Probert, *Marriage Law and Practice*, p. 41.
[14] (1705) 6 Mod 155; 87 E.R. 913 at 913.

might appear to provide unambiguous support for Scott's claim, but it must be read in context. The actual question before the court in *Collins* v. *Jessot* was which court – ecclesiastical or secular – should try the question of whether there had been a contract of marriage. From the mid seventeenth century, different remedies had been available in different courts if a contract of marriage was not followed by solemnisation in church. An aggrieved individual could choose between an action for breach of promise of marriage in the common law courts (for which the remedy was damages), and an action to enforce the contract in the ecclesiastical court. In the latter, the powers of the court varied according to whether the contract was expressed in words of the present tense ('I take you as my wife/husband') or the future tense ('I will take you as my wife/husband'). If the contract was expressed in words of the present tense, the court could require the parties to solemnise their marriage in church. If, however, there had been no more than a future promise of marriage (and no proof of a subsequent sexual relationship between the parties[15]), the recalcitrant party could only be admonished rather than compelled.

The result was that there were two potential actions available in relation to a future promise of marriage, but only one if the vows had been expressed in the present tense. If, therefore, there had been an exchange of vows in words of the future tense, the matter could be dealt with in either the common law court or the ecclesiastical court;[16] if, however, the contract had been expressed in words of the present tense only the ecclesiastical court had jurisdiction. Unsurprisingly, Holt CJ refused to prevent the ecclesiastical court from hearing the case: the mere fact that the contract might turn out to be *de futuro* rather than *de praesenti* did not justify a prohibition as the ecclesiastical court had jurisdiction in either case. Thus *Collins* v. *Jessot* was not a decision that a contract *per verba de praesenti* was in fact a marriage, with all the attendant rights of one celebrated in church, but simply a decision that whether or not there was such a contract was a matter for the ecclesiastical court to decide.

By describing an exchange of vows in words of the present tense as being 'as much a marriage in the sight of God as if it had been *in facie ecclasiae*', Holt CJ was merely signifying that it would be binding on the

---

[15] In which case the promise would be treated as one of present rather than future consent.

[16] See H. Swinburne, *A Treatise of Spousals, or Matrimonial Contracts*, 2nd edn (London, 1711), p. 232.

parties.[17] That a contract did not have the same consequences as a marriage in church is clear from his very next words: 'with this difference, that if they [i.e. the contracted couple] cohabit before marriage *in facie ecclesiae*, they are for that punishable by ecclesiastical censures'.[18] The fact that this important qualification did not appear in some reports[19] (and was not mentioned by Scott) may have contributed to subsequent misunderstandings of the case. Indeed, in *Dalrymple* Scott actually suggested that consummation would be presumed if it was proved that the parties had exchanged vows in words of the present tense. But it would be perverse if the law had presumed that contracted couples had done something that they were actually forbidden to do, and there is no authority for this proposition prior to *Dalrymple*.

Scott's third authority was another century-old case, namely *Wigmore's Case*.[20] This was another decision of Holt CJ, who stated that '[i]f the contract be executed, and he does take her, 'tis a marriage, and the Spiritual Court cannot punish for fornication'.[21] Again, this statement needs to be read with care. That the ecclesiastical courts could not punish a contracted couple for the specific offence of fornication did not mean that they could not punish them at all: it is unlikely that Holt would have forgotten what he had said in *Jesson* v. *Collins*, only two years earlier. They were not treated in the same way as couples not bound by any contract (who would have been punished for fornication), but neither were they treated in the same way as couples who had solemnised their marriage in church, in that they were punishable for contempt for anticipating the ceremony.[22]

---

[17] And this was how the case was interpreted by contemporaries: see e.g. *R* v. *The Inhabitants of Luffington* (1744) Burr. Sett. Cas. 232, No 79, in which counsel noted Holt's comments in *Wigmore's Case* (1707) Holt K.B. 460; 90 E.R. 1153 and argued that in the latter, which referred to a contract *per verba de praesenti* as a marriage, 'he can only mean what he here [i.e. in *Collins* v. *Jessot*] explicitly says with Respect to the very Parties themselves, that they could not release one another, or dissolve their own mutual Agreement'. Sir J. Burrow, *A Series of the Decisions of the Court of King's Bench upon Settlement Cases* (London, 1768), p. 234.

[18] At p. 155.   [19] See e.g. Holt K.B. 457; 90 E.R. 1152; 2 Salk 437; 91 E.R. 380.

[20] (1707) 2 Salk 438; 91 E.R. 380.   [21] At p. 438.

[22] See e.g. *Bunting's Case* (1580) Moo. K.B. 303; 72 E.R. 510: 'contempt encounter un edict del Esglise, que avoit phibite carnal copulacōn devant espousals solemnised in facie Ecclesiae'. For the practice of the ecclesiastical courts, see R. A. Marchant, *The Church under the Law: Justice, administration and discipline in the Diocese of York, 1560–1640* (Cambridge, 1969), p. 137. And note too that in *Hilliard* v. *Phaly* (1723) 8 Mod 180; 88 E.R. 132 the judge reasoned matters differently, suggesting that there was 'no better proof that there was no marriage than sentence that they were guilty of fornication'.

And again, the context – and the report cited by Scott – is important. All of the reports of *Wigmore's Case* are brief, but certain facts can be pieced together. The couple obtained a licence to marry, but the actual ceremony was conducted by a Baptist minister, who was not in orders. The wife then sued the husband for alimony in the ecclesiastical court. The outcome of this is not clear, but the fact that the common law courts were discussing the issue of punishment, together with the fact that the case resulted in a prohibition being issued to the ecclesiastical court, might suggest that the ecclesiastical authorities, on learning the circumstances of the marriage, had sought to punish the couple for fornication. Another possibility is that the prohibition related to the granting of alimony: that the wife was not entitled to it can be inferred from the second report of the case.[23]

What, then, did Holt CJ mean when he referred to the contract being 'executed'? Was he referring to the ceremony that had taken place between the parties, or to the fact that they had engaged in sexual relations? None of the reports offer any assistance on this point, but it is clear from the slightly longer account in Holt's own reports that matters are not quite as simple as the quotation that Scott chose would suggest:

> In the case of a Dissenter, married to a woman by a minister of the congregation, who was not in orders; it is said, that this marriage was not a nullity, because by the law of nature the contract is binding and sufficient; for though the positive law of man ordains that marriages shall be made by a priest, that law only makes this marriage irregular, and not expresly void: but marriages ought to be solemnised according to the rites of the Church of England, to intitle the privileges attending legal marriage, as dower, thirds, &c.[24]

The passage reads as if Holt is setting out the arguments advanced by counsel ('it is said'), only to reject the implication that the wife should be entitled to alimony in the final line. It shows how the courts simply did not know how to deal with the rare examples of marriages celebrated by Dissenting ministers. The 'law of nature' might well accept such a ceremony as a marriage, but the 'positive law of man' insisted on a priest – i.e. an episcopally ordained clergyman. But why would eighteenth-century judges have had any difficulty in determining the status of such a marriage if an exchange of vows in words of the present tense was regarded as a marriage?

---

[23] See Holt K.B. 459, pp. 459–60, and see further below.   [24] *Ibid.*; 90 E.R. 1153.

Finally, Scott referred to an unreported decision of the ecclesiastical courts, *Fitzmaurice* v. *Fitzmaurice*, decided in 1732. It had been held in this case that a contract *per verba de praesenti* that had been proved in writing was binding on the parties and that the marriage should be solemnised in church.[25] Once again, this proves that a contract *per verba de praesenti* was binding on the parties, but not that it was a marriage in and of itself.

All four cases relied upon by Scott are more consistent with the view that a contract *per verba de praesenti* was a binding contract, a marriage before God but not before man, treated differently from a regular marriage and needing solemnisation for the completion of the marriage. As Lord Lyndhurst astutely noted some years later in *R* v. *Millis*:

> The opinion of Lord Stowell in *Dalrymple* v. *Dalrymple* . . . has, I think, been supposed to be much more decisive in favour of the validity, as a marriage, of a mere contract *per verba de praesenti*, than, upon a careful examination of what he there says, it appears to be.[26]

It is also worth pointing out that these were by no means the only four cases relevant to the issue. There was a far broader jurisprudence on which Scott could have drawn.[27] That he did not should be taken into account in evaluating his understanding of the law of this period.

The impact of *Dalrymple*

Scholars have questioned the extent to which Scott was an innovator,[28] and it is clear from *Dalrymple* that he saw his role in this case as that of restating the law. It is therefore surprising that the case should have led to a change in the way that contemporary courts dealt with the problematic cases of marriages celebrated in British territories overseas.

Only three years earlier, in *R* v. *Brampton*,[29] Lord Ellenborough and Le Blanc, Bayley and Grose JJ had struggled with competing interpretations

---

[25] For an account of the case, see *Love without Artifice: or, the Disappointed Peer: A History of the Amour between Lord Mauritio and Emilia, being the Case of Elizabeth Fitz-Maurice, alias Leeson, and the Lord William Fitz-Maurice, Relating to a Marriage-Contract Between Them* (London, 1733).

[26] *R* v. *Millis* (1844) 10 Cl. & F. 534, 769; 8 E.R. 844, 981.

[27] See the cases and commentaries discussed in Probert, *Marriage Law and Practice*, ch 2.

[28] See R. A. Melikan, 'Scott, William, Baron Stowell (1745–1836)' in *Oxford Dictionary of National Biography* (Oxford, 2004).

[29] (1808) 10 East 282; 103 E.R. 782.

of an exchange of consent. That case involved the issue of Lydia Hudson's settlement, and required the court to assess the evidence of her marriage, which had been celebrated in Saint-Domingue (now Haiti) in 1795. The evidence was that Edward Hudson, a sergeant in the 26th Light Dragoons, went through a ceremony of marriage with Lydia, the widow of a fellow soldier. The wedding took the form of a public ceremony of marriage in a chapel in the town, conducted by a person they had reason to suppose was a priest,[30] and according to what they assumed was the marriage service of the Church of England (read in French and interpreted for the parties by a person officiating as a clerk). A complicating factor was that Saint-Domingue was a Roman Catholic country. This added a further layer of uncertainty to the status of the person celebrating the marriage: was he a priest at all, and, if so, was he a Roman Catholic priest? And what would the status of the marriage be in either case?

In reading the judgments in the case, it should also be borne in mind that the common law courts did not have jurisdiction to decide on the validity of a marriage. This remained a matter for the ecclesiastical courts. All the court had to decide in this case was whether there was sufficient evidence of a marriage to resolve the disputed question of Lydia's settlement in England.

It was decided by the court that there was sufficient evidence that this was a marriage that would be good both by the law of England and (in default of evidence to the contrary) by the law of Saint-Domingue. It is however interesting to note that those contending that this was *not* a valid marriage argued that even before the 1753 Act it had been necessary for a marriage to be celebrated 'by a person in holy orders'; those arguing for its validity cited *Jesson* v. *Collins* in support of their contention that an exchange of consent constituted an actual marriage. The ambiguities of *Jesson* have already been considered; for now the important point to note is that the judgment of Lord Ellenborough shows him to be wavering between these two different ideas. He noted that a contract *per verba de praesenti* would have been binding on the parties, but also attached importance to the status of the celebrant. The fact that the celebrant in this case may have been a Roman Catholic priest led to further difficulties, with Ellenborough rather desperately reasoning that such a person 'would be recognized by our Church as a priest capable of

---

[30] As Lord Ellenborough noted at p. 285, he was 'habited like and believed to be a priest, and officiating as such'.

officiating as such, upon his mere renunciation of the errors of the Church of Rome, without any new ordination'.[31]

While he ultimately decided that it was to be regarded as a marriage for the purpose of determining the wife's settlement, Ellenborough was clearly influenced by the fact that the couple had lived together as husband and wife for eleven years: 'every presumption is to be made in favour of its validity'.[32] Of the other judges in *Brampton*, Grose J was more confident that it would constitute a valid marriage by the law of Saint-Domingue than he was regarding its status in English law. Le Blanc and Bayley JJ both attached importance to the fact that the marriage was celebrated by a person in holy orders, but it is not entirely clear whether this was in the context of English law or the law of Saint-Domingue.

The most significant aspect of the case for present purposes is the sense of uncertainty and confusion that pervaded the judgment: the judges all reached the same conclusion but for very different reasons. The uncertainties expressed by the judges in the case reflect the fact that it was a lifetime since the courts had been called on to answer this question. The validity of marriages in England and Wales were of course governed by statute, and many of the early British colonies had also enacted legislation to deal with the issue. It was only as British influence and territories overseas expanded that the domestic courts might be called upon to determine the status of a marriage celebrated outside well-established infrastructures.

But by the time that *Latour* v. *Teesdale*[33] was decided, five years after *Dalrymple*, all the uncertainties expressed in the earlier case had apparently disappeared. The facts of the case were very similar to those in *R* v. *Brampton*: British subjects living in Madras had gone through a Roman Catholic ceremony of marriage there and subsequently lived together as husband and wife. The reasoning of the court, however, was very different. The serjeant for the plaintiffs, arguing that the marriage was valid, noted confidently that the subject had received exhaustive treatment in *Dalrymple* v. *Dalrymple*, and claimed that there was a 'distinct and uniform' line of authority that 'a contract *per verba de praesenti* was a valid marriage without the intervention of a priest'.[34] The serjeant for the defendants, arguing against its validity, did not even attempt to challenge the authority of *Dalrymple*, but argued that it was not applicable as the canon law has been displaced by local regulations. The court decided that the canon law was applicable, and that as the parties had mutually

---

[31] At p. 288. [32] At p. 289. [33] (1816) 8 Taunt 830, 129 E.R. 606. [34] At p. 834.

consented to marry in words of the present tense they had been validly married in Madras.

Yet there are hints in the case that matters were not quite as straight-forward as they were presented as being. The serjeant for the plaintiffs brushed aside the line of cases that might have challenged his contention that the case law was 'distinct and uniform', stating that '[i]t is unnecessary to enter on doubted points, whether dower, community of goods &c. follow on a marriage without a priest'.[35] Gibbs CJ also acknowledged the uncertainty that had existed prior to *Dalrymple*: 'the judgment of Sir William Scott has cleared the present case of all the difficulty which might, at a former time, have belonged to it'.[36] And throughout his judgment all his remarks on the applicable law were prefaced by 'it appears that . . .': *Dalrymple*, rather than any more ancient authority, was his sole authority for the applicability of the canon law and the idea that an exchange of consent constituted an 'actual marriage'.

The impact of *Dalrymple* on the process of legal reasoning and the language employed by the courts was subtle but significant. In practical terms, the case led to men and women being convicted of bigamy who would not previously have been regarded as guilty of such a crime.[37] It is only in the wake of *Dalrymple* that we begin to find references to 'marriage *per verba de praesenti*' as opposed to a 'contract of marriage *per verba de praesenti*'.[38] And doubt was replaced by certainty: with the apparently authoritative judgment in *Dalrymple*, there was no need for subsequent judges to investigate earlier authorities. The ambiguities of those earlier authorities were therefore airbrushed out of the story.

Scott's own change of mind

In trying to identify why a particular judge put forward a certain line of argument, the historian might delve into that judge's past, to identify for-mative influences and ideas. The puzzle about Scott's claim in *Dalrymple* is

---

[35] At p. 834.   [36] At p. 837.

[37] See further R. Probert, '*R v. Millis* reconsidered: Binding contracts and bigamous marriages' (2008) 28 *L.S.* 337–55.

[38] A search of the electronic version of the *English Reports* yields no mention of the term before the decision in *Dalrymple* in the nineteenth century, while only one example appears in the electronic database *Eighteenth-Century Collections Online* – which contains the full text of all the 150,000-or-so books published in England in the eighteenth century – and this one reference related to the marriage law of Holland, not England.

that it was inconsistent with one of his own earlier judgments, *Lindo* v. *Belisario*.[39] *Lindo* concerned the validity of a Jewish ceremony of marriage, and Scott contrasted the situation of the parties before him, having gone through such a ceremony, with that of a couple who had exchanged vows in words of the present tense:

> There is then, on this state of the parties, more than the mere *contract per verba de praesenti* in the Christian Church, which was a perfect contract of marriage law, though public celebration was afterwards required by the rules and ordinances of the canon law.[40]

It is important to read this statement in the light of the earlier eighteenth-century authorities rather than through the prism of Scott's later pronouncements in *Dalrymple*. The early cases show that a contract *per verba de praesenti* should be understood – at least in the context of England and Wales before 1754 – as a contract to marry, rather than as a marriage in itself. This explains why Scott in *Lindo* describes it as a 'mere' contract, and notes the requirement of public celebration.

Yet it was a contract that was binding on the parties. If the exchange of consent could be proved to the satisfaction of the ecclesiastical court it would be legally binding and enforceable.[41] Even if it could not be proved, the parties remained morally bound to each other: married 'in the sight of God' or 'in nature'. So it is common to find references to a contract *per verba de praesenti* as a marriage, but with crucial qualifications of this kind – as in *Lindo* itself, in which Scott suggests that in Scotland, as in England and Wales before 1754, 'a mutual engagement, or betrothment, is a good marriage, without consummation, according to the law of nature, and binds the parties accordingly, as the terms of other contracts would do, respecting the engagements which they purpose to describe'.[42] Here, the implication is that the contract is binding on the parties, in that it requires them to solemnise their marriage in church, but it is only a marriage 'in nature', not in the eyes of the law.

Similarly, in *Lindo* Scott cites Swinburne with approval to the effect that 'it is a present and perfect consent, the which alone maketh matrimony, without either public solemnization or carnal copulation, for neither is the one nor the other the essence of matrimony, but consent only'.[43] Again, this needs to be read in context. Swinburne was referring

---

[39] (1795) 1 Hag. Con. 215; 161 E.R. 530.   [40] At p. 242.
[41] See further Probert, *Marriage Law and Practice*, ch. 2.   [42] At p. 232.
[43] *Ibid.*, quoting Swinburne, *A Treatise of Spousals*, p. 28.

to the fact that a contract *per verba de praesenti* was binding on the parties, as distinct from a contract *per verba de futuro* (which he discussed on the preceding page). In this context it was appropriate to say that consent was of the essence of marriage – although of course such consent had to be proved before an ecclesiastical court would uphold the contract. For other purposes, solemnisation was necessary – as Swinburne went on to explain.[44] It is also significant that Scott does not appear to have interpreted Swinburne as stating that a contract *per verba de praesenti* would create a marriage that was good for all purposes – had this been his understanding of the law, much of the discussion in *Lindo* would have been redundant.

So what changed between *Lindo* and *Dalrymple*? It is possible that a key influence on his decision came from across the Atlantic rather than the Channel, from a contemporary American case rather than the ancient canon law of Europe, namely the decision of the New York Supreme Court in *Fenton* v. *Reed* in 1809.[45]

Elizabeth Reed claimed to be the widow of William Reed and as such entitled to a payment of 25 dollars per year from the Provident Society, of which William had been a member. The problem for Elizabeth was that she had previously been married to John Guest, who had disappeared in 1785. In 1792 it was reported that he had died, whereupon Elizabeth married William Reed. John Guest then turned up alive and well, but made no claims upon Elizabeth, and died in 1800. Elizabeth continued to live with William Reed until his death in 1806. The court decided that Elizabeth was entitled to the annuity, and this was affirmed by the Supreme Court of New York on the different ground that a marriage could be presumed to have taken place between Elizabeth and William after the death of John Guest. The court drew on English precedents to hold that the fact that the parties had cohabited and were reputed to be married was evidence from which a marriage might be inferred. Most significantly for current purposes, it claimed that:

> No formal solemnization of marriage was requisite. A contract of marriage made *per verba de praesenti* amounts to an actual marriage, and is as valid as if made *in facie ecclesiae*.

---

[44] Thus he explains that the principal effect of a contract was that the parties were 'bound by the Laws Ecclesiastical of this Realm, to perform their promise, and to celebrate Matrimony together accordingly' (p. 222); and that a woman contracted to a man who subsequently died was not entitled to dower (pp. 233–4).

[45] 4 Johns (NY) 52 (1809).

The key source for this was, again, *Collins* v. *Jessot*, discussed above, in which Holt CJ had stated that a contract *per verba de praesenti* was 'as much a marriage in the sight of God as if it had been *in facie ecclesiae*'.[46] But the court in *Fenton* v. *Reed* mistakenly assumed that if a contract was as *binding* as if the parties had married in church, it was therefore as *valid* as if the parties had married in church. And from this misunderstanding – which did not go uncontested[47] – sprang the idea that the exchange of consent sufficient to constitute a marriage could be inferred from cohabitation and reputation.[48]

Given that Scott does not refer to *Fenton* v. *Reed*, the argument that it influenced his decision must rest on circumstantial evidence. A brief review of this evidence shows that the dates all fit: in 1795 Scott describes a contract *per verba de praesenti* as a contract rather than an actual marriage; in 1808 this is still the prevailing view in *R* v. *Brampton*, although an opposite view is advanced based on *Jesson*; in 1809 there was a clear assertion in *Fenton* v. *Reed* that a contract *per verba de praesenti* was an actual marriage, it being assumed that this was the case in English law prior to the Clandestine Marriages Act; two years later, in 1811, there is an equally clear assertion by Scott in *Dalrymple* to the same effect, and by 1816 the court in *Latour* v. *Teesdale* regards the matter as recently settled by *Dalrymple*. It is possible that this is no more than a coincidence – but to attribute at least some influence to *Fenton* would explain both why Scott changed his views and also why he did so when he did.

But why was his version accepted by other judges in England? There are a number of possible answers. The first is that Scott himself was held in high regard. By the time of his decision in *Dalrymple* he had been presiding over the London Consistory Court for over thirty years. His judgment in *Dalrymple* was extremely lengthy, and clearly learned. Thus one finds Lord Campbell, who adopted Scott's view in *R* v. *Millis*, heaping praise upon it:

> I believe it is universally allowed that Lord Stowell was the greatest master of the civil and canon law that ever presided in our Courts, and that this is the most masterly judgment he ever delivered. I have read it over and

---

[46] See text at n. 14, above.

[47] See e.g. *The Inhabitants of the Town of Milford* v. *The Inhabitants of the Town of Worcester* (1810) 7 Mass. 48.

[48] For the subsequent development of the law, see O. E. Koegel, *Common Law Marriage and its Development in the United States* (Washington, 1922), ch. 7.

over again, and always with fresh delight. For lucid arrangement, for depth of learning, for accuracy of reasoning, and for felicity of diction, it is almost unrivalled.[49]

The second is that none of his contemporaries had any practical experience of the law as it was before 1754 either. Sixty years had elapsed since the Clandestine Marriages Act, and there wasn't a lawyer alive who had practiced in England and Wales before 1754. All had commenced their careers long after the canon law had been supplanted by statute. The two points are intertwined: anyone wishing to challenge the authority of *Dalrymple* would have to engage in a considerable amount of research rather than contradicting his claims from personal knowledge. Who was in a position to challenge so great an authority as Scott? As Lord Lyndhurst acknowledged in *R* v. *Millis*:

> Ever since the case of *Dalrymple* v. *Dalrymple*, there has naturally been a prevailing opinion consistent with what was supposed to be the doctrine of so great an authority as Lord Stowell. The question in these cases was not the subject of investigation and argument, such as we have had the benefit of in this case; and the opinions so expressed were rather assents to the doctrine so laid down, from the deference to the authority from which it proceeded, than from any judgment exercised as to the grounds upon which it was founded.[50]

A third possible reason for the enthusiastic acceptance of the central claim in *Dalrymple* was that it was a convenient idea for its time. The case of *R* v. *Brampton* shows how the courts were struggling with issues of the status of marriages celebrated overseas. The British were in the process of acquiring more and more territories overseas, which were not always bountifully supplied with Anglican clergymen.[51] If the Episcopal ordination of the celebrant was to be made a prerequisite for the validity of each and every marriage celebrated between British subjects in British territories overseas, then many would be invalid. The potential problem stirred Lord Brougham to characteristically powerful rhetoric in *R* v. *Millis*:

> marriages innumerable have been contracted both by sectarians in this country, and by persons of all descriptions in our vast possessions beyond the seas, possessions on which the sun never sets, all of which are now

---

[49] *R* v. *Millis* (1844) 10 Cl. & F. 534, 769; 8 E.R. 844.   [50] *Ibid.*, p. 982.
[51] See generally L. Colley, *Britons: Forging the nation 1707–1837* (New Haven, CT, 1992); R. Hyam, *Empire and Sexuality: The British experience* (Manchester, 1990).

found out to be void, all these parties fornicators and concubines, all their issue bastards.[52]

Similarly, in the wake of *Millis*, it was noted that the effect of requiring Episcopal ordination 'would be to pronounce a vast number of marriages that have taken place in India during the past 250 years, invalid', and the judge accordingly mused that it 'behoved the Court to be very well assured in the convictions before they could venture to emit a decision fraught with such stupendous and deplorable effects'.[53] The idea that a marriage could be created by a simple exchange of consent avoided any debate about the status of the celebrant, and allowed the courts to uphold marriages celebrated by Nonconformist missionaries[54] and Catholic priests.[55] The acceptance of *Dalrymple* by later judges may thus simply be because it was right for its time, rather than right in itself: it would, after all, be naive to believe that considerations of practicality and convenience never infiltrated judicial reasoning.

Conclusion

Sir William Scott's judgment in *Dalrymple*, and its subsequent reception by later judges, provides a fascinating case study of judges and judging. It shows how a single judge can change the way in which the law is understood, how a parade of learning on one issue can disguise weaknesses in reasoning, and how the convenience of a particular idea may secure its acceptance.

In arguing that Scott misunderstood the law of England and Wales as it stood prior to 1754, it is not my intention to suggest that the actual outcome of *Dalrymple* would have been different had it been heard in that jurisdiction in the first part of the eighteenth century. Johanna Gordon would have brought a suit in contract, rather than one for restitution of conjugal rights, but John Dalrymple's marriage to Laura Manners could have been set aside on the basis of the written evidence of

---

[52] *R* v. *Millis* (1844) 10 Cl. & F. 534, 737–8; 8 E.R. 844.

[53] *Maclean* v. *Cristall* (1849) Perry's Oriental Cases 75, 79.

[54] See e.g. *Maclean* v. *Cristall* (1849) Perry's Oriental Cases 75 (marriage celebrated by a Congregationalist missionary at Surat in the East Indies). On the role of nonconformist missionaries in the empire more generally, see B. Stanley, *The Bible and the Flag: Protestant missions and British imperialism in the nineteenth and twentieth centuries* (Leicester, 1990).

[55] See e.g. *James* v. *James and Smyth* (1881) 51 LJ (P) 24 (marriage celebrated by a Roman Catholic priest in British Burma).

the contract that Johanna produced. Dalrymple would then have been ordered to marry Johanna: 'in case of Divorce for Precontract, the Person before Contracted is bound, by the Decree of the Spiritual Court, to marry the person with whom the first contract was made'.[56] The point is that Johanna would have succeeded on the basis that the contract was binding, rather than on the basis that there was a valid marriage.

Scott's obiter assertion that a contract *per verba de praesenti* was a valid marriage was to have a highly significant impact on both the way in which the history of marriage was perceived and on subsequent marriages. And, although it was of no practical relevance within the confines of England and Wales, the decision validated marriages celebrated other than according to local rites across the burgeoning British Empire. That Scott's judgment in *Dalrymple* was influential cannot be denied. At some point mistakes become so well entrenched that they cannot be challenged. Yet this should not obscure the fact that the law was once otherwise.

---

[56] R. Grey, *A System of English Ecclesiastical Law*, 4th edn (London, 1743), p. 146.

6

The politics of English law in the nineteenth century

MICHAEL LOBBAN[*]

Law and legal institutions have not been well served by historians of nineteenth-century England. In their recent volumes for the New Oxford History of England, Boyd Hilton, K. Theodore Hoppen and G. R. Searle have produced fine volumes for the early, middle and late years of the nineteenth century, covering the political, social, economic and cultural history of England for the general reader.[1] But none has a chapter on the history of law or legal ideas and, in each, developments in law only filter occasionally into broader discussions. This is a pity, not merely for those who earn their crust by studying the history of law. For we miss something vital in our understanding of the political culture of nineteenth-century England if we overlook the world of the law.

For much of the early nineteenth century, law reform was a subject regularly debated in Parliament. The era before 1850 is often spoken of as an 'age of reform',[2] when the legal disabilities of religious Dissenters were removed, the electoral franchise for Parliament widened, and the 'old corruption' of sinecure offices gradually removed.[3] It is in this era

[*] I am grateful to the British Academy for the award of a Research Readership, during the tenure of which I undertook much of the research used in this article. I should also like to thank Joshua Getzler, Tariq Baloch, Déirdre Dwyer, Catharine MacMillan and Richard Ireland for their kind help in Oxford.
[1] B. Hilton, *A Mad, Bad and Dangerous People? England, 1783–1846* (Oxford, 2006); K. T. Hoppen, *The Mid-Victorian Generation, 1846–1886* (Oxford, 1998); G. R. Searle, *A New England? Peace and war 1886–1918* (Oxford, 2004).
[2] See A. Burns and J. Innes (eds.), *Rethinking the Age of Reform: Britain 1780–1850* (Cambridge, 2003).
[3] See W. D. Rubinstein, 'The end of "old corruption" in Britain, 1780–1860' (1983) 101 *Past and Present* 55–86; P. Harling, *The Waning of 'Old Corruption': The politics of economical reform in Britain, 1779–1846* (Oxford, 1996); A. Howe, 'From "old corruption" to "new probity": The Bank of England and its directors in the Age of Reform' (1994) 1 *Financial Hist. Rev.* 23–41.

that the English court system was significantly reformed and modern-ised. In itself, the story of the reform of the courts is an important political story; but it is one largely overlooked in the general histories of the period. This is because, at least after the end of Lord Eldon's chancellorship in 1827, it did not generate the degree of party contention that was found with (for instance) Catholic Emancipation or the Reform Bill. Reform of civil law was generally the result of pressure from legal and commercial interest groups, which attracted support from both Whig and Tory politicians.

The reforms which took place before 1852 significantly altered the institutional structure of English law. The inefficient court of Chancery was transformed by a series of reforms of structure and procedure which by 1852 made it a court much better able to deal with the large number of commercial questions which would come before it in the second half of the nineteenth century.[4] The arcane system of bankruptcy law of the early nineteenth century was also rationalised after 1831, and continued to be revisited and overhauled throughout the nineteenth century, in an effort to make it fit the needs of a growing commercial society.[5] The common law courts were also reformed.[6] The Whig reforms of the 1830s effectively revived the business of the Common Pleas and Exchequer, redressing the balance of the 1820s, when two-thirds of business went to the King's Bench. There were other procedural reforms in these courts in the 1830s, which served to complicate matters for some time, but by 1854, a further set of reforms simplified pleading. As with the Chancery, the common law courts were therefore streamlined by the 1850s. More significant still of course was the passing in 1846 of a County Courts Act, which set up a new set of local courts to replace the moribund local courts of the ancient common law, and the various non-professional courts of requests which had been created in an ad hoc manner in various towns since the mid eighteenth century.[7]

---

[4] See M. Lobban, 'Preparing for fusion: Reforming the nineteenth century Court of Chancery' (2004) 22 *Law and Hist. Rev.* 389–427, 565–99, and P. Polden, 'The Court of Chancery, 1820–1875' in W. Cornish *et al.*, *The Oxford History of the Laws of England* (Oxford, 2010), XI, pp. 646–91.

[5] V. M. Lester, *Victorian Insolvency: Bankruptcy, imprisonment for debt and company winding-up in nineteenth century England* (Oxford, 1995), and M. Lobban, 'Bankruptcy and insolvency' in *The Oxford History of the Laws of England*, XII, pp. 779–833.

[6] See P. Polden, 'The superior courts of common law' in *The Oxford History of the Laws of England*, XI, pp. 569–645.

[7] P. Polden, *A History of the County Court, 1846–1871* (Cambridge, 1999).

Culminating in the 1875 fusion of the courts of law and equity, these reforms transformed the structure of the English legal system. Yet they never attracted much attention from those historians exploring the nineteenth-century revolution in government, which traced the rise of the administrative and regulatory state[8] – for the law courts, it seemed, were not engaged in government or administration. The common law was seen as the background landscape, the neutral terrain on which reformist politicians worked. Yet it was a vitally important forum of governance in the nineteenth century; in an age when the dominant political ideology favoured laissez-faire and non-intervention by the executive government, many rules which regulated social interaction were developed by the judiciary resolving disputes between litigants.

The volume of litigation grew greatly in the nineteenth century.[9] Where, in the eighteenth century, litigation was a relative rarity, in 1830 one person in thirty-three went to court for a civil dispute. By 1860, there was one civil suit for every twenty-one people. Much of the increase was due to the county courts, the great venue for debt recovery litigation, where the number of plaints grew from under half a million a year in the early 1850s to well over a million by the end of the century. While these figures suggest that Victorian England was, once again, a litigious society, it is noteworthy that the volume of litigation in the superior courts did not rise proportionately. The number of cases commenced in the superior courts of common law rose from 63,241 in 1823[10] to 72,424 in 1853.[11] It fell back slightly in the 1870s, and reached 71,980 again in 1900. Moreover, in contrast to the county courts, the number of

---

[8] See O. MacDonagh, 'The nineteenth century revolution in government: A reappraisal' (1958) 1 *Historical J.* 52–67; O. MacDonagh, *A Pattern of Government Growth 1800–60: The Passenger Acts and their enforcement* (London, 1961); Henry Parris, 'The nineteenth century revolution in government: A reappraisal reappraised' (1960) 3 *Historical J.* 17–37; L. J. Hume, 'Jeremy Bentham and the nineteenth century revolution in government' (1967) 10 *Historical J.* 361–75; A. Brundage, 'The landed interest and the New Poor Law: A reappraisal of the revolution in government' (1972) 87 *English Hist. Rev.* 27–48; V. Cromwell, *Revolution or Evolution: British government in the nineteenth century* (London, 1977); S. Conway, 'Bentham and the nineteenth century revolution in government' in R. Bellamy (ed.), *Victorian Liberalism: Nineteenth century political thought and practice* (London, 1990), pp. 71–90.

[9] The history of litigation has been importantly explored by C. W. Brooks: see his collection, *Lawyers, Litigation and English Society since 1450* (London, 1998), and his 'The longitudinal study of civil litigation in England, 1200–1996' in W. R. Prest and S. L. Roach (eds.), *Litigation: Past and present* (Sydney, 2004), pp. 24–42.

[10] First Report of Common Law Commission, HCPP 1829 (46), IX, p. 1 at pp. 146–9.

[11] HCPP 1854 (364), LIII, p. 383.

cases which actually went to trial was small. Only 3.5 per cent of cases begun actually went to a hearing in 1875, for instance. The growth of Chancery's caseload was also not spectacular. Where in 1820, 2,110 bills were filed in Chancery, by the 1860s, an average of roughly 3,200 cases were commenced each year in that court.

Although the number of cases heard and determined in the superior courts remained small, and diminished proportionately, we should not infer from this that they were unimportant. Quite the contrary, for the larger system of county courts, unlike the courts of requests they replaced, were part of the same system of courts. After the creation of the Court of Appeal in 1875, appeals from the county courts could go directly to this court, generating important questions of law for the superior judges to settle. With the mid nineteenth-century boom in legal publications – both in periodical and treatise form – the decisions of the superior judges were disseminated and discussed on a national stage in a way not possible in the eighteenth century, where the transmission of legal ideas occurred far more informally, through oral culture and the circulation of manuscripts.

The superior court judges were thus the tip of an iceberg of legal governance. But they were the men who made the rules, for what these courts did set the tone for all the courts. The very fact that the superior courts only heard a few thousand cases each year meant that their personnel could remain small in number. In 1875, on the eve of the union of the courts, there were only five judges in the Court of Chancery, and fifteen in the Common Law Courts. These men determined the content of the rules of common law and equity, insofar as it was not regulated by legislation. They heard cases both at first instance and on appeal; and while their decisions could be overturned by the House of Lords, the number of appellate lords sitting on this body was before 1876 very limited. The number of judges increased with the Judicature Act reforms, but not by much. In 1900, there were twenty-one judges in the High Court and five members of the Court of Appeal: a grand total (below the House of Lords) of twenty-six.[12] These judges were often required to develop rules in areas left unregulated by the legislature. In an era of laissez-faire and free trade, very many economic matters were left unregulated by central government. Yet rules were needed to stake out what could be done by businessmen, and remedies were needed

---

[12] There were in addition four Lords of Appeal in the House of Lords, who could be supplemented by other peers who had legal qualifications.

when things went wrong. Unlike the legislature, judges could not decline to intervene: when presented with the pressing claims of litigants, judges had to come to a decision.

The politics of the judges

We are led naturally to consider the politics of the judges. It is tempting to focus on the political views of individual judges. But this is a topic which requires some care, for we must recall the increasing collegiality of the judicial benches, which increased over time. It is certainly true that in the early nineteenth century, when the King's Bench dominated the common law side, the politics of that court, and hence of the common law as a whole, might be set by the politics of the chief justice. As might be expected, given the general political landscape, the chief justices before 1832 – Lords Ellenborough and Tenterden – were High Tories. They were both defenders of private property, suspicious of constitutional change, and hostile to Radicalism. The High Tory Lord Eldon, who was Chancellor for some twenty years before 1827, was also known to be a defender of the rights of property, and a resolute opponent of reform proposals, whether of the 'bloody code' of criminal law or his own jurisdiction in the Chancery.[13] One might plausibly try to argue for a 'High Tory' law before about 1830, though such a categorisation might find it hard to explain the approach of these judges to a number of modern commercial questions. But it becomes more difficult to argue for a single political position in the higher courts thereafter.

The Lord Chancellor's remained a political position, and the holder of the Great Seal therefore changed with governments. From 1827 to the end of the Chancery as a separate court, no Chancellor would hold office for longer than six years at a time. Equally importantly, switching the Great Seal between parties often did not import a significant change in political direction in the office in the middle years of the nineteenth century. For instance, Lord Cottenham (who sat from 1836–41 and 1846–50) clearly owed his preferment to combining legal skill with party loyalty. In the view of the conservative *Law Magazine*, he 'surpassed even Lord Eldon in political bigotry', and used his patronage to advance Whigs. However, even this journal conceded that he never 'imported political bias into the

---

[13] For Eldon's politics, see R. A. Melikan, *John Scott, Lord Eldon, 1751–1838: The duty of loyalty* (Cambridge, 1999).

Court of Chancery'.[14] Moreover, mid century occupants of the woolsack generally lacked the political clout enjoyed by Eldon and Brougham before 1834. They spent much of their time in Parliament concentrating on law reforms, rather than having a major impact on broader political questions. Although in the era of fusion, Chancellors like Lord Selborne and Lord Cairns did play a more significant role in the wider world of party politics than their mid century predecessors on the woolsack had done, their greatest impact was also in the area of law reform, where they were prepared to co-operate in a non-partisan manner. The other judges of the court – the Master of the Rolls and Vice Chancellors – were not removed when governments changed. Their politics ranged across the board, from Lord Langdale, who had been one of Bentham's radical followers in the 1820s (but who had lost his radical edge by the 1830s),[15] to Sir James Knight-Bruce, who was politically conservative.[16]

As for the common law side, the Tory Tenterden was replaced by the Whig Thomas Denman, who remained chief justice of the King's (then Queen's) Bench until 1850.[17] By then, this court was no longer the dominant one, for the Exchequer had begun to take more business. While the Queen's Bench was largely Whig in the era before 1850 – including John Williams,[18] the scourge of Eldon in the 1820s – it also

---

[14] See G. H. Jones, 'Charles Christopher Pepys' in *Oxford Dictionary of National Biography*, online edn (Jan. 2008), www.oxforddnb.com [*ODNB*], and 'Lord Chancellor Cottenham' in (1851) 15 (n. s.) *Law Magazine* 280–8 at 281: 'a more unflinching partisan never earned a coronet. The judicial excellence which he displayed after his elevation was a matter of surprise to all.' Cottenham did however display an antipathy to Sir James Knight-Bruce, whose politics were very different.

[15] T. D. Hardy, *Memoirs of the Rt. Hon Henry, Lord Langdale*, 2 vols. (London, 1852). See also the critical view in (1852) 17 *The Law Review* 1–45. Langdale accepted Melbourne's appointment on the condition that he was not expected to support the government politically in the Lords. See also the non-political obituary in (1851) 14 (n. s.) *Law Magazine* 283–93.

[16] See G. F. R. Barker, rev. H. Mooney, 'Sir James Lewis Knight-Bruce' in *ODNB*, and the obituary in *The Times*, 8 Nov. 1866, col. 7e. Appointed as one of the new Vice Chancellors in 1851 by a Whig administration, it was commented that: 'The politics of Sir J. Knight Bruce are a proof of the estimate high of his judicial merits, which could alone have induced the government to promote an opponent of their policy and party', (1851) 15 (n. s.) *Law Magazine* 273 at 274. He was also praised as 'the most effectual of law reformers [in equity], without going one step in aid of the legal bouleversement, so fashionable in certain quarters'. The same journal later devoted an article to praising him as a judge, which did not discuss his politics: 'Lord Justice Knight Bruce' (1858) 5 (3rd ser.) *Law Magazine* 244–60.

[17] J. Arnould, *Memoir of Thomas, 1st Lord Denman*, 2 vols. (London, 1873); 'Memoir of Lord Denman' (1854) 21 (n. s.) *Law Magazine* 166–70.

[18] 'Sir John Williams' (1847) 6 (n. s.) *Law Magazine* 59–71.

included some political conservatives, such as the High Church Tory John Taylor Coleridge.[19] What were the politics of the Exchequer? Again, the answer is mixed. The Chief Baron of the court from 1834 to 1844 was James Scarlett, Lord Abinger B.[20] Although he started his political career as a Whig, he had definitely converted to the Tory side by the time of the Reform Act. Abinger was famously subjected to criticism in the House of Commons in 1843 for his handling of Chartist trials. He was joined on the bench in 1834 by Sir James Parke, who sat until 1856. Parke, who was first appointed to the King's Bench in 1828, was largely non-political.[21] He was known in the profession for his devotion to the technicalities of special pleading; and it was he, rather than Abinger, who dominated the court. The other prominent member of the court in this era, Edward Alderson, was also largely non-party-political: never an MP, he made his name as a law reporter, before consolidating his reputation for legal learning with an extensive practice as a Chamber counsel.

After mid century, we can again find judges with strong political views, some of whom seem to reflect the dominant ideology of the age. The judge most often cited in this context is George Bramwell, who dominated the Court of Exchequer for twenty years after 1856. Bramwell was a liberal, and a vocal champion of laissez-faire, whose hostility to socialism led him to be a leading member of the Liberty and Property Defence League.[22] But again care is needed, for the Chief Baron between 1844 and 1866 was Sir Frederick Pollock, who was a Tory MP in the early 1830s and had been Peel's Attorney-General. Although dominated by Bramwell later in his career, he was a powerful force on the court in the 1850s. Moreover, he was succeeded by another conservative former Attorney-General as Chief Baron Fitzroy Kelly.[23]

---

[19] T. J. Toohey, *Piety and the Professions: Sir John Taylor Coleridge and his sons* (London, 1987). Although he contemplated standing as a Tory candidate on a number of occasions, he 'was not a political creature' (p. 86). After his elevation to the bench, his 'interest in politics diminished considerably' (p. 178).

[20] P. C. Scarlett, *A Memoir of the Rt Hon James, First Lord Abinger* (London, 1877).

[21] G. H. Jones, 'James Parke' in *ODNB*; 'Lord Wensleydale' (1869) 27 (3rd ser.) *Law Magazine* 15–22.

[22] See the articles in the symposium published in (1994) 38 Am. J. Leg. Hist.: R. A. Epstein, 'For a Bramwell revival' (p. 247); D. Abraham, 'Liberty and property: Lord Bramwell and the political economy of liberal jurisprudence, individualism, freedom and utility' (p. 288); A. Ramasastry, 'The parameters, progressions and paradoxes of Lord Bramwell' (p. 322). See also P. S. Atiyah, *The Rise and Fall of Freedom of Contract* (Oxford, 1979), pp. 374–80.

[23] *The Times'* obituary of Kelly (20 Sep. 1880, col. 8a) said that 'because he was a Conservative, he was never, when on the Bench, a mere technical lawyer. He was

We should also note that the two mid century judges who were most praised for their legal skill and influence, James Shaw Willes[24] of the Common Pleas and Colin Blackburn of the Queen's Bench,[25] had no strong political affiliations.[26] While Willes was known to have liberal sympathies and to be enthusiastic for law reform, his fame rested on his extraordinarily extensive knowledge of English case law and the clarity of his thought in searching for legal principles. Blackburn similarly had no known political views, though his brother was a Conservative MP.[27] But both men were steeped in commercial law, Willes having developed his early practice in shipping (while taking time to edit his friend J. W. Smith's *Leading Cases*), and Blackburn having written an influential book on sale, which displayed his knowledge of civilian learning as well as common law doctrine.[28] If it is true that the Exchequer had a greater share of the business than the other courts, it must be recalled that before 1875, review on questions of law (not appeals as such) from one common law court went to the Court of Exchequer Chamber, whose judges comprised the judges of the other two courts. Legal doctrine had to emerge by persuasion, not pure politics.

On the equity side, we can see a similar balance. The Master of the Rolls, Sir John Romilly, was a Liberal, as was the Vice Chancellor, Page Wood. But the other Vice Chancellors, Stuart and Malins, were Conservatives, and ardent protectionists.[29] Moreover, if Bramwell had the most purist views of political economy, in the 1860s and early 1870s it was often Malins and Stuart who had to clear up the mess when companies failed. It might thus be paternalist Tories who dealt with the fallout of capitalist failure, rather than the ardent economists. And

accustomed to judge by what he thought the merits of the case, and remembered the ancient equitable side of the Court of Exchequer.'

24 He was a judge on the Common Pleas from 1855–72. See E. Manson, *The Builders of Our Law*, 2nd edn (London, 1904), pp. 184–91; R. F. V. Heuston, 'James Shaw Willes' (1965) 16 *N.I.L.Q.* 193.

25 He was a judge in the Queen's Bench from 1859–76, then a Lord of Appeal in Ordinary until 1887.

26 Heuston, 'Willes', p. 201 notes his liberal views. See C. H. S. Fifoot, *Judge and Jurist in the Reign of Victoria* (London, 1959), pp. 15–18. See also R. Stevens, *Law and Politics: The House of Lords as a judicial body, 1800–1976* (London, 1979), p. 108.

27 A. W. B. Simpson, 'Sir James Shaw Willes' in *ODNB*; *The Times*, 10 Jan. 1896, col. 6a.

28 C. Blackburn, *A Treatise on the Effect of the Contract of Sale* (London, 1845).

29 Stuart's 'decisions were almost always reversed on appeal': B. Borret, 'Personal recollections of English law courts I: The Chancery Courts' (1899) 11 *Green Bag* 277, 279. For Stuart, see *The Times*, 27 Mar. 1871, col. 10f. On Malins, whose decisions were also often reversed, see *The Times*, 17 Jan. 1882, col. 4a.

even the Liberals, Romilly and Wood, had a keen sense of what moral conduct was required. Page Wood was often keen to proclaim in court on the need for truth and fair dealing, and indeed himself gave lectures on truth at Exeter Hall.[30]

After 1875, the two jurisdictions of law and equity merged, and appointments were made to ensure that the two branches of the profession would 'mingle'.[31] Once again, we can find our supporters of liberal political economy, notably the Master of the Rolls, Sir George Jessel (1873–83).[32] But again, the politics were mixed. Among the common lawyers, Charles Bowen was broadly Liberal in his political views, but was another man whose fame rested on legal rather than political skill. If he was a wiser lawyer, he was generally dominated in the Court of Appeal by W. B. Brett, who was a Conservative, having been Disraeli's Solicitor-General. Brett was another who took a highly moralistic view of the common law. For him, the law should protect the rights of individuals from being harmed by others. He was also notoriously hostile to trade unions.[33] Given that there were Conservative governments for twenty-one out of twenty-nine years after the union of the judicatures, it is hardly surprising that we can find more conservative than liberal judges, particularly given Lord Halsbury's penchant for appointing judges 'as much for their political reliability and political services performed as for any other reason'.[34] But once more, we can find technicians, such as Nathaniel Lindley, who succeeded Brett as Master of the Rolls in 1881, and who was regarded by Frederick Pollock as his 'master in the law', the teacher who imparted to him the lesson that law was 'a science'.[35]

---

[30] *The Memoirs of the Right Honourable Sir John Rolt* (London, 1939), p. 123.

[31] P. Polden, 'Mingling the waters: Personalities, politics and the making of the Supreme Court of Judicature' (2003) 61 *C.L.J.* 575–611.

[32] I. Finestein, 'Sir George Jessel, 1824–83' (1958 for 1953–5) 18 *Transactions of the Jewish Historical Society of England* 243–83; R. St. G. Stubbs, 'Sir George Jessel: Master of the Rolls' (1951) 29 *Can. Bar. Rev.* 147–67. See also D. O'Keeffe, 'Sir George Jessel and the Union of Judicature' (1982) 26 *Am. J. Leg. Hist.* 227–51.

[33] A. Jelf, 'In memoriam Viscount Esher, Master of the Rolls' (1898–9) 24 *Law Magazine* 395; 'Builders of our law: Lord Esher' (1902) 36 *Am. L. Rev.* 526.

[34] Stevens, *Law and Politics*, p. 85.

[35] N. Duxbury, *Frederick Pollock and the English Juristic Tradition* (Oxford, 2004), p. 22. Lindley translated part of A. F. J. Thibaut's *Pandektenrecht*, as well as composing his own works on partnership and company law: N. Lindley, *An Introduction to the Study of Jurisprudence, being a translation of the general part of Thibaut's System des Pandekten Rechts* (London, 1855); *A Treatise on the Law of Partnership* (London, 1860–3). Like Brett, however, he was very hostile to trade unions.

The conclusion from this brief survey is that the politics of the judiciary could be mixed. Despite historians' repeated invocations of the names of Bramwell and Jessel as totems of a judiciary keen to advance the particular economic interests – whether those of trade and industry or finance and banking – there was always a strong countermeasure of conservative voices on the bench, which became more prominent as the century drew to a close. As has been seen, in many cases, what made a legal reputation, and what helped to build law, was not a political reputation but legal mastery. Indeed, many of the most innovative judges in the Victorian era were either non-party-political or Conservative: decisions which constituted startling innovations in legal doctrine might therefore make no discernible impact on the wider world of political debate.

We need to be cautious of laying too much stress on the political views of individual judges for another reason. Any judge had to persuade other judges on the bench of his view of law; and this view in turn might be tested on appeal. At the same time, there were constraints on judgment, since all decisions had to be justified in terms of legal precedent. We also need to bear in mind the professional identity of the lawyers at this time. This identity had been fostered in a number of ways. The 1830s and 1840s saw the growth of new professional bodies, in London and the provinces, such as the Incorporated Law Society, which obtained its charter in 1833. This era also saw the rise of pressure groups, such as the Law Amendment Society, founded in 1844, and dominated by barristers. A proliferation of legal journals helped foster a sense of collective identity. What we are looking for is therefore less the particular politics of individual judges, but the institutional politics of the courts.

The judges who contributed to the development of this institutional politics had to take into account several things not generally found in legislatures. First, they had to resolve disputes between parties, evaluating conduct which had happened rather than explicitly making policy for the future. Secondly, they had to give reasons for their decisions which would be persuasive to other judges and stand up to scrutiny. If this was politics, it was a highly reasoned form of it. Thirdly, judges had to maintain consistency in the law and fidelity to its past. Judges were praised for being able to articulate principles which they found in cases. This was in part an exercise in interpreting the needs and feelings of the wider community, for the common law was recognised as being rooted in the customs of the English people. But it was also a technical and analytical exercise, one of marshalling the precedents and identifying the structure of law. Many of the most admired judges had made their names as treatise writers early in their careers, seeking to collect and make sense of areas of law. The search for principle was encouraged by the movement – which began in the first half of the century, but only bore fruit in the second half – to revive legal education, both at the Inns of Court and in the universities, and to encourage the study of Roman law.[36] But lest we get too romantic about the developing politics of the law, we need to bear in mind that the courts often acted in an *ad hoc* manner, and one which was also *post hoc*. Judges responded to social and economic problems as they came before them, and often had to fill in gaps left by unclear or imperfect legislation. Their work was therefore often experimental, haphazard and changeable.

The political background

Before analysing the politics of the courts, it is useful to sketch out some of the general trends identified by political historians for the nineteenth century. We can divide the period roughly into three. The first era, running roughly from the 1820s to 1850, has been described by Boyd Hilton as one dominated by evangelical religion and the teachings of political economy. It was also a period of political instability, with the radical and Chartist challenges to the status quo.[37] This was an age of mild reform, but also an age of anxiety, spawned by the great changes wrought by massive population growth, economic change and popular protest. According to Hilton, the heirs of Pitt reacted to this by taking a mechanistic view of human action and government. Their views gained ascendancy over the more organic, paternalistic and moralistic views of the older Tory aristocracy, which had been dominant to the early 1820s. The new view suggested that all governments could do was to put in place institutions which would allow the natural laws of the economy and society to prevail. Government was to be small and largely concerned with maintaining sound economic policy, with a currency based

---

[36] See R. Cocks, *Foundations of the Modern Bar* (London, 1983), chs. 2–3; C. W. Brooks and M. Lobban, 'Apprenticeship or academy? The idea of a law university, 1830–55' in J. A. Bush and A. Wijffels (eds.), *Learning the Law: Teaching and the transmission of English law, 1150–1900* (London, 1999), pp. 353–82; and J. H. Baker, *Legal Education in London, 1250–1850*, Selden Society Lecture 2005 (London, 2007).

[37] The historiography of Chartism is extensive; for an introduction, see M. Taylor, 'Rethinking the Chartists: Searching for synthesis in the historiography of Chartism' (1996) 39 *Historical J.* 479–95.

on the gold standard that would encourage 'sound' commerce without permitting insubstantial enterprises to grow. This ideology, Hilton suggests, was informed by evangelical religion, which taught that man's salvation lay in his choosing good over evil, and that he had to use reason to control his passions. Those who failed, in business or in life, deserved their fate since they had failed to make the right moral choices. This was a harsh moral world, where people were to be punished by the rigid laws of political economy for their failings.

This pessimistic view of the world changed mid century, in what used to be called the age of equipoise, running from the late 1840s to the early 1870s.[38] The mid Victorian era has long been seen as one of prosperity and optimism, as the economy grew with free trade, and as the political threat of Radicalism faded away. In Hilton's interpretation, the dissipation of the evangelical *Angst* is most clearly exemplified by the passing of legislation in 1855 which permitted joint stock companies to incorporate freely with limited liability. Investors could now safely be speculators, secure in the knowledge that if the enterprise failed, they would not lose every penny they possessed, but only the value of their share. It was not a sin to trade and fail: the new law would cushion you.[39]

Free trade, laissez-faire and freedom of contract clearly dominated mid century politics. Free trade famously triumphed in 1846, with the repeal of the Corn Laws. In this year, the vested interests of the protectionist landed aristocracy finally gave way to cheap bread for the masses and high commercial dividends for the middle classes. Repeal of the Corn Laws split the Conservative Party. The legislation was passed by its leader, Sir Robert Peel, who (as a *Liberal* Tory) had long been convinced of the errors of agricultural protection. But it was resolutely opposed by the heirs of Eldon's High Tories, who were outraged by Peel's betrayal. Most of Peel's followers (including Gladstone) gradually gravitated to

---

[38] See W. L. Burn, *The Age of Equipoise: A study in the mid-Victorian generation* (London, 1964). See also M. Hewitt (ed.), *An Age of Equipoise? Reassessing mid-Victorian Britain* (Aldershot, 2000); P. Harling, 'Equipoise regained? Recent trends in British political history, 1790–1867' (2003) 75 *J. of Modern Hist.* 890–918.

[39] B. Hilton, *The Age of Atonement: The influence of evangelicalism on social and economic thought, 1785–1865* (Oxford, 1988). Other historians have however stressed that in the mid century there continued to be suspicion of the acquisitive individualism associated with speculative markets, and many sought (and struggled) to set out the rules of commercial morality. See G. R. Searle, *Morality and the Market in Victorian Britain* (Oxford, 1998) and M. Lobban, 'Commercial morality and the common law: or, Paying the price of fraud in the later nineteenth century' in M. Finn et al. (eds.), *Legitimacy and Illegitimacy in Nineteenth-Century Law, Literature and History* (Basingstoke, 2010) pp. 119–47.

the Liberal side, while the protectionist Tories remained in the wilderness. Between 1848 and 1874, Liberal governments were in power for all but two years. Their free-trade ideology embraced not merely the notion that there should be no tariffs on trade, but a wider ideology of minimal state interference, and maximal individual liberty. In terms of economics, business was to be left largely unregulated (save in the case of large monopolies, such as railways or utilities). It was, as it were, a guilt-free, optimistic version of the Liberal Tory ideology of the 1820s and 1830s, and left little space for old-fashioned moralistic paternalism.

In turn, this was replaced in the late nineteenth century by another era of uncertainty and rapid change. Mid Victorian complacency was dealt a blow after 1873, when the economy began to slow (in common with all Western ones). If manufacturing industry suffered, things were far worse in agriculture, where cheap imports from distant overseas markets generated a severe agricultural depression. This lowered rents for landlords, and drove unemployed farm workers into the towns. Urban poverty again became more visible and a source of social anxiety, leading to fears of social degeneration. Labour unrest grew once more, finding organisational focus in the new unionism of the late 1880s. Reform Acts in 1867 and 1884 extended the franchise and made working-class voters much more important, especially to the Liberal Party. The mid Victorian commitment to free trade and laissez-faire was thus increasingly challenged by those who called for collectivist intervention. Governments responded not by implementing socialist or collectivist programmes, but by increasing intervention. Particular attention was devoted to the social fabric – public health, housing – and there was a marked retreat from the 'dismal science' of political economy.

The thumbnail sketch I have just given of the political history of mid nineteenth-century England fits very well with Patrick Atiyah's theory that the nineteenth century saw the rise and fall of 'freedom of contract' which matched the rise of the dominance of classical political economy, replacing an older moral economy, and its subsequent decline with the rise of a welfare state. It is certainly true that the legislative framework of the eighteenth-century moral economy was dismantled in the early nineteenth century. Nineteenth-century magistrates were no longer expected to regulate the price of bread or set fair wages. But for the poor, the moral economy was not replaced by freedom of contract. Instead, there was a new system of regulation created by Parliament. In place of paternalism, a Tory government enacted the Master and Servants Act of 1823, making it a criminal offence for a labourer to break his contract of employment, and a Whig government enacted the New Poor Law, which sought to discipline, rather than to relieve the poor.[40] Judges famously joined in with what has been called the creation of 'class law' by Paul Johnson,[41] with repeatedly hostile judgments respecting trade unions,[42] and the development of the rule of common employment which shielded employers from claims for accident compensation.[43] When it came to the politically disenfranchised nation, the judiciary was even less interested than the legislature in developing rules which would protect the common people from economic hardships.[44]

In fact, the main focus of attention for the early and mid nineteenth-century judiciary was not on issues relating to the disenfranchised, but on economic questions which were of central interest to the politically enfranchised nation. Questions concerning property were those which came most often before the courts. In 1860, for instance, the judges of the common law courts heard 1,437 cases which were concerned one way or another with questions to do with real or personal property rights. They heard only 613 tort cases, of which only 156 were personal injury or negligence cases.[45] Of the cases to do with property rights, only 245 concerned issues arising from land. The common law courts, it may be said, dealt very prominently with the issues growing out of commercial society. Chancery was also a court of property *par excellence*, though here the business pertaining to real property was clearly larger. But in the

---

[40] See D. Simon, 'Master and servant' in J. Saville (ed.), *Democracy and the Labour Movement: Essays in honour of Dora Torr* (London, 1954).

[41] P. A. Johnson, 'Class law in Victorian England' (1993) 141 *Past and Present* 147–69. But contrast the argument of M. C. Finn, 'Working class women and the contest for consumer control in Victorian county courts' (1998) 161 *Past and Present* 116–54.

[42] J. V. Orth, *Combination and Conspiracy: A legal history of trade unionism, 1721–1906* (Oxford, 1991); M. J. Klarman, 'Judges versus the unions: The development of British labor law, 1867–1913' (1989) 75 *Va. L. Rev.* 1487–602.

[43] See P. W. J. Bartrip and S. B. Burman, *The Wounded Soldiers of Industry: Industrial compensation policy, 1833–1897* (Oxford, 1983); M. A. Stein, 'Victorian tort liability for workplace injuries' [2008] *Illinois L. Rev.* 933–84.

[44] Gareth Stedman Jones argued that by the late 1840s, the sting of Chartism was drawn when Parliament demonstrated its willingness to legislate in the interest of the disenfranchised poor (with the repeal of the Corn Laws and the passing of legislation such as the 1842 Mines Act: 'The language of Chartism' in J. Epstein and D. Thompson (eds.), *The Chartist Experience: Studies in working-class Radicalism and culture, 1830–1860* (London, 1982) pp. 3–58. It was after this decade that the judiciary most keenly developed the 'common employment' rule.

[45] Figures taken from the 'Judicial statistics 1860', HCPP 1861 (2860), LX, p. 477.

era after 1852, an increasing amount of its time was spent dealing with the problems arising from commercial investment.

In what follows, three areas will be examined where lawyers and the courts developed policies for regulating economic activity. If the mid nineteenth-century state favoured a policy of laissez-faire and retrench-ment, commercial activity could not be carried on without a base-set of rules. In the first area, the law of contract, Parliament did not intervene, and it was left largely to the judiciary to develop the framework of rules within which trading activity would take place. In the second, company law, Parliament did create a framework of rules, but these rules were found in practice to leave many questions unanswered. Here, again, it was left to the judiciary to devise the rules. In the third area, the law of insolvency, it was the legislature which created the framework. However, insolvency law was not politically contentious. Instead, it was a system largely fashioned by lawyers and law reformers. In developing the law in these areas, lawyers and judges were not simply promoting freedom of contract and maximizing business opportunity.

Contract law and *caveat emptor*

The notion of freedom of contract was not one new to the nineteenth century. The principle of *caveat emptor*, which established (for instance) that a seller gave no guarantee either of the quality of goods, or even that he had a full title to sell them, was a principle as familiar to equity judges as common law ones, and one for which authority was found in seventeenth-century law manuals.[46] Whereas English law in the eight-eenth century had rejected any formal principle of good faith in con-tracting, nineteenth-century judges sometimes qualified and amended this view and developed a set of moral principles regulating the con-tracting process. This was not to do with setting fair prices, or ensuring that needs were met – the topics we associate with E. P. Thompson's notion of a 'moral economy'. It had to do rather with preventing fraud

---

[46] See *Medina* v. *Stoughton* (1701) 1 Salk. 210; *Sprigwell* v. *Allen* (1648) Aleyn 91, 2 East 448n; Thurlow's comments in *Lowndes* v. *Lane* (1789) 2 Cox 363; J. Fonblanque (ed.), *A Treatise of Equity*, 2nd edn (London, 1799), I, p. 120; W. Noy, *The Grounds and Maxims, and also an Analysis of the English Laws*, 6th edn (London, 1794), p. 107. The mid eighteenth-century notion that a fair price implied a warranty of quality was regarded as 'exploded' by *Stuart* v. *Wilkins* (1778) 1 Doug. 18. See J. Chitty, *A Treatise on the Laws of Commerce and Manufactures and the Contracts relating thereto*, 4 vols. (London, 1824), III, p. 303.

and ensuring fair dealing. The common law certainly took a highly individualistic approach, but it was a conservative view of individualism, one based on protecting individuals from being cheated, rather than giving them the chance to cheat.

In analysing how the judges developed rules for the market, we need to recall the artificial forum in which they made rules. Instead of developing rules in the abstract to promote business, judges responded to problems posed by individual litigants when things went wrong. As Mackenzie Chalmers pointed out, 'lawyers see only the pathology of commerce and not its healthy physiological action, and their views are therefore apt to be warped and one-sided'.[47] Their views of how law should develop were shaped therefore by the sharp practice which came before them.

In many areas of contract, early and mid nineteenth-century judges sought to develop a moral view which did not always go down well with the values of the commercial community. This can be seen in two approaches taken by the judges. First, courts sought to protect buyers, to ensure that sellers would not be able to cheat them with sharp practice, passing off substandard goods. Secondly, and sometimes running counter to the first, judges also sought to protect owners of property where they had been cheated out of their goods. In both areas, the courts protected potential victims of fraud, but in ways which were not always good for business – for which free trade might best be promoted by upholding the validity of transactions, even at the cost of the occasional fraud.

The first approach can be seen in the early nineteenth-century development of implied warranties of quality in the sale of goods.[48] As they sought to figure out what was entailed by contractual relations, judges qualified the principle of *caveat emptor* in an attempt to protect buyers. Lords Ellenborough and Tenterden of the King's Bench and Best CJ of the Common Pleas in particular developed the idea that there was an implied warranty of merchantability of goods sold for a purpose. It is interesting to note that their decisions caused disquiet among those who felt that the rule would be bad for business, since it would encourage litigation over how durable goods should be.[49] But these Tory judges felt

---

[47] *The Sale of Goods Act*, 5th edn (London, 1902), p. 129.

[48] In general, see P. Mitchell, 'The development of quality obligations in sale of goods' (2001) 117 *L.Q.R.* 643–63 and M. Lobban, 'Contractual terms and their performance' in *The Oxford History of the Laws of England*, XII, pp. 475–85.

[49] [A. Hayward], 'Mercantile law VI: The contract of sale' (1830) 3 *Law Magazine* 180–99 at 196.

that the buyer should get what he ordered. It was not that the judges wanted to make contracts for parties in a paternalist way. Ellenborough, indeed, was therefore happy enough to throw all the risks on the buyer if the contract stipulated a sale 'with all faults',[50] where the price would be lower. But it was to ensure that parties dealt fairly with each other.

The rule was qualified over time. It became established that where one bought existing goods, *caveat emptor* applied, whereas if one had goods manufactured to purpose or bought fungible goods, there was an implied term. Judges and jurists put forward various theories to explain this doctrinally, at the heart of which was the issue of what the parties had in mind when one person ordered goods and the other agreed to supply them. One might assume there was a tension between judges who favoured *caveat emptor* fighting those who wanted protection, and that each might have staked out claims to territories of doctrine. But it was not a party political matter. The rule, that where one bought existing goods one assumed the risk, was developed by judges including the Tory Abinger,[51] the neutral Parke, and the Peelite Cresswell.[52] In 1847 and again in 1862, the Exchequer decided that there was no implied warranty of quality when a carcass of meat was sold for human consumption, since it was an existing thing which could be checked by the buyer. Certainly, the decisions came from the apparently pro-business Exchequer – but they were handed down respectively by Parke B and Pollock CB. It was not that the Tory Pollock was suddenly happy for bad meat to be foisted on an unsuspecting public. But he was aware that in the modern age, when railways brought large supplies of meat to London from all over the country, the retail butcher who bought from intermediary salesmen who imported it were in as good a position to judge its quality.[53] The moral economy which was developed was not paternalist or protectionist, but was a way of establishing a fair rule for the market.

Implied warranties of title were slower to develop, but here again the courts came to focus on the buyer's expectations. Here, the trajectory is perhaps unexpected. The mid century defender of the rule that a vendor only sold what title he had was Parke B, in the 1849 case of *Morley* v. *Attenborough*. Here, it was held that a pawnbroker selling forfeited goods only passed such title to goods as he had, and was hence not liable

---

[50] *Baglehole* v. *Walters* (1811) 3 Camp. 154 at 156.
[51] *Chanter* v. *Hopkins* (1838) 4 M. & W. 399 at 405.
[52] *Ollivant* v. *Bayley* (1843) 5 Q.B. 288.
[53] *Emmerton* v. *Mathews* (1862) 7 H. & N. 586 at 594.

to repay a purchaser who lost them when the true owner turned up.[54] Parke's decision was not a ringing endorsement of freedom of contract (for he said a different rule might apply to the sale of unascertained goods). It was rather a decision designed to protect pawnbrokers, whose right to sell forfeited goods was highly regulated. Pawnbroking was of course an essential source of credit for the working class, and pawnbrokers had in earlier times been defended by such morally minded judges as Lord Kenyon.[55] For Parke B, those who bought from pawnbrokers knew the risks they ran. The judge who sought to make an implied warranty of title the default rule (leaving an exception for men such as pawnbrokers and sheriffs) was Erle J, the Whig liberal defender of freedom of trade at common law.[56] Erle J's decision – that where one bought goods from a shop or warehouse, one expected to obtain property in the goods – was a sensible enough decision, again protecting the buyer to ensure that he got what he wanted. Freedom of contract meant receiving what you wanted, not the freedom to cheat.

The second approach can be seen in how judges handled fraudulent sales. Just as judges were concerned to protect the buyer, so they sought to give a high level of protection to owners of property. Protecting rights in property was often regarded as more important than protecting freedom of contract. The results of their attempts were often not good for business and were themselves incoherent, as can be seen from the common lawyers' attitude to the acts of commercial agents. From the viewpoint of merchants, it was essential that those who had been entrusted with apparent ownership of property should be able to pass it. The risk of losses caused by fraud were not regarded as sufficiently significant to outweigh the need to be able to deal confidently with goods. As Bowen LJ observed in 1883, 'credit, not distrust, is the basis of commercial dealings; and mercantile genius consists principally in knowing whom to trust'.[57] One area where this was particularly important was when dealing with factors – agents who bought and sold goods on behalf of other merchants. Throughout the middle years of the century, judges repeatedly frustrated the desire of the commercial community to allow factors to deal fully with the goods of others which

---

[54] *Morley* v. *Attenborough* (1849) 3 Ex. 500 at 509.
[55] *Parker* v. *Patrick* (1793) 5 T.R. 175.
[56] *Eicholz* v. *Bannister* (1864) 17 C.B.N.S. 708 at 723. For Erle's views on freedom of trade, see his *The Law Relating to Trade Unions* (London, 1868).
[57] *Sanders* v. *Maclean* (1883) 11 Q.B.D. 327 at 343.

remained in their possession. It had been settled in the eighteenth century that factors could sell, but not pledge, the goods of their principals.[58] But in fact, it was often in the business interest of both principal and factor to allow the latter to raise money on the faith of the goods, waiting for a turn in the market. In the commercial world, it was essential to be able to raise money on the credit of goods pledged; but in order to do so merchants had to be entirely confident that the loan was secure. Merchants seem to have been largely unaware of the rule regarding pledges until the early 1810s, when after the bankruptcy of a number of factors (during a collapse in the West Indian coffee market), principals recovered the value of their goods from lenders. Lord Ellenborough's decisions showed that the common law protected the owners, and not the lenders, even when the factor had not been guilty of any fraud in pledging the goods.[59] There was mercantile uproar and a Factors Act followed in 1823 which sought to protect the lender. Yet the Act was soon restrictively interpreted by the judges, led by Lord Tenterden[60] and Parke B,[61] who instinctively sought to protect the original property owner. After amending legislation was passed in 1843 to protect the lenders, another series of restrictive interpretations was put on the new Act by Blackburn J[62] and Willes J.[63] In taking these views, the judges, regardless of their political views, were keen to prevent fraud. It was a view which may have seemed odd to merchants. Judges like Willes were worried that a law which expanded the doctrine of apparent ownership, which existed in the realm of bankruptcy, would promote fraud. The view of these technical judges was one which was commercially conservative, and protective of property.

If this was bad for business, it was also often incoherent. This can be seen when judges dealt with the vexed question of whether a seller who had been cheated out of his goods could recover them. Early nineteenth-century judges began to assert that where goods had been acquired by fraud, no property passed (which went against the eighteenth-century

---

[58] *Paterson v. Tash* (1743) 2 Stra. 1178; *M'Combe v. Davies* (1805) 7 East 6.

[59] *Martini v. Coles* (1813) 1 M. & S. 140 at 146. See also *Graham v. Dyster* (1816) 2 Stark 21. In *De Leira v. Edwards* (unreported) he did hold that where a factor by the assent of the principal exhibited himself to the world as owner, then the principal was liable: 1 M. & S. at 147. See also his comments in *Whitehead v. Tuckett* (1812) 15 East 400.

[60] *Monk v. Whittenbury* (1831) 2 B. & Ad. 484.

[61] *Phillips v. Huth* (1840) 6 M. & W. 572 at 598.

[62] *Baines v. Swainson* (1863) 4 B. & S. 270 at 285–6.

[63] *Fuentes v. Montis* (1868) L.R. 3 C.P. 268 at 276, 282. The case was affirmed by the Exchequer Chamber in (1868) L.R. 4 C.P. 93.

criminal rule). If someone bought goods without intending to pay for them, it was said, no property could pass. This view was taken by the Tory Tenterden.[64] The Whig Lord Denman confirmed in 1835 that no property could pass where there was fraud.[65] In bankruptcy cases, where property had been obtained via fraud, courts held that the doctrine of apparent ownership did not apply, and the original owners could recover the property which would not go to the bankrupt's creditors. But by the 1840s, the common law judges had begun to change tack, now saying that contracts for goods induced by fraud were voidable, and not void, so that if the seller affirmed the contract, or an innocent third party acquired rights, the seller would have to bear the loss, as property had passed. Lord Abinger[66] and Parke B[67] led the way here.

Just as this rule was put in place to protect innocent buyers, so another one was found to protect sellers. In 1856, in *Kingsford v. Merry*, the Exchequer and then Exchequer Chamber heard a commercial case where the plaintiff had sold a cargo of acid to a merchant, William Anderson, who claimed (falsely) to be acting as factor to another merchant. The plaintiffs gave him delivery orders for the goods, which he used to obtain dock warrants for them. He used these in turn to raise a loan from the defendants. The crook in question here obtained goods by pretending to be the factor of another. In the Exchequer, Pollock CB applied the recently developed rule as to fraud, and said that property had passed, and that the plaintiffs could no longer recover it. In his view, commerce could not be carried out if lenders could not rely on the security of these warrants.[68] But his decision was overturned in a court whose leading judgment was given by Coleridge J, the nephew of the well-known high priest of early nineteenth-century conservatism, who held that here no property passed since, by a correct analysis of the contractual relation, the parties were not in the position of vendor and vendee. While property passed where there was fraud, it did not pass where the nature of the deception was such that the crook could not be held a party to the

---

[64] *Hawse v. Crowe* (1826) R. & M. 414. See also *Ferguson v. Carrington* (1829) 9 B. & C. 59.
[65] *Peer v. Humphrey* (1835) 2 Ad. & El. 495. See also *Earl of Bristol v. Wilsmore* (1823) 1 B. & C. 514 at 521. Note also *Duke de Cadaval v. Collins* (1836) 4 Ad. & El. 858, where Lord Denman held property did not pass in a case of fraud.
[66] *Sheppard v. Shoolbred* (1841) C. & M. 61.
[67] *Load v. Green* (1846) 15 M. & W. 216 at 219; *Stevenson v. Newnham* (1853) 13 C.B. 285 at 302.
[68] *Kingsford v. Merry* (1856) 11 Exch. 577.

contract.[69] The mercantile community was soon up in arms at the decision,[70] feeling that such warrants should be considered as secure as bank notes for the lender. Public meetings were called, but no reform was passed, and subsequent judges pointed to the inability of the merchants to agree to a change to show that they must have been right. This case helped pave the way for the decision in *Hardman* v. *Booth* in 1863, often seen as the first mistake-of-identity case, where the Exchequer held that no contract was made when a supplier of goods sold to a man who had lied about his identity, so that an innocent buyer in the market could not retain the goods bought.[71] The leading judgment here was given by Pollock CB. These decisions seem an odd move away from the line taken in fraud. Commercially speaking, they were odd. It was surely easier commercially to put the risk of loss due to fraudulent sales on the seller than on the buyer in the market; and certainly a supplier was in a better position to insure. It is therefore hard to explain these decisions, though the fact that in both cases the perpetrator of the fraud had been convicted and gaoled may have influenced the courts' moral views of the cases. It may also be significant that in both cases the innocent third party was someone lending money on a pledge of goods – in other words, someone the courts felt should have taken more care. But in any event, the result left the still troubling doctrine that contracts obtained by fraud are voidable, but those obtained by mistake of identity are void.

Despite the ideology of freedom of contract, then, it is hard to see the development of this area of law as notably *political* or in thrall to commercial interests. In general, lawyers developing the law of contract sought a doctrine which was coherent and systematic. At the same time, however, we can perceive a kind of moral economy at work, which looked at the wellbeing of the individual property owner and property seeker. The dominant political language here was not one which left people free to enter whatever contracts they liked, being left to their fate if they chose badly. It was a view which sought to protect the individual from fraud. This law was not often very pro-business. In fact, the

---

[69] According to the court, the contract was made between the plaintiff and the broker instructed by Anderson, and not by Anderson himself.

[70] The case caused some consternation in the city: see *The Times*, 24 Dec. 1856, col. 5a; 'Commerce v. Law' (1857) 3 *Saturday Review* 99.

[71] *Hardman* v. *Booth* (1863) 1 H. & C. 803. This case has been closely examined by Catharine MacMillan in 'Rogues, swindlers and cheats: The development of mistake of identity in English contract law,' (2005) 64 *C.L.J.* 711–44. See also her *Mistakes in Contract Law* (Oxford, 2010).

mercantile community often disliked the rules elaborated by the judges, and so contracted out of them, or developed their own forums of dispute settlement. But the rules, often developed in commercial contexts, generated a body of contract law which county courts would apply to consumers.

Investment and enterprise

For mid century ideologues, such as Robert Lowe, freedom of contract did not, of course, mean the set of technical rules which governed the sale of goods. It meant the freedom to invest in enterprises of one's choice, including limited liability firms, without requiring any particular governmental authorisation. However, the highly non-interventionist company law regime created by legislation proved insufficient to resolve many of the practical problems encountered by investors who needed the courts to sort them out. It was in this area that the courts' concern with fraud was so central. It is also here where we can see a divergence in the politics of the courts and the politics of the legislature.

The legislative history of joint stock enterprise follows Hilton's model very clearly.[72] Until 1844, any joint enterprise seeking corporate powers needed to get either a statute to incorporate it or be granted corporate status by royal charter. Corporate status – which might (but need not) include limited liability for shareholders – was a privilege, and was not available as a right. Any unincorporated joint stock enterprise was a partnership, in which every member had unlimited liability. The 1844 Joint Stock Companies Act changed this. Under the Act, every partnership with more than twenty-five members, and any enterprise with freely transferable shares, had to register as a company. It had to register twice: first, provisionally, giving details of its projected activities and directors; and secondly when it could commence business, at which point the firm gained full corporate status. This Act also made a large number of regulatory provisions over how companies were to operate, but it did not grant limited liability. This was granted in 1855 to any firm of at least twenty-five members. In 1856, limited liability was extended to all companies of seven people, and a legal regime was introduced which

---

[72] See R. Harris, *Industrialising English Law: Entrepreneurship and business organization, 1720–1844* (Cambridge, 2000); J. Taylor, *Creating Capitalism: Joint stock enterprise in British politics and culture, 1800–1870* (Woodbridge, 2006); and M. Lobban, 'Joint stock companies' in *The Oxford History of the Laws of England*, XII, pp. 625–31.

removed most of the regulatory controls established in 1844. By 1856, England had the most liberal company law regime in Europe, and had set out a legal framework which was to remain largely in place for the rest of the century. This history seems to reflect a move in 1844 away from paternalistic discretion – with the state having the power to incorporate at will, but with continued hostility to speculative activity – to a mechanical form of regulation, which was more welcoming to joint stock activity. The 1844 Act aimed at providing publicity so that those who invested would see which companies were safe and which were not; but if they chose badly, they would suffer unlimited liability. This looks like an appropriately Peelite piece of lawmaking. In 1856, it was thought that the protection the regulation seemed to offer was wholly deceptive. People should be left wholly to themselves to choose; and they should be left to their own devices in supervising and administering companies. But if they chose badly, they were to be cushioned from losing their fortunes. This seems to reflect an optimistic laissez-faire approach.

If the *legislative* history fits Hilton's historiographical model, it is not clear that the history of judicial attitudes reflects it so well. We should recall that there was a good deal of unincorporated joint stock enterprise before 1844, particularly in the life insurance sector. Moreover, there were periodic booms in joint stock company flotations. In 1825, there was a notorious stock market crash, with a large number of failures. It is well known that in this era, Tory judges like Tenterden and Eldon expressed views very hostile to joint stock enterprise, and applied the Bubble Act of 1720 which made it illegal for unincorporated companies to deal in shares. At first glance, this seems to endorse the historians' view that reckless speculative investors were to be left to their fate so they would be punished for their sins. But we should look more closely. Generally, these judges were seeking not to punish the *investor* but the speculating *dealer*. Tenterden and Eldon did not share the evangelists' dismal theology. Take the case of *Josephs* v. *Pebrer* in 1825. Here, Tenterden applied the Bubble Act and condemned the 'gaming and rash speculation' which had occurred on the Stock Exchange and spoke of the need for 'fair mercantile transactions' where each party would 'reap a profit in his turn'.[73] But in this case, significantly, the loser was the stockbroker who was suing an investor who failed to pay for the shares when the market collapsed. The court refused to order the customer to pay him. It was therefore the dealer who was punished for his

---

[73] *Josephs* v. *Pebrer* (1825) 3 B. & C. 639 at 644.

trade, not the customer who had wanted to buy. In another case of the same year, *Nockels* v. *Crosby*, the King's Bench judges refused to apply the Bubble Act in a way which would have prevented an investor recovering money he had put into a project which had failed. Echoing the approach taken in sales of goods, the court found that he should not pay when the project he was investing in never got off the ground. Again, the court protected the investor who had been caught in a speculative transaction.[74]

If courts gave relief to the investor who wanted to join a company which turned out to be a fraud, they were less keen on helping out those who merely regretted their investment. Eldon's approach to companies in effect put them beyond the help of the law, at least where it came to internal disputes. The court would only interfere in any internal matters if a firm was to be dissolved, and to dissolve a partnership there had to be proper notice given to all partners, which might be practically difficult. Eldon's hostility to joint stock enterprise translated into effective laissez-faire, as he well knew. As he put it in one case, companies generally had the good sense to avoid going to court:

> as they were usually governed by some moral principle, which was found sufficient for all their purposes, and as they took care to do justice for themselves to all persons who were in a situation to claim anything from them, they went on without inconvenience.[75]

Companies were effectively left to run themselves.

The result of Eldon's approach was also, paradoxically, to give unincorporated joint stock companies the perpetual existence which was the hallmark of incorporated ones. In practice, his technical doctrine shielded companies both from disgruntled shareholders and from creditors. A company could generally find ways to sue its debtors (if its company deed were well-enough drafted),[76] but if sued by creditors it could claim that not all the members had been named. Even where a creditor won at law, he might not gain his money. For although shareholders had unlimited liability, this did not help creditors who did not know the names of shareholders and who might be given power to sue only an impecunious officer. So, we

---

[74] *Nockels* v. *Crosby* (1825) 3 B. & C. 814. See also *Kempson* v. *Saunders* (1826) 4 Bing. 5.

[75] *Van Sandau* v. *Moore* in *The Times*, 16 Aug. 1826, col. 2f. This case involved the British Annuity Company, which had obtained a statute. See further *Van Sandau* v. *Moore* (1826) 1 Russ. 441.

[76] By the late 1830s, the courts were content to allow directors to sue for the body of shareholders: see *Taylor* v. *Salmon* (1838) 4 M. & Cr. 134.

may conclude that the courts in the 1820s were concerned to protect the innocent investor from frauds where possible, but otherwise to leave business largely unregulated. This was hardly a legal regime which was hostile to commerce, or tough on naive investors. Dour evangelicalism clearly did not reach company law.

The courts' willingness to protect the naive investor can be seen once more in the 1840s in the era of railway failures, when legions of widows and clergymen sank their savings into projected railway lines which failed. The legislative framework was sloppy and the courts had to sort out the mess, and decide who was to pay when firms failed. As was so often the case with nineteenth-century company law reforms, legislation served to confuse rather than to clarify.[77] When the disputes came to courts from the late 1840s, they took a sympathetic view of those who had invested in failed firms. For instance, the gentlemen who had agreed to act as provisional committeemen for railways – that is, the first directors of the company – were protected by the courts. Pollock CB ruled that such men were not to be seen as partners in a concern seeking to make a profit, but rather like members of those committees set up to build 'a proprietary school, or literary institution, or assembly-room'.[78] Pollock was sympathetic to such men, men like him. Provisional committeemen were seen as part of a genteel world of improvement, not as part of the world of trade. This meant that such a gentleman would only have to pay for any goods he had personally ordered. Once more, the commercial creditor was the one who suffered. The investing public was also protected.[79] Those who subscribed for and had been allotted shares were not regarded as partners in a firm. Even those who had bought and traded 'scrip' – the certificates giving an entitlement to a share – could recover their money if the firm had failed, again on the principle that those who bought something should get what they ordered.[80] Once again, it was

---

[77] For since 'provisionally' registered companies were not fully formed companies, it was unclear what was to happen when they failed. For instance, investors in railway companies anticipated they would obtain limited liability. But this would only be given by a statute which the provisionally registered company would attempt to have passed. If this company failed before passing its act, any shareholder's liability would not be limited. The legal problems caused by the railway mania are discussed in R. W. Kostal, *Law and English Railway Capitalism, 1825–1875* (Oxford, 1994) and M. Lobban, 'Nineteenth century frauds in company formation: *Derry* v. *Peek* in context' (1996) 112 *L.Q.R.* 287–334.

[78] *Reynell* v. *Lewis* (1846) 15 M. & W. 517 at 529.

[79] This principle of protecting the sharebuyer can also be seen in a case of the 1830s: *Pitchford* v. *Davis* (1839) 5 M. & W. 2.

[80] Again here, the principle was an older one: *Kempson* v. *Saunders* (1826) 4 Bing. 6.

commercial creditors who picked up the tab,[81] since the company they lent to often turned out to be only an empty shell. Nor should we identify this with a decline in the hold of evangelical guilt: for the arguments which courts used, and the precedents they cited, often derived from the 1820s.

This was, in effect, a paternalistic approach to the naive investor often inspired by Tory judges.[82] But it was matched by a continued unwillingness to interfere in the internal affairs of a company. The leading case – one still cited in current textbooks – was *Foss* v. *Harbottle*, decided in 1843.[83] The case was brought by members of the Victoria Park Company – a company incorporated by statute to develop and sell some property near Manchester. It turned out that some of the directors had sold their own property to the company at a profit. Since this defrauded the company, some shareholders sought to sue the directors. But the Vice Chancellor, Sir James Wigram, held that any action could only be brought by the company as a whole, not by individual shareholders. If shareholders disapproved of the action of the directors, they had to deal with it within the corporation, and could not ask the court to intervene for them. In effect, companies were regarded as little democracies, so that minority shareholders could not ask for the intervention of courts. This looks very much like a key principle of laissez-faire. But we should note that it was settled early – three years before the repeal of the Corn Laws – and by a Conservative Vice Chancellor.[84] The decision was not an ideological one nor one driven by political economy theory.

What of the period after 1855? As has been seen, Parliament abandoned the aim of regulating company formation, feeling that any regulations would be a snare rather than a safety net. In this era, governments took the view that it was up to shareholders to exert the maximum control over their companies, rather than leaving it to the paternalistic control of state regulation. Protecting shareholders by a strong regulatory regime, Lowe and his cohorts felt, was a pointless attempt to protect shareholders who needed to exert their own controls. As for creditors, they were best protected by knowing what the firm's capital was and by

---

[81] The same approach was taken by courts of equity from the late 1840s when deciding who should be liable for the debts of provisionally registered companies being wound up.

[82] See e.g. *Walstab* v. *Spottiswoode* (1846) 15 M. & W. 501. See also the approach of the Whig Chief Justice of the Common Pleas Sir Thomas Wilde in *Wontner* v. *Shairp* (1847) 4 C.B. 404.

[83] *Foss* v. *Harbottle* (1843) 2 Hare 461.

[84] Wigram was Conservative MP for Leominster for three months in 1841.

knowing that it had limited liability. In the event, harsh business reality revealed Parliament's ideological framework to be miscued. While shareholders could, if they chose to, take control of the company, the information they most needed was information about the prospects of the company at the moment of its formation. Once they had taken control, it was often at a late stage when they discovered the firm's inherent insolvency and had to recover assets from fraudulent promoters. They then discovered in addition that they really did not have limited liability, since most firms until the 1880s called up only a small proportion of the nominal capital of the firm. As for creditors, they were the very people who needed to know the real solvency of the firm, which would have been available through published audits.[85]

The result was that the non-regulatory model of the liberal free-trade state broke down in the real world, where a regulatory framework was needed to sort it out. The court where much of this business went in the 1860s and 1870s was the Chancery or the Chancery Division of the new High Court. The men who dealt with these disputes were the Vice Chancellors, Masters of the Rolls and Lords Justices of the Chancery Court of Appeal. Long-term judges in these courts before fusion included John Romilly, William Page Wood, George Turner,[86] Richard Kindersley, John Stuart and Richard Malins. Although they represent a fair spread of Liberals and Conservatives, they all subscribed to a business morality concerned to protect investors and curtail fraud. They also had a keen sense of natural equity in the law of obligations. They were not free-trade ideologues but felt the need for good faith in contracting. Romilly MR[87] and Page Wood VC,[88] for instance, applied the doctrine of undue influence so as almost to put the onus on anyone receiving a large gift to prove that the donor understood what he was doing in giving it. Stuart VC wanted to extend the rules of undue influence to protect poor

---

[85] While the compulsory accounting requirement included in 1844 was dropped in 1856, most companies used the model form of articles of association given in the Act, or created their own version, making some provision for accounting: see J. R. Edwards and K. M. Webb, 'Use of Table A by companies registering under the Companies Act 1862' (1985) 15 *Accounting and Business Research* 177–97; J. R. Edwards and K. M. Webb, 'The influence of company law on corporate reporting procedures, 1865–1929: An exemplification' (1982) 24 *Business History* 259–79; and J. M. Reid, 'Judicial views on accounting in Britain before 1889' (1987) 17 *Accounting and Business Research* 247–58.

[86] Turner was a liberal conservative MP for Coventry between 1847 and 1851. S. Hedley, 'Sir George James Turner' in *ODNB*.

[87] *Hobday* v. *Peters (No. 1)* (1860) 28 Beav. 349 at 351.

[88] *Phillips* v. *Mullings* (1871) L.R. 7 Ch. App. 244 at 246.

borrowers from money lenders. In 1866, he observed that the repeal of the usury laws brought into operation 'that principle of the Court which prevented any oppressive bargain, or any advantage exacted from a man under grievous necessity and want of money, from prevailing against him'.[89] Malins VC also took a tough view on money lenders, stating in one case that he would not allow money lenders 'to entrap persons by offers of easy terms and then charge exorbitant ones'.[90] In an age of freedom of contract, such judges were keen to apply ideas about unconscionable bargains – which were often associated with the eighteenth-century Chancery – to new contexts in which they felt the economically vulnerable needed protection. Men like Romilly, Malins and Stuart were also among those keenest to extend the doctrine that a person would be held by a court of equity to make one's promises good, even where they were not backed by consideration. In their view, it would be a fraud for a person to go back on a relied-on promise, especially one relating to a vested right.[91]

In practice, poor men and women were not likely to be able to get before the Chancery Division to ask for its help against money lenders. By contrast, middle-class investors who had been duped by bad promoters were in a much better position to seek the aid of Chancery judges. When they got to court, they found that the judges were willing to develop doctrine which protected their interests. Two developments are particularly significant. The first was the development of the rule that an investor could rescind a contract to buy shares in a company, where the prospectus had been misleading without being fraudulent. Rescission of executed contracts for non-fraudulent misrepresentations was not a remedy which had been available in early nineteenth-century equity.[92] But it began to develop mid century. Perhaps the most

---

[89] *Barrett* v. *Hartley* (1866) L.R. 2 Eq. 789 at 794–5.

[90] *Helsham* v. *Barnett* (1873) 21 W.R. 309, where Malins VC in addition stated that 10% interest was a reasonable rate; *Neville* v. *Snelling* (1880) 15 Ch. D. 679. On money lending, see further M. Lobban, 'Consumer credit and debt' in *The Oxford History of the Laws of England*, XII, pp. 858–69.

[91] See M. Lobban, '*Foakes v Beer* (1884)' in C. Mitchell and P. Mitchell (eds.), *Landmark Cases in the Law of Contract* (Oxford, 2008), pp. 223–68.

[92] According to Francis Vesey, at the start of the nineteenth century, courts of equity might refuse specific performance if a vendor made 'a verbal representation which is not correct, though he believe it to be so'; but if the contract had been executed, the purchaser was without remedy if the representation had not been guaranteed by a term in the contract and it had been made 'without any fraud on the part of the vendor'

important figure in its development was Sir George Turner, who in a series of cases sought to weave together a series of equitable strands to give relief to shareholders misled by untrue prospectuses. Turner LJ held that a shareholder could rescind a contract to buy shares in a company when his consent was induced by the fraud of a promoter, on the ground that the company could not retain property obtained by fraud. He also held that where a statement was not fraudulent, but misleading, a party could rescind. This was because he felt that a company which issued information had to be taken to warrant its truth. Turner died in 1867, but by the early 1870s, his arguments had won over other judges dealing with company cases,[93] and in the aftermath of fusion, the equitable notion that executed contracts for the purchase of shares or businesses could be rescinded where there had been a non-fraudulent misrepresentation became firmly rooted.[94] It was in many ways a position which was

(*Wakeman* v. *Duchess of Rutland* (1796–7) 1 Ves Jr Supp 368; cf. *Legge* v. *Croker* (1811) 1 Ball & Beat 506). Some element of fraud was required (see e.g. *Edwards* v. *M'Leay* (1815) G Coop 308 at 311). In the first half of the nineteenth century, judges seeking to explain what counted as such fraud often drew parallels with what counted as fraud at common law (see e.g. Lord Lyndhurst's comments in *Small* v. *Atwood* (1831) Younge 407 at 460–1). The parallel march of the thinking of the jurisdictions can be seen in *Gibson* v *D'Este* (1843) 2 Y and C 542, and *Wilde* v. *Gibson* (1848) 1 HLC 605. In the first case, Knight-Bruce's approach echoed that of those common law judges who were experimenting in the early 1840s with a notion of 'legal' (as opposed to 'moral') fraud in cases on the action of deceit; and he consequently rescinded a conveyance even though the vendor had acted in good faith (though her agent had stated something which was false to his knowledge). In the second case, which overruled Knight-Bruce's judgment, the approach of the Lords echoed the view which came to be established at common law, that no action (for deceit) could be sustained without 'moral' fraud on the part of the defendant. It was only from the 1860s that the approaches of common law and equity judges began to differ. See further M. Lobban, 'Misrepresentation' in *The Oxford History of the Laws of England*, XII, pp. 411–15 and also R. Meagher *et al.*, *Meagher, Gummow and Lehane's Equity: Doctrines and remedies*, 4th edn (Chatswood, NSW, 2002) [13–080].

[93] See his views in *Rawlins* v. *Wickham* (1858) 3 De G. & J. 304; *Nicol's Case* (1859) 3 De G. & J. 387; *Conybeare* v. *New Brunswick and Canada Railway and Land Company Ltd* (1860) 1 De G. F. & J. 578; *In re Reese River Silver Mining Company. Smith's Case* (1867) L.R. 2 Ch. App. 604; cf. *Reese River Silver Mining Company* v. *Smith* (1869) L.R. 4 H.L. 64. See further the discussion in *The Oxford History of the Laws of England*, XII, pp. 417–25.

[94] See the judgment of Jessel MR in *Redgrave* v. *Hurd* (1881) 20 Ch. D. 1 at 12–13. However, the rule was soon qualified: in *Seddon* v. *North Eastern Salt Co Ltd* [1905] 1 Ch 326, Joyce J. held that there could be no rescission of an executed contract for the purchase of all the shares in a company if the misrepresentation was innocent. He regarded the misrepresentation in question as innocent, since there had been no allegation of fraud. In coming to his conclusion on the law, Joyce controversially followed the judgments in two cases involving the sale of land: *Wilde* v. *Gibson* (1848) 1 HLC 605 and *Brownlie* v. *Campbell* (1880) 5 App Cas 925. The former pre-dated the development of equity's approach to rescission for negligent misrepresentation in cases

necessary – almost in a legislative sense – to protect investors. But it produced doctrinal problems. In *Derry* v. *Peek*, the House of Lords famously rejected the idea that one could also have damages for negligent misrepresentations, rejecting a rule (initially wanted by Lord Kenyon) that people must be held to warrant the truth of all their statements. This put the common law into opposition to the equitable view. Ironically, while the decision in *Derry* v. *Peek* was repealed by legislation in respect of companies, Turner LJ's notion – that one could rescind for negligent misstatements – was generalised by treatise writers to mean that the buyer of goods could rescind a contract entered into on a negligent misrepresentation, even if the matter about which the representation was made was a minor one, the breach of which (were it a term) would not justify termination. The doctrine developed by judges in response to problems presented to them in cases was hence not always elegant or coherent.

The second area is the set of rules developed in the 1870s which set forth that promoters of companies owed fiduciary duties to companies they formed and to the investors in those companies.[95] These rules derived from a series of cases arising from the failure of speculative ventures formed in the early 1870s. Here, we can see the judges as a collective body developing a set of protective rules. And as they figured it out, so their positions changed. In 1875, for instance, Malins VC, in *Phosphate Sewage Company* v. *Hartmont*, fulminated against the fraudulent acts of a promoter, and groped towards a notion of fiduciary duty applying negative sanctions to repress misconduct.[96] But Bacon VC in *Gover's Case* opted for a view which allowed promoters to buy assets and

---

of share purchases. In the latter, where Lord Selborne said that equity would not set aside an executed conveyance for a misstatement in the particulars of sale 'unless there be a case of fraud, or a case of misrepresentation amounting to fraud, by which the purchaser may have been deceived' (at 937), the purchaser had contracted to take the risk of errors in the particulars. The principle articulated in *Seddon* that executed contracts could not be rescinded for innocent misrepresentations was applied in *Angel* v. *Jay* [1910] 1 K.B. 666 (a case concerning the lease of a house, in which a misrepresentation concerning the state of the drains was held to have been innocent). The decision in *Seddon* came in for extensive criticism in the twentieth century, particularly from Lord Denning (see *Solle* v. *Butcher* [1950] 1 K.B. 671 at 695, *Leaf* v. *International Galleries* [1950] 2 K.B. 86 at 90). See also H. A. Hammelmann, 'Seddon v. North Eastern Salt Co' (1939) 55 *L.Q.R.* 90–105. This rule was overturned by s. 1 Misrepresentation Act 1967.

[95] See further M. Lobban, '*Erlanger* v. *New Sombrero Phosphate Co.* (1878)' in Mitchell and Mitchell, *Landmark Cases in the Law of Restitution*, pp. 123–62.

[96] *Phosphate Sewage Company* v. *Hartmont* (1877) 5 Ch. D. 394. See also M. Lobban, 'Commercial morality and the common law'.

sell them to companies they formed without disclosing their interest, seeing it as a mere commercial transaction. Malins VC therefore changed his approach in *Erlanger v. New Sombrero Phosphate Company*, following the 'free contract' model of the earlier case, which seemed to have been endorsed by the Court of Appeal. But in the Court of Appeal, a fiduciary principle was articulated by Jessel MR. In the same year Jessel would tell a select committee than no more protection should be given investors – the same committee Malins had asked for more protection for investors. The Lords in *Erlanger* endorsed Jessel's view.[97] In *Twycross v. Grant*, the Court of Appeal further developed the duties of promoters, in a case where Bramwell B's view that investors should not be pampered was not followed.[98]

As these developments show, there were clear limits to freedom of contract in company matters: even at the height of the mid Victorian boom, courts looked to moral duties. The drive to these moral duties was in part driven by equity judges with a moral and often Tory disposition. But the course of judgments did not divide on neat party lines. Rather there was a framework of policy developed by the judges collectively, stepping in when Parliament was inactive and injustices and inefficiencies seemed to demand correction.

Regulating enterprise: bankruptcy

There is another commercial area where the politics of English law seems out of kilter with the characterisation of political trends described above: the law of insolvency.[99] The law here saw repeated legislation, and frequent parliamentary debates. But the framework of insolvency law was created by, and tinkered with, by lawyers, rather than being a party matter. When dealing with the problem of insolvency, the law at the start of the nineteenth century was in many ways 'mechanical' and tough-minded, for it gave creditors an undifferentiated power to gaol (or release) debtors who failed to pay, and gave little power to the judges to intervene. A series of reforms starting in 1813 and continuing into the mid Victorian era gave judges an increasing power to decide whether

---

[97] *Erlanger v. New Sombrero Phosphate Company* (1878) 3 App. Cas. 1218.

[98] *Twycross v. Grant* (1877) 2 C.P.D. 469.

[99] See Lester, *Victorian Insolvency*; B. Kercher, 'The transformation of imprisonment for debt in England, 1828 to 1838' (1984) 2 *Aust. J. Law & Soc.* 60–109; and M. Lobban, 'Bankruptcy and insolvency'.

creditors should be able to imprison their debtors. This power was a discretionary one, and led judges in insolvency cases to evaluate the moral conduct of the debtor. At the time when the ideology of laissez-faire was reaching its apogee, the law of insolvency turned judges into arbiters of commercial morality.

The early nineteenth-century English law of debt was notoriously tough. It was assumed that all people were solvent, and only failed to pay their debts because of fraud. Imprisonment lay at the root of the law of debt. The easiest way to get a debtor to pay up was to arrest him. Imprisonment on mesne process was designed to force the debtor to come to court and answer to the debt, but it was generally used to coerce the debtor to pay up. If he refused to do so, and a judgment was obtained in court, he could be imprisoned on 'final' process. The debtor would remain in prison until he paid, but the court was often powerless to reach his money. At the same time, the application of the law was haphazard, for the instrument of punishment was not a court, but a creditor. There was nothing inevitable about being imprisoned for financial failure. Everything was left to the discretion of the creditors.

If the idea of a tough law, which allowed any debtor to be punished for his failure to pay, seems to fit Hilton's picture of a society which sought evangelical atonement for the sin of over-trading, it is also the case that by the early nineteenth century there was increasing unease at the notion that innocent debtors were being punished by imprisonment at the suit of their creditors. A system which allowed insolvent debtors to defy their creditors, and which allowed malicious creditors to imprison their debtors, seemed irrational and unfair. From 1810 onwards, we can see increasing attempts to distinguish between fraud and innocent failure, and to give courts the power to determine which was which. In 1813, an Insolvent Debtors Court was set up, which freed non-trading debtors after they had been imprisoned, provided that they gave up their assets.[100] The court would investigate the conduct of the debtor, and refuse to release him if it suspected fraud. This was only a start on the road to giving the courts full control. For, since the creditor had the power to imprison, he also had the power to release even if the court felt there had been fraud.

The debate over imprisonment for debt continued to rage from the late 1820s. In the late 1830s, imprisonment on mesne process was abolished. One was not to be gaoled without a trial first. After much

---

[100] It may be noted that the court was the brainchild of a High Tory, Lord Redesdale.

debate, however, reformers chose to retain imprisonment after judgment (on failure to pay). This was on the assumption that there had to be a means to punish fraudulent debtors and that the best way to do this was to continue to allow prison for all debtors, and then to release the innocent after they had petitioned the Insolvent Debtors' Court. Legislation in 1842 went one step further, allowing ordinary debtors to petition the Court of Bankruptcy prior to imprisonment. If the court decided that the debt had not been contracted in a fraudulent way, or without 'reasonable assurance' of being able to be paid, then protection from imprisonment would be given.[101] Judges hearing the petitions of insolvent debtors were thus asked to make judgments about the character of the debtor's conduct. If protection was not given, the creditor (but not the court) could enforce imprisonment. The regime of allowing imprisonment for debt at the suit of the creditor remained in place until the 1860s, though various mechanisms were put in place to ensure that the innocent were released. The 1840s saw one further important development. The County Courts Act of 1846 provided for imprisonment for small debtors. But under this act, the debtor was to be gaoled not for debt, but for fraud, on the judgment of a judge, and not on arrest by a creditor. Fraud was very broadly defined, and included the incurring of debts when one did not have the means to pay them. But the Act is indicative of both the desire to judicialise the process of imprisonment for debt and to distinguish between good moral behaviour by the debtor and bad conduct.

We can see a moralistic dimension more clearly in the law of bankruptcy. The law of debt was different, depending on whether one was a trader or not. Since Tudor times, bankruptcy laws had empowered the Lord Chancellor to seize the property of traders unable to pay their debts and to distribute it among their creditors. They could still be gaoled, but unlike non-traders, they could not keep their money. However by the eighteenth century, bankrupt traders were given protection from imprisonment if they were granted a certificate of conformity by the bankruptcy commissioners.[102] In fact, the decision whether or not to grant a certificate to a bankrupt remained entirely in the hands of the creditors. As Lord Eldon noted in 1811, it was not his task 'to look into the moral life of the bankrupt'.[103] If Eldon's view seems odd for someone we think

---

[101] 5 & 6 Vict. c. 166, s. 4.   [102] 4 & 5 Anne c. 17, s. 19.

[103] *Ex p. Joseph* (1811) 18 Ves. Jun. 340 at 342. See also the comments of Tindal CJ in *Browne* v. *Carr* (1831) 7 Bing. 508 at 516.

of as a Tory paternalist, it may seem odder that by the 1840s, reformers wanted precisely to ask the judges to make these moral judgments. An Act of 1842 sought to judicialise the process of granting certificates to the bankrupt. Under the Act, the court was to decide whether the certificate was to be withheld, after considering the 'conduct of the bankrupt as a trader before as well as after his bankruptcy'.[104] Judges were increasingly keen to inspect exactly how and why the debtor had got into debt. The bankruptcy commissioner Cecil Fane, for instance, argued in 1847 that the courts should be given the power of imprisoning for up to a year any one who contracted debts through gross improvidence.[105] This moralistic view reached its high point in 1849, when a consolidating Bankruptcy Act was passed. This Act introduced three different classes of bankruptcy certificate, to distinguish between the degrees of blameworthiness in the trader's conduct prior to bankruptcy.[106] It made no difference in law whether one's certificate was of the first, second or third class; but the judge was to give a signal to the commercial world as to the moral worthiness of the trader. In deciding whether to grant a certificate, the judge was also to take into account the nature of the trader's conduct prior to his bankruptcy. The result was quite odd. As one bankruptcy judge, Commissioner Goulburn, stated in 1850,

> it was no part of the duty of the Court to punish the bankrupt for having been engaged in a foul conspiracy to defraud the credulous, even if he were guilty. Other courts possessed abundant powers for that purpose. His [the Commissioner's] duty was to determine upon the conduct of the bankrupt as a trader.[107]

It was to be a court of morals and not of punishment, which was still left in the hands of the creditors. But in the 1850s, the bankruptcy commissioners were regularly quite moralistic in examining the conduct of traders.

At the same time that courts dealing with companies were showing themselves keen to protect those who had been defrauded by businessmen, those dealing with bankruptcy were being asked to make comments

[104] 5 & 6 Vict. c. 122 s. 39. The court could suspend the certificate or impose conditions. The punitive aspects of this were weak, however, since no creditor who had proved his debt could take action against the debtor.
[105] 8 *Law Times* 456 (20 Feb. 1847).
[106] Bankruptcy Law Consolidation Act 1849 (12 and 13 Vict. c. 106) s. 19. The form of the certificate was given in Schedule Z.
[107] The case of William Thomas Ferris, *The Times*, 8 Jan. 1850, col. 7c. Since he had acted most fraudulently, his certificate was denied.

on the commercial morality of traders. This, it may be noted, was
happening in the 1850s, the era generally associated with the high
point of freedom of contract and commercial laissez-faire. Mid
nineteenth-century courts, no less than social commentators, were
extremely concerned about commercial morality, and were not content
to leave all be. In practice, however, a system which gave *lawyers* the say
over commercial morality and *merchants* the say over imprisonment
proved controversial with both traders and lawyers. The system was
reformed again in 1861 and 1869. In 1869 – just about the time that
equity courts were beginning to develop the moralistic rules we have seen
regarding company promotion – a system was developed which was
much more liberal. In that year, imprisonment for debt was finally
abolished, except for small debts in the county courts. After 1869, a
new philosophy permeated this area of law. Anything which was
regarded as criminal was to be left to the criminal courts. Anything
which was to be seen as commercially immoral was to be left to merchants to judge. Under the Act, a debtor would get his certificate if he
paid a 50 per cent dividend; if he did not, his creditors were to decide if he
were to get one. There was no room now for the court to make discretionary judgments, and the structure of the bankruptcy courts was
largely dismantled, with control of bankrupt estates being given to the
creditors. But we should note that this was less an ideological change of
direction than a pragmatic one. The old system was perceived by merchants not to work. In particular, there was concern about legislation
passed in 1861, which had made it easy for debtors to obtain a discharge
from prison. Merchants were afraid that the old harsh system could be
used collusively by insolvent people, getting an associate to imprison
them, and then securing their release. They felt that a reform which put
matters back in the hands of creditors would prevent the 'whitewashing'
of debts.

This regime was not to last. By 1883, the merchants themselves asked
again for greater court involvement to police morality. A London committee of merchants declared in 1879 that commercial morality was a
public matter and that it should not be left to creditors to expose the
faults of an insolvent. There was also worry that the 1869 Act left too
much power with the debtor to come to voluntary arrangements without
any scrutiny. The 1883 reform was piloted by the Liberal President of the
Board of Trade, Joseph Chamberlain. Chamberlain noted that bankruptcy was a matter of public interest. Henceforth, it was to be supervised by the Board of Trade. A public official would examine the person

seeking bankruptcy and would report on his conduct. Granting a certificate again became a matter for the court, and not the creditors. The court was once again to be a moral agent, if not such a crude one as in 1849. As the Inspector General in Bankruptcy, John Smith, declared in 1887, 'full publicity and exposure of commercial irregularities' had 'a powerful effect in repressing the grosser forms of misconduct, and in promoting a healthier tone of commercial morality'.[108] Writing in an age which was anxious about the depression of trade, Smith was of a view (which we might also see in the 1840s) that commercial failures were often due to misconduct rather than misfortune, and that misconduct had to be exposed and made an example of.

Conclusion

We tend to associate the nineteenth century in England with an era of laissez-faire and limited government. The law was supposed to be a neutral territory, the oil in a machine powered by the laws of political economy. But as we have seen, in practice things were more complex. Judges dealing even with the most commercial subjects still saw the law as a moral enterprise, and sought to ensure that commerce was not conducted in an illegitimate manner. We can see something of this in the comment of Brett MR:

> The law of England is not a science. It is a practical application of the rule of right and wrong to the particular case before the Court, and the canon of law is, that that rule should be adopted and applied to the case, which people of honour, candour and fairness in the position of the two parties would apply in respect of the matter in hand.[109]

Such a view did not make life easy for the courts, for it was often unclear exactly what commercial morality demanded.

To return to the beginning, uncovering the politics of the courts can be a difficult enterprise, not least because the currents were subject to change. But the courts remained a crucial venue of governance, setting the rules for many areas of growing importance. Historians should not overlook this venue, and should not assume that the laissez-faire proclaimed at Westminster was replicated in Westminster Hall.

---

[108] 'Fourth Report' of the Board of Trade under s. 131 Bankruptcy Act 1883 (1887) (C (2nd ser.) 5194), LXXV, p. 1 at p. 18.

[109] Quoted in (1898–9) 24 *Law Magazine* at 403.

7

Judges and the criminal law in England 1808–61

PHIL HANDLER

Nineteenth-century judges, with a few notable exceptions, do not enjoy high reputations as criminal lawyers. They are notorious for their defence of England's 'bloody code'; they resisted later attempts to codify the law and displayed a marked reluctance to develop general principles of fault liability through the common law. Reformers castigated the judges as reactionaries, whose instinctive opposition to change seriously inhibited attempts to create a uniform, rule-based system of justice. Some historians have echoed this view. In Gatrell's recent assessment, the criminal law judges 'confront us with a peculiar and diminished species of being in whom benevolence, sympathy, love, and the imaginative faculties were denied'. He argues that it was 'to the last ditch, and vindictively that these men defended their power to hang people'.[1]

Implicit in Gatrell's account and in many others, is the idea that the judges were clinging to a model of justice that was in terminal decline. In 1808, Sir Samuel Romilly began a parliamentary campaign against the widespread use of the punishment of death that led to a series of movements that, in concert, transformed the face of English criminal justice. The 'bloody code' was swept away in the 1830s leaving only a handful of felonies punishable with death. In 1836, the Prisoners' Counsel Act allowed defence counsel the right to address the jury directly for the first time. Over the next quarter of a century the first sustained efforts were made to rationalise the substantive law and to establish a court of appeal in criminal law. These attempts enjoyed mixed success but were intended to set the foundations for a new, uniform and consistent criminal justice system. In 1861 the death penalty was confined to murder; and a number of consolidating Acts further rationalised the

---

[1] V. Gatrell, *The Hanging Tree: Execution and the English people, 1770–1868* (Oxford, 1994), pp. 499–500.

range of felonies and so marked the culmination of the reforming efforts that had been made over the preceding half century.

The period marks a watershed in the history of English criminal justice: the point of transition from a discretionary, severe regime aiming to deter and sanction, to a more regular and centralised system that emphasised and underpinned notions of legality and personal responsibility according to rule.[2] This paradigm of rational modernisation has dominated the history of nineteenth-century English criminal law.[3] The repeal of the capital laws in the 1830s in particular is usually understood to signify the end of what King describes as the 'golden age of discretion'.[4] Rather than using the terror of the scaffold as a deterrent, the law would instil discipline through impersonal processes, clearly defined offences and strictly proportionate punishments. These were certainly the aims of nineteenth-century reformers, but recent research has demonstrated that they were, at best, only partially achieved at lower levels of the administration of justice. Historians have increasingly emphasised the lack of uniformity in prison administration, in law enforcement and in the proceedings of quarter sessions. Magistrates, for example, routinely ignored the letter of the law in the exercise of their discretion leading to widespread local variations.[5]

This chapter argues that the higher judiciary's attitudes towards the criminal law, as expressed in political debates and in the courts, provide further cause to revise the paradigm. The judges did not share the reformers' agenda. They successfully resisted core elements of the proposed reforms and, more significantly, retained discretion to shape the criminal law according to their own beliefs at the assizes and at the Old Bailey. The first part of the chapter attends to the political debates over the capital laws which led to the collapse of the 'bloody code', the second examines judicial attitudes towards other key attempts at criminal law reform, and the final part explores how those attitudes translated into practice in the felony trial. The focus is on those aspects of the judges' approach that emphasise

---

[2] See J. Beattie, *Crime and the Courts in England, 1660–1800* (Princeton, 1986), pp. 633–7. For the emergence of a new model, see M. Wiener, *Reconstructing the Criminal: Culture, law and policy in England 1830–1914* (Cambridge, 1990), pp. 46–91.

[3] For a valuable overview of the historiography, see M. Finn, 'The authority of the law' in P. Mandler (ed.), *Liberty and Authority in Victorian Britain* (Oxford, 2006), pp. 159–78.

[4] P. King, *Crime, Justice and Discretion in England, 1740–1820* (Oxford, 2000), p. 1. See also A. Norrie, *Crime, Reason and History*, 2nd edn (London, 2001), pp. 1–4, 15–31.

[5] King, *Crime, Justice and Discretion*, pp. 160–4. See also P. King, *Crime and Law in England 1750–1840* (Cambridge, 2006), pp. 1–69.

important continuities with the discretionary mode of justice that is
assumed to have declined in the period, in particular the relationship
between the trial judge and the jury and sentencing.

I

The judges' attitudes towards criminal law reform were clearly expressed
in their contribution to parliamentary debates and in their evidence
before numerous select committees and commissions. Their approach
to the question of penal reform in the 1810s and 1820s set the tone for
subsequent decades. The Lord Chief Justice, Lord Ellenborough, and the
Lord Chancellor, Lord Eldon, were the most vociferous opponents of
attempts to mitigate the severity of the law. When Romilly proposed to
abolish the death penalty for shoplifting, Ellenborough reacted with
alarm: 'we shall not know where to stand; we shall not know whether
we are upon our heads or our feet'.[6] In view of this type of remark, it is
perhaps unsurprising that in the 1810s Romilly ignored the convention
of consulting the judges when preparing criminal law bills and, more
significantly still, the highly influential 1819 Select Committee on the
Criminal Laws did not consult the judges.[7] The debate was hard fought,
but for many historians the judges and their parliamentary allies had lost
it before it had begun. In the words of McGowen, 'the battle was fought
by a rear guard against ideas that had already invaded the citadel'.[8]

The penal reform debate is conventionally portrayed in bipolar terms.
On the one side were reformers who advocated certain and mild forms of
punishment and, on the other, their opponents who advocated harsh,
discretionary justice. The collapse of the 'bloody code' in the 1830s is
seen as a triumph for the reformers' model of justice in its entirety. As
Hilton has pointed out in a reappraisal of Peel's role as a law reformer,
this way of presenting the debate seems too one-dimensional, too
'Whiggish'.[9] The judges were not all High Tories locked into the sort

---

[6] 19 HL Deb (1st ser.), 30 May 1810, vol. 19, Appendix (Debates in the year 1810 on Sir
Samuel Romilly's Bills), col. 118.

[7] HC Select Committee on the Criminal Laws, HCPP (1819) (585), VIII, p. 1, and see
P. Handler, 'Forging the agenda: The 1819 Select Committee on the Criminal Laws
revisited' (2004) 25 *J. Legal Hist.* 249–68.

[8] R. McGowen, 'The image of justice and reform in early nineteenth-century England'
(1983) 32 *Buff. L. Rev.* 89, 123.

[9] B. Hilton, 'The gallows and Mr Peel' in T. Blanning and D. Cannadine (eds.), *History and
Biography: Essays in honour of Derek Beales* (Cambridge, 1996), pp. 91–2.

of reactionary mode of thought exemplified by Ellenborough's comments above. Even Eldon had serious misgivings about the infliction of the death penalty in particular cases.[10] Ellenborough's and Eldon's successors as Lord Chief Justice and Lord Chancellor, Tenterden and Lyndhurst, took a softer line and co-operated in many of the more limited efforts made towards reform. Subsequent Lord Chief Justices, Denman and Campbell, were moderate Whigs and law reformers. When the exceptional Brougham was Lord Chancellor, a number of key reforms were initiated from the woolsack. The politics of the higher judiciary were mixed therefore, especially after 1830. Even Lyndhurst, although a Tory, had liberal sympathies in his youth and was thought by many, including Denman, to have chosen his political course on the basis of expediency rather than principle.[11]

It is also important to note that holders of high judicial office seldom tried felonies. Romilly complained of Ellenborough's lack of knowledge in criminal matters, whilst Eldon openly admitted that he had very limited experience.[12] The puisne judges did the majority of the work but it is difficult to discern any uniform political outlook amongst them. Many had no strong partisan links at all. In his detailed study of judicial appointments in the period 1727-1875, Duman found that just over half of judges appointed in the period were MPs. He argues that political allegiance was sometimes influential in appointments to puisne judgeships but was 'by no means an essential criterion for appointment'.[13] From the 1830s onwards ability became the key factor, and even before that time the number of judges appointed solely on the basis of connection was few.[14]

If judges did not conform to a particular type, nor did the men usually labelled as criminal law reformers, who again present a range of different philosophical and political outlooks. For example, Mackintosh's Whiggish ideas about the need for the criminal laws to develop in accordance with an organically evolving society were at odds with the

[10] This is reflected in Eldon's approach to the work of the Council that met to determine the fate of those convicted of capital offences at the Old Bailey. See R. Melikan, *John Scott, Lord Eldon 1751-1838: The duty of loyalty* (Cambridge, 1999), p. 258.

[11] See G. Jones, 'Three very remarkable nineteenth-century lawyers: Lyndhurst, Denman and Campbell' in G. Rubin and K. O'Donovan (eds.), *Human Rights and Legal History: Essays in honour of Brian Simpson* (Oxford, 2000), p. 178.

[12] 19 HL Deb (1st ser.), 30 May 1810, col. 110.

[13] D. Duman, *The Judicial Bench in England, 1727-1875* (London, 1982), pp. 78, 80.

[14] *Ibid.*, pp. 81-2.

Benthamite approach to law reform.[15] The debates over penal reform in the period are best understood with reference to the key substantive issues at stake, rather than the political allegiances of the participants. The two key areas of dispute concerned, first, the desirable level of severity in the administration of the criminal law and, secondly, the desirable level of discretion.[16]

The eighteenth-century criminal justice system was 'shot through with discretion'.[17] At every stage a variety of actors held discretion to shape outcomes and these practices were understood and accepted as part of the normal operation of justice. In the late eighteenth and early nineteenth centuries, however, they became the object of sustained criticism from reformers concerned to institute more certainty and predictability into the criminal process. The reformers explained the prevalence of discretionary practices by reference to the severity of punishment. The existing law was condemned as a 'bloody code' that had alienated public opinion and which operated to deter jurors, prosecutors and witnesses from playing their crucial part in enforcing the law.[18] The divide between public sentiment and the law was fatal to the administration of justice. According to Mackintosh: 'We cherished a system, which in theory was odious, but which was impotent in practice, from its excessive severity.'[19]

Parliamentary campaigners against the capital laws in the 1810s and 1820s singled out for criticism the power of the judge and in particular his discretion to determine whether the sentence of death would be carried out. Romilly thought the power 'highly dangerous' and accused the judges of having created a 'lottery of justice'.[20] Mackintosh agreed: 'It was by the extent of discretion left to the judge in criminal cases, that we were now distinguished from, and opposed to every other country in the world.'[21] They condemned a system of criminal justice that appeared to depend on the whim of individuals.

---

[15] See the discussion in Hilton, 'The gallows and Mr Peel', pp. 102–7.   [16] *Ibid.*, p. 92.

[17] King, *Crime, Justice and Discretion*, p. 1.

[18] For a typical and forceful expression of this argument see the speech of Thomas Fowell Buxton in an 1821 Commons debate on forgery which was also published as a pamphlet: 5 HC Deb (2nd ser.), 23 May 1821, cols. 900–52; T. Buxton, *Severity of Punishment: Speech in the House of Commons on May 23 1821 on the Bill for Mitigating the Severity of Punishment in Certain Cases of Forgery* (London, 1821).

[19] 9 HC Deb (3rd ser.), 21 May 1823, col. 397.

[20] 19 HC Deb (1st ser.), col. 12 and 11 HC Deb (1st ser.), col. 397, cited by McGowen, 'The image of justice', p. 100.

[21] 7 HC Deb (1st ser.), 4 Jun. 1822, col. 794.

For the judges, these charges were barely comprehensible. In their opinion the retention of the death penalty was essential if the law was to preserve its effect. According to Ellenborough: 'After all which has been stated in favour of this speculative humanity, it must be admitted, that the law, as it stands, is but seldom carried into execution, and yet it ceases not to hold out that terror which alone will be sufficient to prevent the frequent commission of the offence.'[22] In the judiciary's view, far from being arbitrary, the prerogative of mercy and discretion were what made the system humane. The judge ensured that the trial was conducted fairly and that the law was tempered where necessary.[23] As Lord Lyndhurst expressed it: 'The whole system of our Criminal Code was founded on discretion.'[24]

In the first decade of the campaign against the death penalty, the judges' 'practical' experience was preferred to the 'speculative theories' of the reformers in the House of Commons. Indeed, Romilly had serious difficulties in attracting attention to his cause and very little success in achieving legislative change.[25] Thereafter a number of scandals, particularly surrounding the crime of forgery, generated momentum for the reform movement and enabled reformers to substantiate their charge that public opinion was set against the severity of the law.[26] The rapid rise in prosecutions at the beginning of the nineteenth century also played a crucial role in shifting perceptions of justice.[27] The consequent increase in capital convictions meant that, after 1815, over 90 per cent of convicts sentenced to death were pardoned.[28] This made the idea of a severe law tempered by mercy difficult to sustain. It also placed the judges, who were responsible for granting pardons in most cases, in an increasingly invidious position. What was really objectionable and unpalatable to the public was not the judge's discretion per se, but his power over life and death. Even Cottu, the

---

[22] 19 HL Deb (1st ser.), 30 May 1810, 89 app.

[23] See Ellenborough's description of the judicial role: 19 HL Deb (1st ser.), 30 May 1810, 112–13 app.

[24] 17 HL Deb (3rd ser.), 7 May 1833, col. 1015. Lyndhurst was Lord Chancellor in 1827–30, 1834–5 and 1841–6.

[25] See Handler, 'Forging the agenda', p. 254.

[26] The reformers' success in constructing 'public opinion' in this period does not of itself evince evidence of a growing distaste for the death penalty. See Gatrell, *The Hanging Tree*, pp. 396–416; Handler, 'Forging the agenda'; P. Handler, 'Forgery and the end of the 'Bloody Code' in early nineteenth century England' (2005) 48 *Historical J*. 683–702.

[27] For the pattern of prosecutions see C. Emsley, *Crime and Society in England*, 3rd edn (Harlow, 2005), pp. 32–3.

[28] Gatrell, *The Hanging Tree*, p. 21.

French admirer of the English criminal justice system, felt obliged to 'confess that there seems something more in so unlimited a power than ought ever to be entrusted to any one man'.[29]

The reformers' success in establishing their critique of the 'bloody code' in the 1820s facilitated the reforms of the 1830s that effectively confined the death penalty to murder and attempted murder. Yet the legislation that mitigated the law also retained many of the discretionary powers of judges and juries and in some instances actually increased them. For example, the statute of 1837, which rendered most forms of serious assault non-capital, gave juries a new power to return a conviction of common assault wherever a felonious assault was charged.[30] Juries continued to have discretion to return partial verdicts in other cases such as murder.

Judges were given a wide sentencing discretion under the new statutory framework. In cases of burglary, for example, the court was empowered to sentence offenders to 'be transported beyond the seas for the term of their natural life . . . or for any term not less than ten years, or to be imprisoned for any term not exceeding three years'.[31] A similarly wide sentencing discretion was bestowed in cases of forgery, serious assaults, robbery and stealing from the person. Some of the statutes specified a minimum or maximum period either of imprisonment or transportation, but generally the discretion given to judges was very wide and there was no guidance as to how it should be exercised.[32]

The judges supported these measures, but many reformers objected to the bills.[33] William Ewart, the most prominent proponent of criminal law reform of the 1830s, when speaking on the Offences against the Person Bill in 1837, stated that he 'objected to the discretion proposed to vest in the judge, though he knew that certain limits in these matters must be allowed to him. But that discretion should be as little as possible; and those limits should be so well defined and fixed, that he should not be readily able to pass them.'[34] Lord Brougham also lamented the fact

---

[29] M. Cottu, *On the Administration of the Criminal Code in England* (London, 1820), pp. 38–9.

[30] 1 Vic. c. 85, s. 11.   [31] 1 Vic. c. 86, s. 3.

[32] 1 Vic. c. 84, s. 1 (forgery); 1 Vic. c. 85, ss. 3, 4 (offences against the person); 1 Vic. c. 87, ss. 3, 5 (robbery, stealing from the person). See L. Radzinowicz and R. Hood, 'Judicial discretion and sentencing standards: Victorian attempts to solve a perennial problem' (1979) 127 *U. Pa. L. Rev.* 1288–349.

[33] Lord Chief Justice Denman reported that the judges supported the measures during the bills' passage through the Lords. 38 HL Deb (3rd ser.), 4 Jul. 1837, col. 1774.

[34] 38 HC Deb (3rd ser.), 24 Apr. 1837, col. 257.

that the bills had been introduced before the Royal Commission on the Criminal Laws had completed its investigation and concurred in the Commissioners' view that 'any partial alteration would inevitably produce great inconvenience, and that the only effectual remedy consisted in an entire revision and re-construction of the whole fabric of the criminal law'.[35] Brougham's and Ewart's objections went unheeded. Thus whilst it is clear that the 1830s legislation substantially mitigated the severity of the law, the problem of discretion in the criminal law remained the subject of controversy and debate.

II

The reduction in the use of the death penalty was only one aspect of a reforming agenda that attempted to overhaul the criminal justice system in this period. Efforts were made to rationalise the law, to introduce a system of criminal appeals and to give prisoners full rights to defence by counsel. For the most part, the judges opposed these measures. They did so for a number of reasons, but at the heart of their position was the desire to retain discretion and ensure that questions of criminal law remained simple and capable of being determined quickly by a jury.

Judges feared that the effect of granting the prisoner's counsel the right to address a speech to the jury would obscure the issues and prolong the trial. Ready appeals raised the prospect of drawn-out criminal proceedings with punishment following weeks or months after sentence. This did not accord with the judges' vision of how criminal justice should be administered. They kept a more-or-less dignified silence in public on the question of prisoners' counsel, but Lord Campbell estimated that twelve out of the fifteen judges opposed the measure, with Justice Park apparently threatening to resign if it passed.[36] In their evidence before the House of Lords Select Committee on Criminal Appeals in 1847 however, the judges made their feelings plain, all of them emphasising the importance of there being, in Baron Parke's words, 'a speedy Determination of every Charge of Crime'.[37] In part, the judicial preoccupation with speed was determined by practical considerations,

---

[35] 38 HL Deb (3rd ser.), 4 Jul. 1837, col. 1786.

[36] *Life of John, Lord Campbell*, ed. M. Hardcastle, 2 vols. (London, 1881), II, pp. 106–7 cited by A. May, *The Bar and the Old Bailey, 1750–1850* (London, 2003), p. 183.

[37] Select Committee of the House of Lords on Administration of Criminal Law Amendment Bill (1847–8) (C (1st ser.) 523), XVI, p. 423 [1848 SC], Minutes of Evidence, p. 4.

specifically the need to get through the assize business in good time.[38] But there were other concerns as well according to Lord Lyndhurst: 'The criminal law depends for the effect . . . which it has in deterring . . . by Example of punishment, upon the speediness with which the Execution of the Sentence follows Trial.'[39]

The presence of defence counsel or long processes of appeal would inhibit this model of quick, exemplary justice and, in the opinion of the judges, could not be justified because difficult or complex questions seldom arose. Judges rejected the reformers' argument that the criminal law should be brought into line with the civil system of appeals.[40] According to Baron Parke: 'in Criminal Cases the Questions submitted to the Jury are, with very rare Exceptions, extremely simple, and the Juries act without any Prejudice'.[41] In contrast, appeals in civil cases were necessary to resolve potentially very difficult questions. Judges drew a clear distinction between civil and criminal matters; in the latter, speedy decisions were of the 'utmost importance to the public'.[42]

The high level of complacency in the judicial responses is noteworthy, if unsurprising. Most claimed to have experienced no incidents of improper convictions and expressed the opinion that they were extremely unlikely to occur. The trial judge could be relied upon to reserve points of law for the consideration of all of the judges or to secure a royal pardon if there was an improper conviction. There was no need for any supervision or other means of redress. A few of the judges conceded that the private system of appealing to the Crown for mercy was imperfect, but none was willing to countenance any of the alternative mechanisms. As a result, despite various attempts throughout the nineteenth century, the only change made was the creation of the Court for Crown Cases Reserved in 1848.[43] This court had a new power to hear cases reserved from the quarter sessions, but its jurisdiction was confined

---

[38] In the event fears that the defence counsel's speech would elongate proceedings proved unfounded as Denman acknowledged to Brougham shortly after the Act: May, *The Bar and the Old Bailey*, p. 197.

[39] 1848 SC, Minutes of Evidence, p. 49.

[40] For the development and rationalisation of appellate procedures in civil cases during the nineteenth century, see W. R. Cornish *et al.*, *The Oxford History of the Laws of England*, XI–XIII, *1820–1914* (Oxford, 2010), XI, pp. 601–2, 799–808. For the contrast with criminal appeals, see P. Handler, 'The Court for Crown Cases Reserved, 1848–1908' (2011) 29 *Law and Hist. Rev.*, 259–88.

[41] 1848 SC, Minutes of Evidence, p. 9.

[42] 1848 SC, Minutes of Evidence, p. 8 per Baron Parke.   [43] 11 & 12 Vict., c. 78.

to points of law that the trial judge saw fit to reserve.[44] The fact that the bill had been prepared by Barons Parke and Alderson may explain its success.[45] It ensured that the judges gave decisions in open court and the court acquired a power to quash convictions, but its overall effect was limited. The court heard a steady trickle of cases each year, but the small volume of cases, together with the judges' reluctance to set out general principles of criminal law, severely limited its influence. There was no effective court of criminal appeal until 1907.[46]

The judges' concern to avoid complications in the criminal law and their distrust of generalising principles were evident in their approach to legislative schemes to consolidate and codify the criminal law. They consistently disparaged attempts to effect sweeping changes, relying upon well-rehearsed arguments about the benefits of flexible common law principles. In one respect this simply reflects the common law mind's distrust of projects of codification, but it was also consistent with judges' attitude towards the criminal law in particular. Peel's very limited reforms of the 1820s met with their approval and co-operation. His bills to consolidate and simplify the law, whilst maintaining capital punishment for most of the felonies that were punished with death in practice, were carried through with the assistance of Chief Justice Tenterden. Tenterden read and amended drafts of bills, and corresponded closely with Peel on bills to be put to Parliament. In relation to the Forgery Bill of 1830, for example, Tenterden made a number of changes to the wording and scope of the bill and Peel was careful to express his gratitude.[47] Tenterden's supervision of the bills in the House of Lords ensured that Peel enjoyed more success than Romilly and Mackintosh had done.

The involvement of judges and lawyers in the drafting of bills often ensured that existing terminology was retained. So in the preparation of the Forgery Bill of 1830, the Attorney-General took exception to the departure from the phraseology of previous Acts and a compromise was reached.[48] This pattern repeated itself in the drafting of criminal laws over subsequent decades, sometimes to the consternation of those who

---

[44] On the history of this court, see Handler, 'Court for Crown Cases Reserved'.

[45] See Parke and Alderson's evidence before the 1848 Select Committee: 1848 SC, Minutes of Evidence, pp. 3–13.

[46] See Handler, 'Court for Crown Cases Reserved'; R. Pattenden, *English Criminal Appeals 1844–1994* (Oxford, 1996), pp. 8–10; D. D. Bentley, *Select Cases from the Twelve Judges' Notebooks* (London, 1997), Appendix 4, Table B, p. 196.

[47] For the correspondence on the bill in the early months of 1830, see Peel Papers BL Add MSS 40399, fos. 410, 419; 40400, fos. 3, 30, 37, 76–80, 89.

[48] Peel to Gregson, 7 Jan. 1830, Peel Papers, BL Add MSS 40400, fo. 14; Tenterden to Peel, 28 Feb. 1830, Peel Papers, BL Add MSS 40400, fo. 78.

wished to simplify and clarify the language of the law. The attempts to codify and consolidate the law following the reports of the Royal Commission on the Criminal Laws provide the clearest examples. In 1853, the Lord Chancellor sought the judges' opinion on the expediency of preparing a statute for the criminal law as a whole and on two bills that had been prepared to amend the law of offences against the person and on larceny. However the judges were uniformly opposed to the creation of any kind of a code and at pains to point out the inadequacies of the bills. They warned of the dangers of the 'court and jury being bound by precise words and expressions' typical of statutes.[49] In the words of Chief Baron Pollock, a new code would 'create very, very much more doubt than now exists'.[50] In contrast, the rules of the common law, according to Baron Parke, were 'clear and well understood'.[51]

Unsurprisingly the judges' attitudes drew criticism from those concerned to ameliorate the criminal law through legislation. The men who had prepared the bills, Charles Greaves and James Lonsdale, published a pamphlet that sought to rebut the judges' objections.[52] The judges' insistence that the common law provided clarity and certainty was particularly objectionable in view of the Royal Commission's extensive criticisms. The Law Review magazine thought the judges' claim 'singular' in view of the state of the common law.[53]

It would be easy to dismiss judicial attitudes towards the legislative amelioration of the criminal law as being narrow-minded and self-interested; but the judges were predisposed to distrust legislation in criminal law on practical grounds. For example, Baron Alderson, having listed a number of problems with a proposed bill relating to rape, bluntly declared: 'All this difficulty comes from defining in words the crime of rape and carnal knowledge.'[54] Underlying this judicial attitude was the belief that questions of criminal law were best decided at the trial where there was sufficient flexibility to ensure that a broad view could be taken of each case. They drew a sharp distinction between criminal and civil

---

[49] 'Copies of the Lord Chancellor's Letter to the Judges and of their Answers respecting the Criminal Law Bills of the Last Session', HCPP (1854) (C (1st ser.) 303), LIII, p. 19 (Justice Wightman).

[50] *Ibid.*, p. 6.   [51] *Ibid.*, p. 7.

[52] C. Greaves and J. Lonsdale, *A Letter to the Lord Chancellor containing Observations on the Answers of the Judges to the Lord Chancellor's Letters on the Criminal Law Bills of the Last Session of Parliament* (London, 1854).

[53] Anon., 'The judges and the criminal code' (1854) 20 *Law Review* 110, 117.

[54] *Copies of the Lord Chancellor's Letter*, p. 10.

matters. In the latter, difficult points arose and appeals were necessary and desirable, but so far as the criminal law was concerned, judges wanted to avoid even the possibility of any difficult questions of interpretation or construction arising. Baron Martin referred to the difficulties involved in interpreting the recent railway and bankruptcy legislation and asked 'what would be the consequence of permitting the criminal law of this country to depend upon reasonings and criticism such as may be found in the reports of these cases'.[55] Baron Parke suggested that the frequent questions for judicial decision that would arise from any code would 'be a great evil, especially in the administration of the criminal law, from which it is now comparatively free, as the points which arise in it are in a striking degree less frequent than in the administration of civil justice'.[56] As is well known, the attempts to codify the law floundered in the 1850s and the intransigent attitudes of the judiciary contributed hugely to this failure. The consolidating statutes of 1861 for the most part retained the language and offences of former Acts.[57]

The judges' attitudes towards projects of criminal law reform were not static or wholly negative. They came to recognise, reluctantly at first, that the effective operation of justice required public support. One of the key rhetorical devices of those who spoke against criminal law reform in Parliament in the 1810s and 1820s was to dismiss the calls for change as speculative or theoretical. The correct mode of proceeding, so they argued, was on the basis of experience and judges had more experience of criminal justice than anyone else. Yet it was less easy to combat arguments against the death penalty in particular, when public opinion seemed set against the law.[58] Even if the reforms of the 1830s left many of the key elements of the trial and discretionary sentencing processes in place, there was a new need to project an acceptable image of justice.[59] The days when judges could openly defy opinion, as when Ellenborough rode, laughing, through the jeering crowd following William Hone's acquittal for blasphemous libel in 1817 before stopping to buy kippers,

[55] *Ibid.*, p. 39.   [56] *Ibid.*, p. 8.

[57] For the history of the legislation, see C. Greaves, *The Criminal Law Consolidation Acts of the 24 &25 Vict with Notes, Observations and Forms for Summary Proceedings*, 2nd edn (London, 1862).

[58] See n. 26, above.

[59] The shift was acknowledged, albeit reluctantly, by Peel: 'in the present spirit of the times, it was in vain to attempt to defend what is established, merely because it is established'. Peel to Lord Liverpool, 12 Oct. 1822, Liverpool Papers BL Add MSS 38195, fo. 120.

were drawing to a close.[60] In an 1832 debate on mitigating the punishment of death for forgery, the future Lord Chancellor, Sir Edward Sugden, stated that 'when one general and universal opinion pervaded the public mind amongst all ranks and classes, let it be right or wrong, the Members of that House were bound to attend to it'. Even the deeply reactionary judge, Lord Wynford, accepted the need for change.[61]

The judges co-operated with some of the bills that were put forward and initiated a number of measures. For example, Denman and Campbell, during their terms as Lord Chief Justice, brought bills to Parliament that aimed to expedite aspects of procedure and evidence. Denman attempted to reform the law of evidence.[62] Campbell's Criminal Procedure Act of 1851 reformed the law relating to indictments by giving judges the power to amend the indictment at the trial.[63] This aimed to reduce the scope for technical acquittals based on very minor errors on the indictment, such as that which had occurred in 1841 in the trial of Lord Cardigan for attempted murder.[64] These measures reflected the new judicial awareness that, with the hugely increased public scrutiny of trial, justice had to be seen to be done. The establishment of the Court for Crown Cases Reserved can be understood in this light because, whilst it effected no real substantial change to the procedure of reserving points, it did force the judges to hear cases openly and to give reasons for their decisions. In trials judges began to express concern in cases where only one side had counsel that having to conduct the examination of witnesses compromised their position of impartiality. For example, in 1844 Justice Cresswell complained of the lack of prosecuting counsel and the impropriety of the judge having to fill his place.[65]

Transforming the public image of justice required much more than simply streamlining procedures and eliminating some of the patent fictions and abuses that had established themselves over preceding centuries. Judges also recognised the need for the criminal justice system to respond to the rapidly growing fears about the threat of crime in the first half of the nineteenth century. Yet they resisted attempts to

---

[60] W. Townsend, *The Lives of Twelve Eminent Judges of the Last and Present Century*, 2 vols. (London, 1846), I, p. 388, cited in Gatrell, *The Hanging Tree*, p. 531.

[61] 14 HL Deb (3rd ser.), 31 Jul. 1832, col. 984; 14 HL Deb (3rd ser.), 13 Aug. 1832, col. 1348. Sugden and Wynford still argued for the retention of the death penalty for certain types of forgery.

[62] See G. Jones and V. Jones, 'Denman, Thomas, first Baron Denman (1779–1854)' in *Oxford Dictionary of National Biography*, online edn (May 2009) www.oxforddnb.com.

[63] 14 & 15 Vic. c.100.   [64] *The Times*, 17 Feb. 1841.

[65] *The Times*, 20 Mar. 1844 (case of William Hazel).

centralise criminal justice through legislation of clearly articulated rules, and they continued to envisage a local, discretionary form of justice as the best means of addressing public concerns. This is evident from judicial attitudes towards two particular and important areas of trial practice: the judge's relationship with the jury and sentencing.

III

Judges and juries worked together harmoniously in felony trials in the eighteenth century. This was important in the context of an assize system that had limited time to deal with cases. Jurors were often experienced which further facilitated the process and obviated the need for detailed judicial instructions.[66] Judges did not seek to exert undue pressure on juries who retained substantial independence and used their discretion to acquit or convict on a lesser charge with regularity. This 'pious perjury', as Blackstone termed it, was tacitly condoned by judges.[67]

In contrast to the eighteenth century, the evolution of judge–jury relations in nineteenth-century criminal trials has not been much studied. As Wiener has recently pointed out, we know relatively little about the judges and jurors of the period or about the sorts of factors that informed their decisions.[68] It has been presumed rather than demonstrated that the discretionary practices common in the eighteenth century declined in the nineteenth as many of the features of the modern trial emerged. Two principal reasons underlie this presumption. The first is that changes within the trial, in particular the increased presence of lawyers, meant that proceedings increasingly met formal professional standards. The second is that legislative reform in the 1830s and the removal of the death penalty in particular removed the scope and incentive for courtroom participants to nullify or modify the law.

The rise of lawyers and of adversarial procedure have been the subject of much scholarly attention over recent years.[69] The admission of

---

[66] See Beattie, *Crime and the Courts*, pp. 406–10; T. Green, *Verdict According to Conscience: Perspectives on the English criminal trial jury 1200–1800* (Chicago, 1985), pp. 267–317.

[67] W. Blackstone, *Commentaries on the Laws of England*, facsimile of the first edn of 1765–9 (Chicago, 1979), p. 239.

[68] M. Wiener, 'Judges v Jurors: Courtroom tensions in murder trials and the law of criminal responsibility in nineteenth-century England' (1999) 17 *Law and Hist. Rev.* 467, 471.

[69] See J. Beattie, 'Scales of justice: Defence counsel and the English criminal trial in the eighteenth and nineteenth centuries' (1991) 9 *Law and Hist. Rev* 239–63; D. Cairns *Advocacy and the Making of the Adversarial Criminal Trial* (Oxford, 1998); J. Langbein,

defence counsel into felony trials in the 1730s wrought a change in the structure of the trial that was eventually to lead to full adversary procedure. The effect of the arrival of lawyers on the judicial role was very significant in the long term. It meant that they retreated from the fray and ceded their fact-adducing role to the lawyers.[70] The coming of lawyers also brought with it an increasingly detailed body of rules of evidence and subjected the judge to more scrutiny. Yet, as Cairns warns, it is important to be wary of over-emphasising the effect of these changes at least insofar as the first half of the nineteenth century is concerned.[71] Indeed, throughout the nineteenth century, most trials continued to be lawyer-free.[72] Where lawyers were present, the effect was not necessarily to instigate more regularity into proceedings. Defence lawyers were bound to exploit jurors' sympathies and encourage them to use mitigating practices. Thus whilst the structure of the trial may have shifted to an adversarial model, there continued to be space in trials for judges and jurors to persist in the sorts of activities that characterised their roles in the eighteenth-century trial.

The reduction in capital offences in the 1830s removed one of the key incentives for the juries' discretionary practices but the legislation left the juries' discretion intact in a number of cases.[73] Defenders of the death penalty contested the reformers' argument that the only reason behind juries' nullification and modification of the law was the death penalty. In 1830, Lord Lyndhurst commented: 'There might be times of great excitement, when a run, if he might so express it, was made upon the humanity of juries, and they became reluctant to find men guilty; but in ordinary times and cases he had seen no such reluctance.'[74] 'Runs', of the sort Lyndhurst referred to, could have substantial effects but they were rare. Juries employed mitigating practices in cases where there was no prospect of the death penalty being imposed. They were actuated by a variety of motives, reflecting a deeply ingrained culture of discretionary decision-making in felony trials.[75]

If the reformers' vision of a new, more certain and predictable system of justice was to be realised in the courtroom, it was the judge's

---

The Origins of Adversary Criminal Trial (Oxford, 2003); A. May, The Bar and the Old Bailey, 1750–1850 (London, 2003).
[70] See Langbein, The Origins of Adversary Criminal Trial, pp. 311–14.
[71] Cairns, Advocacy and the Making, p. 54.
[72] D. Bentley, English Criminal Justice in the Nineteenth Century (London, 1998), p. 108.
[73] See n. 30, above.   [74] 25 HL Deb (2nd ser.), 1 Jul. 1830, col. 844.
[75] See Handler, 'Forging the agenda', pp. 249–68.

responsibility to ensure that the law was applied by tightening controls over the jury's discretion. In certain areas, judges sought to curb the more merciful instincts of juries in order to put the law into force.[76] In their evidence before numerous select committees and commissions in the mid nineteenth century, judges seldom expressed dissatisfaction with juries, suggesting that the good working relationship that they had enjoyed in the eighteenth century continued. For example, Baron Martin extolled the virtues of the jury: 'My notion is that juries almost always find a correct verdict, that they are as good a tribunal as can exist, and that they find an honest verdict upon all occasions.' He had only known one case in which a woman was charged with the murder of her child and the jury returned an unexpected conviction. 'I thought that the jury would at once have found her guilty of manslaughter and accordingly I summed up in very few words.'[77] Martin was 'very much surprised' that they needed to retire and then 'astonished' that they returned a guilty verdict. The fact that Martin did not see the need for much of a summing up is revealing of the general level of trust that he had in the jury. Some judges did not direct juries at all. The City judges at the Old Bailey routinely omitted a summing up in the 1830s and 1840s, a practice that continued, albeit less frequently, for the remainder of the century.[78]

Writing in 1863, Fitzjames Stephen shared his brethren's trust of the jury. He argued that the jury's verdict supplied 'as high a standard of certainty as can be expected for any practical purpose, and it must never be forgotten that the administration of the criminal law is a practical matter, and not a process of philosophical inquiry. It is absolutely essential to the objects in view, that the process should be short and decisive.' Stephen took a pragmatic view of the administration of justice as a 'rough expedient' and one of the key advantages of this brand of justice was that it commanded public support. He was quite willing to accept that even 'after all possible public exhortations have been delivered to juries on the duty of putting the law in force ... the jury still retain a certain regard to the consequences, and modify their verdict

---

[76] In his detailed study of Victorian homicide, Wiener argues that, as concerns over drunken, impassioned and violent behaviour, particularly towards women, increased, judges sought to narrow the grounds of exculpation for murder. M. Wiener, 'Judges v Jurors', pp. 476–81; M. Wiener, *Men of Blood: Violence, manliness, and criminal justice in Victorian England* (Cambridge, 2004).

[77] Capital Punishment Commission Report (1866) (C (1st ser.) 3590), XXI, p. 1, Minutes of evidence, p. 43.

[78] Bentley, *English Criminal Justice*, pp. 274–5.

accordingly'. This was beneficial because to the public 'who take a rough view of the matter, and care more for particular results than for general rules, this tends to make the administration of justice popular'.[79]

Other commentators expressed dissatisfaction at the juries' continued willingness to mitigate the law through partial verdicts and acquittals. In his 1845 pamphlet, 'The Juryman's Guide', George Stephen declared that 'all humane minds rejoiced at the general abolition of capital punishments', but they also 'felt and reasonably expected that when this apology for weakness was removed, jurymen would discharge their duty with firmness and make up in certainty, the influence which our law might be thought to lose by being shorn of its greatest terrors; that reasonable expectation has been miserably disappointed'.[80]

The persistence of the jury's discretionary practices after the collapse of the 'bloody code' can be seen in the law relating to felonious assaults. In felony trials for assault in the period 1803–61, juries routinely reduced charges of assault with intent to cause grievous bodily harm to the lesser offences of common assault or unlawful wounding after they had been given the power to do so in 1837.[81] Commenting on this practice in 1866, Bramwell doubted whether in 'one case out of 10 the jury find the greater crime where they can find the less'.[82] Baron Wensleydale (formerly Parke) referred to the 'natural inclination' of juries to find prisoners guilty of a lesser offence where possible.[83] Yet judges did not make a sustained attempt to narrow the jury's discretion and secure more convictions for the crime of assault with intent to commit grievous bodily harm. As often as not they were content to leave the jury to interpret key fault terms such as malice and intention with a minimum level of guidance. The judges had a wide sentencing discretion, which gave them scope to express their own view of the seriousness of any particular assault in the punishment. Even the minor assault carried a maximum penalty of three years in prison with hard labour. The boundaries between the different grades of assault that were consolidated in 1861 therefore remained very fluid. The law in this particular area did not accord with the reformers' vision of having clearly defined offences and graded punishments.

---

[79] J. Stephen, *A General View of the Criminal Law of England* (London, 1863), p. 208.
[80] G. Stephen, *The Juryman's Guide* (London, 1845), p.138.
[81] See P. Handler, 'The law of felonious assault in England, 1803–1861' (2007) 28 *J. Legal Hist.* 183–206.
[82] Capital Punishment Commission Report, Minutes of Evidence, p. 30.   [83] *Ibid.*, p. 54.

The practice in relation to felonious assault accords with the general tenor of the evidence given by the judges before parliamentary committees about their relationship with juries. The judges' general level of satisfaction with the relationship suggests that acquittals entirely against the evidence were uncommon. Of course judges were frequently frustrated by jury recalcitrance. They pushed for convictions in certain instances and expressed clear opinions on the facts in their summings up when they thought it necessary.[84] They were not concerned, however, to establish general standards of acceptable conduct through the enunciation and uniform enforcement of rules.

Consistency took second place to pragmatism in judicial minds. This is clearly manifest in their approach to sentencing. The wide discretion granted to judges, together with the almost complete lack of supervision, meant that even if all the judges had been committed to securing uniformity, the goal would have been difficult to achieve. But judges were not committed and did not measure their sentences according to any generally accepted criteria. The need to suppress a particular offence in a given area continued to be a significant factor. For example, one judge on assize in Liverpool referred to the 'brutal mode of conducting their quarrels for which this county is so remarkable' as a reason to impose the relatively severe punishment of ten years' transportation for an assault with intention to do grievous bodily harm.[85] Contemporary criticism of inconsistency in sentencing had little effect on judicial practice in trials, although in 1892 it prompted the Council of Judges to propose a court of appeal with a power to review sentences.[86] Nothing came of the proposal and the widespread disparities in sentencing practices persisted into the twentieth century.[87]

The judges retained faith in exemplary and discretionary justice, putting the ideas that they expressed in public debates on criminal law reform into practice in felony trials. This persistent belief has implications for our understanding of the operation of justice during a period which is conventionally associated with upheaval and change. The

---

[84] See Bentley, *English Criminal Justice*, p. 275.

[85] *The Times*, 16 Aug. 1847, p. 7, col. a, Samuel Irish.

[86] See 'Return of report of the judges in 1892 to the Lord Chancellor recommending the constitution of a Court of Appeal and revision of sentences in criminal cases', HCPP (1894) (C (2nd ser.) 127), LXXI, p. 173 at pp. 177–8.

[87] For details of the disparities in practice through the Victorian period, see Radzinowicz and Hood, 'Judicial discretion', pp. 1307–13. For the practice in relation to felonious assault, see Handler, 'The law of felonious assault', pp. 203–5.

reformers' demands for certainty and uniformity in the criminal law depended in large part on trial judges but, in the absence of an over-arching legislative framework or an active review court, there was little to constrain them from acting on their own beliefs. This is not to say that judges were able to preserve the existing system in isolation from or opposition to wider cultural forces. The judges shared the increased general fears about crime in the period and they sought to use the criminal law to suppress it. But whereas reformers sought to make the law an instrument of discipline that would hold people responsible for their own actions with unswerving consistency, the judges preferred to use the law as a selective, discretionary tool that could be utilised according to local and pragmatic considerations. This individualistic approach allowed for a continued tolerance of discretionary practices, which in turn meant that community standards retained a key role in shaping the law. The judges' view of the criminal law as a 'rough expedient' helped ensure that, whilst the administration of criminal law in felony trials changed significantly in this period, it did not do so out of all recognition. In his 1883 history of the criminal law, Stephen reflected: 'I do not think that the actual administration of justice, or the course of trials has altered much since the beginning of the reign of George III.'[88] This statement undoubtedly underestimates the impact of lawyers amongst other things, but it serves as a useful reminder that, from the bench at least, continuity was at least as important a feature of this period as change.

---

[88] J. Stephen, *A History of the Criminal Law of England*, 3 vols. (London, 1883), I, p. 425.

8

Bureaucratic adjudication: The internal appeals of the Inland Revenue

CHANTAL STEBBINGS[*]

Introduction

While the orthodox personification of the judicial function in English legal history is found in the regular judiciary of the courts of law, an integral element of the legal system was a wide acceptance of, and dependence on, lay adjudication. Through Justices of the Peace and juries, and also through arbitration, ordinary people were accustomed to having their disputes and transgressions adjudicated by their peers. The judicial function was both integrated and paramount, for the function of the lay adjudicators was primarily to decide issues of fact, and any issues of law which might arise would be dealt with by a formal appeals process to the courts of law. Inherent in amateur lay adjudication, therefore, was the underlying safeguard of access to the regular courts, staffed by independent and qualified judges. In the implementation of tax law the legal system maintained, to some extent, this orthodoxy of lay adjudication of fact and professional adjudication of law.[1] The law of direct taxes was administered entirely by lay commissioners with no legal training, and, with the important exception on policy grounds of the income tax, some provision was made for appeals to the regular courts on questions of law.

Tax law, however, did not sit entirely comfortably within this established paradigm. Not only was the administration of tax by untrained lay adjudicators of constitutional importance, reflecting the fundamental principle of taxation only by popular consent, there were inevitable tensions in the

[*] This research formed part of a wider project on the legal protection of taxpayers' rights in the nineteenth century funded by the Leverhulme Trust, which support is gratefully acknowledged.
[1] H. J. Stephen, *New Commentaries on the Laws of England*, 4 vols. (London, 1844), III, pp. 622–3.

integration of the judicial and the lay adjudicative functions. It was essential in taxation to provide robust avenues of appeal against assessments. Governments had long understood that the levying of taxes depended on voluntary compliance, and that the taxpaying public had to consent to tax in a real and not just a formal sense. And this real consent was achieved in large measure by providing comprehensive routes of appeal to challenge assessments or raise complaints. There were, however, equally powerful reasons of public policy for discouraging appeals to the regular courts in tax cases.[2] Not only were tax disputes too minor, factual and numerous for their consignment to the already overburdened judges of the regular courts, but the inevitable flood of appeals would delay unacceptably the flow of revenue to the Exchequer. As a result, appeals to the regular courts were permitted either only on points of law by case stated or denied altogether and the decisions of the various lay adjudicators held to be final.[3] These tensions between political, popular and fiscal imperatives led to the development within the tax field of a parallel or additional species of adjudication, namely the determination of tax disputes by adjudicators who were not part of the judicial establishment but were instead unambiguously civil servants, full-time permanent paid officers of the central government departments charged with the administration of taxes,[4] and as such unequivocally an arm of the executive. The nature of the personnel who acted as judges, and their relationship to both the taxing authorities and to the legal system, made their functions utterly different from the traditional judicial function, both professional and amateur. Nevertheless they exercised a unique and important judicial function within the legal system. It is one which reveals the difficulties in achieving a balance of accepted norms of judicial conduct, the pragmatic demands of a specialist branch of the law and irresistible political exigencies.

Adjudication in tax disputes

Adjudication of tax appeals by the revenue organs of the executive was found in a number of tax regimes in the nineteenth century, notably that for excise

---

[2] *Allen* v. *Sharp* (1848) 2 Ex. 352 at 363 per Parke B.

[3] Income tax appeals to the regular courts were permitted only in 1874: 37 Vict. c. 16, ss. 8–10.

[4] The organs of central government were the revenue boards. The Boards of Stamps and Taxes and of Excise existed separately before being consolidated to form the Board of Inland Revenue in 1849: 12 & 13 Vict. c. 1.

duties and the taxation of commercial income. In the excise duties there existed special courts in London, staffed by officers of central government with a wide but specific jurisdiction, both civil and criminal. In income tax, bureaucratic adjudication had two aspects: the first was the Special Commissioners of Income Tax who had assessing and appellate functions and were civil servants working for the Board of Inland Revenue, the organ of central government which was charged with responsibility for the administration of the public revenue from the direct taxes; the second was the process whereby the board itself would hear appeals from a variety of tax decisions.

The assignment of adjudication in excise matters to a specially appointed and discrete tribunal created from within the central government department was one of the earliest and most striking expressions of bureaucratic adjudication. In most of the country excise cases were tried by Justices of the Peace, but in London minor breaches of the excise laws were tried before a specialist bureaucratic court known as the Excise Court of Summary Jurisdiction.[5] The jurisdiction of the court consisted primarily of very wide discretionary powers for the recovery of the severe penalties characteristic of the excise laws[6] and the hearing of complaints,[7] and was an example of an extensive jurisdiction, both criminal and civil, in a bureaucratic body. An appeal lay to a Court of Excise Commissioners of Appeal.[8] In income tax, bureaucratic adjudication took the form of the jurisdiction of the Special Commissioners, a statutory tribunal originally created in 1805[9] whose powers were considerably extended in 1842.[10] Commercial taxpayers subject to the income tax were given the option of being assessed either by local lay commissioners, which was the norm, or by the Special Commissioners, and they could also elect to appeal against an assessment to the Special Commissioners.[11] And in Ireland, the

---

[5] Founded by 20 Car. II c. 24, s. 45 (1660). See too 7 & 8 Geo. IV c. 53, s. 65 (1827).

[6] 7 & 8 Geo. IV c. 53, ss. 69, 78, 98.

[7] Ibid., s. 120; but see 4 & 5 Will. IV c. 51, s. 26 (1834).

[8] This was a non-bureaucratic court staffed by barristers: 7 & 8 Geo. IV c. 53, ss. 81, 82. It fell into disuse by the early nineteenth century and was abolished by 4 & 5 Vict. c. 20, ss. 25, 26 (1841) when the power of appeal was given to a Baron of the Exchequer.

[9] 45 Geo. III c. 49, s. 30. For a comprehensive account of the functions of the Special Commissioners, see J. Avery Jones, 'The Special Commissioners from Trafalgar to Waterloo' [2005] British Tax Rev. 40 and J. Avery Jones, 'The Special Commissioners after 1842: From administrative to judicial tribunal' [2005] British Tax Rev. 80.

[10] 5 & 6 Vict. c. 35, s. 131; Minutes of Evidence before the Select Committee on the Income and Property Tax, HCPP (1852) (C (1st ser.) 354), IX, p. 1 at questions ['qq.'] 1036–314; HC Deb (3rd ser.), 18 Apr. 1842, vol. 62, cols. 657–8, per Sir Robert Peel.

[11] 5 & 6 Vict. c. 35, ss. 130–1 (1842).

Special Commissioners constituted the prime appellate body hearing all appeals against assessments to income tax.[12] The cases heard by the Special Commissioners often involved considerable sums of money, and though their jurisdiction was narrow and specific, it ultimately came to dominate their work and would prove of increasing and enduring importance.

The Board of Inland Revenue itself was involved in tax adjudication. By statute all the members of the board were *ex officio* Special Commissioners[13] and in the first years of the Victorian income tax they participated regularly in their determinations.[14] There also existed a well-established tradition of appeals directly to all the central revenue boards as such in relation to those taxes of the Inland Revenue that were centrally administered, namely the excise and stamp duties, including the legacy and succession duties.[15] In relation to these taxes, bureaucratic adjudication was naturally regarded as the normal and proper course. In relation to the locally administered taxes, however, an appeal to the central board was not self-evident, as the theory underlying these was that their administration should be entirely and exclusively local and lay in nature. The practice of bureaucratic appeals to the board as such, and indeed to the Special Commissioners, was therefore remarkable in such cases because it appeared legally anomalous. Nevertheless it is clear from the minutes of the board's proceedings in the nineteenth century that the board was deluged with written applications of various kinds, some major but most minor, comprising complaints, memorials, petitions, inquiries and appeals from individual taxpayers covering every aspect of tax law and administration relating to all the taxes in the board's charge.[16] The status of these various applications is not clear, for some of the board's appellate functions were of a general nature and not necessarily related to a specific statutory provision. Some were formal legal

---

[12] 16 & 17 Vict. c. 34, s. 21 (1853); Minutes of Evidence before the Select Committee on Inland Revenue and Customs Establishments, HCPP (1862) (C (1st ser.) 370), XII, p. 131 at qq. 408–9.

[13] 45 Geo. III c. 49, s. 30 (1805).

[14] Minutes of Evidence before the Select Committee on the Income and Property Tax, HCPP (1852) (C (1st ser.) 354), IX, p. 1 at qq. 1064–6, 1121, 1126–7; see too The National Archives [TNA] PRO IR 86/1, Board Order of the Special Commissioners, 20 Aug. 1844.

[15] See Minutes of Evidence before the Select Committee on Inland Revenue and Customs Establishments, qq. 2156, 2211, 2318, 2320.

[16] See Second Report of the Commissioners of Inland Revenue, HCPP (1857–8) (C (1st ser.) 2387), XXV, p. 477 at p. 508.

appeals, notably the statutory appeal by way of case stated from the appellate decisions of the Special Commissioners,[17] itself a striking example of an unambiguously legal device adopted unaltered for use in a bureaucratic context.[18] Others were informal applications for relief or repayment,[19] or complaints about decisions taken.[20] Although the board broadly maintained the theoretical finality of local commissioners' decisions in the direct taxes,[21] it clearly exercised a de facto wide-ranging appellate jurisdiction.

Problems with tax adjudication

This extensive use of bureaucratic adjudication in tax cases was sufficiently prominent to attract the attention of critics in the legal and political establishments throughout the nineteenth century. It was problematic in two particular respects: it was adjudication without formal legal knowledge or skills; and it was adjudication by a body lacking independence from the parties and the subject matter of the dispute under consideration. It thus raised fundamental questions of the personal requirements for effective adjudication which did not arise in the context of the judicial function in the regular courts and arose in a different way in the context of traditional lay tax adjudication.

The first problem was the lack of legal knowledge in the civil servants undertaking judicial work. The Special Commissioners and members of the revenue boards had no formal legal training, unless by chance they happened to have qualified as lawyers, and certainly no legal qualification was required of them. The lack of specialist legal skills was viewed with concern because it meant that laymen were deciding on technically demanding matters such as the construction of often intricate statutes. It could also undermine the standard of justice delivered by the bureaucratic tribunals, for they had no training to enable them to decide on points of evidence. It was a major

---

[17] 5 & 6 Vict. c. 35, s. 131; Minutes of Evidence before the Select Committee on the Income and Property Tax, qq. 1067, 1124.

[18] The provision was virtually identical to that in the founding Act of the assessed taxes, though there the appellate body was one of the superior courts of Common Law: 21 Geo. II c. 10, s. 10 (1748). It was re-enacted in the Income Tax Act 1918, apparently in addition to the right introduced in 1874 to appeal in income tax cases to the High Court by way of case stated.

[19] See e.g. TNA PRO IR 31/141, Minute of Board of Inland Revenue, 1 Jan. 1849.

[20] Minutes of Evidence before the Select Committee on Inland Revenue and Customs Establishments, qq. 1361–3.

[21] *Ibid.*, q. 196; TNA PRO IR 31/141, Minute of Board of Inland Revenue, 1, 2, 15, 16 Jan. 1849.

objection to their exercise of any criminal jurisdiction, notably in the excise cases in London and in Ireland. In Ireland the problem was particularly serious, since there, as in London, excise cases had been taken out of the ordinary processes of the administration of law by giving them their own extraordinary bureaucratic jurisdiction, but the judicial powers were invariably delegated to much more minor, and arguably less able, revenue officials. The question of legal expertise was also specifically raised in connection with the Special Commissioners, for it was regarded as 'illogical'[22] and 'anomalous'[23] that there existed stringent requirements for the appointment of a county court judge with a jurisdiction limited to small amounts, and none at all for Special Commissioners who had an unlimited jurisdiction and 'the rights and duties of a judge and jury'.[24]

An even greater problem with bureaucratic adjudication in tax cases was that of a lack of independence. It was contrary to the rules of natural justice that judges in a cause should be interested, particularly in a pecuniary way, in the outcome of the disputes which came before them for determination. The adjudication of tax disputes by members of the taxing department of the executive unequivocally breached this rule, for there was a clear conflict of interests between their judicial duties and their administrative function as organs of the executive in charge of making the assessments to tax. This lack of independence constituted a major undermining of the safeguard of the appeals process. Again, it was an issue of particular concern in the exercise of a criminal jurisdiction. The Irish Excise Courts, described as 'courts formed by a meeting of Revenue officers, who act alternately as prosecutors, witnesses and judges',[25] were condemned in 1824 as 'subversive of all principles of justice' and 'in theory and principle, indefensible'.[26] This condemnation was later adopted to reflect views on the London Excise Court[27] and was the principal factor in recommendations for its abolition.[28] The issue of

---

[22] Minutes of Evidence before the Royal Commission on the Income Tax HCPP (1919) (Cmd 288), XXIII, p. 1 at q. 23,891.

[23] *Ibid.*, q. 24,001.　　[24] *Ibid.*, q. 23,891.

[25] Ninth Report of the Commissioners of Inquiry into the Collection and Management of the Revenue arising in Ireland and Scotland, HCPP (1824) (340), XI, p. 305 at p. 310.

[26] *Ibid.*, p. 312 per John Foster.

[27] Third Report of the Commissioners of Inquiry into the Excise Establishment: Summary Jurisdiction, HCPP (1834) (C (1st ser.) 3), XXIV, p. 87 at pp. 96–100.

[28] Despite these objections, the fact that the courts worked so well in practice led the inquiry to allow the Excise Court of Summary Jurisdiction to continue until the department as a whole was reformed. The power of the Commissioners of Excise to hear and determine informations for penalties was only finally abolished in 1890. All informations were thereafter to be

independence was only gradually recognised in relation to civil adjudication, despite it being striking in the case of the Special Commissioners. They too were permanent employees of the very government department whose function was the direction and control of the systems necessary to raise the revenue and were entirely under the control of the board.[29] Furthermore, being appointed from the ranks of surveyors or inspectors of taxes, they shared the same professional background and a common appointment by the Crown with one of the parties to every dispute they adjudicated upon. One commentator observed that this duality of function was unacceptable, and that the distinction between administrative and judicial functions was one which 'is carefully preserved in all other judicial bodies in this country'.[30]

Official justification

Despite these criticisms, the Board of Inland Revenue maintained that its internal appellate processes were justified, arguing that they were both proper and indeed necessary. First, they were legally sound. The board's statutory duty was the 'care and management' of all the excise and stamp duties, the assessed taxes, the land tax and the income tax.[31] Despite its fundamental importance as the central phrase in determining the nature and extent of the duties and powers of the board, it was not defined in any statute nor had it been the subject of judicial consideration. Furthermore, the board's parent Act was not comprehensive in its provisions, and left much to be deduced from copious and often obscure earlier legislation.[32] The legislature thus imposed a statutory duty of immense breadth, with undefined and equally extensive powers, on the board. This permitted, and resulted in, the adoption of the widest managerial discretion by the board, for it interpreted it as an overarching duty to manage the inland revenue efficiently with authority to address any problems which interfered with that. The shortfall in the revenue due to a reluctance to make full disclosure to local commissioners was one such, as was the lack of

---

heard and determined by a court of summary jurisdiction, as defined by 52 & 53 Vict. c. 63, s. 13(11) (1889).

[29] See e.g. TNA PRO IR 86/1, Board Orders of the Special Commissioners, 17 Jun. 1843.

[30] Minutes of Evidence before the Royal Commission on the Income Tax, q. 23,891 per Randle Holme, solicitor, on behalf of the Law Society. See his specific criticism of the board's power to hear appeals from the decisions of the Special Commissioners in TNA: PRO IR 75/90, Income Tax Consolidation Bill 1918 and Memoranda thereon and in Minutes of Evidence before the Royal Commission on the Income Tax, q. 23,898.

[31] 12 & 13 Vict. c. 1, s. 1 (1849).   [32] Ibid., s. 3; 53 & 54 Vict. c. 21, s. 1(2) (1890).

appellate machinery in Ireland. Legislation gave express authorisation for these, but in the absence of such unambiguous and specific statutory authority, the board justified virtually any activity, including its system of internal appeals, under this overriding statutory duty. It viewed its internal bureaucratic appeals as a legitimate means of exercising its control over its taxes, to ensure their swift and efficient administration and to promote that uniformity of administration which was one of its main objectives.[33] This extensive discretion in the central revenue boards was possible only because of a lack of control from the Treasury. In theory all the central revenue boards were sub-departments of the Treasury and so under its control, a status confirmed by the boards' founding Acts and the patents appointing their members.[34] In practice and in appearance, however, the boards were independent in character and function, and this independence of action subsumed their real, subordinate status. This lack of clarity in the constitutional relationship between the boards and the Treasury, the breadth of the statutory duty placed on the boards and the indefinite nature of their powers combined to make the revenue boards pre-eminent in virtually every aspect of tax administration. So while there was some official acceptance of the condemnation of the criminal jurisdiction of the Excise Court on the grounds of principle, partiality and inconsistency, its civil jurisdiction with respect to proceedings to secure the single duty, and proceedings on complaints, was maintained as acceptable because it related:

> to questions of a description which must in a great degree be common to every department of revenue, and for the determination of which the discretionary powers vested in the Commissioners of Excise, in the course of their ordinary duties relating to the collection and management of this branch of revenue, must be deemed as sufficient.[35]

The second official justification of the bureaucratic adjudication of tax disputes lay in a number of pragmatic considerations. The availability of appropriate adjudicative machinery was a recurring theme in tax administration. To create new taxing machinery was expensive, difficult, uncertain in its efficiency and of the utmost political sensitivity. Routine tax litigation was unsuitable for the regular courts, and the revenue boards generally held the

[33] See e.g. 4 Geo. IV c. 23, s. 1 (1823).

[34] See 7 & 8 Geo. IV c. 53 (Board of Excise); Patent appointing the Commissioners of Excise in 1833, reprinted in Twentieth Report of the Commissioners of Excise Inquiry, HCPP (1836) (C (1st ser.) 22), XXVI, p. 179 at p. 340.

[35] Third Report of the Commissioners of Inquiry into the Excise Establishment: Summary Jurisdiction, pp. 95–6.

view that local lay commissioners and their officers were incompetent and inefficient, and that Justices of the Peace in excise cases were biased against the Crown and would find for the taxpayer if they possibly could.[36] If no specific and suitable machinery existed, the simplest and cheapest option was to employ the permanent staff of the executive department. It was the absence of appropriate machinery which provided the justification for making the Special Commissioners the sole appellate body for income tax in Ireland: there existed no other body to which the task could be allocated.

Thirdly, and specifically with respect to the taxation of commercial income, the Board of Inland Revenue justified its use of bureaucratic appellate adjudication on the basis of political and fiscal necessity. When Robert Peel reintroduced the income tax in 1842 in order to address the financial crisis faced by his government, he was determined it should tap the vast new commercial and industrial wealth of the expanding British economy. This had been hindered when income tax was last in force by the old problem of privacy. The commercial community were intensely reluctant to disclose their financial affairs to the local lay commissioners who traditionally administered the tax and who were themselves usually businessmen, often rivals in trade to the taxpayer.[37] The reason was, over and above a natural dislike of publicising personal financial matters, a fear that the information would be used to undermine their trade or would affect their ability to attract credit.[38] Though there was no real evidence of any public revelation of confidential information, the suspicion of inadvertent or deliberate disclosure persisted and it inevitably had an effect on its fiscal yield, whether by fraud or a general lack of co-operation. Peel's solution was to introduce a large and important element of bureaucratic adjudication into the income tax administrative process by extending the appellate powers of the Special Commissioners and giving the taxpayer the option of recourse to a tribunal which was independent of his commercial colleagues in his locality and whose processes were confidential.

Lastly, though expressly and principally, bureaucratic adjudication was maintained as a practical necessity: the tax laws, it was argued, could only be administered by specialists in the field. The argument was a powerful one.

---

[36] *Ibid.*, pp. 148, 152.

[37] Minutes of Evidence before the Royal Commission on the Income Tax, pp. 555–6. See generally C. Stebbings, 'The Budget of 1798: Legislative provision for secrecy in income taxation' [1998] *British Tax Rev.* 651.

[38] See HC Deb (1st ser.), 17 Mar. 1816, vol. 33, cols. 26–7; HC Deb (3rd ser.), 4 Apr. 1842, vol. 61, cols. 1272–3; *Exeter and Plymouth Gazette*, 13 Jan. 1871 and 1 Dec. 1871.

Tax law was acknowledged as being particularly complex and technical. Illogical arrangement, ambiguous language, poor drafting, innumerable amendments, the practice of reading a number of sections in different Acts 'as one' and the invariable tradition of incorporating earlier Acts into a new taxing Act merely by reference, meant that tax Acts were notoriously long, obscure and complex. Furthermore there existed a large body of material incorporating the interpretation of tax legislation by the central boards, instructions to tax officials as to how they were to deal with certain cases or certain groups of taxpayers, regulations issued by the boards and countless circulars and orders embodying the daily implementation of tax law. This practice of the revenue departments was central to the implementation of tax law, and was utterly inaccessible to anyone outside the closed circles of the central revenue boards.[39] In the context of the government's unrelenting demand for revenue, and a commercial context which was daily becoming more sophisticated as the industrialisation of the country grew, it was believed that specialist practitioners were needed to understand the law, to master the revenue regulations which underpinned it, to apply it accurately and, ultimately, to adjudicate fairly upon it. This was assumed rather than widely articulated and needed no special promotion, for the nature of the tax legislation was only too clear to everyone involved in the process. And tax adjudicators who lacked these specialist skills, whether laymen or the judges of the regular courts, were frequently criticised for an inability fully to appreciate the nature of the issues they had to decide.[40]

The skills of the bureaucratic adjudicators were above all, therefore, those of specialist tax expertise, and it was an expertise they undoubtedly possessed. The Commissioners of Excise, later the Commissioners of Inland Revenue, members of the central boards who presided in the Excise Court, were highly experienced. The exclusive jurisdiction of the court in London and the popularity of its swift, cheap, certain and undoubtedly expert processes meant it was widely used.[41] Through the large numbers of cases they heard,[42] the members of the court developed a profound knowledge and expertise in personal adjudication. They were knowledgeable as to the excise laws because they were the only laws they had to

[39] See e.g. Twentieth Report of the Commissioners of Excise Inquiry, p 221.

[40] See Minutes of Evidence before the Royal Commission on the Income Tax, qq. 1571, 1667–72 per G. O. Parsons, accountant and secretary to the Income Tax Reform League.

[41] Third Report of the Commissioners of Inquiry into the Excise Establishment: Summary Jurisdiction, pp. 99, 149.

[42] *Ibid.*, pp. 94–5, 140, 143.

administer and were involved with them every day of their working lives. It was said they had a 'superior competency'[43] to administer the law and had 'a more precise knowledge'[44] of the cases than magistrates.

For reasons of inadequate publicity[45] rather than any public reservations about the tribunal's lack of independence or legal knowledge, the Special Commissioners were relatively little used for most of the nineteenth century, but they nevertheless acquired a profound understanding of tax law and practice, with an expertise that went far beyond that of all lay bodies of commissioners. Their professional backgrounds in the Inland Revenue and a measure of internal specialisation[46] ensured a thorough knowledge of tax matters, while an expertise in personal practical adjudication was acquired through a sustained exercise of their jurisdiction in appeal hearings. By the end of the century it had become clear to anyone working in the field of tax that they were the best tribunal to handle complex appeals and those involving any question of law.[47]

The judicial abilities of the general members of the Board of Inland Revenue were less clear. While contemporary sources suggest the formal appeal to the board from the appellate decisions of the Special Commissioners was rarely used,[48] it is not possible with any accuracy to quantify the informal appeals to the board, primarily because, unlike the Special Commissioners and the Excise Court, the appeals were not distinguished as such in official statistics, were not public and in the eyes of the board itself were regarded as part of its daily work of managing the revenue. Certainly the members of the board met daily and undertook a great deal of business at each session. They considered some fifty different issues every day, each one requiring a determination of some sort, suggesting it was well-used as an appellate body by taxpayers. The board members' work in income tax thus consisted of a considerable and constant amount of practical application, albeit on the basis of written reports rather than personal advocacy. In this respect at least, therefore, their adjudicative skills were highly developed. They undoubtedly also possessed a wide knowledge of tax policy, law and practice. Some were

---

[43] *Ibid.*, p. 97.   [44] *Ibid.*, p. 140.

[45] C. Stebbings, 'Access to justice before the Special Commissioners of Income Tax in the nineteenth century' [2005] *British Tax Rev.* 114.

[46] Minutes of Evidence before the Select Committee on Inland Revenue and Customs Establishments, q. 405.

[47] Minutes of Evidence before the Royal Commission on the Income Tax, q. 15,921 per A. M. Bremner, barrister.

[48] *Ibid.*, q. 23,898.

drawn from the revenue services themselves,[49] while others were appointed from various public offices unconnected with the revenue departments as such.[50] So though the members as individuals were not necessarily expert in revenue matters on appointment, they acquired an unparalleled overview of the duties and an understanding of their practical implementation through the numerous and technical papers which came daily for their consideration and decision and which addressed all the duties of the Inland Revenue.[51] Of course the members of the boards were always able to counter any accusation of inadequate legal knowledge by showing that they had free and constant recourse to their own legal department.[52]

Perceptions of the judicial function

The various organs of bureaucratic adjudication in tax matters were of substantial jurisdiction, indubitable specialist tax expertise, varying degrees of accessibility, limited legal knowledge and, perhaps most strikingly, they were in their status entirely lacking in independence from executive government. The evidence suggests that taxpayers appearing before them were on the whole satisfied with the service they received, and that bureaucratic adjudication played a significant and effective role in the overall body of tax litigation. The absence of legal training and of independence from the executive would not have been tolerated in the judges of the regular courts of law and yet the voices raised in criticism were a small minority and bureaucratic adjudication survived. In relation to the Excise Court of Summary Jurisdiction these criticisms proved fatal, but only in relation to its criminal jurisdiction which was perceived as exceptional in its nature. In all civil tax disputes, bureaucratic adjudication increased in scope rather than diminished.

The existence and acceptance of bureaucratic adjudication in the nineteenth century is revealing of the legal system and the values

---

[49] For the career of Charles Pressly, see Seventh Annual Report of the Commissioners of Inland Revenue, HCPP (1863) (C (1st ser.) 3236), XXVI, p. 205 at pp. 228–9.

[50] Minutes of Evidence before the Select Committee on Inland Revenue and Customs Establishments, qq. 35–7, 489–91.

[51] In 1862 the members of the board met every day to discuss and dispatch their business. They divided into three committees to deal with excise, stamp duty and tax matters respectively on a daily basis, and less frequently to deal with other matters. They met as a full board every day once their committee business was completed. For the conduct of the board in 1862 see *ibid.*, qq. 39–40.

[52] The Excise Board had a particularly extensive legal department: Twentieth Report of the Commissioners of Excise Inquiry, p. 644.

which permeated it. It was the outcome of an overtly pragmatic approach to dispute resolution in Victorian England. The primary and, generally, the sole object of taxation was the raising of public revenue. To achieve this, the administration of tax had to be efficient, and efficiency meant uniformity and, necessarily, strongly centralised control. Appeals could not be allowed to disrupt the smooth and consistent raising of revenue, but since a measure had to be allowed in the interests of justice and to make taxation publicly acceptable, as well as to address the disputes that would inevitably arise, it was better if it could be placed in the hands of expert bureaucrats who understood their field of operation and could interpret the law as the executive thought it should be interpreted. And in practice all indications were that bureaucratic adjudication worked well: the taxpaying public used it, and there were few complaints in the form of further appeals to the courts of law where that was permitted.

The lack of legal knowledge was felt to be outweighed by the specialist expertise possessed by the tax officials and adequately dealt with in times of need by the legal departments of the boards, while the absence of theoretical independence was regarded as unimportant in view of the tax officials' assertion of their impartiality in practice[53] and practical arrangements ensuring that as far as possible the officials who made an administrative decision did not subsequently hear any appeal against it. In practice the Special Commissioners avoided the hearing of an appeal by the same two Commissioners who signed the assessment, though as for many years they numbered only three in total, this was not always possible.[54] In the Excise Court of Summary Jurisdiction the judges were the same officials who decided which cases to prosecute and so instituted all the criminal proceedings in their own court. They maintained that it was the chairman or his deputy who made those decisions and, as they did not personally sit in the court, they did not try them.[55] These practical arrangements and assertions of impartiality rather missed the point, since justice was manifestly not seen to be done; yet the lack of separation of powers was accepted by the government and the public, and the lack of theoretical independence was endured as the price

---

[53] Minutes of Evidence before the Select Committee on Income Tax, HCPP (1906) (Cd 45), IX, p. 659, q. 2709. See too Minutes of Evidence before the Royal Commission on the Income Tax, qq. 13,582 and 13,588; Third Report of the Commissioners of Inquiry into the Excise Establishment: Summary Jurisdiction, p. 139.

[54] Minutes of Evidence before the Royal Commission on the Income Tax, qq. 13,781–3.

[55] Third Report of the Commissioners of Inquiry into the Excise Establishment: Summary Jurisdiction, p. 153.

to pay for knowledgeable adjudication. The position was accepted because in taxation the taxpaying public were more concerned with the tax tribunals' independence from the locality rather than their independence from the executive. Justices of the Peace in London would be mainly tradesmen or merchants and inevitably connected with the litigants appearing before them and, whether favouring or prejudiced against a litigant, their impartiality was compromised. This was an issue of particular moment in relation to income tax, which was administered entirely by local men. So while many witnesses giving evidence to the inquiries into the Excise Court accepted that it was theoretically unsound, they argued that nevertheless it should be maintained because it was effective. In 1833 the anomaly of adjudicators in the Excise Court being judges in their own cause was recognised, but it was maintained that 'it has been a jurisdiction of such long standing, and has been found to work so well, that the theoretic objection appears to be of no real weight in the present day'.[56]

It appeared, therefore, that pragmatic considerations in the implementation of tax law transcended any inconsistencies or weaknesses of legal theory. However, if bureaucratic adjudication had indeed been theoretically unsound, undermining the fundamental tenets of adjudication as conceived by the judges of the regular courts of law, it would be unlikely that it would have been left untouched by the rationalising and reforming zeal of the Victorian legislators. The Victorians were indeed highly pragmatic legislators, but they were equally rational and recognised the importance of a coherent legal system. Accordingly in the early 1870s the Judicature Commissioners were highly critical of the specialised and local courts which were then permanent constituents of the legal system.[57] They recommended their abolition, saying they did not fit into the new and rationalised legal system to which the Victorian legislators aspired. Highly specialised litigation with its own courts was the very thing they wanted to avoid in their pursuit of the reformed legal order of a free-flowing legal system. And yet despite this policy the organs of bureaucratic adjudication in tax disputes was left almost entirely untouched, a state of affairs which A. V. Dicey, once junior

---

[56] *Ibid.*, p. 144 per Hart Davies. In the case of the Excise Court, however, the official view which ultimately prevailed, because of the criminal nature of the jurisdiction, was that the objection on principle outweighed any other consideration.

[57] Second Report of the Judicature Commissioners, HCPP (1872) (C (2nd ser.) 631), XX, p. 217 at p. 234.

counsel to the Board of Inland Revenue, implicitly criticised later in the century.[58] Though the Excise Court was condemned by a parliamentary inquiry in 1833 for an unacceptable absence of independence, it not only survived for some further sixty years, but less than a decade after its condemnation the legislature created the Special Commissioners, identical in that respect to the Excise Court, as an appellate body. Furthermore, not only were the Special Commissioners created and permitted to continue, there was a largely uncritical acceptance of their avowed impartiality, and public confidence in the tribunal was high throughout the nineteenth century.[59]

The reason why bureaucratic adjudication in tax was permitted to continue was because its acceptance did not constitute the condoning of a theoretical inconsistency. Rather it was evidence that no theoretical inconsistency existed at all. It is this which is most revealing not only of the tax bureaucratic adjudication system itself, but of the Victorian legal system as a whole and the judicial function in particular. Central to the existence and acceptance of bureaucratic adjudication in tax is the notion that the settling of appeals in the tax sphere was not regarded as a judicial act.[60] The Board of Inland Revenue did not consider its various adjudicatory powers as discrete, let alone judicial. It saw them as part of its duty to manage the Inland Revenue and so merely an aspect of the administration of tax. Tax appellate adjudication was perceived as nothing more than a step in the process of assessing an individual to tax, and this view prevailed until well into the following century.[61] The reason for this was that the overall objective of the tax legislation, and therefore of the executive bodies implementing it, was to arrive at a correct assessment to tax, and in

---

[58] For a discussion of A. V. Dicey's views on the dispute resolution function of tribunals in general, see C. Stebbings, *Legal Foundations of Tribunals in Nineteenth-Century England* (Cambridge, 2006), pp. 108–9, 329–30.

[59] See the evidence of G. O. Parsons who said in 1919 that he felt the taxpayer received 'the best of treatment': Minutes of Evidence before the Royal Commission on the Income Tax, q. 1853. This confidence proved to be enduring: see Report of the Committee on Ministers' Powers, HCPP (1931–2) (Cmd 4060), XII, p. 341 at pp. 432–3.

[60] The right to appeal to the superior courts of law by way of case stated on points of law was allowed in relation to the assessed taxes from the eighteenth century, but withheld for the income tax on policy grounds until 1874: see n. 3 above. And although the writs of mandamus and prohibition were frequently employed in relation to the tax tribunals, the problematic status of tribunals as courts of law meant that certiorari did not apply until the end of the nineteenth century. See C. Stebbings, *The Victorian Taxpayer and the Law: A study in constitutional conflict* (Cambridge, 2009), pp. 131–45

[61] See Report of the Royal Commission on the Income Tax, HCPP (1920) (Cmd 615), XVIII, p. 97 at para. 340.

determining an appeal they were achieving the last step in that admin-istrative task.[62] No clear delineation was drawn between the two func-tions of making the original assessment and hearing an appeal, and the determination of any appeal could legitimately be said to constitute the making of the assessment. Any judicial powers given to the executive bodies had not been given to them as an end in themselves, as stand-alone powers, but solely as part of the process of raising tax and as such were subsumed by the overall administrative purpose. As administrative bodies with merely incidental judicial powers, they were not exercising the judicial power of the state, so they were not courts and could not be constituents of the judicial system. Context was everything.

That tax was not perceived as law in the generally accepted sense of the term was the prevailing view within the legal profession. It was also a perception which was more persistent in tax than in other fields. Railway regulation, for example, a subject more novel than taxation, was condemned in the 1850s by the judges as being mere regulation and therefore unsuitable for the regular courts of law, and yet only twenty years later it was being proposed that there should be a railway division of the High Court. It was not solely because tax law was complex. After all, Victorian lawyers were accus-tomed to highly technical law, notably the land law, and in the nineteenth century tax law was not as technically demanding as it was later to become. It was, rather, due to its own special composite nature. It was part adminis-tration, part accountancy, and only part law, factors which combined to make tax law perceived as something other than ordinary law, and as such foreign to lawyers who were notoriously uncomfortable with it.[63] Tax law was found in the statutes and their interpretation by the judges, but the details and mechanics of its application lay with a highly specialised, skilled bureaucracy. These tax practices were integral to the law, and yet were physically inaccessible to lawyers, and to some degree intellectually inaccessible since their full understanding demanded some specialist accounting knowledge. Tax law, furthermore, was unlike most other branches of law in that it had an immensely strong political context and constitutional basis. Tax administration formed a self-sufficient system, isolated by its persistent classification as pure administration

---

[62] See *IRC* v. *Sneath* (1932) 17 T.C. 149, per Greer LJ at 164, per Romer LJ at 168. Note that until 5 & 6 Geo. VI c. 21 (1942) sch. 10 at paras. 3, 4, income tax assessments under Schedule D had to be 'allowed and confirmed' by the General or Special Commissioners, and assessments which were subject to an appeal could only be allowed once the appeal had been heard: 8 & 9 Geo. V c. 40, ss. 122, 123 (1918).

[63] Twentieth Report of the Commissioners of Excise Inquiry, p 644.

and essentially inward-looking, a culture fostered by the developing civil service and bureaucratic state and the special nature of tax. This resulted in the tax adjudication systems having no effect on either the wider legal system or even on the emerging system of statutory tribunals in the nineteenth century. Indeed, tax law and institutions were ignored by lawyers, government and the public in that context.

As adjudication in tax was regarded as part of an administrative and not a judicial process, it followed that it stood outside the judicial system and that it was legitimate to maintain that it should be untouched by the values and standards – and indeed the controls – of that system. While an absence of legally qualified adjudicators and of independence was totally unacceptable in the regular courts of law, which maintained a long and profound training in the law and an unimpeachable independence as its two salient features, in tax they were portrayed, if not as virtues, then certainly as proper and legal. Legal training was neither necessary nor appropriate for an administrative function. Indeed, a different kind of expertise altogether was required: that of specialist knowledge of tax administration. In the same way independence was irrelevant where the process was not judicial, and so the Board of Inland Revenue saw no need to assert its independence and accordingly rarely did so. Viewed in this context, bureaucratic adjudication was the only proper instrument in tax disputes.

Conclusion

Bureaucratic adjudication in tax survived the rationalisation of the legal system in Victorian England because it was not regarded as being judicial in any sense, and so stood outside the fundamental values and formal controls of the regular legal system. It not only survived, but increased in scope and authority, because it served the interests of the immensely powerful and largely uncontrolled revenue departments of the executive. Being regarded as part of the administrative process of tax assessment, bureaucratic adjudication undoubtedly promoted one of the executive's principal aims, namely uniformity and control in taxation. Its existence, coupled with limited appeals to the regular courts, ensured the tax laws were administered in conformity with the boards' own 'correct' views. This persistence of bureaucratic adjudication in tax matters was of particular concern to taxpayers. It was worrying in its own right, namely that tribunals which clearly lacked independence from the executive were determining a significant number of tax disputes, but worrying in its wider context. The notion of real consent to taxation, which was a deeply held ideal for the British taxpayer, was being eroded throughout the nineteenth century. The administration of direct taxes by lay commissioners in the taxpayer's locality, one of the oldest and most important legal safeguards for the taxpayer, was gradually, insidiously and continually undermined throughout the nineteenth century by an encroaching executive anxious to take over as much of the administration of tax as possible, in the interests of efficiency and uniformity. Furthermore, formal parliamentary consent to taxation was being diminished by the movement which culminated in the Parliament Act 1911[64] whereby the House of Lords was taken entirely out of any influence in money bills and full authority in taxing matters was left with the House of Commons. While arguably this was constitutionally proper, the growth of the party system, the decline in the influence of the private member and the inability of most Members of Parliament to engage with complex tax legislation in any meaningful way, meant that that chamber was increasingly dominated by the executive. The resistance of the system of internal appeals of the Inland Revenue, namely the informal appeals to the board and the formal appeals to the Excise Court and the Special Commissioners, to informed criticism and reform was promoting its increasingly secure establishment in tax administration, and accordingly constituted one more instance of the dominance of the executive in tax matters. Both in law and in the public perception this dominance of the executive considerably reduced the potency of the legal safeguards which the taxpayer enjoyed, and left him significantly more vulnerable to executive abuse in taxation at the end of the Victorian period than he had been at its beginning.[65]

---

[64] 1 & 2 Geo. V c. 13 (1911).
[65] See generally, Stebbings, *The Victorian Taxpayer and the Law.*

II

Continental law

9

Remedy of prohibition against Roman judges in civil trials

ERNEST METZGER*

Civil trials in classical Rome were conducted by lay judges, appointed for a single case and occasionally sitting together but more often alone.[1] Knowledge of the law and dedication to the task of judging could vary widely among their number. This was no real hindrance to the conduct of trials, which were largely unguided by rules of evidence and procedure. Instead of using rules as such, Roman law supervised the conduct of trials by *managing the judge*. The judge had a finite number of positive tasks to perform, and a finite number of pitfalls to avoid, and beyond these the trial would proceed in its own way, steered mainly by rhetorical conventions and the whims of the advocates.[2] In this chapter I discuss one important way in which the law managed the judge: a largely

---

* The author thanks Professor Boudewijn Sirks for his helpful comments.

[1] Historians differ in their use of the term 'classical Rome'. Here it refers to Rome from the late republic to the middle third century CE. It marks a period of energy in the juristic sources. It also marks a span of time in which the formulary procedure – a creative form of litigation unique to the Romans – prospered and then declined. A separate form of procedure (*cognitio*), which occasionally required the participation of a delegated judge (*iudex pedaneus*), appeared at an unknown time in the early empire. The *iudex pedaneus* is not the subject of this discussion, nor should he be confused with the lay judge of the formulary procedure. See S. Liva, 'Ricerche sul *iudex pedaneus*: organizzazione giudiziaria e processo' (2007) 73 *Studia et Documenta Historiae et Iuris* 161–5, 168, n. 34 (analysing references in the edictal commentaries); cf. W. Turpin, '*Formula, cognitio*, and proceedings *extra ordinem*' (1999) 46 *Revue Internationale des Droits de l'Antiquité* (3rd ser.), pp. 522–3. Ambiguities in judicial terminology do arise in discussions of *provincial* procedure, where a proceeding may share certain attributes of the formulary procedure (e.g. bifurcation and the use of formula). See M. Kaser and K. Hackl, *Das römische Zivilprozessrecht*, 2nd edn (Munich, 1996), pp. 168–70. Provincial procedure, however, is no part of the present discussion.

[2] The conduct of trials was an area that the classical jurists ceded to advocates. See J. A. Crook, *Legal Advocacy in the Roman World* (Ithaca, 1995), pp. 6–7, 17–21, 178–9, and most recently, B. W. Frier, 'Finding a place for law in the High Empire: Tacitus, *Dialogus* 39.1–4' in W. Harris and F. de Angelis (eds.), *Spaces of Justice in the Roman World*, Columbia Studies in the Classical Tradition (Leiden, 2010), pp. 67–87.

unremarked procedure for preventing judges from giving judgment when doing so would be inappropriate.[3]

Briefly, a suit came to the judge as follows. A plaintiff seeking a civil lawsuit against another would appear before a magistrate (a praetor or aedile or, outside Rome, a local magistrate), bringing along with him the person he wished to sue. The plaintiff would then request permission to bring a particular kind of action; the defendant, for his part, might request the inclusion of a particular defence. This proceeding, though brief, might require the parties to recount their 'stories': how one's opponent had failed to pay, stolen a thing, agreed not to pursue a debt, etc. The magistrate who listened to these stories was guided by the edict he had published on taking office. The edict, though expressed as a series of conditional promises to grant certain actions and defences, was in effect a series of 'acceptable stories'. If the parties' own history with one another corresponded to an acceptable story, they would win the right to bring the action before a judge for trial, along with any relevant defences.[4]

As soon as the magistrate passes the lawsuit to a judge, the magistrate has no further control over the lawsuit. He has no say in how the trial is conducted. The plaintiff and defendant could conceivably go before the judge and tell an entirely different story from the story they told to the magistrate. The magistrate, however, communicates a set of precise instructions to the judge, and these instructions, though exerting no real

---

[3] I partly addressed this subject in a previous article: E. Metzger, 'Absent parties and bloody-minded judges' in A. Burrows and A. Rodger (eds.), *Mapping the Law: Essays in memory of Peter Birks* (Oxford, 2006), pp. 455–73. At that time I omitted a crucial piece of evidence, noting that it needed reconstruction and re-examination after a less than satisfactory *editio princeps. Ibid.*, p. 459, nn. 18–19. It is the fragment of a fourth-century parchment from Antinoopolis: C. H. Roberts (ed.), *The Antinoopolis Papyri* (London, 1950), I, no. 22 (*recto*) (commonly cited Pap. Ant. 22 recto). I have since had the opportunity to examine the parchment on several occasions, and can now present a provisional reconstruction. I am grateful for the assistance of the staff in the Papyrology Rooms, Sackler Library, University of Oxford, where the parchment is held.

[4] I should make clear that the precise nature of this proceeding, and particularly the extent to which the parties would be obliged to 'plead their facts' before the magistrate, is not well understood. The magistrate was alert to specific issues, such as the suing of one's patron or suits involving free status, which required a lengthier conversation or even a preliminary trial. But there were other suits – and one imagines that suits for a simple debt would fall into this class – where the parties could simply indicate the actions and defences they wished to carry forward to the judge. The consequences of making bad choices fell hard on the parties themselves, suggesting that the magistrate sometimes would have little interest in the underlying merits of the parties' submissions.

control over the procedure at trial, do keep the judge's attention to the matter at hand. These instructions are indeed the principal instrument by which the magistrate manages the judge.

The instructions take the form of what the Romans called a formula.[5] The formula is usually only a few sentences long, and describes mixed questions of law and fact. It explains the conditions under which the judge should condemn or absolve the defendant. To modern eyes it is a peculiar hybrid: a statement of the law, a summary of the pleadings,[6] and a judicial commission. Crucially it gives the magistrate indirect control over the fate of the action he has granted. The magistrate cannot, from a distance, prevent the parties from feeding the judge irrelevant facts or arguing irrelevant law. But with the formula as his instrument, the magistrate controls what the judge listens to. The trial itself can be disorganised and chaotic, but the judge is being effectively managed to listen and sift and sort and take from all the chaos only what is relevant to the lawsuit.

The judge must fulfil his commission carefully and thoroughly. The reason for this lies in the nature of the formula itself. When the formula has been prepared and the judge has been ordered to adjudicate,[7] the Romans would say that issue was joined. This is an important moment, because the plaintiff's original claim against the defendant in essence disappears. In exchange, the plaintiff receives a new claim based on the formula:

> Gaius, *Institutes* 3.180. Nam tunc obligatio quidem principalis dissolvi-
> tur, incipit autem teneri reus litis contestatione: sed, si condemnatus sit,
> sublata litis contestatione, incipit ex causa iudicati teneri.

---

[5] For more detail, see E. Metzger, 'Formula' in S. N. Katz (ed.), *The Oxford International Encyclopedia of Legal History* (New York, 2009); D. Johnston, *Roman Law in Context* (Cambridge, 1999), pp. 112–18. A catalogue of formulae is given in D. Mantovani, *Le Formule del Processo Privato Romano*, 2nd edn (Milan, 1999).

[6] The parties presented their allegations orally to the magistrate. (For an argument that they read from tablets, see E. A. Meyer, *Legitimacy and Law in the Roman World* (Cambridge, 2004), pp. 82–3.) The allegations were then compressed into the formal edictal language and inserted into the so-called *intentio* and *exceptio* of the formula. Peter Birks and Grant McLeod, in their translation of Justinian's *Institutes*, chose to translate '*intentio*' as 'principal pleading', which is jarring but in fact correct. P. Birks and G. McLeod (eds.), *Justinian's Institutes* (London, 1987), p. 154.

[7] The 'order to judge' (*iudicare iubere*) appeared as part of the formula itself, at least judging by the scanty documentary evidence. See TPSulp. 31, in G. Camodeca, *Tabulae Pompeianae Sulpiciorum (TPSulp.): Edizione critica dell'archivio puteolano dei Sulpicii* (Rome, 1999), pp. 97–8.

> [For at that moment [i.e. joinder of issue], though the original obliga-
> tion is dissolved, joinder of issue imposes a new obligation on the
> defendant. Then if the defendant is adjudged liable, joinder of issue
> loses its effect, and the judgment imposes a new obligation.]

Gaius is describing a plaintiff who claims a right under a subsisting obligation, for example a contract. At joinder of issue, that right is dissolved and replaced by a new right defined by the formula. In effect, a new contract is replacing the old. If judgment is in favour of the plaintiff, the new contract, in turn, is dissolved and replaced by the judgment, which itself serves as the foundation of a new obligation. The same legal effects apply to property claims, though there are differences in nuance.

The result is that a plaintiff who successfully passes joinder of issue receives something of great value, but also gives something up. He receives a short, clear statement of his complaint and the opportunity to bring it before a judge. He gives up the opportunity of ever going before the magistrate and telling the same story again. Thus a plaintiff with a formula in hand, we imagine, is pleased but nervous. As he considers the judge – a non-professional with an uncertain degree of commitment to the task at hand – he may silently express the hope that the judge will not spoil his one chance at a remedy.[8]

Enforcing the formula

The judge was answerable for failing to fulfil the instructions set out in the formula. He was, in fact, at risk of becoming personally liable. Unfortunately this species of liability is not perfectly understood due to the scarcity of sources. It is often discussed under the general head of 'the judge who makes the case his own' (*iudex qui litem suam facit*), a phrase (apparently) drawn from the praetor's edict[9] and listed by

---

[8] I am omitting here any discussion of how judges were selected, though in fact the selection procedures would ameliorate though not cure the plaintiff's anxieties. The parties' own wishes strongly affected the choice of judge, and in many cases the parties could avoid submitting the matter to an obviously incompetent judge. On judicial selection in Rome, see, most recently, L. Bablitz, *Actors and Audience in the Roman Courtroom* (London, 2007), pp. 101–3. For a summary of the judicial selection procedures revealed in the *lex Irnitana*, see E. Metzger, *A New Outline of the Roman Civil Trial* (Oxford, 1997), pp. 61–6.

[9] For discussion of the edictal evidence see G. MacCormack, 'The liability of the judge in the republic and principate' in H. Temporini and W. Haase (eds.), *Aufstieg und Niedergang der römischen Welt* (Berlin, 1982), ii: 14, p. 9; F. de Martino, 'Litem suam

Justinian among the four quasi-delicts in his *Institutes*.[10] Newly discovered evidence, however, has confirmed that judges' liability was also the subject of an Augustan 'judicature act'.[11] The relation between that act and the edict is uncertain: it is not entirely clear which acts of misconduct are covered by each.[12] A consensus has nevertheless formed around the proposition that a judge who fails to follow the basic procedural requirements of his office, including the duty to give judgment, will put himself in danger of liability.[13]

The offence of 'failing to give judgment' is sometimes straightforward: the most vivid example is given by Macrobius, describing drunken judges rushing to the forum to hear their assigned cases, fearful of being late 'lest they make the case their own'.[14] There are also subtler ways of failing to give judgment; one of our less ambiguous items of

---

facere' (1988) 20 *Bullettino dell'Istituto di Diritto Romano* (3rd ser.) 10, 36. On the pre-edictal law and its possible relation to the edict, see MacCormack, *ibid.*, pp. 4–6.

[10] Justinian, *Institutes* 4.5 pr. Justinian's treatment of the quasi-delict has been the special object of study in a series of pieces by O. F. Robinson. See 'Justinian's institutional classification and the class of quasi-delict' (1998) 19 *J. Legal Hist.* 245–50; 'The "iudex qui litem suam fecerit" explained' (1999) 116 *Zeitschrift der Savigny-Stiftung für Rechtsgeschichte*, romanistische Abteilung 195–9; 'Justinian and the compilers' view of the *iudex qui litem suam fecerit*' in H.-G. Knothe and J. Kohler (eds.) *Status Familiae* (Munich, 2001), pp. 389–96; 'Gaius and the class of quasi-delict' in *Iuris Vincula: Studi in onore di Mario Talamanca* (Naples, 2001), pp 120–8. Robinson argues that many of the texts from the justinianic compilation do not refer to the *unus iudex* of the formulary procedure, but to the 'judge deputy' (*iudex pedaneus*) of the later *cognitio* procedure.

[11] A *lex Iulia de iudiciis privatis* of the late first century BCE. This new evidence is the *lex Irnitana*. See n. 20, below, and accompanying text.

[12] The terminology is not helpful: Pomponius refers to *litem suam facere* in discussing a type of judges' liability that might well have been treated in the *lex Iulia*, a statute which appears to have used instead the term *iudici lis damni sit*. See Pap. Ant. 22 (*recto*), cited in Roberts, *The Antinoopolis Papyri*. Are we therefore justified in treating the offence as unitary regardless of its source, as most writers do? See, most recently, Á. Gómez-Iglesias, 'Lex Irnitana *cap.* 91: lis iudici damni sit' (2006) 72 *Studia et Documenta Historiae et Iuris* 468–9: '[N]o parece que pueda haber duda acerca de que las expresiones utilizadas en este capítulo (*lis iudici damni sit*) no son sino otro modo de dar forma, aquí legal, al concepto del *litem suam facere* que ya concíamos como acuñado por los comentarios jurisprudenciales.' By 'legal' Gómez-Iglesias means 'statutory': he argues that *lis damni sit* refers to the statutory sanction contemplated by the conduct described by *litem suam facere*. *Ibid.*, pp. 490–1.

[13] For a survey of the sources (excluding the *lex Irnitana*) supporting the view, see MacCormack, 'The liability of the judge in the republic and principate', pp. 18–25. See also the literature cited in Metzger, 'Absent parties and bloody-minded judges', p. 458, n. 16.

[14] Macrobius, *Saturnalia* 3.16.15. The events Macrobius describes will have taken place in the middle second century BCE. This is well before the passage of the *lex Iulia*, and if Macrobius is sensitive to his chronology, then what he describes does not necessarily comport with the later law.

evidence is in Gaius (*Institutes* 4.52), describing the judge who ignores the formula's injunction to condemn for a certain sum and condemns for some other sum, or who exceeds the 'ceiling' (*taxatio*) fixed by the formula for condemnation.[15] Gaius adds the tag '*alias enim similiter litem suam facit*' ('he makes the case his own in other ways as well'), which allows us to predict with some confidence that a judge who ignores the formula altogether, and attempts to adjudge some other, ungranted action, has equally breached the 'order to judge'. Under any of these scenarios the plaintiff is seriously aggrieved by the judge's failure to give judgment. The foundation of the plaintiff's original claim has disappeared, and the new foundation – the obligation created by the granting of the action – remains unadjudicated.

Liability in giving judgment

The principal subject of this chapter is the counterpart to the one just described: not 'failing to give judgment', but 'giving judgment when judgment should not be given'. This is an aspect of judges' liability that is less often discussed in the literature for the simple reason that many of the sources are new. One of the older and more familiar sources is the jurist Julian, writing in the second century CE. Julian is discussing, not the rule of liability directly, but the problem for which the rule of liability was the solution.

> Digest 42.1.60 (Julian 5 *digestorum*). Quaesitum est, cum alter ex litigatoribus febricitans discessisset et iudex absente eo pronuntiasset, an iure videretur pronuntiasse. Respondit: morbus sonticus etiam invitis litigatoribus ac iudice diem differt. Sonticus autem existimandus est, qui cuiusque rei agendae impedimento est. Litiganti porro quid magis impedimento est, quam motus corporis contra naturam, quem febrem appellant? Igitur si rei iudicandae tempore alter ex litigatoribus febrem habuit, res non videtur iudicata. Potest tamen dici esse aliquam et febrium differentiam: nam si quis sanus alias ac robustus tempore iudicandi levissima febre correptus fuerit, aut si quis tam veterem quartanam habeat ut in ea omnibus negotiis superesse soleat, poterit dici morbum sonticum non habere.

---

[15] The problems sometimes ran deeper than this because the praetor, in an effort to be fair, occasionally gave relief both to a party who claimed too little, and to a party against whom too much was claimed. See Gaius, *Institutes* 4.57. The possible effects on the judge's liability are discussed in Gómez-Iglesias, 'Lex Irnitana *cap. 91*: lis iudici damni sit', pp. 473–4.

[It was asked whether judgment is deemed to have been lawfully given when either of the litigants left in a fever and the judge gave judgment in his absence. The answer was that a definite and legitimate illness effects an adjournment, even if the litigants and judge are unwilling. It is, moreover, regarded as 'definite and legitimate' if it hinders the trans-action of any business. And what hinders a litigant more than the aberrant shaking of the body called fever? So if either of the litigants takes a fever at the time the matter is adjudged, the matter is not regarded as adjudged. Even fevers, however, can be distinguished one from another: so if a person who is otherwise well and strong is hit with a fairly light fever at the time of judging, or if he suffers the kind of chronic quartan fever that he can usually surmount in all his affairs, one could say he does not have a 'definite and legitimate illness'.]

From the passage we take the following. Judges and litigants sometimes fail to show for judgment on account of illness. In that event, there was a general rule that 'a definite and legitimate illness effects an adjournment, even if the litigants and judge are unwilling'. The words 'effects an adjournment' (literally 'puts off the day'; more usually expressed 'divides the day') indicate something more significant than simply 'rise for the day', because the consequence of failing to adjourn is to vitiate any judgment given in contravention of the rule. This is not necessarily a rebuke to the judge, who has no ready way of knowing whether a litigant's illness is serious or not. It is rather an assurance to an ill litigant that his absence is not fatal to his case. Julian is asked: how far does this assurance extend? Does it extend to litigants who, though ill, never-theless put in an appearance? In reply Julian (or the unnamed jurist he quotes[16]) is satisfied to recite the general rule (including the portion 'even if the litigants and judge are unwilling', which is unnecessary to the point being raised).[17] Thus litigants who fall ill and leave during trial are

---

[16] The text of Digest 42.1.60 appears to preserve the views of two jurists. The first, unnamed, has answered the question that is put in the opening sentence. The second, Julian himself, has given an opinion on how fevers may be distinguished one from another. This reading, however, turns on Mommsen's emendation, *respondit* for *respondi*. Intruded between the two views are comments on the nature of the term *sonticus* ('definite and legitimate'), some of which comments may be interpolated.

[17] The general rule therefore predates Julian. Some form of the general rule, including the terms 'illness' and 'divide the day', was found in the Twelve Tables. See Digest 2.11.2.3 (Ulpian 74 *ed*.): 'Et ideo etiam lex duodecim tabularum, si iudex vel alteruter ex litigatoribus morbo sontico impediatur, iubet diem iudicii esse diffissum.' ('And so even the law of the Twelve Tables demands that the day of trial be postponed if the judge or either of the litigants is hindered by a definite and legitimate illness.') For a reconstruction of *XII Tab.* 2.2, with sources, see M. H. Crawford (ed.), *Roman Statutes* (London, 1996), II, p. 623.

protected by the general rule, and need not fear any judgment given in their absence.

The principal value in the passage is in giving us a glimpse of the general rule: serious illnesses 'divide the day' and deprive judgments of their force. The trial must be adjourned. But the passage tacitly introduces a problem without giving a ready answer. The judge, after all, is bound by the formula[18] to give judgment, and faces the threat of personal liability if he does not. And yet from Julian we understand that, under certain circumstances, the judge must *not* give judgment. The question is: how did the rules on judges' liability negotiate between 'the duty to give judgment' and 'the duty not to give judgment'?

The answer came only in 1981 with the discovery of the *lex Irnitana*.[19] The *lex Irnitana* is one of several statutes, each closely similar, drafted on the exemplar of a law passed in 78 CE under the emperor Vespasian. Each of the statutes drafted on that exemplar are in the nature of 'town charters' for various Spanish *municipia*. The *lex Irnitana* is the most complete of the statutes that survive, and sets out in terse but plain language a series of rules for local institutions, including civil lawsuits which, for all relevant purposes, were to be conducted as if they took place in Rome.[20] In setting out rules for civil lawsuits, the *lex Irnitana* reveals how the liability rules negotiated between the 'two duties'.

The *lex Irnitana* treats liability in chapter 91.[21] This part of the statute is slightly unusual: instead of reciting the relevant rules, it tells the residents of the community that if they wish to know about certain procedural matters, among them adjournment and judges' liability, they should consult the rules governing these matters in Rome.[22] If this were all the statute gave us we would know little more than we

---

[18] Strictly speaking, by the *iudicare iubere* ('order to judge') that accompanies the formula.

[19] One source, known before the *lex Irnitana*, gives a hint of what the *lex Irnitana* would later reveal more fully: Pap. Ant. 22 (*recto*). This parchment fragment, like the *lex Irnitana*, associates adjournment with judges' liability, but lacks the fuller treatment of 'events that prompt adjournment' given in the latter source. It is discussed below.

[20] The principal critical texts of the *lex Irnitana* are J. González, 'The *lex Irnitana*: A new copy of the Flavian Municipal Law', tr. M. Crawford (1986) 76 *J. Roman Stud.* 147–243; F. Lamberti, '*Tabulae Irnitanae'. Municipalità e 'ius Romanorum'* (Naples, 1993).

[21] González, 'The lex Irnitana', pp. 179, 197–8; Lamberti, '*Tabulae Irnitanae'. Municipalità e 'ius Romanorum'*, pp. 362–7.

[22] Or more specifically, that for these purposes they should treat local lawsuits as if they were *iudicia legitima*, a class of lawsuit which took place in Rome, between Roman citizens, and before a single judge. See Gaius, *Institutes* 4.104.

knew before, but fortunately the drafter pauses in places and inserts brief explanations of what it means to conduct a Roman-style trial in Spain. It is these short parentheses that help to complete our picture of judges' liability. The following is the crucial section of chapter 91, which includes both a referral to the practice at Rome, and a parenthesis.

> *Lex Irni.*, c. 91, tab.10B, ll. 10–19. Itaque iis omnibus . . . diem diffindendi iudicandi in foro eius municipi aut ubi pacti erunt dum intra fines eius municipi utique ex isdem causis dies diffindatur diffissus sit utique si neque diffissum e lege neque iudicatum sit per quos dies quoque loco ex hac lege iudicari licebit oportebit, iudici arbitrove lis damni sit . . . siremps lex ius causaque esto atque uti si praetor populi Romani inter cives Romanos iudicari iussisset . . .
>
> [So in all those matters [i.e. in the private lawsuits treated in this chapter], for dividing the day and for judging in the town forum (or where the parties agree, so long as it is within the town boundaries), the statute, law, and position shall be as if the praetor of the Roman people had ordered adjudication between Roman citizens, so that the day shall be divided, or shall have been divided, for the same reasons [i.e. as obtained in Rome], and so that if the day has not been divided according to the statute and judgment has not been given on those days and in the place which, under this law, is right and appropriate for adjudication, the suit may be against the judge or arbiter for the loss . . .]

The text brings two valuable matters to our attention.

1. Causes for dividing the day. The *lex Irnitana* speaks of 'causes' in the plural, and thus a trial conducted in Rome recognised other causes, beyond 'serious illness', for dividing the day. This confirms a long-standing belief. For example, the Twelve Tables would divide the day if – the language is obscure – a litigant had a court appointment with a foreigner. Also, the *lex Coloniae Genetivae Iuliae* (a charter for a Spanish colony from the first century BCE) recites several valid excuses for absence from a proceeding (though not a private trial). Noteworthy among these excuses, and perhaps applicable to private trials in Rome generally, are service as a magistrate and conflicting court appointments.[23] One supposes that the *lex Iulia*, to which the words '*diffissum e lege*' in the quoted passage apparently refer,[24]

---

[23] See respectively *XII Tab.* 2.2, in Crawford, *Roman Statutes*, ii, p. 623; *Lex Col. Gen. Iul.*, c. 95, in Crawford, *Roman Statutes*, ii, p. 407.

[24] Cf. D. Mantovani, 'La "diei diffissio" nella "lex Irnitana"' in *Iuris Vincula* (n. 10 above) pp. 245–7.

contained a specific list of causes. If any of these mostly unknown causes arose, the judge would adjourn without giving judgment.[25]

2. The basis for liability. The key language is: 'si neque diffissum e lege neque iudicatum sit ... iudici arbitrove lis damni sit' ('if the day has not been divided according to the statute and judgment has not been given ... the suit shall be against the judge or arbiter for the loss'). The *lex Irnitana* puts us at a slight disadvantage because this language, though valuable, is properly speaking only an echo of the 'true' liability language set out in the *lex Iulia*. The residents of this Spanish town are directed to consult the *lex Iulia* and are given only a glimpse of that statute in the quoted language. The language nevertheless explains the most important point: how a judge, charged with giving judgment but charged also in certain instances with stopping proceedings, could incur personal liability. The act of 'failing to give judgment' is insufficient on its own, given the possibility of a 'cause for dividing the day' arising. But when the judge has not given judgment, *and* no cause has divided the day, then the judge may indeed be liable. Thus the liability language recites two conditions to liability: no dividing of the day for cause, and no judgment. The quoted language concludes with a threat rather than a penalty: the judge may face a lawsuit. (In Michael Crawford's elegant translation this is rendered: 'the case may be at the peril of the iudex or arbiter'.[26])

If we consider the fragment of Julian together with the new information provided by the *lex Irnitana*, we arrive at the following. A trial is underway. A litigant is seriously ill and does not appear, or appears but then leaves. A serious illness is a so-called cause for dividing the day, requiring the judge to stop proceedings. If the judge does indeed stop, he will not face a lawsuit for his failure to give judgment, because he has satisfied only one of the two conditions for such a lawsuit. If however the judge carries on in the litigant's absence and gives judgment, he may face a lawsuit. This is because his judgment is ignored (Julian: 'the matter is not

---

[25] For a different view, namely, that judges were obliged to give judgment on a fixed day, and escaped this obligation by offering one of several enumerated excuses, see Mantovani, 'La "diei diffissio" nella "lex Irnitana"', pp. 213–72; J. G. Wolf, '*Diem diffindere*: Die Vertagung im Urteilstermin nach der *Lex Irnitana*' in P. McKechnie (ed.), *Thinking Like a Lawyer* (Leiden, 2002), pp. 15–41; and most recently Gómez-Iglesias, 'Lex Irnitana *cap. 91*: lis iudici damni sit'. Cf. Metzger, 'Absent parties and bloody-minded judges', pp. 467–72.

[26] González, 'The lex Irnitana', p. 198.

regarded as adjudged') and both conditions are satisfied (*lex Irnitana*: 'the day has not been divided . . . and judgment has not been given').

If a judge's actions prima facie fall within the liability language, he is not necessarily condemned for the loss, as already noted. The problem of absent litigants must have been common, and judges will rarely have been in a position to know, at trial, whether a litigant is absent 'for cause' or not. Some judges will wrongly adjourn, while others will wrongly continue to conduct the trial, but in most cases neither mistake is so serious that reconvening and giving a valid judgment could not cure it. A real danger of loss will arise only in cases where the time period for giving judgment expires without judgment,[27] or where the ostensible winner gains an advantage over his opponent through the invalid judgment (for example, by execution). Thus the truly disobedient judge is not the one who assumes wrongly that cause exists but nevertheless reconvenes at a later time, nor the one who gives an invalid judgment in a litigant's absence but nevertheless gives a valid one later. The truly disobedient judge is the one who gives no valid judgment and cannot justify his disobedience by pointing to an adjournment for cause. This is what the liability language punishes and, one assumes, what the proceedings against the judge sought to determine.

What is described above is an aspect of judges' liability that is not developed in the literature. We have known for some time that a judge who failed to give judgment could make himself liable. What we did not know until the discovery of the *lex Irnitana* is that a judge who gives judgment when he should not is in danger of committing the same offence.

A further cause for dividing the day: false tutors

The discussion to this point has considered causes for dividing the day and offered the very simple example of illness. The discussion below offers a more exotic example. It comes from the text of a classical jurist (probably Ulpian[28]) preserved on a small corner of parchment, provisionally dated to the fourth century CE. It was discovered in Egypt almost

---

[27] Eighteen months: Gaius, *Institutes* 4.104; *lex Irni.*, c. 91, tab. 10A, l. 53 – tab. 10B, l. 2; ll. 17–18.

[28] De Zulueta provided a commentary for the fragment's first publication (Roberts, *The Antinoopolis Papyri*; see n. 3, above), where he convincingly showed that the fragment belonged to a commentary by Ulpian on the edict, of which fragments remain at Digest 27.6.

one hundred years ago,[29] but a reconstructed text was first published only fifty years ago.[30] Unfortunately the editor was sometimes careless in his readings, and in fact the final text he produced does not properly account for all of the readings he accepted. The text I offer below is based on new readings. Though it is only a provisional reconstruction, none of the variant readings affects the thesis.[31]

The issue discussed in the text is similar to the issue discussed by Julian. An event occurs in the middle of a trial, and at that moment the judge must adjourn. Here the event concerns a slightly fussy point of procedure concerning guardians and wards.

In order to be a defendant, a person must agree to be sued. A defendant who participates in joinder of issue, and allows the formula to create a new legal relationship between himself and his opponent, does so willingly.[32] However, if the defendant is a child (*impubes*) or a woman, then the defendant cannot give consent on his or her own authority. The defendant will be constrained by the Roman institution of guardianship (*tutela*) and will require the permission of his or her guardian (*tutor*).[33] This is not so much a 'procedural disability' as an expression of the principle that a ward (*pupillus*) may not make a decision to the detriment of certain property that, on the ward's death, would pass to another.[34]

From time to time a ward would find himself as defendant in a lawsuit to which his guardian had not given permission. This would occur where no permission was extended (the ward being treated as an ordinary defendant), or where permission was extended by a person who was not in fact the

---

[29] The find is described in J. de M. Johnson, 'Antinoë and its papyri: Excavation by the Graeco-Roman branch, 1913–14' (1914) 1 *Journal of Egyptian Archaeology* 168–81.

[30] Roberts, *The Antinoopolis Papyri*; see n. 3, above.

[31] The fragment has been written on extensively. Much of the literature is cited in E. Metzger, 'A fragment of Ulpian on *intertium* and *acceptilatio*' (2006) 72 *Studia et Documenta Historiae et Iuris* 116, n. 16, from which I would single out for special mention Mantovani, 'La "diei diffissio" nella "lex Irnitana"', pp. 254–9, and Wolf, '*Diem diffindere*: Die Vertagung im Urteilstermin nach der *Lex Irnitana*', p. 32. See, most recently, Gómez-Iglesias, 'Lex Irnitana *cap. 91*: lis iudici damni sit', pp. 477–9. In light of my new readings and reconstruction, but also on reflection, I have revised some of the views I expressed in Metzger, *A New Outline of the Roman Civil Trial*, ch. 11.

[32] See Kaser and Hackl, *Das römische Zivilprozessrecht*, pp. 289–90.

[33] A male *impubes* became independent of guardianship at the age of fourteen; a female remained under guardianship for life. An introduction to the main features of guardianship, with sources, is given in J. F. Gardner, *Women in Roman Law and Society* (London, 1986), pp. 14–26; and J. A. Crook, *Law and Life of Rome* (London, 1967), pp. 113–16.

[34] See Crook, *Law and Life of Rome*, pp. 113–14.

ward's guardian (a so-called *falsus tutor*). If the rules were followed strictly, then each and every time a plaintiff sued a ward without a guardian's permission, the plaintiff would lose the suit and would not be permitted to sue again on the same action. He would be barred because the basis of his original claim, for instance a contract, would have been extinguished as soon as issue was joined. But in reality the law was not so unforgiving. Our text gives a notion of how far the law protects an honest plaintiff.

> Pap. Ant. 22 (*recto*) (provisionally restored). . . . pupillo siue . . . [non] obstabit exceptio aut restitutorium iudicium dabitur. Quodsi sciens cum pupillo egit sine tutore auctore lis peribit iure praetorio. Item Pomponius scribit si falso tutore auctore minime[35] fuerit diffisus dies edictum quidem cessare at[36] iudicem quia neque diffidit neque sententiam dixit litem suam fecisse . . .
>
> [. . . . pupil either . . . the defence will fail or a restitutory trial will be granted. But if he sued a pupil knowingly without tutorial authority [sc. of his defendant's guardian] the action will be lost by praetorian law. Similarly Pomponius writes that when the day has not been divided in a case where the authority of a false guardian arises, though the edict ceases to apply, yet the judge, because he has neither divided nor pronounced judgment, has made the case his own . . .]

The text considers the case of a plaintiff who sues a ward lacking the permission of a guardian. The matter has proceeded to trial, and perhaps even to judgment. When the irregularity comes to light, the magistrate will hear the plaintiff out. The first two sentences spell out the relief

---

[35] The word *minime* (translated here as 'not [been divided]') appears on the parchment as an *m* with a faint macron over the right portion (indicating abbreviation). The first editor, reading a diagonal bit of stain as a mark of abbreviation, suggested *m(ale)*, and some have followed this resolution. It would give the meaning 'wrongly adjourned'. Gómez-Iglesias may be correct that, if a 'wrong adjournment' is equivalent to 'no adjournment', then there is no logical inconsistency in the text. Gómez-Iglesias, 'Lex Irnitana *cap. 91*: lis iudici damni sit', pp. 478–9; Metzger, *A New Outline of the Roman Civil Trial*, pp. 135–6 (same point). But it would open an entirely new issue: what is a 'wrong adjournment' and is it serious enough to bring liability? See e.g. F. J. Cremades and I. Paricio, 'La responsibilidad del juez en el derecho Romano' (1984) 54 *Anuario de historia del derecho español* 179–208 at 182. A later suggestion, with some support in other sources, is *m(inus)*: see T. Giménez-Candela, 'Una revision de Pap. Ant. 22' in *Estudios de derecho Romano en honor de Alvaro D'Ors* (Univeridad de Navarra, Pamplona, 1987) pp. 570–3; Metzger, *A New Outline of the Roman Civil Trial*, 135–37. It expresses 'not' though, as Mantovani notes, with insufficient peremptory force for the context. Mantovani, 'La "diei diffissio" nella "lex Irnitana"', v, p. 256, n. 115. The suggested resolution *m(inime)* is my own.

[36] The *at* is emended for *et*: see Mantovani, 'La "diei diffissio" nella "lex Irnitana"', v, p. 255, n. 114.

afforded the plaintiff under the edict. If the plaintiff was unaware he was suing a ward (a fact inferable, though not preserved, in the mutilated first sentence), he will be given another trial and, if the matter had proceeded to judgment, the ward will not be permitted the defence of *res judicata*. The magistrate's remedies acknowledge that the ward's objection ('no permission by the guardian') is too petty to be indulged. On the other hand, a plaintiff who goes into the affair with his eyes open – he knows the defendant is a pupil with no guardian – receives no relief from the magistrate ('the action will be lost by praetorian law').

In the last sentence, the background facts change. A person has falsely represented himself as a guardian, and has given permission for the ward to be sued. Issue is joined, and the case goes to trial. At some time during the trial, it comes to light that the guardian is false and that joinder of issue should not have taken place. The text suggests that when the true state of affairs comes to light, the judge's duty is to adjourn. Thus the final portion of the text is describing a cause for dividing the day, to be treated in a manner analogous to serious illness.[37] Discovering that a guardian is false is the same as discovering that a party is seriously ill: judgment should not be given. If the judge does not adjourn but proceeds to judgment then, on analogy with 'serious illness', the case is not regarded as adjudged (*res non videtur iudicata*, as Julian says). The text states that the protections of the edict, discussed in the two foregoing sentences, no longer apply; in failing to heed the rule to divide the day the judge has 'neither adjourned nor given judgment' and the judge has made the case his own.

The text ends here, and the question it leaves open – a question already raised in the context of serious illness – is whether condemnation of the judge follows these facts as a matter of course. The question is complicated by the fact that the text uses the formula 'makes the case his own', while the *lex Irnitana*, otherwise describing the same legal position, uses the formula 'the suit may be against the judge'. Some judges, we suspect, will be in a poor position to discover the true state of affairs during trial, and it seems harsh to expect a judge to decide the falsity of a tutor on the spot, at the risk of certain condemnation on getting it wrong. The presence of a false tutor is, moreover, a simple problem to mend. If a judge adjourns and it later emerges he was mistaken, the trial can simply resume. If a judge fails to adjourn and gives an invalid judgment, it will occasionally be possible to begin an entirely new trial without loss to either party. The truly, irredeemably misbehaving judge is the one who

---

[37] Cf. Metzger, *A New Outline of the Roman Civil Trial*, pp. 134–7.

utterly refuses to adjourn – here the force of *minime*[38] may be justified – and steps away from his commission with no valid judgment whatsoever. As in the case of illness, the proceedings against the judge give the first real occasion to weigh the judge's wrongdoing.

Conclusion

Making judges personally liable for procedural mistakes always raises eyebrows. Obviously it is not the way we do things now. Modern writers sometimes explain the Roman system by pointing out that the Romans at this time did not have a system of appeals, and suggesting that an action against the judge served as a kind of substitute.[39] This is undeniably true, but we should not misunderstand the motives underlying the action. The Romans did not adopt judges' liability to soothe a frustrated desire for appeals. They recognised, as we do, a division between a higher and lower judicial authority, but preferred to give the higher authority the first pass: the magistrate determined once-and-for-all certain crucial questions of law and fact, matters that we would leave to an appeal. The magistrate also possessed wide equitable powers to restore an earlier, pretrial state of affairs. Litigants were never wholly at the mercy of the lay judge, even without judges' liability.

Judges' liability was a tool of administration. It gave the magistrate a way to manage the judge from a court that otherwise operated at a distance from the judge's court. A judge undertook the task of adjudication as a one-off commission, and was bound to perform that commission properly. Liability was only a remote threat; the nearer threat was a *proceeding* in which the magistrate could consider the propriety of an adjournment or the validity of a judgment. The worst of the judges would be condemned, but for many it was an opportunity to hear the magistrate say: 'You thought you were finished; you're not; please finish.'

---

[38] See n. 35, above. The judge who utterly refuses to acknowledge a cause for adjournment is possibly the subject of Ulpian's famously mysterious text. Digest 5.1.15.1 (Ulpian 21 *ed.*): 'Iudex tunc litem suam facere intellegitur, cum dolo malo in fraudem legis sententiam dixerit (dolo malo autem videtur hoc facere, si evidens arguatur eius vel gratia vel inimicitia vel etiam sordes), ut veram aestimationem litis praestare cogatur.' ('A judge is treated as having made the case his own when he has fraudulently given judgment contrary to the *lex* [*Iulia*?] (and he is regarded as having done so fraudulently when partiality, enmity, or even corruption is clearly shown), at which point he is compelled to pay the true assessment of the case.') The relation of this text to the parchment fragment and the *lex Irnitana* will be discussed elsewhere.

[39] See e.g. MacCormack, 'The liability of the judge in the republic and principate', p. 24; J. M. Kelly, *Roman Litigation* (Oxford, 1966), p. 117.

10

The spokesmen in medieval courts: The unknown leading judges of the customary law and makers of the first Continental law reports

DIRK HEIRBAUT[*]

The problem: the great judges of customary law are largely unknown to us because judgment was a collective act

Legal historians studying customary law in northern France, the Low Countries and Germany can only be envious of their colleagues working on the *ius commune* or the early history of the common law. They can identify the makers of the law they study, whether these are legislators, professors, notaries, judges, serjeants, attorneys or advocates. Hundreds of their names have come down to us and, even though this is not always easy, one can identify their individual contributions to the development of the law. Moreover, some great jurists have deservedly become famous and they have given a certain 'star quality' to the history of the law they created. Continental customary law lacks these great lawyers. True, a few of them, like Beaumanoir[1] or Eike von Repgow have become household names amongst legal historians,[2] but that makes us even more aware of the fact that we do not know much about their colleagues. Here, one can quote Susan Reynolds about Eike von Repgow: 'He was what I would call

---

[*] I would like to thank Prof. em. dr. R. van Caenegem, P. Carson, G. Sinnaeve, B. Debaenst, B. van Dael and B. Quintelier who read a draft version of this text, for their comments. I would also like to thank Dr Paul Brand for revision of the English of this chapter and for other help. Needless to say any remaining errors are entirely my own.

[1] See e.g. J.-M. Carbasse, 'Philippe de Beaumanoir: Coutumes de Beauvaisis' (2002) 22 *Revue d'histoire des facultés de droit* 135–54.

[2] e.g. the exhibition Heiner Lück organised about Eike, first in Germany and then also in Brussels as capital of the EU. For the catalogue see H. Lück *et al.*, *Sachenspiegel und Magdeburger Recht. Saxon Mirror and Magdeburg Law. Eike von Repgow. Grundlagen für Europa. The groundwork for Europe* (Magdeburg, 2005). The texts of a 2007 symposium in Brussels on Eike will be published in the series *Iuris scripta historica*.

an expert, and he cannot have been the only one in Germany to have gained his legal expertise in courts rather than in schools.'[3]

Indeed, Eike was not the only one, but the individual contributions of his colleagues to the development of customary law have been forgotten. Indeed, customary law is sometimes even said to have been created by the 'people', though most of it was made by judges whose judgments were later condensed into legal rules.[4] If there was not a single judge, but a group of them (whether *echevins* or a feudal lord's tenants), the court's judgment was seen as a collective act.[5] Even if the legal historian knows who the judges were, he does not know their individual contributions to the judgment. He may safely assume that a few of them were more important than their colleagues in reaching a decision, that they were the real makers of customary law, but they remain hidden by the presence of their lesser brethren.

An exception: the judges acting as spokesmen for the Lille castellany court around 1300

Most of our sources may give the impression that the judgments of customary law courts were collective acts, but the reality was somewhat different, as a Flemish text from around 1300 proves. The *Lois des pairs dou castel de Lille* contains a hodgepodge of legal rules and case law from the feudal court of the count of Flanders in the castellany of Lille.[6] The president of this court was the comital bailiff of Lille and its judges were comital vassals who held their fiefs of the castle of Lille. The Lille castellany court had jurisdiction not only in feudal but also in criminal cases and was the 'head'[7] of

---

[3] S. Reynolds, 'The emergence of professional law in the long twelfth century' (2003) 21 *Law and Hist. Rev.* 365. Reynolds would have done better to choose another example, as Eike seems to have received some formal schooling, though in theology, rather than in law, and there is even a (small) chance that the canonist Johannes Teutonicus was one of his teachers: see P. Landau, 'Der Entstehungsort des Sachsenspiegels. Eike von Repgow, Altzelle und die anglo-normannische Kanonistik' (2005) 61 *Deutsches Archiv für Erforschung des Mittelalters* 73–101 and H. Lück, *Über den Sachsenspiegel. Entstehung, Inhalt und Wirkung des Rechtsbuches* (Dößel, 2005), esp. p. 23.

[4] Cf. J. Gilissen, *La Coutume* (Turnhout, 1982), pp. 78–80.

[5] See e.g. F. d'Hoop, *Recueil des chartes du prieuré de Saint-Bertin à Poperinghe, et de ses dépendances à Bas-Warneston et à Couckelaere* (Bruges, 1870), no. 102, pp. 113–14 (1263); Archives départementales du Nord (Lille), Ser. B, 4058/4150 (1299).

[6] For the *Lois de Lille*, see D. Heirbaut, 'The oldest part of the *Lois des pers dou Castel de Lille*' (2007) 75 *Tijds. Rgeschied.* 139.

[7] P. Godding, 'Appel et recours à chef de sens à Brabant. Wie hoet heeft die heeft beroep' (1997) 65 *Tijds. Rgeschied.* 281.

the castellany's lower courts, which asked for its advice when their judges were unable to solve a case themselves.[8]

The *Lois de Lille* show how the collective judgments of the Lille judges came to be reached. As in other Flemish courts, proceedings consisted of a series of questions by the court's president, the lord or his representative, who asked the court to judge, on the one hand, and of answers by the judges, on the other.[9] Other texts give us the impression that the judges answered their president collectively, which may have been possible for simple questions where a rote formula could be used (for example, as to whether the sun had risen, so that the court could start its activities), but when legal and factual issues were more complex this would have led to chaos, because some judges would have contradicted the others. One can only imagine what a cacophony of shouts and brawls would have resulted from any more-or-less complicated question put by the court's president. Moreover, not everyone sitting in a court was an expert, so that some judges would have remained silent.[10] For this reason and also to avoid confusion, in Lille one of the judges who was more of an expert than the others acted as a spokesman for his fellows and, after he had spoken, they followed suit: 'Se rendy che jugement, Jehan de le Heye, chevaliers, et l'ensïuy . . .'[11] That all the judges did so was only possible because they had first withdrawn to debate the matter and reach agreement.[12] During this discussion, the later spokesman came to the fore and he can be seen as the intellectual author of the court's judgment. This means that the spokesmen were the leading judges and, as such, the real

---

[8] On the feudal castellany courts in Flanders, see D. Heirbaut, *Over heren, vazallen en graven. Het persoonlijk leenrecht in Vlaanderen, ca. 1000–1305* (Brussels, 1997), pp. 172–89; A. Koch, *De rechterlijke organisatie van het graafschap Vlaanderen tot in de 13e eeuw* (Antwerp, 1951), pp. 173–88, 199–205.

[9] R. van Caenegem, *Geschiedenis van het strafprocesrecht in Vlaanderen van de XIe eeuw tot de XIVe eeuw* (Brussels, 1956), pp. 138–9.

[10] In one 1280 Flemish case the judges were so ignorant that they all remained silent, so that in the end their more experienced president, the bailiff of Douai, had to trade places with a member of the court: E. Hautcoeur, *Cartulaire de l'abbaye de Flines*, 2 vols. (Lille, 1873) (hereinafter abbreviated to HFl), I, no. 216, pp. 237–9.

[11] R. Monier, *Les lois, enquêtes et jugements des pairs du castel de Lille. Recueil des coutumes, conseils et jugements du tribunal de la Salle de Lille, 1283–1406* (Lille, 1937) (hereinafter abbreviated to Lille), no. 290, pp. 183–4 (1292). Cf. HFl, I, no. 224. pp. 245–6 (1281).

[12] See e.g. Groenenbriel Abbey, Charters, 71, State Archives Ghent (1260–1); M. Gysseling, *Corpus van Middelnederlandse teksten (tot en met het jaar 1300)* (The Hague, 1977), I(4), no. 1694, pp. 2537–9 (1298); A. d'Herbomez, 'Histoire des châtelains de Tournai de la maison de Mortagne Preuves' (1895) 25 *Mémoires de la société historique et littéraire de Tournai* 74–5 (1240).

creators of customary law in the Lille area.[13] The usual terminology of 'judgment by peers' is somewhat misleading here. In the feudal hierarchy the judges may have been the peers of the parties, but their spokesman was first among these peers and, literally, a leading judge.

Not only do the *Lois de Lille* describe the activities of the spokesmen quite well, but they also contain the names of eight of them: Pasquier Li Borgne, Robert Brunel, Peter of Sainghin, John of La Haie, Giles of Linsselles, Walter of Douai, Walter of Reninge and Peter of Le Més.[14] It is not that interesting just to know their names, but once we do know them this can be the starting point for detailed prosopographical research, which helps us to discover the common characteristics of these leading judges.[15] For this, Peter of Le Més's biography is not very useful as not much is known about him. The others, however, have in common a pattern of activities. All these spokesmen acted as legal advisers of others, whether to judges, arbiters, parties in court or even the count of Flanders. All acted as the presidents/summoners of courts, either as lords or as their representatives (bailiffs, seneschals etc.). Pasquier Li Borgne, Robert Brunel, Peter of Sainghin, Walter of Douai and Walter of Reninghe were all lords who had their own tenants and thus had their own courts over which they presided. Moreover, Pasquier Li Borgne, Robert Brunel, John of La Haie, Peter of Sainghin and Walter of Reninge, all acted as bailiffs, or in a like capacity in which they presided over the courts of others. Thus, all the spokesmen were presidents/summoners of courts at one time or another during their lives. All were also judges in courts other than the Lille castellany court. At the central level, in the count's *curia* we can find Robert Brunel, Walter of Douai, John of La Haie and Walter of Reninge; in other castellany courts, Walter of Reninge in Ypres, Walter of Douai and Peter of Sainghin in Douai; in local courts, whether feudal or not, Pasquier Li Borgne, John of La Haie, Peter of Sainghin and Giles of Linsselles.

What these data show is that the Lille spokesmen, even though they were only semi-professionals,[16] were not just the leading judges of their court, but also the legal experts *par excellence* in the Lille area. If someone has been

---

[13] However, the city of Lille had its own customary law, written down by its clerk Roisin around 1300: R. Monier, *Le livre Roisin: Coutumier lillois de la fin du XIIIe siècle* (Paris, 1932).

[14] For detailed references, see Heirbaut, 'Oldest part', p. 144.

[15] For these prosopographies, see D. Heirbaut, 'Une méthode pour identifier les porte-paroles des jurisdictions de droit coutumier en Europe du Nord au Haut Moyen-Age, basée sur une prosopographie des porte-paroles de Cassel et Lille autour de 1300' in V. Bernaudeau *et al.* (eds.), *Les Praticiens du droit du Moyen Âge à l'époque contemporaine: Approches prosopographiques Belgique, Canada, France, Italie, Prusse* (Rennes, 2008), pp. 26–38.

[16] It is clear that they had received no training in the learned law and that they were still far behind the professional lawyers to be found at the same time in England. On these see

identified as a spokesman of the castellany court, he can be considered a major player in the world of law in Lille and, in many cases, not just there, as some of the Lille spokesmen were also active elsewhere. Still, while this may be interesting for specialists in local legal history, the Lille material only becomes really useful if it can be proven that spokesmen of this kind can also be found in other times and places, since it is possible that this type of leading judge was typically Flemish and only a recent phenomenon. In the last decades of the thirteenth and the first decades of the fourteenth century Flemish feudal law underwent great upheavals. By then the count of Flanders had a network of local feudal courts, but originally he had only one feudal court, the central *curia*.[17] Because of the count's preponderance in Flanders, he had the most vassals and his court set the tone for all the other courts. Early Flemish feudal law was identical to the comital *curia*'s feudal law. For various reasons, local comital feudal courts, the feudal castellany courts, came into existence in the second half of the twelfth and the first half of the thirteenth century. Before 1244 these were only of secondary importance as comital feudal courts and their impact on the development of Flemish law was very limited. However, in 1244, when Countess Margaret came to power, the central *curia* ceded its jurisdiction over most comital fiefs to the castellany courts, so that it could concentrate on more important issues. During the first generation, the vassals in these courts still stuck to the old common feudal law of the central *curia*. The next generation (which, in Lille, we encounter from 1280 onwards) did not remember the old common law that well and in this generation the unity of Flemish law disappeared, as in each castellany the central court developed its own version of a formerly common law.[18] The Lille spokesmen might have been just one of the new phenomena and unique to Lille. However, they were not, as the following paragraphs will show.

P. Brand, 'The professionalisation of lawyers in England' (2006) 28 *Zeitschrift für Neuere Rechtsgeschichte* 7–19; P. Brand, *The Origins of the English Legal Profession* (Oxford, 1992); P. Brand, 'The origins of the English legal profession' in P. Brand, *The Making of the Common Law* (London, 1992) (first published in (1987) 5 *Law and Hist. Rev.* 31); P. Brand, 'Edward I and the transformation of the English judiciary' in P. Brand, *The Making of the Common Law* (London, 1992).

[17] The Flemish *curia* probably already existed in the tenth century, but we have reliable data only from 1024 on (Heirbaut, *Heren*, pp. 152–3, n. 130 there needs to be corrected in the light of B. Meijns, *Aken of Jeruzalem? Het ontstaan en de hervorming van de kanonikale instellingen in Vlaanderen tot circa 1155* (Leuven, 2000), pp. 368–81) and its early history, including its activity as a feudal court, still needs to be studied in detail.

[18] Heirbaut, *Heren*, pp. 152–64, 172–89; D. Heirbaut, *Over lenen en families. Het zakelijk leenrecht in Vlaanderen, ca. 1000–1305. Een studie over de vroegste geschiedenis van het leenrecht in het graafschap Vlaanderen* (Brussels, 2000), pp. 81–7, 133–6.

Leading judges as spokesmen in Flanders before 1300

The great Lille judges around 1300 were the founding fathers of a new customary law, which henceforth distinguished the Lille castellany from other Flemish customary laws and, therefore, their names have been preserved for posterity. However, this does not mean that there were no spokesmen in Flanders before them. We do not know their names, but that does not mean they did not exist. After all, without the *Lois de Lille* the spokesmen commemorated there would also have been forgotten. Without evidence we could not be certain of the existence of these older spokesmen. Fortunately, two of the tens of thousands of charters relating to Flanders dating from before the end of the thirteenth century[19] explicitly mention spokesmen. One is from 1122, the other from 1148.

In 1122 Count Charles the Good mentions two proceedings before his court in which a leading judge acted as spokesman.[20] In the first, the judges were described as experts in law and among them count Eustace of Boulogne[21] is singled out (*comite Eustachio et prudentioribus patrie*). This makes it very likely that he was their spokesman. In the second the count called upon his barons to retire and give him a judgment: 'Domini, obtestor vos per fidem quam michi debetis, ite in partem et judicio irrefragabili decernite, quid Ingelberto, quid monachis conveniat responderi.' When they returned, Robert of Bethune was their spokesman, and this time there can be no doubt about that: 'Qui euntes communicato consilio redeuntes, per Robertum advocatum[22] responderunt.' In the 1148 charter countess Sybil, her husband Thierry being absent, called upon the barons to judge: 'adiuratis baronibus meis ... precepi ut ... iudicarent', and the barons answered

---

[19] On the sources of Flemish feudal law, see D. Heirbaut, 'The quest for the sources of a non-bureaucratic feudalism: Flemish feudalism during the High Middle Ages (1000–1300)' in J.-F. Nieus (ed.), *Le vassal, le droit et l'écrit* (Louvain-la-Neuve, 2007), pp. 97–122.

[20] F. Vercauteren, *Actes des comtes de Flandre (1071–1128)* (Brussels, 1938), no. 108, pp. 247–51.

[21] On the relationship between the counts of Boulogne and Flanders, one can consult H. J. Tanner, *Families, Friends and Allies: Boulogne and politics in northern France and England, c.879–1160* (Leyden, 2004), or the more balanced J.-F. Nieus, 'Aux marges de la principauté: les comtés vassaux de la Flandre, fin Xe–fin XIIe siècle' in *VIe Congrès de l'association des Cercles francophones d'histoire et d'archéologie de Belgique* (Mons, 2002), pp. 309–24.

[22] Robert, lord of Bethune and peer of Flanders, was advocate of Saint Bertin at Saint Omer and also advocate of the abbey of Saint Vaast: E. Warlop, *The Flemish Nobility before 1300* (Courtrai, 1975–6), II(1), no. 65, p. 664. But his title of advocate in these years was linked to Bethune (*advocatus Betuniae*) e.g. in Vercauteren, *Actes*, no. 67, pp. 158–9.

through their spokesman, the seneschal Anselm of Houdain,[23] 'Communicato itaque consilio omnes unanimiter per Anselmum de Husdenio nobilem virum et dapiferum nostrum iudicaverunt.'[24] Once again there can be no doubt that a leading judge had acted as spokesman for the court. The 1122 and 1148 charters prove that the spokesmen were not new at the end of the thirteenth century and that there was a continuity between the late thirteenth century and the twelfth, although there are some differences between the twelfth-century charters and the Lille material. For example, in the twelfth century the judges and, most of all, their spokesmen are persons of a higher social standing, the count of Boulogne in 1122 being more of a neighbouring prince than a Flemish vassal.[25]

Leading judges as spokesmen outside Flanders

Spokesmen can also be found outside Flanders. One can for example quote the count of Hainaut in 1281: 'par le jugement de mes hommes, c'est à savoir monsigneur Rasson de Gavre, signeur de Liedekierke, sour cui li jugement fi tornés, et l'en sivirent notre autre homme ki i furent'.[26] This brings to mind the *Lois de Lille*'s formula: *se rendy che jugement ... et l'ensïuy* .... Hainaut was next to Flanders, but the activity of spokesmen is also recorded for the *curia* of the kings and emperors of the Romans, for which there are also charters containing references to spokesmen.[27] These sometimes also clearly indicate that someone spoke first (*Primam iudicii sententiam dedit*) and that then others followed his opinion (*quam secutus est*).[28] However, a more detailed study of these spokesmen outside Flanders still needs to be made.

Although this chapter is mainly concerned with the Continent, it should be mentioned that there are also indications of the activity of spokesmen in England. For example, in a 1121 lawsuit in the feudal court of the bishop of Bath an anonymous person acted as spokesman: 'Those who were older and more learned in law left the crowd and weighed subtly and wisely all the

---

[23] See about him, T. de Hemptinne and A. Verhulst, *De oorkonden der graven van Vlaanderen (juli 1128–1191)*, II(1), *Regering van Diederik van de Elzas (Juli 1128–17 Januari 1168)* (Brussels, 1988), p. 136, n. 5.

[24] de Hemptinne and Verhulst, *Oorkonden*, no. 111, pp. 179–82.   [25] See n. 21, above.

[26] C. de Reiffenberg, *Monuments pour servir à l'histoire des provinces de Namur, de Hainaut et de Luxembourg* (Brussels, 1844), I, no. 45, pp 372–3 (1281).

[27] See e.g. B. Diestelkamp and E. Rotter, *Urkundenregesten zur Tätigkeit des deutschen Königs- und Hofgerichts bis 1451*, I, *Die Zeit von Konrad I. bis Heinrich VI. 911–1197* (Cologne, 1988), no. 284, p. 218 (1150).

[28] *Ibid.*, no. 255, pp. 192–3 (1147).

arguments they had heard and settled the case. After they came back, the following pronouncement was made by one man's mouth for them all, who said . . .'[29] In the 1164 trial of Thomas Becket at Northampton, it was: 'The noble man Robert, at the time earl of Leicester, most honoured among the honoured, who had been asked to act as spokesman.'[30] Needless to say, the context was different. For example, Robert of Beaumont, earl of Leicester, was chief justiciar of England and as such hardly a person who needs to be saved from obscurity,[31] and in general the English legal profession is already well known.[32] However, this is only true at the central level, as local lawyers, apart from someone like Hugh Tyrel of Mannington, who is the subject of an article by Paul Brand,[33] remain largely unknown. Reading Brand's article it seems that the English local lawyers are not that different from their Lille counterparts, as they are also the 'jacks of all legal trades' in their region. Moreover, some of them acted as spokesmen of the county courts.[34]

Leading judges not explicitly identified as spokesmen: the charter material

Once it has been established that spokesmen could be found not only in Lille around 1300, but also in other times and places, a way needs to be found of identifying judges who have not been expressly named as spokesmen. For Flanders, one can construct a model of a spokesman in a Flemish feudal court around 1300 with the data about the Lille spokesmen and use that as a pointer to other leading judges who acted as spokesmen. A person who acted as a legal adviser, judge in and president/summoner of courts and interacted with spokesmen was likely to have been a spokesman

---

[29] 'Secedentes ergo a turba qui majores natu vel juris peritiores esse videbantur, singula juxta quod audierant subtiliter et discrete pensantes, causam dijudicaverunt. Quibus iterum introgressis, sic unius ore pro omnibus relatum est.' R. van Caenegem, *English lawsuits from William I to Richard I, Part I*, Selden Society, vol. 106 (London, 1990), no. 226, pp. 192–3.

[30] 'Nobilis vir Robertus, tunc Leicestriae comes, inter honoratos honoratior, in cujus ore verbum positum fuerat': van Caenegem, *Lawsuits*, no. 421C, pp. 446–457 at 455.

[31] On him, see D. Crouch, *The Beaumont Twins: The roots and branches of power in the twelfth century* (Cambridge, 1986).

[32] See e.g. the publications by Paul Brand quoted in n. 16, above.

[33] P. Brand, 'Stewards, bailiffs and the emerging legal profession in later thirteenth-century England' in R. Evans (ed.), *Lordship and Learning: Studies in memory of Trevor Aston* (Woodbridge, 2004).

[34] For an example, see *Curia regis rolls*, X, Trinity term 1222, 344–6 (cf. *Curia regis rolls*, I, Easter term 1201, I, 445–6). (I am very much indebted to Paul Brand for these references.)

himself.[35] Moreover, very valuable information is given by the lists of judges in the charters. The *Lois de Lille* indicate that the first judge to be mentioned is the spokesman and those who follow him in the list are those who spoke after him, following his opinion.[36] The same order is found in the charters. For example, charters of lower courts, in which one of the known leading judges of the Lille castellany court is present, will, with one exception,[37] award him the first place,[38] which can only be taken as meaning that he also acted as spokesman of the lower court. This impression is strengthened by looking at the position of the known Lille spokesmen in other courts, where they are also likely to be mentioned first,[39] unless a more expert colleague was present.[40] Likewise, charter evidence for Robert Brunel and Walter of Douai – that is, other sources than the *Lois de Lille* – show that they took first place in Lille.[41] A final indication of the fact that the first place in the list of the court's members went to its spokesman is to be found in another Flemish text, the *Loy et jugemens des hommes de le baillie de Cassel*. This comes from the end of the thirteenth century and is about the law of the castellany of Cassel.[42] It explicitly identifies Philip of Ypres once as the spokesman of the Cassel castellany court,[43] and thrice mentions him in first place,[44] a place he also occupied in lower courts in that region.[45] In short, in

---

[35] Heirbaut, 'Méthode', pp. 38–42.

[36] Lille, no. 290, pp. 183–4 (1292): 'Se rendy che jugement, Jehan de le Heye, chevaliers, et l'ensïuy . . .'. Cf. de Reiffenberg, *Monuments*, I, no. 45, pp. 372–3 (1281).

[37] Pasquier Li Borgne in the feudal court of the castellan of Lille (E. Hautcoeur, *Cartulaire de l'église collégiale de Saint-Pierre de Lille*, 2 vols. (Lille, 1894) (hereinafter abbreviated to HStP), I, no. 802, p. 568 (1299)). This personal court of the comital castellan, composed of the castellan's own vassals, is not to be confused with the castellany court, composed of comital vassals. At that time Pasquier had not yet been spokesman of the castellany court (see Heirbaut, 'Méthode', pp. 26–7), so this does not count. Moreover the two persons preceding him had already been pre-eminent in the castellan's court in 1284 (HStP, I, no. 716, pp. 504–5).

[38] HFl, I, no. 319, p. 337 (1292); M. Vanhaeck, *Cartulaire de l'abbaye de Marquette* (Lille, 1937–40), I, no. 302, pp. 287–8 (1290); HStP, I, no. 800, p. 566 (1298); Lille, no. 298, pp. 188–9 (1296).

[39] HFl, I, no. 291, pp. 316–19 (1290); de Reiffenberg, *Monuments*, I, no. 18, pp. 22–3 and no. 59, pp. 202–3 (1284).

[40] e.g. in Cassel Walter of Reninge had to give way to his kinsman Philip of Ypres (on whom see below): E. de Coussemaker, 'Loy et jugemens des hommes de le baillie de Cassel' (hereinafter abbreviated to Cassel), (1873) 32 *Annales du comité flamand de France* 216–17 (1288).

[41] Robert: E. de Coussemaker, 'Sommaire des chartes de la Chambre des comptes à Lille, et du Grand-Cartulaire de Saint-Bertin où se trouve mentionné Philippon de Bourbourg' (1886–8) 4 *Bulletin du Comité flamand de France* 88 (1292); Walter: HStP, I, no. 721, p. 507 (1285).

[42] See on this text below.   [43] Cassel, no. 11, p. 208 (1276).

[44] Cassel, no. 14, p. 209 (1276); no. 23, p. 212; no. 32, pp. 216–7 (1288).

[45] J. Haigneré, *Les Chartes de Saint-Bertin, d'après le grand cartulaire de Dom Ch.-J. Dewitte* (Saint-Omer, 1886–99), II, no. 1237, pp. 157–8; no. 1236, pp. 155–6 (1282). In

Flanders a spokesman can easily be found, because the leading judge does not only lead his colleagues during the proceedings, but also in our documentation. Nevertheless, this is not yet proven to be an unbreakable rule and it is best always to corroborate this with other evidence. For example, a 1279 charter makes it highly likely that Christian of Wicres was a Lille spokesman, by putting him ahead of the other Lille judges.[46] That he belonged with the other leading judges is proven by the *Lois de Lille*, in which he is acting together with Pasquier Li Borgne and Giles of Linsselles as adviser of Robert Brunel,[47] and by a 1286 charter in which his advice is asked together with that of Walter of Douai.[48]

The two charters from the first half of the twelfth century confirm that the first place in the list of witnesses belongs to the spokesman. In 1122, both the count of Boulogne and Robert of Bethune are singled out and the latter is explicitly identified as a spokesman. Both their names are the first in the respective lists of judges. In the 1148 list the name of the spokesman, Anselm of Houdain, is not the first, but those preceding him were the young Baldwin, the designated heir to the county of Flanders and some high-ranking members of the clergy, although these persons had not sat in the court. However, of those who had, Anselm's name comes first. Although some caution is called for, it seems that already in the first half of the twelfth century it was not unusual in Flemish charters to award the first place in the list of the judges to the spokesman. Unfortunately, it is not always that easy. It seems likely that in the charters of neighbouring Hainaut this practice was also followed,[49] but it was certainly not always so in Germany.[50]

Leading judges not explicitly identified as spokesmen: the earliest law reports on the Continent

The origin of the oldest part of the Lois de Lille in the private notes of the Lille judges

If one wants to identify more spokesmen, it is helpful to look more closely at the *Lois de Lille*, the text that was the starting point of this article. It is a strange mixture of legal rules and case law, containing reports and abstracts

these charters Philip was a judge in Walter of Reninge's feudal court and thus Walter's man, but this did not bar him from preceding his lord in the castellany court.

[46] E. Gachet, 'Le Couvent de l'Abbiette à Lille' (1852) 64 *Messager des sciences historiques, des arts et de la bibliographie de Belgique* 56–7 (1279).

[47] Lille, no. 304, pp. 194–5 (1298).   [48] HStP, I, no. 727, pp. 510–12.

[49] De Reiffenberg, *Monuments*, I, no. 45, pp. 372–3 (1281).

[50] A detailed study of this is in preparation.

of cases from 1283 until 1407. Five later manuscripts have been preserved, of which only one (E) is a copy of another surviving manuscript. This still leaves four (A, B, C and D) and none of these can be considered closer to the original text than the others.[51] In fact, at first there were several texts and these have then been brought together, separated, amended and abridged by different authors in different ways. The upshot is such a confusion that the editor, Monier, initially put all four manuscripts on an equal footing.[52] The chaotic origins of the texts also mean that, to us at least, there seems to be no logic in their composition. Some cases, or legal rules derived from them, are found in all four manuscripts,[53] some are not, and sometimes one manuscript is our only source.[54] Moreover manuscripts which agree with one other manuscript on one point, may not on another.[55] Manuscripts may contain a very elaborate report of a case with the parties' arguments, the court's decision and remarks by later compilers of the *Lois de Lille*[56] or just a mere abstract, the legal rule but not the original case.[57] One manuscript might have a short discussion for one case, whereas another discusses it in detail.[58] Even if two manuscripts are alike in the amount of attention they pay to a certain case, they may focus on different aspects; for example one report may concentrate on a problem concerning witnesses and another on the arguments of the parties.[59] The impression of shoddy workmanship is greatest when a manuscript contains several reports of the same case,[60] or when the text contradicts itself and solves the same legal problem in different ways.[61]

---

[51] Heirbaut, 'Oldest part', p. 140.   [52] Monier, *Lois*, pp. 14–16.

[53] e.g. Lille, no. 1, p. 19 (1286).

[54] e.g. Lille, no. 304–22, pp. 194–203 have only been preserved in manuscript C.

[55] Manuscripts B and D have the same content most of the time, but there are exceptions (see below). The order of the texts in B and D may also vary in significant ways: e.g. Lille, no. 298 (pp. 188–9) (1296) and no. 219 (pp. 139–41) (1297) relate to two proceedings concerning the same case. Manuscript D tries to show this and so has the two reports following one another, whereas in manuscript B they have been placed far apart.

[56] e.g. Lille, no. 219, pp. 139–41 (1297); no. 298, pp. 188–9 (1296); no. 237, pp. 151–3 (1297).

[57] e.g. Lille, no. 7, p. 22 (end of the thirteenth century; date based on its place in manuscript A).

[58] e.g. manuscript C contains an extensive report of a case (Lille, no. 304, pp. 194–5 (1298)), whereas the others only have an abstract of it (Lille, no. 52, pp. 49–50).

[59] e.g. Lille, no. 121, pp. 78–9 (1298) and the report of the same case edited in the note there.

[60] e.g. manuscript A contains two versions of a 1305 case (Lille, no. 42, pp. 43–4; no. 118, p. 77). The same is probably also true for no. 53 (p. 50) and no. 219 (pp. 139–41) (1297) in manuscripts B and D, which also contain the report of another proceeding related to this one (no. 298, pp. 188–9) (1296).

[61] e.g. the contradictions between Lille, no. 16, pp. 27–8; no. 20, p. 30; and no. 85, p. 62.

The editor of the *Lois de Lille*, Monier, could not really name any text like it, but in a footnote he tentatively suggested that they might be compared to the Year Books,[62] although he did not elaborate upon this, in all likelihood because the Year Books were largely unknown to him.[63] His hesitation is justified. True, the *Lois de Lille*, at times, share with the Year Books an interest in pleading strategies and arguments, in the way the judgment had come to be produced[64] ('the possible moves in the recondite games of legal chess played by pleaders in an open court' as Baker calls them),[65] rather than in the legal rule it expressed. Moreover, the earliest English law reports[66] were as chaotic, varied and creative as the *Lois de Lille*.[67] Yet one cannot deny the differences since in many cases the *Lois* do not contain a report of the court's proceedings but an abstract of its judgment and real verbatim reports are rare and short.[68]

It would be better to make another comparison, not with the Year Books, but with their predecessors. The contradictions of the *Lois de Lille* already indicate that it was composed of several chronological layers, each stating the law as it was at that time, hence in conflict with earlier or later legal rules. Its oldest stratum covers the years from 1283 until 1308/ 1314 and it is the one which contains the names of the Lille spokesmen around 1300. In fact, these leading judges were the originators of this oldest part. There was no formal training in local law available to them, but the courtroom could be their school. For their own information or the training of their successors some of them took notes and out of these private notes, which were copied and continued by friends and pupils, grew the texts which we now know as the *Lois de Lille*. The link between the spokesmen and the *Lois de Lille* explains why these also contain lawsuits in which these judges themselves or their family members were involved. Moreover, it is even possible to discover which judges took the notes which resulted in the *Lois de Lille* and to link them to the

---

[62] Monier, *Lois*, p. 15, n. 2.

[63] He seems to have been unaware of the existence of J. Lambert, *Les Year Books de langue française* (Paris, 1928), a book in his own language, which might have given him valuable insights; cf. T. Plucknett, *A Concise History of the Common Law* (London, 1956), p. 268, n. 2.

[64] See e.g. Lille, no. 235, pp. 148–50 (1300); no. 236, pp. 150–1 (1291) where several remarks have been added to the report.

[65] J. H. Baker, *An Introduction to English Legal History* (London, 2002), p. 179.

[66] Edited in P. Brand, *The Earliest English Law Reports*, Selden Society, vols. 111–12 and 122–3 (1996–2007).

[67] P. Brand, *Observing and Recording the Medieval Bar and Bench at Work: The origins of law reporting in England*, Selden Society lecture 1998 (London, 1999).

[68] See e.g. Lille, no. 305, pp. 195–6.

manuscripts we now have. Manuscript A contains nothing useful, but manuscript C can be linked to Pasquier Li Borgne and manuscripts B and D to Robert Brunel and Peter of Sainghin. This does not mean that they wrote these manuscripts, for all three contain a lot of later material. It does not even mean that all of their notes (or at least the notes of someone close to them) were used by the compilers of these three manuscripts. It means only that in manuscript C more is preserved of Pasquier's notes, and in manuscripts B and D more of Robert's and Peter's.[69]

Similarities between the Lois de Lille and the forerunners of the law reports in England

Any comparison with English material should not be made with the later *Lois de Lille*, but with the notes of Pasquier and of Robert and Peter. In that case, their closest counterpart are the first English experiments from the 1250s and later of putting to parchment what happened in court.[70] In England too, we have notes taken by lawyers, which could contain anything from mere dicta of judges to longer reports,[71] and which can be seen as the forerunners of the law reports. In fact, one is struck by the similarities between the *Lois de Lille* and *Brevia Placitata* or *Casus Placitorum* and the excellent studies English scholars have made of texts like these and the earliest English law reports can help to explain some hitherto unresolved puzzles. Originally, in England reports were written down in court on small slips of parchments, which were then preserved in bags and only later were they copied into books.[72] Given this, it is easy to see why in Lille some years are better documented than others (some pieces of parchment simply got lost), though the Franco-Flemish war

---

[69] Heirbaut, 'Oldest part', 146–8.

[70] J. H. Baker, 'Case-law in Medieval England' in J. H. Baker, *The Common Law Tradition: Lawyers, books and the law* (London, 2000) (first published in J. H. Baker (ed.), *Judicial Records, Law Reports, and the Growth of Case Law* (Berlin, 1989), pp. 136–8). It may be useful here to stress that the following is not about records – 'kept by the court as an official memorial of what it has done' (J. H. Baker, 'Case-law in England and Continental Europe' in Baker, *Common Law Tradition* (first published in Baker, *Judicial Records*, p. 110) – but about reports – 'an account (usually unofficial) of how a case was argued or what motivated a decision' (*ibid.*).

[71] Baker, 'Case-law in Medieval England', p. 138.

[72] W. Dunham, *Casus Placitorum and Reports of Cases in the King's Courts, 1272–1278*, Selden Society, vol. 69 (1952), pp. xlviii–lv. Dunham edited some of these slips of parchment in Appendix III to his introduction (*ibid.*, pp. xc–xciv).

around 1300 also played a role.[73] If the notes came out of the bag as unordered as they went in, it is no wonder that the text made with them was so chaotic.[74] Another interesting element suggested by what is known of early English law reporting is the existence of a lot of mutual assistance and co-operation between the note-takers and their successors. The circulation of several slips of parchment containing different accounts of the same case also help to explain the later chaos and variety.[75] This is also evident in Lille, where the notes of Robert Brunel and Peter of Sainghin were already being brought together at an early date, maybe even in 1311–14 by Peter of Sainghin himself.[76] (One should not overestimate the difficulty of this, as the whole operation may have amounted to nothing more than Peter asking Robert's heir for his father's bag of notes and shaking it out into his own bag.)

Of course, the similarities should not make us forget the differences. For example, in Lille the knights Peter of Sainghin and Robert Brunel did not exchange notes with their colleague Pasquier Li Borgne who, being a burgess of the city, was their social inferior.[77] Moreover, texts like *Brevia Placitata* and *Casus Placitorum* already belonged more to the classroom than to the courtroom.[78] Yet, the main differences with the *Lois de Lille* came to be only later. In England the notes evolved into a continuous, standardised series of verbatim reports,[79] whereas the *Lois de Lille* took off in a completely different direction. From reports of cases and other notes the Lille text gradually became a book of legal rules. Because the focus was on fixed rules and not on ever-changing arguments and strategies, there was no need of a continuous series of reports. In fact, after a certain period of time, when most of the rules had been fixed, there was not much need for any report of events in court at all. Hence, the oldest group of cases in the *Lois de Lille* is the largest and the more recent groups 2, 3 and 4 in the *Lois de Lille* are each smaller than their

---

[73] During the fighting the Lille court was not in session (cf. Lille, no. 55, p. 51); no. 306, p. 196 (1303): 'a che jour estoit were et ly plet souspendut').

[74] Dunham, *Casus Placitorum*, pp. xxx–xxxii.   [75] *Ibid.*, p. lii.

[76] Heirbaut, 'Oldest part', pp. 147–8.   [77] *Ibid.*

[78] P. Brand, 'Courtroom and schoolroom: The education of lawyers in England prior to 1400' in *The Making of the Common Law* (first published in (1986) 60 *Historical Research* 147); P. Brand, 'Legal education in England before the Inns of Court' and J. Beckerman, 'Law-writing and law-teaching: Treatise evidence of the formal teaching of English law in the late thirteenth century' in J. Bush and A. Wijffels (eds.), *Learning the Law: Teaching and transmission of law in England, 1150–1900* (London, 1999).

[79] This all happened rather fast, with already a breakthrough of larger-scale law reporting in 1291 (Brand, *Observing and Recording*, p. 16).

predecessor.[80] The evolution from reports to rules was not completely achieved in the *Lois de Lille*, as it still contains some more elaborate texts. In one case, we can even see the process of abridgement at work. Manuscript A sometimes has only the abstract of a case which is extensively reported in the other manuscripts,[81] but in nos. 42 and 118 manuscript A has both an abstract and a longer report, whereas the other manuscripts only have the longer report.[82] The compiler of A must have forgotten that he already had the abstract and no longer needed the longer text.

Hidden Continental law reports as possible sources for the identification of judges as spokesmen

The evolution from reports and other extensive notes to abstracts was not unique to Lille. For example, the *Loy et jugemens des hommes de le baillie de Cassel* contains reports of cases, *dicta* of judges, legislation and customs from the feudal castellany court of Cassel for six years between 1276 and 1292.[83] That the text deals only with six years indicates that it also started as notes written by one of the judges on slips of parchment. For most years these were lost, though their existence may be presumed.[84] Their loss was of no great concern at the time because there is a second text, the *Statut ordené en l'enqueste faite à Cassel* of 1324,[85] which contains legal rules only. However, many of these have their origin in cases and ordinances of the period 1276–92.[86] In one generation these had been turned into abstract legal rules and consequently the original documentation, the first slips of parchment, could be discarded. (One can only wonder why some of them were not.) If we had only the Cassel *Statut* and not the Cassel *Loy*, we would have remained unaware of its origins in case law and legislation, and, likewise, if we had for Lille only the final result of the evolution from reports

---

[80] Heirbaut, 'Oldest part', pp. 142–3.

[81] Lille, no. 52, pp. 49–50 is a shorter version of no. 304, pp. 194–5 (1298).

[82] Lille, no. 42, pp. 43–4; no. 118, p. 77 (1305).

[83] Edited in E. de Coussemaker, 'Sources du droit public et coutumier de la Flandre maritime' (1873) 11 *Annales du comité flamand de France* 204–19.

[84] Cf. references to earlier decisions in *Cassel Loy*, no. 6, p. 206; no. 9, p. 207; no. 21, p. 212 (1280); nos. 36–9, p. 218 (1289); no. 41, p. 218 (1291). That in these cases there was a text can be proven by a comparison with the 1324 text (see n. 86, below).

[85] De Coussemaker, 'Sources du droit public', pp. 220–34.

[86] e.g. *Cassel Statut*, no. 18, p. 223 was based on an ordinance (*Cassel Loy*, no. 34, pp. 217–18 (1289)) and no. 3, p. 221 on case law (more specifically *Cassel Loy*, no. 2, p. 204 (1276)), as also no. 52, p. 231 (more specifically, *Cassel Loy*, no. 40, p. 218 (1291)) and no. 61, pp. 232–3) (more specifically *Cassel Loy*, no. 33, p. 217 (1288)).

of cases to abstract legal rules. In how many other cases do we now have only the end product?[87]

A new study of medieval law texts on the Continent is needed, because, if, as has been shown for Lille and as seems likely for Cassel, there is a link between some embryonic law reports (some of which may, at first sight, look like mere collections of legal rules) and spokesmen, any study of the latter is likely to teach us more about the former. The reverse is also true. A study of spokesmen will lead us to a new appraisal of the infancy of law reporting not only on the Continent, but also in England. In the light of what happened in Lille and Cassel in the last quarter of the thirteenth century, England does not seem to be that much ahead of North-western Europe as far as the first steps into law reporting are concerned – only a few decades and not more than a century later as has been assumed.[88] (One has to admit, though, that the infancy of law reporting lasted for much longer on the other side of the Channel.)[89] The opinion of this author is that discoveries may still be made, because texts like the *Lois de Lille* or the Cassel *Loy* have been neglected by historians who prefer more polished, more finished texts like Beaumanoir's, whereas their raw predecessors may contain more interesting data, although it is much harder to unearth them.

Conclusion: a general study of the spokesmen as leading judges of customary law is needed

The spokesmen were the makers of customary law. A general study of these leading judges of customary law should therefore be undertaken, or legal historians are likely to miss certain crucial elements. For example, how can one evaluate the role and importance of the few great names of customary law we have, like Beaumanoir and Eike von Repgow, if we ignore their 'lesser' brethren? This may lead us to overestimate their contacts with learned law, because we have looked at them from that angle and neglected their normal environment.[90]

A study of the spokesmen as leading judges of customary law can also help us to understand it better. For example, for northern France and the southern Netherlands several clusters of customs have been identified,

---

[87] See for further examples, Heirbaut, 'Oldest part', pp. 150–1.

[88] Baker, 'Case-law in Medieval England', pp. 110–12.

[89] Cf. J. Hilaire and C. Bloch, 'Connaissances des décisions de justice et origine de la jurisprudence' in Baker, *Judicial Records*.

[90] This does not mean that such studies should not be made. In fact, they are necessary, but they should not be the only ones.

but explanations for the existence of these groups have not always been satisfactory.[91] Looking at the influence of spokesmen who were active in several courts may be useful here. For example, at the end of the thirteenth century a new rule appeared in the law of inheritance in Artois and Lille: henceforth the eldest son had to grant a fifth of his fief to his younger siblings.[92] It is strange that these regions suddenly shared a new rule, the more so when one takes into account the fact that that they are on either side of the the border between Flanders and Artois. What united these territories was the person of Robert Brunel, an Artois lord and a Lille spokesman and one can in fact prove that he brought the new rule from Artois to Lille.[93] The spokesmen, as leading judges, clearly contributed to the spread of legal rules from one region to another. Moreover, within a certain region, like the Lille castellany, spokesmen of the higher court, the castellany court, were also active in lower courts, which ensured that the rules of the former would seep into the jurisprudence of the latter.[94] Of course, the practice of asking the advice of the higher court, the 'head' court, also contributed to that, but one can only wonder in how many cases this was not necessary because the great judge from the higher court was already present in the lower one. In short, both the 'migration' of legal rules from one region to another and homogeneity within a region may, in part, be explained by the activity of spokesmen.

Given these and other new insights to which a study of the spokesmen and their embryonic law reports can lead us, the conclusion of this chapter can only be that a general search for these forgotten leading judges of customary law is long overdue.

---

[91] For a survey, see P. Godding, *Le Droit privé dans les Pays-Bas méridionaux du 12e au 18e siècle* (Brussels, 1987), pp. 318–21.

[92] Heirbaut, *Lenen en familie*, pp. 81, 85.

[93] D. Heirbaut, 'Who were the makers of customary law in medieval Europe? Some answers based on sources about the spokesmen of the Flemish feudal courts' (2007) 75 *Tijds. Rgeschied.* 265.

[94] Of course, the practice of asking the advice of a higher court also contributed to this.

11

Superior courts in early-modern France, England and the Holy Roman Empire

ULRIKE MUESSIG

Introduction

The issue: supreme jurisdiction as a driving force for early-modern monarchies

In the registers of the Parlement de Paris there is the following statement in an entry dated 5 December 1556: 'la souveraineté est si étroitement conjointe avec la justice que séparée elle perdrait son nom et serait un corps sans âme'.[1] While the pre-Bodinian concept of sovereignty is not my topic the absence of any abstract conception of comprehensive royal power should be noted here. Accordingly, there is no entry for the word *souveraineté* in the 1549 French–Latin dictionary. The adjective *souverain*, however, is explained as the final jurisdiction of a *parlement*.[2] This concept of final jurisdiction as sovereign jurisdiction is the central issue of my chapter. Does the development of a supreme jurisdiction correspond to success in the process of early-modern state-building?

Three considerations guide us to this central issue: (a) for the effective administration of justice one needs a strong power to provide and secure access to the courts; (b) law itself is not at the disposal of the sovereign – however as the provision of justice is a central duty of the ruler, royal jurisdiction may have been an appropriate way to influence the

---

[1] Archives Nationales, X^{IA} 1583, 5 Décembre 1556.

[2] 'Les cours souveraines: Curiae jurisdictionis ultim, jurisdictionis summae – jugement souverain, comme par arrest d'une cour de parlement : res primum et ultimum iudicata – par main souveraine: pro iure maioris imperii'; cited in D. Klippel, 'Staat und Souveränität VI-VIII' in O. Brunner *et al.* (eds.), *Geschichtliche Grundbegriffe, Lexikon zur politisch-sozialen Sprache in Deutschland* (Stuttgart, 1990), VI, p. 34; cf. also S. Dauchy, 'Introduction historique' in R. van Caenegem, *Les Arrêts et jugés du Parlement de Paris sur appels flamands* (Brussels, 2002), III, p. 135.

development of law; (c) feudal and ecclesiastical courts are natural rivals to royal courts and therefore the genesis of a supreme jurisdiction emerges alongside the struggle between monarchic centralism and feudal particularism.

This last assumption motivates the choice for historical comparison of the systems of France, England and the Holy Roman Empire. The history of the courts in France begins with a variety of jurisdictions, that of the English courts is characterised by early centralisation and the development of a supreme jurisdiction in the Holy Roman Empire was weakened *ab initio* by the competition between the *Reichsgerichte* (imperial courts) – that is, between the *Reichskammergericht* (the Imperial Chamber Court) and the *Reichshofrat* (the Aulic Council) and by the number of privileges against appeal (*privilegia de non appellando*) granted to all the major territories of the empire.

Method and structure

A comparative history of European superior courts is a methodological challenge. Even the term 'supreme court' does not have a fixed or universally agreed meaning. Therefore one has to define the basis of comparison very carefully, taking into account the fact that some scholars plead for the uniqueness,[3] or even the incomparability,[4] of certain judicial institutions. Among the courts to be considered here are the French *parlements* and the jurisdiction in cassation of the *Conseil du Roi privé*; the English common law courts and the House of Lords; as well as the Imperial Chamber Court (*Reichskammergericht*) and the Aulic Council (*Reichshofrat*) at the imperial level, and the highest appellate courts (*Oberappellationsgerichte*) at the territorial level. There are considerable differences in respect of personnel (the numbers of judges; the criteria for the admission of lawyers), structure (the hierarchy of courts) and functions. Whereas the *Parlement de Paris* was the final court of appeal within its jurisdiction, the English common law did not adopt the practice of appeals from Romano-canonical law, and the appeal jurisdiction of the *Reichsgerichte* was weakened by the already mentioned *privilegia de non appellando*.

---

[3] G. Zeller, *Les Institutions de la France au XVIe siècle*, 2nd edn (Paris, 1987), p. 147; J.-P. Royer, *Histoire de la justice en France*, 2nd edn (Paris, 1996), p. 47.
[4] Cf. J. F. Baldwin, *The King's Council* (Oxford, 1913), pp. 6 *et seq.*

What all supreme courts have in common is their origin in the *curia regis*. Their emergence from the *curia regis* provides the supreme courts with a kind of superior authority, which is realised through control of inferior courts or by the suppression of feudal and ecclesiastical courts. This superiority in turn encourages the emergence of judge-made law, which subsequently requires professionals trained to handle it. Professional and learned judges tend to be more self-confident, even against the monarch as fountain of justice. And so, professionalisation in the judiciary fosters a sort of rivalry between the supreme courts and the monarch.

Superior courts in comparison

France

Parlements, in particular the *Parlement de Paris*, and their control of other courts

The *Parlement de Paris* originated between 1254 and 1260 during the reign of Louis IX, who detached court sittings (*grand assises*), which were institutionalised as a 'law council', out of the *section judiciaire* of his *curia regis*. The first registers of 1254 ('*Olim*') prove that these law court sessions no longer followed the royal court, but were held independently of the king's presence.[5]

Added to its initial competence as a court of peers of first instance, as early as the thirteenth century, was its function as a general court of appeal, which resulted in the *Parlement de Paris* becoming a court of justice for the whole realm.[6] At the same time, innumerable '*Ordonnances*' were enacted, laying down detailed rules for the organisation and procedure of the *Parlement*.[7]

Recourse to appeal was the exception in the feudal monarchy. It was only available in cases of default of justice (*appel de défaute de droit*) or wrongful judgment (*appel de faux jugement*).[8] With the reception of the learned law and replacement of the monarchy's feudal administrative structures, a hierarchy of courts was established, so that a case would be

---

[5] G. Ducoudray, *Les Origines du Parlement de Paris* (1902), I, pp. 24, 44.

[6] Ducoudray, *Les Origines du Parlement de Paris*, p. 45; M. Fournier, *Essai sur l'histoire du droit d'appel* (Paris, 1881), p. 187.

[7] See for details Ducoudray, *Les Origines du Parlement de Paris*, pp. 65 *et seq.*

[8] Royer, *Histoire de la justice en France*, p. 39; Fournier, *Essai sur l'histoire du droit d'appel*, pp. 140 *et seq.*

taken by the *prévótes*, then by the *baillages* or *sénéchaussés* and finally by the *parlements*. This did not take the form of a revolution but of a synthesis of local customary law and Romano-canonical law.[9] As a result, by the fourteenth century at the latest, royal jurisdiction dominated, and feudal *justice seigneuriale* and ecclesiastical jurisdiction as *justice concédée* both became subordinate to royal jurisdiction.[10]

The centre of French supreme jurisdiction remained the *Parlement de Paris*. Even after new *parlements* had been established, it claimed supremacy as the *cour capitale et souveraine du royaume*, first and foremost because its jurisdictional area covered half of France.[11]

Legal profession and judge-made law

The replacement of feudal judges by officials of the royal court went hand in hand with the growing professionalism of those 'councillors' (*maîtres*).[12] In the middle of the fifteenth century, *parlementaires* (like all other royal officials) were declared irremovable from their office. At the same time, the *Parlement* itself was clearly organised by the *Ordonnance ou Établissements pour la reformation de la justice* of *Montils-les-Tours*, of 15 April 1453,[13] which remained in force until 1771. The appointment of new judges through co-option provided the foundation for the distinctive political assertiveness of the *Parlement*. This was the origin of a

---

[9] S. Dauchy, 'Cours souveraines et genèse de l'état. Le Parlement de Paris' in B. Diestelkamp (ed.), *Oberste Gerichtsbarkeit und Zentrale Gewalt* (Köln, 1999), p. 71; Fournier, *Essai sur l'histoire du droit d'appel*, p. 178.

[10] B. Basdevant-Gaudemet and J. Gaudemet, *Introduction historique au droit* (Paris, 2000), pp. 175 et seq., 235; J. H. Shennan, *The Parlement of Paris* (London, 1968), p. 82.

[11] F. Olivier-Martin, *Histoire du droit français des origines à 1815*, 2nd edn (Paris, 1951), p. 538: 'le plus ancien de tous et celui qui a toujours joué le rôle le plus important'. See also J. Brissaud, *Cours d'histoire générale du droit français public et privé à l'usage des étudiants en licence et en doctorat* (Paris, 1904), I, p. 880. The supremacy of the *parlement* of Paris was one of prestige. In theory each of the different *parlements* was one and the same institution. How far the other *parlements* became eventually subject to the jurisdiction of the *parlement* of Paris is still an open question.

[12] A.-É. Lair, *Des hautes cours politiques en France et à l'étranger et de la mise en accusation du Président de la République et des ministres, étude de droit constitutionnel et d'histoire politique* (Paris, 1889), p. 73. Cf. the *Ordonnance* of 1364 (*Ordonnance contenant réglement sur l'administration de la justice aux requêtes du palais, les devoirs des magistrats, ceux des advocats et des sergens, Novembre 1364*), cited in A. J. Leger Jourdan *et al.* (ed.), *Recueil général des anciennes lois françaises depuis l'an 420 jusqu'à la révolution de 1789*, 29 vols. (Paris, 1821–1833), V, pp. 224 et seq. J. P. Dawson, *A History of Law Judges* (Cambridge, MA, 1960), pp. 39–94

[13] *Ordonnance ou Établissements pour la réformation de la justice, Montil-les-Tours*, Apr. 1453: *Recueil général des anciennes lois françaises*, IX, pp. 202 et seq.

stable social class of judges (*gens du Parlement, noblesse de robe*) with extensive privileges, a clearly defined process of professional formation and career structure (study at the Parisian colleges, the study of canon law in Paris, the study of Roman law in Orléans), a common way of life and shared culture, and a closely interwoven social network.

Judges were recruited from advocates at the *parlements*,[14] who had gained in number and importance during the thirteenth century due to the control over the admission of advocates. Professional qualifications for judges and advocates were loosely formulated. An *ordonnance touchant les avocats* of 1344 required only the selection of suitable candidates and the rejection of inexperienced ones.[15] So, complaints about ignorant advocates found in fifteenth-century sources should not surprise us. Nor should the recommendations of the *Ordonnance des parlements de Paris* cause any surprise. They were, for one thing, not to accept any appointment without thorough prior practical experience and, for another, to learn the *stilus curiae* and the *modus advocandi* of more experienced advocates.[16] It is impossible to say to what degree this resulted in an institutionalised practical training. A university education in Romano-canonical law for judges as well as for advocates did not exist before modern times.[17] However, a chronological (and probably also a causative) connection can be seen between the development of a distinct legal profession and the evolution of supreme jurisdiction. It was the *Parlement de Paris* that brought about the monopoly of representation

---

[14] Zeller, *Les Institutions de la France au XVIe siècle*, p. 152.

[15] Art. 1: 'Ponantur in scriptis nomina advocatorum; deinde, rejectis non peritis, eligantur ad hoc officium idonei et sufficientes.' Cited in *Recueil général des anciennes lois françaises*, IV, p. 506.

[16] 'Quia circa advocationis officium facti experientia, et observantia stili curiae multum prodest, advocati, qui de novo ad hujusmodi officium, per curiam sunt recepti, abstinere debent, propter eorum honorem, et dampnum quod partibus propter eorum forsitan negligentiam provenire posset, ne ex abrepto et imprudenter advocationis officium exerceant; sed per tempus sufficiens advocatos antiquos, et expertos audiant diligenter, ut sic de stilo curiae, et advocandi modo primitus informati, suum patrocinium praestare, et advocationis officium laudabiliter, et utiliter possint et valeant exercere': *Recueil général des anciennes lois françaises*, IV, p. 508.

[17] Dauchy, 'Cours souveraines et genèse de l'état. Le Parlement de Paris', pp. 45, 59 *et seq.*, unfortunately provides no evidence. The earliest order touching the subject I have found is in the *Ordonnance sur l'administration de la justice en Provence* of 1535, ch. III [IIII is meant], art. 1: 'Premièrement avons inhibé et défendu, inhibons et défendons à tous graduez et advocats, d'eux ingérer de postuler ne patrociner en icelle nostre dite cour de parlement, qu'ils ne soient receux en icelle, et qu'ils ayent presté le serment en tel cas pertinant, et soient escrits en la matricule: et qu'ils ne soient receux s'ils ne sont graduez in altero jurium.' *Recueil général des anciennes lois françaises*, XII, p. 457).

by properly admitted and accredited advocates and so the need for advocates to be familiar with the *stilus curiae* and the *modus advocandi*.

The authority of the *parlements* promoted the development of private law reports, the first of which are the *Quaestiones* by Jean Lecoq (also Le Coq) of the fourteenth century.[18] In the fifteenth century there are only a few relevant collections,[19] but by the sixteenth century a great number of *recueils d'arrêts* (collections of judgments) were in circulation.[20] Because judgments of the *parlements* did not contain any reasons,[21] these *recueils* mostly record only the legal arguments of the parties as understood by the author and, despite the term '*motifs*',[22] do not allow for the reconstruction of any of the judicial reasoning.[23] Because advocates used the *recueils* in preparing for actual cases, they are also called sources of law (*sources de droit*).[24] It is hard to say to what extent these reports also influenced the judges themselves, lacking as they did the legal reasoning of the judges. Nevertheless, French experts do speak of a '*jurisprudence des arrêts*'.[25]

According to the unanimous opinion of modern scholars, official collections of judgments did not exist and excerpts from registers were issued solely for internal use by the court.[26] However, as my research in the French national archives has confirmed, almost all these excerpts

---

[18] See the introduction to du Breuil, *Stilus suprême curie parliament Parisiensis* (Paris, 1512).

[19] C. du Moulin, *Omnia quae extant opera ex variis librorum apothecis, in quibus latebant nunc primum eruta et simul typis commissa permultisque mendis, quibus sensim scatebant* (Paris, 1681), III, pp. 23 *et seq.*

[20] Dauchy, 'Cours souveraines et genèse de l'état. Le Parlement de Paris', pp. 68 *et seq.*

[21] Cf. T. Sauvel, 'Les Demandes de motifs adressées pas le conseil du roy aux cours souveraines' (1957) 35 *R.H.D.* 528–48.

[22] Cf. *Brillon dictionnaire* (1711), IV, p. 497, subject index 'Motifs', cited in F. Olivier-Martin, 'Notes d'audiences prises au Parlement de Paris, de 1384 à 1386, par un practicien anonyme' (1922) 1 *R.H.D.* 513, 517.

[23] S. Dauchy, 'Les Recueils privés de jurisprudence aux temps modernes' in A. Wijffels (ed.), *Case Law in the Making* (Berlin, 1997), I, p. 245 with further references; G. Walter, 'Frankreich, Rechtsprechungssammlungen' in H. Coing (ed.), *Handbuch der Quellen und Literatur der neuen europäischen Privatrechtsgeschichte* (München, 1976), II(2), pp. 1223 *et seq.*, 1239; J. P. Dawson, *The Oracles of the Law* (Ann Arbor, 1967), p. 298.

[24] Dauchy, 'Les Recueils privés de jurisprudence aux temps modernes', p. 246.

[25] Walter, 'Frankreich, Rechtsprechungssammlungen', pp. 1237 *et seq.*

[26] Their judgments were entered by the court's scribes (*greffiers*) into registers, which were kept by the court's chancery and were seemingly kept private. For the registers, see D. Jousse, *Traité de l'administration de la justice, ou l'on examine tout ce qui regarde la jurisdiction en général* (Paris, 1771), II, pp. 272 *et seq.*; Dawson, *Oracles of the Law*, pp. 327 *et seq.*

invoke the royal printing privilege. This suggests that the compilations were only printed after a royal official had read and authorised them. This renders problematic the allegedly internal character of the register excerpts. The printing privilege prohibits reprinting but only through public circulation did the excerpts run the risk of being reprinted.

Rivalry with the monarch

Rivalry in judicial matters As part of the *cour du roi*, the *Parlement de Paris* was not subject to any superior authority (hence the term *Cours souveraines*). Decisions that were seen as decisions made by the king himself could not be attacked using any of the regular remedies.[27] The only possible option was the *proposition d'erreur*, common from the Middle Ages onwards, which provided an opportunity to claim that errors had been committed, initially before the king or his council, and then before the *parlement* itself. A parallel development during the fifteenth century was the so-called *requête civile*, an informal remedy which by 1667 had superseded the *proposition d'erreur*.[28]

The monarch himself was able to intervene by means of evocation, bringing cases from the *parlement* to his own council, the *Conseil du roi* (*Conseil privé du roi*), and annulling decisions of *parlement* by virtue of the royal prerogative. The absence of detailed arrangements for cassation allowed a considerable scope for discretion, to the benefit of the *Conseil privé*. A first hint of the use of cassation can be found in art. 92 of the *Ordonnance de Blois* of 1579.[29] Errors of law made by the *parlements* could be attacked by cassation at the *Conseil privé du roi*. The *ordonnance* of 1667 (tit. I, art. 7)[30] allowed nullification of illegal decisions made by *parlements*, requiring, however, that the illegality of the

---

[27] S. Dauchy, *Les Voies de recours extraordinaires: proposition d'erreur et requête civile* (Paris, 1988), p. 17 with a reference to art. 12 of the 1303 *ordonnance*: 'volumus, santimus et etiam ordinamus quod judicata, arresta et sententie, que de nostre curia seu nostro communi consilio processerunt, teneantur et sine appellatione aliqua executioni mandentur.'

[28] Dauchy, *Les Voies de recours extraordinaires*, pp. 47 et seq. This was abolished by tit. XXXV, art. 42 of the 1667 ordonnance: *Recueil général des anciennes lois françaises*, XVIII, p. 180.

[29] 'Declarons que les arrêts de nos cours souveraines ne pourront estre cassez ne retractez, sinon par les voyes de droit, qui sont requeste civile et proposition d'erreur, et par la forme portée par nos ordonnances, ni l'exécution d'iceux arrests suspenduë ou retardée sur simple requeste à nous presentée en nostre conseil privé': *Recueil général des anciennes lois françaises*, XIV p. 404.

[30] *Recueil général des anciennes lois françaises*, XVIII p. 106.

contested decision be evident.[31] The consequence was the subordination
of *parlements* to the royal council, as sought by Louis XIV.[32]

Rivalry in respect of political issues   A further field of rivalry between
parlements and the monarch was legislation. Having originated in the
advisory circle of the *curia Regis*, the *Parlement de Paris* demanded
control of royal legislation. *Ordonnances* and *edits* were valid only if,
and insofar as, they had been registered and published by the *Parlement
de Paris*, and for the provinces by the other *parlements*. This developed
into the right to review as yet unregistered royal decrees and, if necessary,
to remonstrate against them.[33] This right to remonstrate before registry
(*droit de remonstrance avant l'enregistrement*)[34] grew into a political
right of control to be exercised against royal legislation, which at the
peak of the *parlements*' resistance on the eve of the French Revolution
escalated into a refusal to register and the obstruction of royal legislation,
turning the supreme courts into the strongest opponents of the Crown
during the eighteenth century.

On the other hand, the monarch was able to order the registration of
decrees during a *lit de justice*, namely a session held in his presence
(literally, a 'bed of justice').[35] Although the term *lit de justice* was
common in the Middle Ages,[36] the enforcement of royal legislation at
such sessions is a phenomenon of the early-modern period. During the
reign of François I (1494–1547) the *lit de justice* was extended to become

---

[31] Tit. I, art. 8: *Recueil général des anciennes lois françaises*, XVIII p. 106. See also G. Jugnot,
Histoire de la justice française (Paris, 1995), p. 49.

[32] *Recueil général des anciennes lois françaises*, XVII pp. 403 *et seq*. See also A. N.
Hamscher, *The Conseil Privé and the Parlements in the Age of Louis XIV: A study in
French absolutism* (Philadelphia, 1987), p. 21.

[33] See A. Grün, 'Notice sur les archives du Parlement de Paris' in E. Boutaric (ed.), *Actes du
Parlement de Paris* (Paris, 1863), I, pp. clxiii–clxv. The phrasing in Olivier-Martin,
Histoire du droit français des origines à 1815, pp. 541 *et seq*., esp. p. 544, suggests that
the sending of the *Ordonnances* to all *cours souveraines* with the goal of registration of
royal decrees could have taken place. However, Olivier-Martin does not give examples.

[34] 'D'ordinaire, avant de modifier la loi qui lui était envoyée à l'enregistrement et surtout
avant de refuser de l'enregistrer, le Parlement addressait au Roi des remontrances pour le
supplier de retirer son édit ou d'y faire les changements nécessaires. C'était, à propre-
ment parler, le seul cas où les remontrances fussent permises aux cours souveraines':
J. Flammermont, *Remontrances du Parlement de Paris au XVIIIe siècle*, I: *1715–1753*
(Paris, 1888), p. xxxvii.

[35] Basdevant-Gaudemet and Gaudemet, *Introduction historique au droit*, p. 294.

[36] Cf. S. Hanley, *The Lit de Justice of the Kings of France* (Princeton, 1983), pp. 14 *et seq*.

a specific demonstration of royal power,[37] and from the middle of the sixteenth century, these sittings were increasingly used to carry through royal decrees against the opposition of the *parlements*.[38]

Already by then resistance had begun to stir among the members of the *parlements*, but without much success. Resistance to the forced registration of tax laws in 1648 caused the most serious governmental crisis of the seventeenth century (the so-called *Fronde*), but resulted only in the abolition of the right to remonstrate (1667, 1673), which finally also led to the abolition of the *lit de justice*.[39]

All in all, remonstrations hardly ever had any substantial consequences.[40] An author expressing the monarchical viewpoint minimised the significance of the requirement of registration as a mere formality: 'Leur enregistrement dans les cours, à qui l'exécution est confiée, n'ajoute rien au pouvoir du législateur; c'en est seulement la promulgation et un acte d'obéissance indispensable dont les cours doivent tenir et tiennent sans doute à l'honneur de donner l'exemple aux autres sujets.'[41] Also, the claims of the various presidents of the *parlements*, that the king was bound by the law, went unheard. The *parlements* were praised in the fourth chapter of Montesquieu's book *Esprit des Lois* as custodians of the state's constitutional laws (*dépôt de lois*),[42] which the monarch could neither change nor abolish. This estimation of *parlements* as constitutional courts (*conseils constitutionnels*) is hardly justified by the evidence cited.

---

[37] E. A. R. Brown and R. C. Famiglietti, *The Lit de Justice: Semantics, ceremonial, and the Parlement of Paris, 1300-1600* (Sigmaringen, 1994), p. 102. Hanley, *The Lit de Justice of the Kings of France*, pp. 48 et seq., considers the *lit de justice* to be a new constitutional institution, one which is not the same as the *lit de justice* of the Middle Ages. Brown, *The Lit de Justice*, p. 16, qualifies this, recognising a difference in meaning, but also attesting to an institutional continuity between the *lit de justice* of the Middle Ages and the early-modern period.

[38] Brown, *The Lit de Justice*, p. 103.

[39] Hanley, *The Lit de Justice of the Kings of France*, pp. 332, 335. N. Henshall, *The Myth of Absolutism: Change and continuity in early modern European monarchy* (London, 1992), p. 52, holds, however, that the removal of the right to remonstration in 1673 only affected *lettres patentes*, and not common *ordonnances* or *édits*. Also, with the reintroduction of the *lit de justice* under Louis XV (1715), compulsory registration was reintroduced at the same time.

[40] Royer, *Histoire de la justice en France*, p. 66.

[41] *Réponse du Régent du 2 juillet 1718*, in Flammermont, *Remontrances du Parlement de Paris au XVIIIe siècle*, I: *1715–1753*, p. 71.

[42] 'Il ne suffit pas qu'il y ait, dans une monarchie, des rangs intermédiaires; il faut encore un dépôt de lois', claims Montesquieu for the *parlements* (*De l'esprit des lois, oeuvres complètes*, ed. Roger Caillois (Paris, 1994), II, p. 249).

England

The common law courts and their control of other courts

Unlike the law of France and the other countries of the *ius commune* the common law of England did not include a right of appeal. Appeals in the Continental sense of the term were not established until the nineteenth century.[43] The *writ of error* (a procedure allowing the review of decided cases) has no more than a marginal similarity to the appeal. The *writ of error* led only to an examination of the record of a lower court; substantive legal matters could not be reviewed in this way.[44] A thorough legal review by means of an appeal was possible only in courts whose procedural law was influenced by the civil law (for example, for decisions of the ecclesiastical courts at the High Court of Delegates). In addition, a review of decisions made on the 'English side' of Chancery (namely the equitable jurisdiction)[45] was possible from the later seventeenth century in the House of Lords.[46] But 'motions in banc' (motions in arrest of judgment, motion for judgment *non obstante veredicto* and motions for a new trial) and the 'reservation of points of law' provided an opportunity for appeal within the central courts before a final decision was taken.[47]

The legal profession and judge-made law

As in France, the common law courts gave birth to a legal profession in England. Chronologically it is comparable to the professionalisation of councillors at the *Parlement* of Paris. The teaching of law is traceable from around 1280,[48] and the inns of court soon became the place where English common law was taught.

The concept of *stare decisis* as a legally binding rule belongs to modern times. The decisive judgment in *Mirehouse* v. *Rennell*[49] brings us to the

---

[43] Cf. J. H. Baker, *An Introduction to English Legal History*, 4th edn (London, 2002), pp. 141 *et seq.*

[44] *Ibid.*, p. 136; W. S. Holdsworth, *A History of English Law*, 7th edn (London, 1956; repr. 1971), I, pp. 362, 370.

[45] In contrast to the Latin side (Baker, *An Introduction to English Legal History*, pp. 100 *et seq.*).

[46] *Shirley* v. *Fagg* (1675) 6 State Tr. 1121; see Baker, *An Introduction to English Legal History*, p. 141. Appeals from the Chancery (English side) to the House of Lords were only recognised in the 1675 decision *Shirley* v. *Fagg*, *ibid.* Cf. Holdsworth, *A History of English Law*, p. 372.

[47] Baker, *An Introduction to English Legal History*, p. 139.   [48] *Ibid.*, p. 159.

[49] *Mirehouse* v. *Rennell* (1833) 1 Cl. & Fin. 527 at 546; 6 E.R. 1015, 1023 per Parke B. (later Lord Wensleydale). See further Lord Bingham, 'The judges: Active or passive' (2005

year 1833. The 'Abridgements', which emerged in the Tudor period, simplified the recourse to precedents and made it a more frequent occurrence.[50] Coke's Reports (1600–15) are often referred to as the origin of *stare decisis*,[51] but, in my opinion, Sir Edward Coke did not yet use the word 'precedent'as a technical term with its later meaning.[52]

Rivalry with the Crown

On legal matters   The rivalry between the common law courts and the English monarchy is characterised by a few peculiarities. On the one hand, the common law as established by the Westminster courts – and conceived as immemorial custom – possessed a unique legitimacy and presented a crucial counterbalance to the royal prerogative, which not even Stuart absolutism was able to override. On the other, the relatively small number of common law judges – particularly in comparison to the French *gens de robe* – led to a markedly elitist status for the judges (maintained to this day) which was reflected in a distinctive self-confidence on the part of the judges, even with regard to the Crown. John H. Baker notes that judges often adjudicated in cases against the Crown without having to fear any personal disadvantages.[53] However, I have myself found only one example: *Dimock's Case*.[54] Also the common reference to the aforementioned Coke, Lord Chief Justice and leader of the common law opposition to Stuart absolutism, cannot serve as a general model, because Coke's fellow judges yielded to all the

British Maccabaean Lecture, Cardiff), esp. at pp. 3–15: www.law.cf.ac.uk/publiclecture/transcripts/271005.pdf).

[50] S. Vogenauer, 'Zur Geschichte des Präjudizienrechts in England' (2006) 28 *Z.N.R.* 48, 57; C. K. Allen, *Law in the Making*, 7th edn (Oxford, 1964), pp. 203 *et seq.*, 380 *et seq.*; W. H. D. Winder, 'Precedent in equity' (1941) 57 *LQR* 246 *et seq.*

[51] e.g. H. J. Berman, 'The origins of historical jurisprudence: Coke, Selden, Hale' (1994) 103 *Yale L.J.* 1651–733.

[52] U. Müssig, art. 'Coke, Edward (1552–1634)' in *HRG*, 2nd edn (2006), I, supplement 4, cols. 871, 873.

[53] J. H. Baker, 'The superior courts in England, 1450–1800' in B. Diestelkamp (ed.), *Oberste Gerichtsbarkeit und Zentrale Gewalt* (Köln, 1999), p. 105, without any references. 'Decisions against the crown' are, in light of the maxim 'The king can do no wrong', probably not to be understood as applying where the king himself was party to the proceedings, but rather, only that the courts restricted his *officials'* sphere of action. For the maxim 'The king can do no wrong' see J. R. Greenberg, *'Our Grand Maxim of State, The King Can Do No Wrong'* (1991) 12 *H.P.T.* 209 *et seq.*; U. Müssig, 'Die englischen Verfassungskämpfe des 17. Jahrhunderts' in U. Müssig (ed.), *Konstitutionalismus und Verfassungskonflikt* (Tübingen, 2006), pp. 37 *et seq.*

[54] *Sir Edward Dimock's Case* (1606–7) Lane 60, 65; 145 E.R. 278, 302–3. Baker, *Introduction to English Legal History*, p. 135. Baker says there are lots of other examples but a statistical evaluation is required.

conditions demanded by James I. Additionally, judges of the royal courts were dismissable at will until the Act of Settlement, and until 1761 their commissions were subject to renewal on the accession of a new monarch, who might occasionally fail to reinstate ('discontinue') a disfavoured judge.[55]

The sovereignty of Parliament, based on the idea of Parliament as the highest common law court   The decisive factor in the relationship between the common law and the royal prerogative is the sovereignty of Parliament which was achieved in 1689; or to put it another way, Parliament's claim to possess the ultimate authority to decide on the public good was the key to resolving the constitutional controversies of the seventeenth century. In those struggles, Parliament never questioned the idea of political balance, never attempted to remove the royal veto in regard to legislation and never endeavoured to introduce a concept of sovereignty similar to Rousseau's *volonté générale*. The parliamentary bill itself represents rather the idea of political balance. An Act of Parliament served the weal of the king, and the weal of his subjects, the Commonwealth. Yet Parliament justified its claim to sovereignty primarily on its ultimate authority to decide on the public good. In accordance with Coke's conception of the common law as being based on reason and Locke's Natural Law theory the seventeenth-century English common law was widely perceived as a body of law providing the most natural and just solution to any question of public good. It was not the monarch's will that decided on the public good but the common law. This position motivated Parliament's claim to be the highest court of common law: 'The High Court of Parliament is . . . a court of judicature, enabled by the laws to adjudge and determine the rights and liberties of the kingdom, against such patents and grants of His Majesty as are prejudicial thereunto, although strengthened both by his personal command and by his Proclamation under the Great Seal',[56] in the words of the Declaration of the Houses in Defence of the Militia Ordinance of 6 June 1642. The concept of Parliament as a court of law is at the heart of the Parliament's claim to sovereignty which was achieved in 1689 by art.

---

[55] Baker, *Introduction to English Legal History*, p. 167; Dan Klerman and Paul G. Mahoney, 'The value of judicial independence: Evidence from eighteenth-century England' (2005) 7 *American Law & Economics Rev.* 1.

[56] S. R. Gardiner (ed.), *The Constitutional Documents of the Puritan Revolution 1625–1660*, 3rd edn (Oxford, 1906), no. 54, pp. 254, 255 *et seq.* Cf. also 'The votes of the Houses for raising an army of 12th July 1642', *ibid.*, no. 56, p. 261.

VIII of the Bill of Rights,[57] because the monarch could veto legislative acts, but he could not veto judgments.[58] Thus Blackstone's well-known comment on parliamentary sovereignty[59] is based on Coke's definition of the (absolute) jurisdiction of the High Court of Parliament.[60]

The Holy Roman Empire: superior courts

The *Reichskammergericht* (Imperial Chamber Court)

A supreme jurisdiction for the empire had its beginnings in the *Hoftag* (imperial Diet) held at Mainz in 1235. Emperor Frederick II created a *Reichshofgericht* as his personal court, over which the emperor himself presided with a body of *assessores* sitting in judgment.[61] This ceased to

---

[57] 'All which Their Majesties are contented and pleased shall be declared, enacted, and established by Authority of this present Parliament, and shall stand, remain and be the Law of this Realm for ever; and the same are by Their said Majesties, by and with the Advice and Consent of the Lords Spiritual and Temporal, and Commons, in Parliament assembled, and by the Authority of the same, declared, enacted, and established accordingly': 1 Gul. & Mar. Sess. 2 c. 2, in T. E. Tomlins and J. Raithby (eds.), *The Statutes at Large, of England and of Great-Britain: From Magna Carta to the Union of the Kingdoms of Great Britain and Ireland*, 20 vols. (London, 1811), III, pp. 275, 278 as cited by D. Willoweit and U. Seif (eds.), *Europäische Verfassungsgeschichte* (München, 2003), p. 248.

[58] 'For that, by the constitution and policy of this kingdom, the King by his Proclamation cannot declare the law contrary to the judgement and resolution of any of the inferior courts of justice, much less against the High Court of Parliament': Declaration of the Houses in Defence of the Militia Ordinance of 6 Jun. 1642, cited in Gardiner, *The Constitutional Documents of the Puritan Revolution 1625–1660*, no. 54, pp. 254, 255 et seq. In the same way, Blackstone's classic commentary on parliamentary sovereignty (W. Blackstone, *Commentaries on the Laws of England*, I: *Of the Rights of Persons* (London, 1765), Introduction, ch. II: 'Of the Parliament', p. 156) is based on Coke's definition of supreme jurisdiction for the High Court of Parliament: 'Of the power and jurisdiction of the parliament, for making of laws in proceeding by bill, it is so transcendendent and absolute, as it cannot be confined either for causes or persons within any bounds. Of this court it is truly said: *Si antiquitatem spectes, est vetustissima, si dignitatem, est honoratissima, si jurisdictionem, est capacissima*'; E. Coke, 'The Fourth Part of the Institutes of the Laws of England concerning the jurisdiction of Courts' in *The Institutes of the Law of England, Second to Fourth Parts* (London, 1797), part IV, p. 36.

[59] Blackstone, *Commentaries on the Laws of England*, p. 156.

[60] Coke, 'The Fourth Part of the Institutes of the Laws of England concerning the jurisdiction of Courts', p. 36: 'Of the power and jurisdiction of the parliament, for making of laws in proceeding by bill, it is so transcendendent and absolute, as it cannot be confined either for causes or persons within any bounds. Of this court it is truly said: *Si antiquitatem spectes, est vetustissima, si dignitatem, est honoratissima, si jurisdictionem, est capacissima.*'

[61] F. Battenberg, art. 'Reichshofgericht' in *HRG*, IV, cols. 615, 618.

act when the emperor was abroad and was dissolved on his death. The court proved incapable of maintaining its prerogatives against the more powerful territorial lords and it lost importance due to the privileges *de non evocando* and *de non appellando* granted to territorial courts. No traces of the *Reichshofgericht* can be found after the middle of the fifteenth century.[62] The *königliche Kammergericht* (traceable from 1415 onwards) met with a similar fate.[63] It remained dependent on the emperor during the fifteenth century, having no regular seat, no regular judges and no independent jurisdiction; it was rented out to the *Reichsstände* for money and was finally merged into the *kaiserliches und Reichskammergericht*.[64]

The *Reichskammergericht* was founded in 1495 as part of the process of imperial reform which took place under Maximilian I, a reform which the emperor granted the *Reichsfürsten* (imperial princes) only because he needed their support in the war against Hungary. It is therefore no surprise that the reorganisation of the *Reichskammergericht* by the imperial estates, the only lasting success of the imperial reform, made the territorial princes emerge all the stronger, having left the empire dismembered and moribund. The Imperial Chamber Court can be distinguished from the old royal *Kammergericht* by the fact that it was not the personal court of the emperor, but the official court of the empire, and it was paid for by the empire and thus not dependent on either the will or the money of the emperor. In the death throes of medieval forms within the ageing empire the *Reichskammergericht* and its *Ordnung* (rules) did produce one new unifying factor: the recognition of the learned law (see § 3 of the *Reichskammergerichtsordnung* (Ordinance) of 1495). There was no longer any coherent German legal tradition to

---

[62] J. A. Tomaschek, 'Die höchste Gerichtsbarkeit des deutschen Königs und Reichs im XV. Jahrhundert' in *Sitzungsberichte der philosophisch-historischen Classe der kaiserlichen Akademie der Wissenschaften*, vol. 49 (1865), pp. 521–63 at 561; O. Franklin, *Das Reichshofgericht im Mittelalter*, II: *Verfassung – Verfahren* (Weimar, 1869), pp. 328, 340; R. Seyboth, 'Kontinuität und Wandel. Vom mittelalterlichen Reichshofgericht zum Reichskammergericht von 1495' in I. Scheuermann (ed.), *Frieden durch Recht* (Mainz, 1994), p. 68.

[63] B. Dick, *Die Entwicklung des Kameralprozesses nach den Ordnungen von 1495 bis 1555* (Köln, 1981), p. 11; H. Mitteis and H. Lieberich, *Deutsche Rechtsgeschichte*, 17th edn (München, 1985), pp. 242 *et seq*. The king or his deputy presided over the *Kammergericht*, which was the king's personal court. The members of the court were now officials of the court. It was generally the legal members of the council who sat in the *Kammergericht*.

[64] W. D. Räbiger, art. 'Kammergericht, königliches' in *HRG*, II, cols. 576–580 at 578.

follow. A uniform procedure and judicature could be created only by recourse to the *ius commune*. Under the 1495 ordinance, it is true, local law was applicable if pleaded before the court but this could only be the case where local laws were written down, and writing them down presented an opportunity to romanise them. The territorial state came at a price, and Germany paid it. It was by rationalising the administration of their principalities that the princes consolidated their power. The princes gained their lead over the estates in the fifteenth century because they alone possessed modern techniques of administration and law, and it was trained lawyers who ensured this monopoly.

The jurisdiction of the *Reichskammergericht* The creation of the *Reichskammergericht* as the highest court of the estates reflected the imperial estates' opposition to the emperor. The choice of a seat for the court was always based on keeping it away from the Habsburgs' sphere of influence.[65] First it resided at different places, then at Speyer (1527–1689), and later at Wetzlar. Article 2 of the *Reichskammergerichtsordnung* of 1495 secured the imperial princes' right to appoint a majority of the court's members.[66] The emperor retained the right to appoint only the chief justice (*Kammerrichter*), who had to be a high-ranking aristocrat, and the two (or later four) presidents of the court's divisions as well as the right to nominate a small number of *assessores*.[67] The rest were nominated by the estates of the empire. Initially, only one half of the *assessores* who rendered decisions were to be 'learned and qualified in the law' (namely Roman law) and able 'to give proper opinions in pending legal cases' – that is, laying out the case in an orderly manner, as only a jurist with his superior training could do. The other half drawn from the knightly class should 'also be learned in the law . . . so far as available, but if not, then experienced and practised in the courts' procedure'. This parity between learned judges and non-graduate gentry was the social compromise between the old

---

[65] H. Duchhardt, 'Das Reichskammergericht' in B. Diestelkamp (ed.), *Oberste Gerichtsbarkeit und Zentrale Gewalt* (Köln, 1999), pp. 1–13 at 3.

[66] 'Item so der urteyler einer oder mer abkeme, sow ellen wir zu yeder zeit mit rate und willen Ket seq., Ff. und der samblung, die desselben jars zusamenkumen werden, oder irer anwelde an des- oder derselben stat andere tugliche personen setzen': H. Angermeier (ed.), *Deutsche Reichstagsakten, Mittlere Reihe* (Göttingen, 1981), V(1), 1, p. 387.

[67] At the *Reichskammergerichtshof* there existed the old class-based and functional differentiation between the process-directing judges (*Kammerrichter*) and the adjudicating assessors (*Assessores*), from whom the presidents of the court were selected.

leaders by right of birth and the new professionals, and this is the explanation for the estimation of the German legal doctorate (Dr. iur) as an attribute of nobility. After 1555 it became necessary for the knights to be learned in Roman law as well.

First and foremost the princes created the Imperial Chamber Court (*Reichskammergericht*) as an instrument to protect the public peace within the empire (*Landfrieden*). This accounts for its competence in matters of *Landfriedensbruch* (breach of the public peace) and for the regulation of *Austrägalverfahren* (arbitral procedure between territories within the realm).[68] In addition, the jurisdiction of the *Reichskammergericht* covered cases of arbitrary imprisonment, pleas related to the treasury, violations of the emperor's decrees or laws passed by the Diet, property disputes between immediate vassals of the empire and, finally, suits against the latter, excepting criminal charges and matters relating to imperial fiefs, which went to the Aulic Council (*Reichshofrat*).

Notwithstanding this, one should not forget the jurisdiction of the *Reichskammergericht* as an appellate court, which it exercised from the fifteenth century onwards. The court managed to subject the weaker parts of the empire to this jurisdiction. Proof of this can be found in law reports dealing with appeals from territorial courts to the *Reichskammergericht*.[69] The *Reichskammergerichtsordnung* of 1495 already reflects a modern view of the hierarchy of courts: 'Item es sol kein appelacion angenomen werden, die nit gradatim gescheen were, das ist an das nechst ordenlich obergericht.'[70] Appeals by the *Austrägalgerichte* (arbitral courts dealing with inter-territorial law suits) were also allowed.[71] Yet no detailed regulation of appeal

---

[68] §§ 28, 30 of the Rules of the Imperial Chamber Court 1495 (Angermeier, *Reichstagsakten*, pp. 411 *et seq.*) and articles II–IV of the Rules of the Imperial Chamber Court 1555, Part II (*ibid.*, pp. 168 *et seq.*).

[69] B. Diestelkamp points this out in 'Vom königlichen Hofgericht zum kaiserlichen Kammergericht' in H. de Schepper (ed.), *Höchste Gerichtsbarkeit im Spätmittelalter und der frühen Neuzeit* (Amsterdam, n. d.), p. 1 (without references). Cf. J. Chmel, *Regesta chronologico-diplomatica Friderici IV romanorum regis (imperatoris III)* (Wien, 1838), for appellate cases of 1443 and 1444. An appellate case of the city of Weissenburg (1452) is cited in H. C. von Senckenberg, *Abhandlung der wichtigen Lehre von der kayserlichen höchsten Gerichtsbarkeit in Deutschland* (Frankfurt a. M., 1760), Beil. XXVII, p. 64.

[70] Cited in Angermeier, *Reichstagsakten*, p. 399.

[71] §§ 28, 30 RKGO 1495 (*ibid.*, pp. 411 *et seq.*). Cf. Dick, *Die Entwicklung des Kameralprozesses nach den Ordnungen von 1495 bis 1555*, pp. 68 *et seq.*

proceedings emerged until the *Reichskammergerichtsordnung* of 1555 (Part II, art. XXVIII et seq.).[72] The right to appeal in criminal cases was denied in § 95 of the *Augsburger Reichsabschied* of 1530 (edicts made at the royal assembly at Augsburg), except for criminal cases in which basic procedural rules had been violated.[73] Appellate jurisdiction might cease at the borders of larger principalities which enjoyed the privilege of freedom from appeals (*privilegium de non appellando*), especially the territories of the electors. The territorial courts in the exempted principalities nevertheless also followed the procedures of the learned law. The *Reichskammergericht* served as the model on which the larger territories reconstituted their courts and procedure, often down to the most minor detail. The *privilegia de non appellando* enabled, and indeed obliged, the principalities to maintain or set up their own jurisdiction. This is explicitly mentioned in the *Jüngster Reichsabschied* of 1654, § 113.[74] The privilege of freedom from appeals was generally obtained by the supreme court of a territory on its creation or renewal, as in the case of Bavaria in 1625 and Brandenburg in 1586.

Judge-made law, law reports and the legal profession at the Reichskammergericht Being an appellate court for the weaker territories and a role model for the stronger principalities the *Reichskammergericht*'s decisions were of considerable importance for the development of law.[75] Collections of opinions and court decisions by Mynsinger (1563), Seiler (1572), Gail (1578), Gylmann (1601) and Meichsner (1601) were widely used and had a strong influence on legal practice.[76]

---

[72] A. Laufs, *Die Reichskammergerichtsordnung von 1555* (Quellen und Forschungen zur höchsten gerichtsbarkeit im Alten Reich, 3: Köln, 1976), pp. 172, 175 *et seq.*

[73] C. Szidzek, *Das frühneuzeitliche Verbot der Appellation in Strafsachen* (Köln, 2002), p. 29.

[74] A. Laufs, *Der Jüngster Reichsabschied von 1654* (Bern, 1975), reclam. 5, pp. 35–42.

[75] Even the rules of the Imperial Chamber Court 1495 allowed for instructions by the Court: § 32. 'Item so hienach am camergericht furfiel, das verrer versehung, ordnung, satzung oder declaration bedurfen wurde, dasselb sullen camerrichter und urteyler yeglichs jars an uns, auch unser Ket seq., Ff. und samlung, die desselben jars durch sich selbst oder ire anwelde beyeinander komen werden, bringen, das wir mit rate und willen derselben samlung daryn zu handeln haben zu furdrung und aufnemung des camergerichts und erfindung des rechten und gerechtigkeit': Angermeier, *Reichstagsakten*, p. 419.

[76] H. Weller, *Die Bedeutung der Präjudizien im Verständnis der deutschen Rechtswissenschaft* (Berlin, 1979), pp. 47 *et seq.* with further references.

Furthermore, certain imperial laws were understood as imposing standards of competence for the *Reichskammergericht* in adjudicating matters
both in their procedural and substantive aspects and held to be generally
binding when in doubt.[77] Cameralist jurists (*Kameralisten*)
deduced despite terminological inconsistencies[78] that both the
Reichskammergerichtsordnung of 1555 (Part II, art. XXXVI)[79] and
the imperial ordinance (*Reichsabschied*) of 1570 (§ 77)[80] allowed the
Reichskammergericht to establish generally binding legal rules. A majority

---

[77] C. F. Gerstlacher, *Corpus iuris Germanici publici ac privati* (Stuttgart, 1789), IV, § 23,
pp. 213–15, 223; J. St. Pütter and G. W. Stock, '*De iure et officio summorum imperii
tribunalium circa interpretationem legum imperii, dissertation (Göttingen, 1758)*' in J. St.
Pütter, *Opuscula rem iudiciariam imperii illustrantia* (Goettingae, 1766), pp. 185–258,
here: § 31 = pp. 212 *et seq.*; § 32 = pp. 216 *et seq.*, § 45 = pp. 234 *et seq.*; E. A. Haus,
Versuch über den rechtlichen Werth des Gerichtsgebrauchs (Erlangen, 1798), § 25, pp. 95
et seq.; § 27, p. 101, n. iii.

[78] See for details Dick, *Die Entwicklung des Kameralprozesses nach den Ordnungen von
1495 bis 1555*, p. 10.

[79] 'Item, ob dieser Ordnung des Process halben des Cammer-Gerichts Zweiffel einfallen,
oder weiter Ordnung und Fürsehung zu thun vonnöthen seyn würde, wollen wir
Cammer-Richter und Beysitzer befohlen haben, jederzeit wann es die Nothdurfft erfor-
dert, des Process halben, diese Ordnung ihres besten Verständnuß zu declariren, zu
bessern, auch weitere nothwendige Fürsehung und Ordnung fürzunehmen und zu
machen, und dieselbig also bis zu der jährlichen Visitation des kayserlichen Cammer-
Gerichts zu halten befehlen, und alsdann dieselbige samt andern Mängeln, den verord-
neten Commissarien und Visitatorn fürzubringen, die dann dieselbig approbiren, oder
sonst derhalben gebührlichs Einsehens thun sollen': A. Laufs (ed.), *Die
Reichskammergerichtsordnung von 1555* (Köln, 1976), p. 217.

[80] 'Damit aber aller Veränderung und Ungleichheit künfftiglich vorkommen werden
möge, ordnen und befehlen Wir unserm Cammer-Richter, etliche Beysitzer insonder-
heit zu verordnen, so die substantial qualitates, darauff die Process, es sey in erster oder
andern Instantz, zu erkennen, zuvorab in Sachen fractae pacis, Pfändungen,
Mandatorum sine clausula, Inhibitionum, citationis contra plures correos diversi fori,
und dergleichen, so täglich fürkommen, zusammen tragen sollen, darnach in pleno
Senatu referiren, darauff sich das Collegium eines einhelligen Brauchs und alten Styli, in
Fundirung unsers Cammer-Gerichts Jurisdiction und Ertheilung der Process, endlich
Vergleichen: darneben auch diejenigen opiniones, so bey den Rechts-Lehrern gantz
streitig / und aber etwan in relationibus causarum mit approbation deß gantzen Raths
angenommen / mit Fleiß colligiren, solches alles in ein sonder Protocoll-Buch, so die
Leser in ihrer Verwahrung haben sollen, mit vorwissen unsers Cammer-Richters, durch
einen Protonotarien, nur per modum conclusionis beschreiben lassen, und in die
Mayntzische Cantzley, durch Uns auf nechstkünfftige Reichs-Versammlung, auf Rath
und Gutachten gemeiner Ständ publiciren zu lassen, schrifftlich überschicken.
Gleichwol sollen Cammer-Richter und Beysitzer, immittelst solcher verglichenen
Puncten, in decernendo processus, & decidendo causas, sich gemäß verhalten': E. A.
Koch (ed.), *Neue und vollständige Sammlung der Reichsabschiede III–IV* (Frankfurt,
1747), p. 333).

of votes was sufficient.[81] The *Reichskammergericht*, however, was not allowed to reverse judgments in *ius commune* or imperial law and its own decisions were valid only if they were not reversed by visitation or the *Reichstag*.[82] In the *Jüngster Reichsabschied* of 1654 (§ 136), the imperial legislature ascribed a certain binding character to decisions made by individual divisions within the *Reichskammergericht* to avoid contradictory decisions.[83]

Identical arguments are adduced for the binding force of the *Conclusa pleni* (decisions of the whole court) on one hand and the *praeiudicia* of the individual divisions on the other. One argument that is always mentioned is the principle of equality.[84] Identical cases should not be adjudged differently.[85] The purpose is to ensure equality in the interpretation of legislation and uniformity in the decisions made by the *Reichskammergericht*.[86] Moreover, the judge's function in the development of judge-made law plays a role. To sum up, the incompleteness of every act of legislation necessitates the concession of a certain influence to judge-made law, and imperial legislation was very fragmentary. Practitioners regarded the published opinions of individual scholars and faculties as being as authoritative as decisions of the *Reichskammergericht* itself.

One should not, however, overestimate the importance of the precedents of the *Reichskammergericht*. The compilation '*Des hochlöblichen Kayserlichen und Heiligen Römischen Raichs Cammer-Gerichts Gemeine Bescheide und andere Raths-Schlüsse, vom Jahr 1497 biß 1711 inclusive Wetzlar 1714*' contains only 239 decisions and they are only of minor

---

[81] Gerstlacher, *Corpus iuris Germanici publici ac privati*, IV, § 23 Anm. 59, p. 223.

[82] *Ibid.*, § 23 Anm, 49 3, pp. 201 *et seq.*

[83] 'So viel aber die bey diesem Puncten von den Assessorn selbsten, in ihrem Anno 1643 nacher Franckfurt denen Deputirten überschickten Bedencken, berührte Contrarietäten und Praejudicia Cameralia anbelanget, welche sich theils auf die Advocaten und Sachwalter nicht unbillig ziehen lassen, sollen die Assessores solche gegen einander laufende Präjudicia, in alle Weg verhüten helfen, und da sich dergleichen Fälle begeben würden, fürderlichst in pleno sich eines Gewissen vereinbahren': H. C. von Senckenberg, *Neue und vollständigere Sammlung der Reichs-Abschiede* (Frankfurt a. M., 1747), Theil III, p. 665.

[84] §§ 75, 78 Reichsabschied 1570: *ibid.*, Theil III, pp. 297 *et seq.* (sometimes Theil IV, p. 297).

[85] 'Quia casus, quos connectat identitas rationis, etiam quoad decisionem non sunt separandi': J. Wolf, *De eo quod iustum est circa praeiudicia iudicialia* (Altdorf [?], 1728), § VII, p. 9.

[86] Gerstlacher, *Corpus iuris Germanici publici ac privati*, IV, p. 323 (§ 24 n. 64); Haus, *Versuch über den rechtlichen Werth des Gerichtsgebrauchs*, § 27, p. 101.

significance.[87] I was not able to find any decisions relating to substantive law in it. Presumably precedents only took effect in the area of procedure and the constitution of the court.

In contrast to the French *nobles* of *parlement* (the *gens de robe*) and the community of common lawyers the *Reichskammergericht* did not possess its own distinctive legal profession. This was prevented from the outset by the differences in social class within the *Reichskammergericht*'s staff, between the judges and assessors on the one side, and the proctors and advocates on the other. Assessors developed a pronounced class-consciousness, numbering only twenty and originating from the territorial or imperial aristocracy. The assessors' separation from the proctors and advocates can be shown in 1700 when marriages between the families of assessors and procurators were strictly banned.[88]

Rivalry with the emperor   The *Reichskammergericht* successfully resisted any direct interference by the emperor (for example, by a dictum of power – the so-called *Machtspruch*).[89] Yet there did exist legal possibilities for the reversing of decisions. Besides visitations, which were able to reverse decisions of the Imperial Chamber Court, the Authentic Interpretation (settled in art. V § 56 IPO of the *Osnabrücker Friedensvertrag* of 1648) was a useful instrument.[90] This meant that the interpretation of an imperial law could be made subject to the Reichstag, although one has to admit that the Reichstag remained mostly inactive in the face of requests for redress.[91] Supplications to the

---

[87] Some examples of the contents of these decisions: that proctors must refrain from unnecessarily long and ill-judged pleadings (no. XIX, p. 5); that the *termini praejudicales* be strictly adhered to (no. CXV, p. 43); and that the *beneficium restitutionis in integrum* be not abused (no. CLXXX, pp. 91 *et seq.*).

[88] A. Baumann, *Advokaten und Prokuratoren: Anwälte am Reichskammergericht (1690–1806)* (Köln, 2006), p. 28.

[89] *Machtspruch* refers to a sovereign decision of the ruler, unrestrained by regular procedure. Cf. B. Ruthmann, *Die Religionsprozesse am Reichskammergericht* (Köln, 1996), p. 568 with reference to B. Diestelkamp, 'Das RKG im Rechtsleben des 16. Jahrhunderts' in H.-J. Becker *et al.* (eds.), *Rechtsgeschichte als Kulturgeschichte, Festschrift für Adalbert Erler* (Aalen, 1976), pp. 435–80 at 457 *et seq.*

[90] Ferdinand III, Kristina von Schweden, Instrumentum Pacis Osnabrugensis, Frankfurt am Main, 1648; Acta Pacis Westphalicae (Nordrhein-Westfälischen Akademie der Wissenschaften in Verbindung mit der Vereinigung zur Erforschung der Neueren Geschichte e.V. durch Konrad Repgen), Serie III Abteilung B: Verhandlungsakten. Band 1: Die Friedensverträge mit Frankreich und Schweden. 1: Urkunden, ed. Antje Oschmann (Münster, 1998), pp. 97–98.

[91] W. Sellert, art. '*Recursus ad Comitia*' in *HRG*, IV, cols. 446–9 at 448.

emperor could aim for revision of the Imperial Chamber Court's decision. Furthermore, in all its business the *Reichskammergericht* suffered from competition with the Aulic Council (*Reichshofrat*).

On the other hand recent research has also brought to light that, particularly in the eighteenth century, the rulings of the *Reichskammergericht* anticipated in many ways the constitutional establishment of civil liberties. For instance, the inviolability of one's housing or the freedom of trade were legally introduced into the empire by court rulings.

The Aulic Council (*Reichshofrat*)

The Jurisdiction of the *Reichshofrat* The reorganisation of the *Reichskammergericht* in 1495 did not prevent the emperor from insisting on having his own personal jurisdiction, and so he reorganised his own court council (later called the *Reichshofrat*) in 1498, as a rival to the *Reichskammergericht* which the Diet had forced upon him. Originally (as stated in the *Hofordnung* of 1498) the *Reichshofrat* functioned not only as a law court but also as a governmental and administrative body, primarily as an advisory body to the emperor in all imperial matters.[92] Later ordinances (*Hofratsordnungen*) of 1559 and 1654 were similarly worded, confirming the Aulic Council as an executive-judicial council for the Holy Roman Empire.[93] The Aulic Council was composed of a president, vice president, vice chancellor, and eighteen councillors, who were all appointed and renumerated by the emperor, with the exception of the vice chancellor, who was appointed by the Elector of Mainz. Of the eighteen councillors, six were Protestants whose votes, when unanimous, were an effective veto, so that a religious parity was to some extent protected. The seat of the Aulic Council was at the imperial residence, namely in Vienna. Upon the death of the emperor, the Council was dissolved and had to be reconstituted by his successor.

The *Reichshofrat* claimed exclusive jurisdiction as against the *Reichskammergericht* in a few matters (in all feudal processes, in criminal matters relating to the immediate feudatories of the emperor and in

---

[92] O. von Gschliesser, *Der Reichshofrat: Bedeutung und Verfassung, Schicksal und Besetzung einer obersten Reichsbehörde von 1559 bis 1806* (Wien, 1942), pp. 14 *et seq.* The administrative and advisory function was only taken over by the *Reichshofrat* with the increasing separation of the *geheimer Rat* (privy council), or rather, the *Reichshofkanzlei* (Gschliesser, p. 15).

[93] W. Sellert (ed.), *Die Ordnungen des Reichshofrates 1550–1766*, II: *1626–1766* (Köln, 1980), p. 18 with further references.

matters concerning the imperial government) but mostly both courts had concurrent jurisdiction. This competition between the Aulic Council and the Imperial Chamber was settled by the priority rule established by the Treaty of Westphalia of 1648 (the so-called *Prävention*). Whichever court was approached first had jurisdiction. The *Reichshofrat* heard mainly first-instance cases; experts suggest that only 25–33 per cent of its cases dealt with appeals.[94] As with the *Reichskammergericht*, this development at the *Reichshofrat* is probably the result of the prevalence of the *privilegia de non appellando*.

Professionalisation, law reports and case law (judge-made law)

Initially the *Reichshofrat* consisted only partially of *gelährte personen* (learned persons), of whom legal knowledge was required (*Reichshofratsordnung* of 1617).[95] Closeness to the monarch seems to have been more important than legal education. Only as late as 1654 did legal learning, as verified by an adequate examination, become a prerequisite for all members of the *Reichshofrat*. Although in the subsequent period complaints about incompetence can still be found,[96] an academic degree or, at the very least, a longer course of studies at a university can be demonstrated for most of the *Reichshofräte*.[97]

As with the *parlements* the *Reichshofrat* did not intend that the reasoning for its decisions should be made public. This applied particularly to the publication of the *Relationes et Causas decidendi*.[98] Only towards the end of the seventeenth century, and thus considerably later than for the *Reichskammergericht*, were legal decisions of the *Reichshofrat* officially published. The influence of these collections on subsequent decision-making has yet to be investigated. Wolfgang Sellert deduces from the stated aims of the publisher (to give information about the work of the *Reichshofrat* and to create a *stilus curiae*) that any substantial influence of these law reports is rather unlikely.[99]

Rivalry with the emperor

It was always possible for the emperor, as possessor of jurisdictional power, or as '*allein obristes haupt und richter*' (sole head and judge)[100] of the *Reichshofrat*, to influence the council's

---

[94] von Gschliesser, *Der Reichshofrat*, p. 35.
[95] Sellert, *Die Ordnungen des Reichshofrates 1550–1766*, p. 38.   [96] *Ibid.*, p. 39.
[97] von Gschliesser, *Der Reichshofrat*, p. 73.
[98] Sellert, *Die Ordnungen des Reichshofrates 1550–1766*, p. 43.   [99] *Ibid.*, p. 44.
[100] *Ibid.*, p. 26.

decisions. The *Reichshofrat* itself fought against this imperial interference. The princes of the empire succeeded in asserting the personal independence of the *Reichhofsräte* and later achieved the emperors' renunciation of direct and indirect interference, the latter being to refrain from reversing the *Reichshofrat*'s judgments regarding common matters.[101]

But this renunciation of subsequent revision of the Aulic Council's decisions did not apply to matters that '*ratio status und andere umbständ mitsichbringen und erfordern*'.[102] In particular the so-called *vota ad imperatorem* helped to enforce the emperor's claims to power and his political interests. For instance, tit. V § 18 of the *Reichhofsratsordnung* of 1645 states that in the case of an equal number of votes or in the case of an exceptionally important matter, the case had to be brought before the emperor.[103] The *votum ad imperatorem* was common practice in cases regarding constitutional law.[104] Ultimately the emperor held a *votum decisivum*. This was regarded by the imperial estates as mere *Kabinettsjustiz* (interference in the course of justice by a sovereign).[105]

The Holy Roman Empire: territorial superior courts

Because of the particular constitutional situation in the Holy Roman Empire – that is, the dualism of territorial lords (*domini terrae* or *Landesherren*) and emperor – territorial superior courts also played an important role in the history of jurisdiction in Germany, especially in those territories where the authority of the imperial courts had been neutralised except for cases of failure of justice by means of *privilegia de non appellando*. The territorial lords' own striving for sovereignty manifested itself in their endeavour to acquire independent judicial supremacy. Some experts even talk about a 'fight over appellate jurisdiction'[106] insofar as appeals to the imperial courts were prohibited.[107]

I confine myself here to discussing the Austrian territories. In 1620 the *Reichshofrat*'s authority as final appellate court for the hereditary lands of the Habsburg monarchy was replaced by territorial courts. Legal matters affecting the hereditary lands of the Habsburg monarchy were

---

[101] *Ibid.*, p. 30.   [102] *Ibid.*, p. 30.   [103] *Ibid.*, p. 29.
[104] *Ibid.*, p. 31 with further references.   [105] *Ibid.*, p. 29 with further references.
[106] J. Weitzel, *Der Kampf um die Appellation ans Reichskammergericht, Zur politischen Geschichte der Rechtsmittel in Deutschland* (Köln, 1976).
[107] K. Modéer, 'Die Gerichtsstruktur in den deutschen Lehen der schwedischen Krone' in N. Jörn *et al.* (eds.), *Integration durch Recht* (Köln, 2003), pp. 123–38 at 123.

detached from imperial legal matters and a separate Austrian chancery (*Hofkanzlei*) was established, which also functioned as the superior Austrian court.[108] This development is a typical example of the emancipation of territorial superior courts from imperial jurisdiction. In the mid eighteenth century the Haugwitz reforms separated justice and political administration through departmentalisation; the *Hofkanzlei*'s function as superior court was taken over by the new *Oberste Justizstelle* (supreme judicial board).[109]

It would appear that there was no such thing as precedent in the law of the Austrian territories. The instructions for the *Oberste Justizstelle* do not define clearly how they were to deal with precedents. They should neither rely blindly on precedent nor should they deliver contradictory judgments. The binding character of precedent was not recognised until 1822.[110] Nevertheless the *Oberste Justizstelle* had an extraordinary influence on the development of the Austrian codification of civil law (*Zivilrechtskodifikation*), as its members were in charge of the code's drafting.

The *Justizstelle*'s relationship to the sovereign is marked by an explicit dependency. Austrian monarchs retained their right to intervene. *Dicta* of power (*Machtsprüche*) were only officially renounced in the *Bürgerliches Gesetzbuch von Westgalizien* (the civil code of Western Galicia)[111] and in the *Codex Theresianus*, which dictated enquiry at the *curia regis* should doubts about the interpretation of a law emerge (I cap. I § V no. 81 ff.). Similar wording can be found in § 437 of the *Allgemeine Gerichtsordnung* (general constitution of the court) of 1781 and in the *Josephinische Gesetzbuch* (Josephinian code of law, I § 26).[112]

---

[108] H. Baltl and G. Kocher, *Österreichische Rechtsgeschichte*, 7th edn (Graz, 1993), p. 139; T. Fellner and H. Kretschmayr, *Die Österreichische Zentralverwaltung*, I. Abteilung, vol. I (Wien, 1907), p. 231. In administrative matters the separation was realised earlier in 1559: Baltl and Kocher, *Österreichische Rechtsgeschichte*; E. C. Hellbling, *Österreichische Verfassungs- und Verwaltungsgeschichte*, 2nd edn (Wien, 1974), p. 242.

[109] O. Lehner, *Österreichische Verfassungs- und Verwaltungsgeschichte*, 7th edn (Linz, 1992), p. 137. More extensively, G. Kocher, *Höchstgerichtsbarkeit und Privatrechtskodifikation, Die Oberste Justizstelle und das allgemeine Privatrecht in Österreich von 1749–1811* (Wien, 1979); G. Kocher, art. 'Oberste Justizstelle (Österreich)' in *HRG*, III, cols. 1162–8; H. M. Scott, 'Reform in the Habsburg monarchy' in H. M. Scott (ed.), *Enlightened Absolutism Reform and Reformers in Later Eighteenth-Century Europe* (Ann Arbor, MI, 1990), p. 54.

[110] Kocher, 'Oberste Justizstelle (Österreich)', cols. 1162–8 at 1165.

[111] W. Brauneder and F. Lachmayer, *Österreichische Verfassungsgeschichte*, 2nd edn (Wien, 1980), pp. 85 *et seq.*

[112] H. Conrad, *Richter und Gesetz im Übergang vom Absolutismus zum Verfassungsstaat* (Graz, 1971), pp. 12 *et seq.*

Conclusion

The key question posed in this chapter, whether the beginnings of supreme jurisdiction correspond in time to the early-modern state-building process, is – on the basis of the findings of this chapter – to be answered in the affirmative. The foundation and exercise of supreme jurisdiction alone expresses the (monarchical) claim to be the arbiter of common interests. The first aspect of our comparison already shows this. Superior courts repressed or effectively controlled the lower courts, in particular those that were independent of the sovereign. Ecclesiastical and feudal jurisdiction were rivals to monarchical jurisdiction.

Supreme jurisdiction as an expression of the early-modern state-building process can also be observed in the second aspect of my comparison: the existence of judge-made law and the establishment of the legal profession. French experts link the concept of the nation to the self-confidence of parliamentary jurists.[113] English scholars unanimously emphasise that access to common and equal legal proceedings fostered the development of a sense of national identity.

The third aspect of comparison, rivalry with the monarch, emphasises the state-building function of the superior courts. The sovereignty of the English Parliament, based on the idea of it being a court of law, leads to a control of the royal prerogative and of the common law courts; the French *parlements* were controlled by the *Conseil du roi*, their resistance to monarchical jurisdiction proving to be a precursor to the Revolution. The *Reichskammergericht* was influenced by the emperor and had to deal with visitations and the instrument of *authentic interpretation* of imperial laws, even though immediate interference by the emperor could be abolished. Decision-making at the *Reichshofrat* was subject to the *vota ad imperatorem*. Control of justice comes with control of jurisdiction.

---

[113] A. Bossuat, 'L'idée de nation et la jurisprudence du Parlement de Paris au XVe siècle' (1950) 204 *Revue historique* 54–61; Dauchy, *Les Voies de recours extraordinaires: proposition d'erreur et requête civile*, p. 30.

12

The Supreme Court of Holland and Zeeland judging cases in the early eighteenth century

A. J. B. SIRKS

I

Under the Burgundian and Habsburg rulers (1384–1581) the various territories of the Netherlands, consisting of most of the present-day Netherlands, Belgium, Luxembourg and a part of north-west France, each had its own court.[1] Wishing to unify these lands the Burgundian rulers established in 1445 the *Grote Raad* (Grand Council), since 1504 permanently established in Mechelen (Malines), to which appeal could be made from the decision of a provincial court. When the northern provinces seceded in 1576 and in 1581 finally renounced their feudal ruler – at that time King Philip II of Spain – since he had broken his oath to them, they naturally no longer accepted this Grand Council. In 1581 the States of Holland had decided to set up a separate supreme court, the *Hoge Raad*, as an appellate court for their province, since travelling to Mechelen was difficult if not impossible due to the war; and this was to develop into an appellate court for the now sovereign northern provinces. The provinces of Holland and Zeeland acknowledged this court but the other provinces (Friesland, Groningen, Overijssel, Gelderland and Utrecht) did not:[2] sovereignty was too a sweet a thing to give up quickly and so only for these two provinces the Supreme Court remained

---

[1] Traditionally the result of the successive expansions of the Burgundians and Habsburgs is called after 1543 the Seventeen Netherlands, but the precise number is a point of discussion and seventeen is rather a symbolic number. They comprised, after 1543: Artois, Flanders, Rijssel-Flanders, Mechelen, Namur, Hainaut, Zeeland, Holland, Brabant with Antwerp, Limburg with Overmaze, Luxemburg, Friesland, Tournai, Utrecht, Overijssel incl. Drenthe and Lingen, Groningen, Gelderland with Zutphen.

[2] In 1572 the Prince of Orange, although formally no longer royal stadholder, but nevertheless acknowledged as such by the province of Holland, instituted the Court of Holland as a pure judiciary court (it previously had been also advisory board) and, as long as

a court of appeal. In the other provinces a second appeal to the same (provincial) court, a revision, was created.[3]

II

The Supreme Court, or to give its full name the *Hoge Raad van Holland, Zeeland en West-Friesland*,[4] consisted of ten judges: nine ordinary judges and one president, all appointed by the States of Holland. After 1596 the procedure was that in case of a vacancy a list of six candidates was drawn up by the Supreme Court and presented to the States. Here one candidate was chosen, usually the one on top of the list, who then was sworn in at the court. Three posts were reserved for candidates from Zeeland, the remaining seven for candidates from Holland. The Zeeland candidates were provided by six towns, in rotation, and the candidate had to hold a municipal post in the town. The practice was, however, that the town whose turn it was to appoint a judge could sell a municipal post qualifying the post-holder for the court to the highest bidder, who then jumped, so to speak, into the court. It was not a nice practice but it was silently allowed.[5] In practice it was not that bad, since it enabled capable outsiders to obtain posts in the court. In Holland the selling of posts was prohibited from 1579 onwards. Since the States of Holland consisted of nineteen members, eighteen representatives of certain of the towns in Holland and one representative of the (almost extinct) nobility of

appeal to the Mechelen court was not possible, as supreme court. In 1577 revision was introduced here as substitute for appeal to Mechelen but this was unsatisfactory. Therefore on 15 Mar. 1581 the States of Holland decided to institute a separate Court of Appeal, the *Hoge Raad*, for Holland. In 1582 the States-General decided to set up a substitute for the entire Republic for the Great Council of Mechelen, but the matter lingered on, while the *Hoge Raad* for Holland functioned. After Mechelen had been conquered by Parma in 1585, Zeeland by treaties of 1586 and 1587 accepted the *Hoge Raad*. The other constituting provinces of the Republic (Friesland, Groningen, Overijssel, Gelderland and Utrecht) and the *land* Drenthe, did not accept it. See A. S. de Blécourt, 'De geboorte van den Hoogen Raad van Holland en Zeeland' (1920–1921) 2 *Tijds. Rgeschied.* 428–59 at 430, 432, 439, 443–5, 448. Also C. M. O. Verhas, *De beginjaren van de Hoge Raad van Holland, Zeeland en West-Friesland* (The Hague, 1997).

[3] See Verhas, *De beginjaren van de Hoge Raad van Holland, Zeeland en West-Friesland*.

[4] 'West-Friesland': the northern part of the later province of Holland formed originally the western part of Frisia and was conquered from 1256 onwards by the counts of Holland. It retained its original name.

[5] See C. Brom, *Urteilsbegründungen im 'Hoge Raad van Holland, Zeeland en West-Friesland' am Beispiel des Kaufrechts im Zeitraum 1704–1787* (Frankfurt a. M., 2007), pp. 38–43. See this book also for the description below of the court and its procedure. In its second part, this book analyses the jurisprudence of the court in the eighteenth century regarding the Roman-Dutch law of sale.

Holland, candidates here had to secure support from many towns. To that end, and since there were more provincial and local appointments to make in future, ingenious schemes of mutual support were drawn up between these eighteen towns. These, like other towns not represented, were ruled by oligarchies which had often drawn up similar 'contracts of correspondence'[6] or agreements of mutual appointments between themselves. In the end the effect of this was that Holland candidates came from the oligarchies of the voting towns, or were favourites of the Prince of Orange if he was stadholder. The prince as stadholder exercised influence since he could choose one of the six candidates proposed and further often directly appointed town functionaries. But in 1650 and 1702 Holland, Zeeland, Utrecht, Gelderland and Overijssel did not appoint a stadholder and enjoyed stadholder-free periods in 1650–72 and 1702–47. In those periods the first candidate on the list would be the one chosen.[7]

Thus the Holland candidates usually came from local oligarchies, with sometimes somebody who was clearly an Orange favourite, while among the Zeeland candidates there could be new men who disposed of sufficient money to buy their place in the court. Bijnkershoek was one such person, as was his later son-in-law Willem Pauw.[8]

Formally university study was not required but in practice, certainly later on, all judges were university-educated lawyers. We need to realise, however, that in the eighteenth century a university degree in law did not have to mean much. It was commonly held that one learned law better through practice and often the candidates for the court were already experienced barristers or syndics of a town; none had previously been a professor of law.[9]

---

[6] See J. W. de Witt van Citters, *Contracten van correspondentie en andere bijdragen tot de geschiedenis van het ambtsgejag in de Republiek der Verenigde Nederlanden* (Den Haag, 1873).

[7] The Frisian Nassaus, who were stadholders in Friesland and Groningen, entertained similar mutual agreements of appointments with the local magnates in order to continue their position.

[8] See Brom, *Urteilsbegründungen im 'Hoge Raad van Holland, Zeeland en West-Friesland' am Beispiel des Kaufrechts im Zeitraum 1704–1787*, pp. 29–34 for the appointment of both; see also O. W. Star Numan, *Cornelis van Bynkershoek, zijn leven en zijne geschriften* (Leiden, 1869), pp. 84–117 for an extensive discussion on the intrigues around Bijnkershoek's appointment in 1724 as president.

[9] Such a judge was Willem Duirkant (1664–1724), who finished his legal studies when fifty-two, and was appointed when sixty years old (also over the 'Zeeland-route') but he did well enough: see A. J. B. Sirks, 'Aantekeningen van de raadsheer Willem Duirkant bij een zitting van de Hoge Raad van Holland, Zeeland en West-Friesland op 5 maart 1726' (2006) 8 *Pro Memorie* 235–45.

Appointments were for life and although theoretically the States could dismiss a member, in practice this did not happen. The Supreme Court was very concerned about its independence, as much from public authorities as from litigants: even the appearance of bribery was to be avoided. Members of the court could not hold other public offices which might give cause for a conflict of interests. Furthermore there were restrictions if family ties might impede an independent judgment.[10]

A judge earned 2,550 guilders or, from 1716 onwards, 3,000 guilders a year; the president earned 4,200 guilders a year. Added to this were emoluments from fees. These could be substantial: a provisional calculation is some 1,500 guilders per year extra for judges. Yet there were certainly big differences in lifestyle between judges. Bijnkershoek had a private income, as did his wife whose father had enjoyed the blessings of the East India Company. This in total brought him an annual income of probably far more than 10,000 guilders per annum, and at his death Bijnkershoek's estate amounted to over 225,000 guilders. But in 1742 there were in The Hague people with an annual income of 50,000 guilders and incomes of 10–20,000 guilders were not uncommon in that year. Keetlaer, a judge with Bijnkershoek, enjoyed an income of 7,000 guilders (including his 3,000 from the court), but his wife disposed of 173,000 guilders capital, which he did not inherit from her, according to our source, probably the assessment for a special war tax in 1743 in connection with the Austrian Succession War. To compare: an alderman and a mayor of The Hague each got 1,500 guilders yearly as a fee, solicitors had incomes of between 2,500 and 4,000 guilders, one baker 2,000 guilders.[11] Thus being a member of the Supreme Court meant that one had, as a lawyer, reached the apex of professional esteem, but certainly not the apex of income. The position helped, however, to marry into the oligarchies and join their fortunes.[12]

---

[10] Such a case in *Obs. tum.* n. 1566 (of 1719), concerning a *tontine*: only five of the ten judges were not disqualified by ties of consanguinity or marriage and the court had to be supplemented with two judges from the Court of Holland. On the case reports *Obs. tum.* and *Obs. tum. nov.*, see n. 27 below.

[11] For these figures, see A. J. B. Sirks, 'Bijnkershoek over de "quade conduites" van Huibert Rooseboom, president van de Hoge Raad (1691–1722)' (2008) 76 *Tijds. Rgeschied.* 49, 53, n. 22. The Austrian Succession War (1740–8) concerned the Republic of the United Netherlands in as far as it held garrisons in cities in the Austrian Netherlands.

[12] For the social position of members of the Supreme Court in the context of society in the Dutch Republic, see L. van Poelgeest, 'De raadsheren van de Hoge Raad van Holland, Zeeland en West-Friesland in de achttiende eeuw' (1988) 103 *Bijdragen en Mededelingen betreffende de Geschiedenis der Nederlanden* 20–51.

III

The usual case before the Supreme Court had originated in a local court and had then been appealed in the Court of Holland, which also was the Court of Zeeland, three of the ten judges being from and appointed by Zeeland. After obtaining leave, a further appeal could be lodged with the Supreme Court. After the second appeal one still could apply for leave of revision and, if granted, the court was doubled with supplementary judges, usually chosen from the Court of Holland and from the advocates of towns. The Supreme Court was also, but exceptionally, the court of first instance. It further could grant a so-called voluntary condemnation (*condemnatio voluntaria*) on agreements, which provided a ready title of enforcement. Such cases were examined both on their factual and legal merits. The Supreme Court was competent for civil, criminal, feudal and public law.

If an appeal was lodged with the Supreme Court, the case was put on the cause list; perhaps a meeting of parties was arranged (a *comparitie*), perhaps pleadings were requested and heard. Then the case was examined by a rapporteur, who drew up a summary of the case facts and arguments and gave his opinion. After that the case circulated amongst the judges, to return to the assembly of between seven and nine, or sometimes all ten, judges. It was a requirement for voting on the judgment (and voting on the judgment was in turn a requirement for sharing in the court fees) to have heard all the pleadings and read all the papers. At the meeting all gave their opinions, first the rapporteur, then the others in line of seniority, starting with the most junior judge and always ending with the president. In his opinion the judge stated whether he allowed or rejected the claim, and why. After this, a discussion could start and at the end of the discussion the opinions, now called sentences or *vota*, were collected. Since the judgment of the court was either to allow the appeal or to reject it, with an ancillary decision as to the process costs, all there was to be done was counting the votes. So it could happen, and did happen, that a majority formed based on differing substantive opinions, which might even not agree with each other.[13] Two such cases are dealt with below. Considering this, Bijnkershoek once uttered with some despair: 'but it is true, one only counts the votes, one does not weigh

---

[13] Such a case in *Obs. tum.* n. 2766 (of 1722), where Bijnkershoek cites: 'Vario igitur medio concludendi usi sunt Senatores, in eo tamen concordantes, utram, quam dixi, sententiam probandam esse.'

them'.[14] And Pauw[15] added to this that the suggestion of Montesquieu, made in the *Lettres Persanes*, that the minority opinion should rather be followed, seemed quite attractive to him.[16]

IV

It was not just the Supreme Court, but all other courts in Holland and the Republic, as well as in those in France, and also the *Reichskammergericht*, that merely upheld or rejected claims, and gave judgment as to costs. Courts did not give reasons for their judgments: the judges believed that to do so would diminish their authority and lessen respect for the court. The giving of judicial reasons was introduced by the French Revolution and only became mandatory in the Netherlands after 1815. Thus in our period, parties remained in the dark as to why their claims had been confirmed or rejected. Nevertheless there were judges, both in the Supreme Court and in the Court of Holland, who collected the judgments given during their time in the court. This they did firstly for their own convenience, since it allowed them to compare the results, if not the *rationes*, of cases. The court registrar (*griffier*) kept records of the opinions given in chambers and of the voting and the resulting resolutions (*resoluties*), as well as noting, next to the cause list, the sentences as promulgated (*gepronuncieerde sententies*) and other ancillary matters concerning the administration of judicial orders. But these *resoluties* were not easily accessible and much depended on how the registrar summarised the actual deliberations of the court as well as its orders.[17] Thus, for individual judges, keeping one's own records had its advantages, particularly if one took the trouble of indexing them. Judges who made such records would keep them secret (as was expected from

---

[14] *Obs. tum.* n. 2678 (24 Mar. 1735): 'Sed verum est, sententias numerari, non ponderari.'

[15] *Obs. tum. novae*, I, 433–4 referring to Montesquieu, *Lettres Persanes*, no. 87.

[16] The complete procedure is too extensive to be described here. See for more information on the procedure before the Supreme Court: C. M. O. Verhas, 'Le Hoge Raad (1582–1795)' in B. Diestelkamp (ed.), *Oberste Gerichtsbarkeit und zentrale Gewalt im Europa der frühen Neuzeit* (Köln, 1996), pp. 127–52; M. C. Le Bailly and C. M. O. Verhas, *Hoge Raad van Holland, Zeeland en West-Friesland (1582–1795)* (Hilversum, 2006); better than this booklet, with the text of the Instruction of 1583 on the procedure, is Brom, *Urteilsbegründungen im 'Hoge Raad van Holland, Zeeland en West-Friesland' am Beispiel des Kaufrechts im Zeitraum 1704–1787*.

[17] The records for the *Hoge Raad* and the *Hof van Holland, Zeeland en West-Friesland* are kept in the National Archives (NA) in The Hague, resp. inv. NA 3.02.02 and NA 3.03.01.01. Theoretically they cover the period 1581–1797 resp. 1428–1811, but in practice there are lacunae, both in time and subject.

them),[18] but some (Naeranus, de Mauregnault, Neostadius, Coren and Loen) used them to select and adapt decisions for public reading in collections of judgments, usually made anonymous. Other collections are still unpublished like van Bleiswijk's;[19] some were published much later on (such as those of Rosa and Ockers). Such collections also existed outside Holland.[20] Further, there are also collections of opinions made by advocates, akin to the nominate reports then emerging in contemporary England.[21]

The most famous case reports are the *Observationes tumultuariae* (*Obs. tum.*) by Bijnkershoek. Cornelis van Bijnkershoek, born in 1673 in Vlissingen, was the son of a rich sailmaker. He studied law at Franeker University and practised in The Hague, after which he became judge of the Supreme Court in 1704. In 1724 he was elected president of the court, which he remained till his death in 1743.[22] He won fame in his lifetime as

[18] When Judge Duirkant died in 1740, the court sent the registrar (*griffier*) to his house to collect his private copy of a *resolutie-boekje*, in order to prevent this from getting into unauthorised hands: *Obs. tum.*, IV, 311. Likewise did Bijnkershoek forbid publication and subsequently Pauw order to destroy their observations if there was no male lawyer descendant: *Obs. tum.*, I, iv–v.

[19] For the *Observationes tumultuariae* of Bleiswijk (NA Collectie Bisdom, inv. nr. 139) see L. van Poelgeest, 'Mr. Johan van Bleiswijk en zijn "Observationes tumultuariae"' (1987) 55 *Tijds. Rgeschied.* 119–22. They are of special interest since they cover the period 1723–41, consisting of 156 decisions, thus coinciding for the greater part with Bijnkershoek's *Observationes*. But they are not as frequently made as the latter's.

[20] J. Rosa, *Memorialen van het Hof (den Raad) van Holland, Zeeland en West-Friesland, van den secretaris Jan Rosa*, Uitgegeven en van een inleiding voorzien door A. S. de Blé court en E. M. Meijers, 10 vols. (Haarlem, 1929–85); H. C. Gall, *Regtsgeleerde decisien. Aan de raadsheer Pieter Ockers toegeschreven aantekeningen betreffende uitspraken van het Hof (1656-1669) en de Hoge Raad (1669-1678) van Holland, Zeeland en West-Friesland* (Amsterdam, 2002); a necessary supplement to this is A. J. B. Sirks, 'De Decisiën van Pieter Ockers (1628-1678)' (2003) 71 *Tijds. Rgeschied.* 197–210. For a full survey see E. M. M. Meijers, 'Onuitgegeven rechtspraak van den Hoogen Raad en het Hof van Holland, Zeeland en Westfriesland' (1918-1919) 1 *Tijds. Rgeschied.* 400–21, repr. in his *Etudes d' histoire de droit* (Leyde, 1973), II, pp. 3–20. In addition see L. van Poelgeest, 'Mr. Johan van Bleiswijk en zijn "Observationes tumultuariae"' (1987) 55 *Tijds. Rgeschied.* 117–22. Decisions of other provincial courts were also published, e.g. J. van de Sande, *Decisiones Frisicae sive rerum in suprema Frisiorum curia iudicatarum libri V* (Leeuwarden, 1647).

[21] e.g. *Consultatien, advysen en advertissementen, gegeven ende geschreven by verscheyden treffelijcke rechts-geleerden in Hollandt*, 6 vols. (Rotterdam, 1645–85) (the so-called 'Hollandsche Consultatien', to distinguish these from e.g. the collection of opinions given by Utrecht lawyers).

[22] The only biography, still authoritative, on Bijnkershoek is Star Numan, *Cornelis van Bynkershoek, zijn leven en zijne geschriften*. In addition, see G. C. C. J. van den Bergh, 'Der Präsident Cornelis van Bijnkershoek. Seine Bedeutung und sein Nachruhm' (1995) 3 *Zeitschrift für europäisches Privatrecht* 423–37.

a formidable lawyer, court president, legal author and polemist, and he is still well known as an author and authority on international law.[23] At home every night after a day in court, Bijnkershoek would make a summary of the case dealt with that day, noting down the legal essence, particulars and, importantly, the discussion between the judges and their personal opinions. He said that these notes were written *tumultuarie* – that is, entered in chronological order without organisation by subject matter – in his *adversarium*, ledger or rough-book. For that reason the notes were called *observationes tumultuariae*. In his *Quaestiones juris privati* Bijnkershoek cited many of them, referring to their number in his books, but now organised according to subject.[24] Bijnkershoek never used real names, except in cases in which the Nassaus were involved. He substituted names like Titius or Sempronius for the litigants' real names. But many of his reported cases can be traced through the resolution books of the Supreme Court with the help of the date and subject of decision, and from these books the full parties' names are often recoverable. Further, they can be traced in some other sources as well.[25] After Bijnkershoek's death his fellow member in the court and son-in-law Willem Pauw continued the *observationes* as *observationes tumultuariae*

---

[23] On account of his works *De dominio maris* (Lugduni Batavorum, 1703), in which he proposed the theory that sovereignty over sea is a derivative of sovereignty over the coast (based on possession) and extends from there over sea as far as guns can reach; *De foro legatorum* (Lugduni Batavorum, 1721); and *Quaestionum juris publici libri duo* (Lugduni Batavorum, 1731). Other works include *Observationum Juris Romani libri quattuor* (Lugdunum Batavorum, 1710). Next to that Bijnkershoek published in 1699, when he was still an advocate, anonymously, the *Ooyevaertjes of Haegse Mercuur*, a sometimes scabrous journal. When elected to the court, he tried to buy all copies. After his death a second edition was published at once in 1744. He also wrote the *Commentarius juris Hollandici et Zelandici*, the *Commentarius juris feudalis* and the *Farragines*, but the whereabouts of these works, only in manuscript, are unfortunately unknown. That is deplorable, since particularly in his *Commentarius juris Hollandici et Zelandici*, already written before he entered the court and which must have been longer than 1,600 pages, Bijnkershoek dealt with all kinds of (doctrinal) questions of law as applicable in the provinces of Holland and Zeeland. See A. J. B. Sirks, 'Bijnkershoek as author and elegant jurist' (2011) 79 *Tijds. Rgeschied.* 229–52.

[24] *Quaestionum juris privati libri quattuor* (Lugduni Batavorum, 1744). Books 1 and 2 were translated into English and published in Pretoria in 1987. It was well known that he kept such a diary, but of course he never showed it to others. In this book the *observationes* have been edited.

[25] The 'Resolutieboeken van de Hoge Raad' are in the National Archive, NA 3.03.02, 631–80, covering the years 1582–1779 (except for the years 1737–40). An alternative source is the 'Register van de Rapport-, Specie- en Comparitiegelden' (the register of fees and dues paid, which always records the parties), NA 3.03.02, 1352–1454, covering, with lacunae, the years 1688–1797. Since all judges were sharing the dues for reporting, we can be quite certain that this source is complete and correct.

novae (*Obs. tum. nov.*) until his own death in 1787, after which the notes remained in the family. Discovered in 1918 in an old bookshop, they were gradually published over the period 1923–2008.[26] The *observationes*, some 5,000 of them, written in a fluent Latin with shifts to and from Dutch, are an incomparable source on the formation of legal opinions within the Supreme Court for most of the eighteenth century (1704–87), and indeed encompass most of the cases dealt with in that period;[27] and crucially the *observationes* provide additional information about the cases that appears in no other sources. In the illustrative cases discussed below the *observationes* are, where possible, supplemented by the records of the resolution books. The latter sometimes fill out with useful forensic and procedural detail the more abstract rendering by Bijnkershoek of his colleagues' arguments. Through a combination of these sources we can begin to discern the qualities of the individual judges.

[26] Contrary to Pauw's wish that they were to be destroyed, the manuscripts of the *observationes* remained in the family, were auctioned in 1889, and lay on a shelf in an antique bookshop until 1919, when E. M. Meijers discovered them and began their publication. They are now in the University Library Leiden, sign. Coll. Meijers ms. 42 for vols. 1–14 of the *Obs. tum.* and Meijers ms. 43 for vols. 1–10 of the *Obs. tum. novae*. The published editions of Bijnkershoek's *Observationes tumultuariae*, cited as *Obs. tum.*, are as follows: ed. E. M. Meijers *et al.* (Harlemi, 1923–6), I: 1704–14; ed. T. J. Dorhout Mees *et al.* (Harlemi, 1934), II: 1714–24; ed. E. M. Meijers *et al.* (Harlemi, 1946), III: 1724–35; ed. E. M. Meijers *et al.* (Harlemi 1962), IV: 1735–43. The published volumes of Pauw's *Observationes tumultuariae novae*, cited as *Obs. tum. nov.*, are as follows: ed. H. F. W. D. Fischer *et al.* (Harlemi 1964), I: 1743–55; ed. R. Feenstra *et al.* (Harlemi, 1967), II: 1756–70; ed. R. Feenstra *et al.* (Harlemi, 1971), III: 1771–88. See, further, A. J. B. Sirks, 'Onuitgegeven teksten uit de *observationes tumultuariae* van Cornelis van Bijnkershoek' (2008) 75 *Tijds. Rgeschied.* 58–94. There are Dutch summaries of the *Obs. tum.* for the first three volumes: for the first two volumes, they are appended to the original, while those for the third volume have been published separately: *Van Bijnkershoeks Observationes (2018–2913) (Deel III)*, ... uitgeg. door A. J. B. Sirks ('s-Gravenhage, 2005). There are translations of a selected number of Pauw's *Obs. tum. novae*: W. Pauw, *Some Cases Heard in the Hooge Raad Reported by Willem Pauw*, ed. and tr. R. Feenstra *et al.* (Pretoria, 1985). There is a systematic index to the *Obs. tum.*: M. S. van Oosten, *Systematisch Compendium der Observationes tumultuariae van Cornelis van Bijnkershoek* (Haarlem, 1962). The 1985 edition of Pauw above has a subject index, while a separate subject register on all *observationes* has been published in Afrikaans: P. van Warmelo, *Registers op die observationes tumultuariae van Cornelis van Bijnkershoek en van Willem Pauw* (Pretoria, 1982). For an index by the authors themselves, see C. van Bijnkershoek and W. Pauw, *Index in observationes tumultuarias*, uitgeg. door A. J. B. Sirks (Werken der Stichting tot Uitgaaf der Bronnen van het Oud-Vaderlandse Recht, 34) ('s-Gravenhage 2005).

[27] A. Bisdom, Prosecutor-General at the Supreme Court 1734–9, and his son who was judge in the Supreme Court from 1788 until 1795, also collected material concerning cases before the court, often criminal cases (National Archives, Coll. Bisdom, NA 1.10.06, nos. 89–125, 216). In Bijnkershoek's *observationes*, in contrast, the large majority of cases are civil.

V

As to the private law applied by the court, it was primarily the customary, mostly written law of Holland and Zeeland, together with the laws of the executive of these provinces. Customary law could differ according to the towns the litigants were citizens of, and there was further a great divide in the law of succession of Holland between the areas of '*aas-*' and '*schependomsrecht*', primarily important regarding succession to real estate.[28] In commercial law, several ordinances and some municipal regulations (like the Amsterdam regulation on cheques) were important. In 1462 Duke Charles issued an instruction for the Court of Holland to judge 'according to the written laws'. By that he meant the Roman law, written down and collected in the *Corpus Juris* of Justinian. That was already the practice in the *Grote Raad* in Mechelen: reception of Roman law had already progressed considerably.[29] The public law was basically governed by the Political Ordinances of 1581 of Philip II, and criminal law by the Penal Ordinance of Charles V of 1532 (the *Constitutio Criminalis Carolina*) and, partially, by the Criminal Ordinances of 1570 of Philip II. These were some of the few unifying measures of the Habsburg rulers which had lasting success.

It would be wrong to assume that, due to the precedence of customary law, the court busied itself much with it. On the contrary, like courts elsewhere in Europe, it had a low opinion of it, often considering it an unattractive jumble of writings not to be taken seriously. Roman law was the law generally applied unless there was an explicit and clear customary law or an ordinance, issued by the former emperors, counts or, now, the States or the States-General. The question was not how Roman law could be applied to particular cases or situations, but whether there was

---

[28] South of the Old IJssel the (Zeeland) *aasdomsrecht* ruled, north of it the (Frisian) *schependomsrecht*. In case of an intestate inheritance and no descendants, the basic difference was that according to the former the estate was divided equally and went to the two ascendants of the *de cuius*, while according to the latter the estate went to the nearest of kin: H. de Groot, *Inleiding tot de Hollandsche rechts-geleertheid*, 2nd edn (Rotterdam, 1631), II.28.3: 'the nearest blood inherits the goods' (het naeste bloed, beurd het goed). See R. W. Lee, *An Introduction to Roman-Dutch Law*, 5th edn (Cape Town, 1953), pp. 393 *et seq.*

[29] See A. Wijffels, *Qui millies allegatur. Les allégations du droit savant dans les dossiers du Grand Conseil du Malines (causes septentrionales, ca. 1460–1580)* (Amsterdam, 1985). To the same effect for the *Reichskammergericht* of the Holy Empire, s. 3 Reichskammergericht Act stipulated that if there was no customary law, Roman law would be applied.

an area of sufficient interest to litigate or to write about in the first place. Areas worth developing included marriage and succession, sale, lease and partnership and general commercial law such as cheques, assignments and secured transactions such as land hypothecs (mortgages) and pledges in financial transactions. Most of this law was ruled by Roman law or strongly influenced by it.[30] Several handbooks on the resulting mixture of Roman and customary law were published, those of Grotius, van Leeuwen and Voet being the best known.[31] In other provinces, where the same fusion took place – with the exception of Friesland, where only Roman law was said to apply, and which Huber most aptly described – similar books were published.[32] Lawyers, and in the courts judges, used and referred to them freely.

VI

The following cases that are extracted from the *observationes* may give some impression of how the Supreme Court worked and applied the law. Here we shall meet questions of matrimonial and inheritance law, the law of sale, and of the validity of foreign judgments.

The first case from the *observationes tumultuariae* involved litigation between the duke of Richmond and his mother-in-law, Cecilia Munter, reported as *Obs. tum.* n. 2888, and decided on 1 March 1735. When Henry Cadogan, quartermaster general to Marlborough and later ambassador to the Dutch Republic, lived in The Hague, he married a Dutch girl, Margaretha Cecilia Munter, in 1704. Margaretha Cecilia was of high bourgeois birth (her grandfather, a very rich merchant, was seven times burgomaster of Amsterdam, her mother a wealthy Trip, her father a

---

[30] See also Brom's analysis of the court's jurisprudence in matters of sale (Brom, *Urteilsbegründungen im 'Hoge Raad van Holland, Zeeland en West-Friesland' am Beispiel des Kaufrechts im Zeitraum 1704–1787*).

[31] De Groot, *Inleiding tot de Hollandsche rechts-geleertheid*; H. de Groot, *The Introduction to Dutch Jurisprudence of Hugo Grotius*, with notes by Simon van Groenewegen van der Made, tr. A. F. S. Maasdorp (Cape Town, 1878); S. van Leeuwen, *Het roomsch hollandsch recht* (Leiden, 1664; many subsequent editions); S. van Leeuwen, *Simon van Leeuwen's Commentaries on Roman-Dutch law*, ed. C. W. Decker, tr. J G. Kotzé, 2nd edn (London, 1921–3); J. Voet, *Commentarius ad Pandectas* (Hagae-Comitum, 1698–1704); *The Selective Voet being the Commentary on the Pandects by Johannes Voet (1647–1713)*, tr. P Gane (Durban, 1955 (repr.)).

[32] U. Huber, *Heedensdaegse rechtsgeleertheyt*, 4th edn (Amsterdam, 1742); U. Huber, *The Jurisprudence of My Time* (Durban, 1939); J. Voorda, *Dictata ad ius hodiernum. Lectures on the Contemporary Law*, ed. and tr. M. Hewett (Amsterdam, 2005), gives an account of Roman and particular law of all provinces for the middle of the eighteenth century.

judge in the Court of Holland). As was usual in such social circles,[33] the parties to the marriage made an antenuptial agreement on 13 March 1704 before exchanging vows. They had two daughters, one of whom, Sarah, married the later second duke of Richmond,[34] the other marrying a son of the first earl of Portland.[35] When Sarah married in 1719, Cadogan promised his future son-in-law a large dowry but paid him only a quarter of it. It may not come as a surprise that when earl Cadogan died in 1726, the duke of Richmond claimed before the Court of Chancery from Cadogan's executor and heir (his brother Charles Cadogan) and his widow, who lived in The Hague, £60,000 sterling, the remainder of the dowry. The widow was not pleased with this. Her defence was that she herself had many claims on the estate, some deriving from her antenuptial agreement and some from Cadogan's testament. The antenuptial agreement entitled her to a lifelong allowance of 4,000 guilders per annum and a usufruct to be exercised over one-third of Cadogan's net estate. She also claimed *doarium* on the entire real estate, namely that the estate was burdened with what we might call a trust for her support. Furthermore she claimed back her dowry (44,000 guilders) and what she had brought into the marriage later on out of her father's inheritance (the *paraphernalia*). A dowry could only be established in Holland by way of antenuptial agreement and in such a case Roman law principles would apply. Apparently Margaretha Cecilia had stipulated for a full return of her dowry in the agreement.[36] All this should take preference over the duke's claim. Her youngest daughter also claimed from her father's estate her share according to her antenuptial agreement or as co-heiress.

The Court of Chancery adjudged on 11 July 1728 that the executor had to pay the remainder of Richmond's dowry first, invest the remainder in real estate so that the antenuptial agreement could be fulfilled, and put Margaretha Cecilia and her other daughter to a choice, between the antenuptial agreement and the testament.

---

[33] In the province of Holland community of property was the rule and in order to avoid that, one had to make an antenuptial agreement: see H. de Groot, *Inleiding tot de Hollandsche rechts-geleertheid*, II.11.8 and II.12; and further, Lee, *Introduction to Roman-Dutch Law*, pp. 66–71. Among the rich this was customary.

[34] Sarah, born 18 Sep. 1705, married Charles Lennox, on 4 Dec. 1719 in The Hague.

[35] Margaret, born 21 Feb. 1707, married Charles John Bentinck, in 1738.

[36] See Voet, *Commentarius ad Pandectas*, XXIII.3.1 and 2 on the establishment and extent of the dowry; *ibid.*, XXIV.4.52 on the full return of the dowry by antenuptial agreement (that the dowry would return to the wife upon the death of her husband was the rule in Roman law, in case of divorce it might be different).

Margaretha Cecilia's reaction was simple. She served a writ of seques-
tration over all the deceased's assets in the Netherlands and had the
executor summoned before the Court of Holland to pay her what was
owed to her under the antenuptial agreement and on other grounds.
According to the law of Holland (applying Justinian's law on dowries),
the antenuptial agreement gave her a preferred claim. The executor
replied with the exception that there was already a lawsuit concerning
this pending in England (the so called *exceptio litis pendentis*). This was
rejected by the Court of Holland.

On appeal all the Supreme Court judges agreed that Margaretha
Cecilia's argument did not lie in respect of the claims outside the antenuptial agreement since these were not the subject of any claim in
England. In respect of those deriving from the agreement, since the
creditor (Margaretha Cecilia) lived in Holland, this upheld the jurisdiction of the court; if the executor had wanted to contest this, he should
have used the exception of incompetence.

There remained the *exceptio litis pendentis*. All the judges thought it
did not apply, but for different reasons. The majority was of the opinion
that Margaretha Cecilia had merely been the defendant in England and
had not submitted a counterclaim to the agreement. Some, on the other
hand, were in doubt. Van der Hoop said that apparently in England a
universal judgment had been introduced, by which everything in a lawsuit, claims and counter-claims, could be adjudicated, even without a
formal counterclaim. Yet even if her claim was denied, such a judgment
would not be valid in Holland and therefore the exception was to be
rejected. Van Hees carried it even further: the lawsuit had been settled by
that and the exception was useless now. Van Bleiswijk, a good civilian,
remarked that it was more in the nature of a *iudicium familiae erciscun-
dae*, the judgment by which an estate was divided between heirs.
President Bijnkershoek was shocked by the stupidity of van der Hoop
and van Hees: nowhere in the world could a claim be granted without it
having first been formally submitted (*hoc abhorreat ab omni praxi,
ubique terrarum recepta*). If that were the case, it would have been in a
lawsuit between Richmond and the widow, not between her and the
executor: they were both defendants in England but in Holland each
other's adversaries. But he kept this to himself and remarked merely that
the *exceptio litis pendentis* was only applicable between the same adversaries. For him that sufficed. Other judges brought still other arguments
forward (which Bijnkershoek did not think quite relevant for the case),
and a majority confirmed the decision of the Court of Holland. And so

the exception was rejected. We may assume that Margaretha Cecilia was in the end victorious before the courts of Holland. In any case, she lived very comfortably afterwards.[37]

We see here the importance of the antenuptial agreement in Holland and the difference from the English common law. In the province of Holland marital community of property was customary law – not only for assets acquired during the marriage, but also for assets owned at the time of marriage (feudal assets excluded); and debts too became common. To avoid the unwanted consequences of this system the Dutch, by virtue of the subsidiary place of Roman law, used the Roman law system of *pacta antenuptalia* or *pacta dotalia*, the dowry agreement, which in classical and Justinianic Roman law did not rule property relations between spouses completely, but did so in Roman-Dutch law. As to succession, the *dotalia* was an agreement under which at the moment the marriage ended, whether by divorce or by death, all property relations between the spouses had to be settled. The marriage had been concluded in The Hague and was, according to Dutch law, ruled by Dutch law – hence Margaretha Cecilia's claim that her claims to the dowry and the *doarium*, evidently based on the *dotalia*, were privileged. At common law, as we have all become aware, they have no value. Also Cadogan's daughters presumably lived under English law: had it been Dutch law, they could have claimed a legitimate portion of their father's inheritance.

VII

Another case, reported as *Obs. tum.* n. 2465 and 2752 and decided on 28 February 1733, also shows the effects of antenuptial agreements. On 4 November 1688 the baron von Heems, an Austrian nobleman (from 1696 ambassador of the German emperor in Berlin, and from 1707 resident in The Hague and extraordinary imperial envoy and ambassador there) married in Berlin one Agneta Heidoorn, widow of Daniel Schadeberg, who had two sons by her first marriage. Agneta and Heems had some assets, Daniel had had nothing. On 20 November, sixteen days after the marriage, they had drawn up an agreement, which Bijnkershoek calls *pacta dotalia*, since it said that the parties had agreed the following before the marriage. As to the two boys, Agneta reserved for them 500

---

[37] According to the tax register, she had in 1742 a yearly income of 20,000 guilders, a coach with two horses, seven maids, a house in The Hague, rent 800 guilders, and a country house, Raephorst (near Haarlem, inherited from her father).

rixdollars each out of her paternal inheritance, with the income from this capital to maintain them until they were sixteen. If Heemst were to die without children, Agneta was to receive a pre-legacy of 500 rixdollars and their goods were to be divided into two halves which would go to the relatives of each spouse, unless one of the contracting parties wanted to bestow on the other by testament something more. As we shall see, the judges were divided over the nature and effect of this complicated agreement. The terms of the agreement barred from the outset the imposition of community of property, but if the baron died without children then this in effect is what would emerge, subject to a reservatory clause allowing a party to reduce its share in favour of the other. Heems died in 1718. He had made a testament, in which he had instituted his brother as his heir, bestowing upon his wife the usufruct of all his possessions. She accepted this and enjoyed it till she died in 1721. Meanwhile, Frans, one of the boys, both of whom had been travelling and studying in Prague and Bresslau, had died. Now a controversy emerged between the count's brother Johann Baptist and the other boy, Ernst, now calling himself more genteelly Ernestus de Schadeberg (though to little avail, as he would turn bad),[38] which by mutual consent they put before the Supreme Court to decide. Ernst claimed half of the estate as remaining and sole heir to his mother. The count's brother contended that according to the law of Vienna, under which Heems had married Agneta, there was no community of property whatsoever, that all his brother had ever possessed had been acquired by him and not by Agneta, and so he, as brother, was now, as sole heir, entitled to all. To be certain, he asked for a declaration by the court that there had been no community between the spouses. Lacking an account of what each spouse had contributed at the moment of marriage, his second argument was frail. The judge-reporter (Keetlaer) remarks that Heems had apparently been

---

[38] In 1729 Ernst was an advocate in The Hague and pretended to be consul of the Genoan Republic and counsellor of the Countess of Wils. Arrested and detained, he confessed that he had obtained secret documents which he had sent to the embassies of Sweden, Denmark and Hanover, offering to provide more in exchange for money. He further had communicated other state secrets to the ambassador of Greater Russia. Other persons too had sold secrets. All this was treason. See the letter of Johan de Mauregnault (judge in the Court of Holland), to Caspar van Citters, pensionary of the States of Zeeland, 6 Jan. 1729 (Archief Zeeland, Verheyen van Citters, 468, at 1, 2, 2, 18). Perhaps he was the banished advocate of *Obs. tum.* n. 2529, decided 1 Jun. 1729, who had still some claims before the Supreme Court. His wife now represented him. Banishment for life would have been the least, but also rather the most likely punishment Ernst could have expected in view of his social position. Thus, although the case, which will have begun before June 1729, is in his name, it is very probable that after January 1729 an agent (his wife?) conducted the litigation.

under the impression that the nuptial agreement had introduced community of property, but that had not been the case. Besides, Agneta had accepted the testament which had replaced the agreement. He therefore decided in favour of Heems. As for the other six judges, de Roovere agreed with Keetlaer; van der Hoop on the other hand was of the opinion that the agreement had introduced community of property, but that by testament it was possible to deviate from this and Agneta had accepted that. Van Hees and Duirkant joined him. Van der Does, on the other hand, considered the agreement a conditional testament, revoked by Heems' subsequent testament. Thus six judges wanted, for different reasons, to award Heems the entire estate. Bijnkershoek came quickly to the point. Antenuptial agreements in the eighteenth century had to be instituted before the marriage. The agreement was saved in this case by the insertion in the deed that it had been agreed, apparently orally (which was possible), beforehand, and only recorded after the marriage. But it did not introduce marital community of property. It only ruled what was to happen after death. What we see here is that the antenuptial agreement almost takes the place of a testament; as in modern German law *Ehe-* and *Erbvertrag* can fuse. The only exception allowed here was the granting by testament to the other spouse of more than half, and this was what the testament did: it gave the usufruct to Agneta over the other half (of Heems), but this did not mean that it could take away Agneta's own half. Unfortunately she had been under the impression that all would go, eventually, to her husband's brother, but this misapprehension had no legal consequences. Apparently Bijnkershoek's argument convinced several of his colleagues, because in his observation he notes that four of the seven followed this reasoning (the various opinions were evidently noted down in the resolutions book before the discussion, and the final vote was not recorded in this case) and assigned Ernst half the estate. It is evident that this was not what the baron had wanted in his testament, but his *voluntas* did not count here, since he had already restricted his *facultas testandi*. Apparently Bijnkershoek was thinking here of the mutual testament which, like the modern German Berliner testament, is an *Erbvertrag*, which cannot generally be revoked without the consent of the other party if this party were to profit from it. That had indeed been the case for Agneta, who possessed much less than the baron and would benefit by receiving half of the joined fortunes.[39]

---

[39] For this, see *BGB* para. 2269. For mutual wills, see Voet, *Commentarius ad Pandectas*, XXIII.4.63 and Lee, *Introduction to Roman-Dutch Law*, pp. 390–1 referring to S. van Leeuwen, *Het roomsch hollandsch recht* (Leiden, 1664), III.2.4.

There were other differences between the parties. Heems's brother also claimed back from Ernst those expenses which the deceased had paid after his sixteenth birthday. Ernst responded with claims of large accounts in Vienna and a house in Berlin which had belonged to his mother. Two judges simply concluded that Heems had never had the intention of claiming these expenses back; van Hees, followed by three other judges, stated that there had been community of property and that these expenses were communal and so, according to D. 17.2.73, burdened the community property. Bijnkershoek again dotted the i's and crossed the t's – he must have been exasperating at times for his fellow judges – stating first that the Roman law rules on *communio omnium bonorum* could be applied to the marital community of property. That is not self-evident and present Dutch law does not entirely accord with that. Furthermore, according to Roman law, if a stepfather supported his stepson while planning to claim back the value, he was not to reclaim: C. 2.18.15. This text says this of a freedman who supports his manumissor's daughter. He did what he should already have done as moral duty. The same went for a stepfather. Secondly, although there was no marital community of property in Rome, the Romans were nevertheless of the opinion that if there was a *communio omnium bonorum* between partners it also included money spent on the children of a partner. D. 17.2.73 stated that if a communion of property between partners had been agreed, it included future acquisitions, but also expenses *ob honorem* for the children. By that the Romans had, of course, meant expenses necessary in seeking an honorific municipal office. But that did not matter. If this was valid for such an office, the more was it valid for such expenses as food, travel and study. Besides, the stepfather was prepared to spend lavishly. Thirdly, according to modern practice and as confirmed by Dutch authors such as Someren, Wesel and Voet, a stepfather was obliged to do this. He had accepted with the marriage the burden of his wife's children from the previous marriage.

VIII

Another case, reported as *Obs. tum.* n. 420, decided on 26 June 1708, also deals with the law of succession. Joannes Vollenhoven (1631–1708), vicar of the Great Church in The Hague, had died on 14 March 1708, leaving a holographic testament with his children as witnesses. With this he instituted his two sons for the legitimate portion, saying that through his protection they had already been blessed with some profitable offices.

Although they received less than the other children, the reference to their advancements makes this postponement reasonable and legally defensible,[40] and it is certainly plausible that a vicar could so promote his children's careers in order to protect their future. Vollenhoven had taken as his second wife a sister of Frederik Rosenboom, member of the Court of Holland, and had through that marriage got into the Orangist clique, which could provide sinecures; as could his brother, a burgomaster of Zwolle and member of the Admiralty of Amsterdam. The remainder of his estate was left for his three daughters, who of course did not have such opportunities.

Still one son, the elder, was not a true Christian. As soon as he came of age he started to contest the will, saying that it was invalid since it lacked a date. The daughters and the other son opposed this and asked the Supreme Court for maintenance and possession of the estate. As the other younger son was content with his legitimate portion, he based himself on Justinian's Code 6.33.3, which says that whoever is first instituted as heir, ought to have possession. The elder son claimed possession on the ground that his father had died intestate. Normally a testament needs a date, but, as Bijnkershoek notes, 'in my Commentarii I have refuted this idea'.[41] Yet here we are dealing with a *testamentum inter liberos* and for that Justinian's Novel 107.1 and the *Authentica Quod sine* (inserted in the Codex after C. 6.23) require explicitly that the time must be designated. That had not been done here and so C. 6.33.3 did not apply.

But the other heirs objected that that was only the case where more than one testament existed. Otherwise it would be impossible to determine which one was the last one. That, however, was not the case here. A daughter who had died less than a year before the testator, had been passed over in the testament. Consequently it had to have been drawn up within this short period. They also cited D. 20.1.34.1. Here a contract of pledge which lacks a date is considered valid. The Supreme Court accepted this exception to the rule since there was but one testament.

---

[40] Lee, *Introduction to Roman-Dutch Law*, p. 355: in the absence of a provision to the contrary, children claiming to share in the estate may only do so on condition of bringing into account property received from the deceased during his lifetime for the advancement of their marriage, business or merchandise, the so-called *collatio bonorums*; referring to, inter alia, Voet, *Commentarius ad Pandectas*, XXXVII.6. The profitable offices were of course not property of the deceased and formally the claiming son had a point here, but substantially it would lead to an unfair benefit.

[41] See n. 24, above: these commentarii were his private writings.

The texts and authors the plaintiff cited (Justinian's Novel 107.1, Sande's *Decisiones Frisicae*, and some *consilia*) followed the formalities of the law, but not its substance. Judge van Vrijhoven also cited Grotius in favour of this, President Admirael reminded the Court that Novel 107 did not sanction omission with nullity and that the Accursian Gloss allowed for exceptions in case of testaments *ad pias causas*, as Gothofredus had done. Already by 26 June the court had decided the case in favour of the pious children.

If you look at Bijnkershoek's report of the case, the Roman law sources are clearly distinct. It would seem as if only this was Roman law and the rest not. Yet that would be a wrong impression. All the rest is Roman law too. In his *Introduction to Roman-Dutch Law* Grotius, when dealing with the testament, simply follows the Roman law. Only after he has described the way a testament is executed according to Roman law does he say that it is permissible to do it thus, but that we – the Hollanders – usually follow custom – namely, execute the testament before a public officer. Also the customary law is that husband and wife may make one testament. Thus customary law is marginal: substantially it is all Roman law. It is Roman-Dutch law, but the Roman part is major. Common law executorship, on the other hand, also known in medieval Continental Europe, was an indigenous invention, but on the Continent it survived only as one particular form of testamentary disposition available to testators.

IX

In other areas of the law, such as contracts, Roman law influence was likewise great. An exception here was insurance, bills of exchange and average gross. A case of a sale, *Obs. tum.* n. 1420 and decided on 25 February 1728,[42] is interesting for the liability of the seller but also for showing the role of the option in trade. On 6 July 1706 Adam van Kempen gave Lucas Condrij an option on 5,000 lbs of whalebones to be delivered between 6 July and 30 November 1706, for a price of up to 41 guilders per 100 lbs. If Lucas had not requested delivery before that date, delivery would take place on 30 November for that price. Because the price increased to 58 or 59 guilders, Lucas claimed delivery on 23 October 1706. But no delivery was made and Adam was cited before the Bench of Amsterdam and adjudged to deliver for the agreed price

---

[42] See now Brom, *Urteilsbegründungen im 'Hoge Raad van Holland, Zeeland en West-Friesland' am Beispiel des Kaufrechts im Zeitraum 1704–1787*, pp. 151–2 on this case.

and also to restore to Lucas the *id quod interest, quanti unquam plurimi*, his full interest in having the delivery made on that date. Adam indeed now agreed to deliver, but as to the damages he merely offered to pay the difference between the 41 guilders and the market price of the whalebones on 23 October.

Adam's appeal being rejected, he appealed up to the Supreme Court. This had had cases like this before and it was its standing opinion that the *interesse* was to be reckoned with reference to the day delivery should have taken place and not the day the claim was raised before the court (or, for example, the day judgment was given). The Supreme Court based this on several texts of the Digest: D. 12.1.22, D. 13.3.4 and D.2.11.12.1, and also Sande, *Decisiones Frisicae* III.4.8. D. 12.1.22 who deals with the question of whether to take the moment delivery was due or the bringing of the claim, or that of the judgment being given, in order to establish the *litis aestimatio* – namely, the value the case has for the claimant. Sabinus's answer in D. 12.1.22 is: the moment delivery was due, unless this was not established, in which case the moment the proceedings started should be taken. D. 13.3.4 says the same, but Cassius here supports the second possibility, the day of judgment. D. 2.11.12.1, not cited in previous cases, states in a general way that the moment at which performances should have taken place is to be taken as determinative. As we see, it is Roman law which dictates the solution. The decision of the Frisian court was the same (which is not surprising, since Roman law was the private law in that province). Furthermore the Supreme Court condemned Adam van Kempen to pay interest on the sum claimed, but only from the moment the claim was initiated. This was contrary to previous decisions, but here the price had gone up since and was at the moment 100 to 110 guilders per 100 lbs, whereas in the previous decisions the price had gone down and delivery had not been in the interest of the buyer.

But Lucas Condrij had claimed both delivery and *id quod interest*, which was possible in Roman law. But was it right in this case? Van Kempen thought not, since it was the practice in Amsterdam and a custom amongst merchants that one could always deliver and be discharged. Bijnkershoek and the court thought otherwise. If the whalebones were delivered – and Condrij could insist on that, since there was still a contract of sale – Condrij could sell them at 100 to 110 guilders per 100 lbs. However, if he would receive in addition to that the price difference as at 23 October, he would be enriched without ground. The *id quod interest* was, in this particular case, what he would get if delivery did not take place. So if there was a delivery, it was not right that he should also be entitled to the *interesse*. Therefore the court confirmed on 25 February 1718 the Amsterdam judgment but with the modification that van Kempen either had to deliver or to pay the *interesse*, leaving it to Condrij to choose which he wanted. We see here, by the way, the slow but irresistible entrée of the unjustified enrichment idea, not unknown in Roman law, but more developed by the canonists.

X

The civil law of sale also had great difficulty with the passing of risk, and this point was the problem in *Obs. tum.* n. 1326, decided on 17 April 1723, a case which concerned the sale of hay.[43] In September 1697 Robeijns bought from Verploeg all the hay still on land which was to be mowed. Before the hay could be delivered the land was flooded. Robeijns tried to withdraw from the contract, but Verploeg insisted on specific performance – namely, that Robeijns should take the hay and pay for it. On 5 October 1697 they agreed that Robeijns, the buyer, would mow the hay as soon as possible and take it away with him, that some hay stacks should be left for another buyer and that arbiters should estimate the damage caused by the flooding. The next day Robeijns' ships took a sizeable part of the hay, but an even larger part remained on the land. The day after, another flood spoiled the remainder of the hay. The seller, Verploeg, now sued Robeijns for the entire price and the third party buyer for the price of the haystacks. The court of Heusden awarded Verploeg his claim, the Court of Holland confirmed this ten years later, in 1710. In 1723 the case went before the Supreme Court, since the buyer had appealed. There had not yet been an estimate of the damages.

The opinions of the judges varied enormously. Some confirmed the judgments of the previous courts, which had based themselves on the rule *periculum est emptoris*: as soon as a sale is perfected, the risk of the yet undelivered thing is on the buyer. Other judges contested this, since this case concerned generic goods and here, as stated in D.18.1.35, 18.6.1 and CJ 4.48.2, the contract was not perfect until the goods had been weighted, counted or measured, individualised as we now say. That had not taken place for the second delivery. As to the first delivery, no estimate of damages had yet been made. They consequently rejected the previous judgments. Bijnkershoek thought this was sensible.

---

[13] See *ibid.*, pp. 168–70 on this case.

Other judges said that individualisation had not taken place because the buyer had been *in mora*, in default. Consequently the risk now lay with him, see CJ 4.48.2. Yet, according to Bijnkershoek, it was not certain that the buyer had been in default either before the first or before the second flooding. Therefore this opinion could not stand, in his opinion.

Lastly, another group of judges, among whom was Bijnkershoek, were of the opinion that the case was not yet ripe for any decision since the facts were too obscure: they were not yet *in forma probanti* — that is, there was insufficient certainty about the facts. This seemed to a majority the best way to go. There was nothing better in case of doubt than to postpone the matter, and in an interlocutory decision the parties were charged to present their case better. As to the third party, with a majority of one vote his claim was adjudicated but not yet promulgated. Of course this was nonsense and Bijnkershoek jotted down his dissatisfaction with it. On 17 April a majority in the court decided that Robeijns had been in default on both occasions, whereas the third party buyer had not been. Thus the judgment of the previous courts was annulled but only in respect to the third party.

XI

The *observationes* of Bijnkershoek show us two things. One is how the judgment of the Supreme Court was reached. It was a case of finding a majority by vote. But behind the vote lay the reasons for voting this way. How did a judge understand the legal aspects of the case? Here opinions could differ considerably and sometimes a majority was found but on completely different grounds and, albeit rarely, on grounds which in themselves could not carry the decision (and the errors are sometimes indeed appalling). To speak of 'the opinion of the court' is to speak of a fiction. Such a fictive intent pertained even if all judges were of the same opinion (which, it must be emphasised, was far more often the case than the examples given above might suggest). The common law way of judges each delivering in public their opinion is more clear and trans-parent, but it makes the search for a *ratio decidendi* (which, actually, is the equivalent of the opinion of the court) a necessary yet often elusive task. But this difference will be due to the formally different role of the judge: here to find and formulate the law, there merely to interpret the law. 'Leges, solae leges, Senatorum animos regunt, et sine his vix quic-quam valet ullius hominis auctoritas' ('The laws, only the laws rule the minds of the judges, and without these the authority of any man is barely good for anything'), wrote Bijnkershoek.[44] Today there is no difference and opinions of the court remain to be constructed by the readers of judgments. Until 1815 it was anyway impossible in Dutch law to distinguish an opinion since the judgments were given without reasons. From the beginning of the nineteenth century a reasoned judgment was generally required in Europe. Where more than one judge is involved in determining a case it means that a seeming consensus has to be constructed. But this may disguise stark differences in opinion between the judges; the published opinion may reflect merely the minimum of agreement necessary to issue the judgment.

Secondly we see here how the reception of Roman law took its course in Holland, and, in principle, everywhere else where it was accepted as subsidiary law. Theoretically, if there was a clear local or customary law, this had to be applied. But as soon as there was a lacuna, Roman law could and would be applied. Practice was, actually, the other way around: Roman law was the basis of jurisprudence and positive law, unless there was an explicit local law. And then this was interpreted narrowly and in a civilian way. There were so many lacunae that the space occupied by Roman law continually expanded and so made the customary law dwindle. In the end custom formed isolated spots in a wide landscape of Roman law. In such a setting, the development of new views would be framed within Roman law concepts and in a Roman law context.

---

[44] *Obs. tum.*, VII, p. vi., in Sirks, 'Onuitgegeven teksten uit de observationes tumultuariae van Cornelis van Bijnkershoek'.

III

Imperial law

13

11,000 Prisoners: Habeas corpus, 1500–1800

PAUL D. HALLIDAY[*]

I began a systematic survey of King's Bench files in the late 1990s, but for any historian working since 2001 on the writ of habeas corpus, especially for an American, there is now a large presentist elephant in the room. I want to begin with a story, telling it in part to acknowledge that elephant, which has been with us since the case of Lakhdar Boumediene and others have followed their shambling courses through US courts. I also tell the story to suggest how I hope to honour my commitments as a historian, all the while aware that any history of habeas corpus will be used by American lawyers and judges who insist that they must base decisions on an understanding of what the writ was in 1789 and the generations preceding.[1]

So first, a story, before delving into the archives from which the story comes, in order to suggest how the English history of such a legal device might be recovered.

One story

Given the names of the ships involved, this may sound like the tale that proves fact stranger than fiction. It was late 1692. Britain and France were at war, and though King James II had been decisively defeated at the Boyne two years earlier, those who supported William and Mary still feared rebellion at home and invasion from Ireland or France. In such circumstances, that an Irishman – John Golding – should have captained

---

[*] My thanks to participants of the 2007 British Legal History Conference for discussion, especially Kevin Costello, James Oldham, and D. E. C. Yale.

[1] The US Supreme Court has said repeatedly that it must use the writ, 'at the absolute minimum . . . "as it existed in 1789"'. The original quotation is from *Felker* v. *Turpin*, 518 U.S. 651, 663–4 (1996), repeated in *INS* v. *St. Cyr*, 533 U.S. 289, 301 (2001). In his opinion for the court's majority in favour of the plaintiffs, Associate Justice Anthony Kennedy reiterated this view: *Boumediene* v. *Bush*, 553 US 723, 746 (2008).

a ship commissioned by Louis XIV called the *Sunn* is a detail made for anyone with an eye for irony. That Golding's ship should then have been captured by an English galley called the *James* is simply too good to be true. Yet there it is, all recounted in the return to the writ of habeas corpus sued by Golding from the court of King's Bench in 1693.

The warrant for Golding's imprisonment, transcribed fully in the return, had been made by the Commissioners for Sick and Wounded Seamen and for the Exchange of Prisoners of War. Their warrant called Golding a 'prisoner at war'. Whether or not he was properly designated such a prisoner was the question Golding asked by using habeas corpus. Upon reading the return to his writ, the justices would have learned that Golding was the king's and queen's subject, and thus not correctly labelled a 'prisoner at war'. So the court bailed him to await trial for treason at the next Admiralty sessions. The trial ended badly for Golding: he was convicted and executed.[2] But habeas corpus had performed precisely as it long had by 1693, providing the court with the opportunity to supervise imprisonment or detention orders made by any authority acting in the monarch's name, and correcting such authorities when they erred.

With one story, we have added 50 per cent to the total of pre-1800 habeas cases examined by scholars concerned with whether or not people called 'prisoners of war' could raise questions about their detention by using habeas corpus.[3] But we can add more to the mix. At least nine more prisoners in five other cases were called 'prisoners at war' or 'enemy aliens' in returns to writs of habeas corpus in the 1690s. Not only did they use the writ, four were released.[4] When we increase the number of known cases concerned with prisoners of war and enemy aliens, we enrich our

---

[2] M. J. Prichard and D. E. C. Yale (eds.), *Hale and Fleetwood on Admiralty Jurisdiction*, Selden Society, vol. 108 (London, 1993), pp. 332–41. For the writ and the order on it, see TNA KB 16/1/3 and KB 21/24/264. There is some confusion in the record: though the date on the writ is 4 Nov. 1693, the order to issue the writ in the Crown side rulebook is dated 8 Feb., in the following Hilary term of 1694. The notation of bail – entered on the return, the usual place for such notation in this period – is quite clear.

[3] The other two are the case of the *Three Spanish Sailors* (1779) and *Schiever's Case* (1759) 2 Black. W. 1324 and 2 Keny. 473, 96 E.R. 775 and 1249.

[4] On prisoners of war, see P. D. Halliday, *Habeas Corpus: From England to Empire* (Cambridge, MA, 2010), pp. 168–74. These nine were: Abraham Fuller, 'prisoner at war', discharged (TNA KB 11/14, 23 Jan. 1690, KB 21/23/362, and PC 2/73/316 and 351); John Depremont and three others, alien enemies, remanded pending prisoner exchange with the French (KB 11/14, 7 Feb. 1690, KB 21/23/367, 370, and 372, and PC 2/73/245, 260, 279, 300, 328, 361, and 366); John Dupuis, French prisoner, remanded pending exchange (KB 16/1/5, 12 Apr. 1695 and PC 2/76/116v); Garrett Cumberford, 'prisoner of war', bailed (KB 16/1/6, 23 Jan. 1697, KB 21/25/120 and PC 2/76/65v); and

understanding of the writ's history. This matters, and not only because lawyers and federal judges in the United States want a history of habeas corpus to tell them what to do. It matters because it suggests a wider problem in the methods and sources used in writing a writ's history. That we know Golding's story at all tells us how we can solve that problem.

The problem is leading case history.[5] Though such an approach to law's past has generally been out of favour among legal historians, habeas corpus remains a legal device whose historical outlines have traditionally been traced along a thin string of some dozens of printed case reports linked in connect-the-dots fashion.[6] That we know Golding's story results from setting aside the reports – even the manuscript ones – until we have first done our work in the appropriate court archives: in this case, those on the Crown side of King's Bench. Golding's case points out the surprises that await us there. If we go further into the archives, if we count such cases in a systematic way, we can begin to see patterns of usage in their full, multi-dimensional shapes, shapes that help us make sense of the leading cases, and more important, of less-than-leading cases like Golding's. But this is a point that hardly needs emphasising here, so let us get to work.

Daniel DuCastre and Francis LaPierre, alien enemies, discharged (KB 16/1/6, 23 Jan. 1697, KB 21/25/149 and 210, and Fortescue 195, 92 E.R. 816).

[5] As Christopher Columbus Langdell, transformative dean of Harvard's law school more than a century ago, put it as he promoted the virtues of leading case learning, 'the vast majority [of cases] are useless and worse than useless'. Quoted by A. W. B. Simpson, 'Legal iconoclasts and legal ideals' (1990) 58 *U. Cin. L. Rev.* 837. Sir Frederick Pollock took a similar view of leading cases compared to those that did not lead: 'Unreported cases are in theory no less binding on the court than reported ones. But here the difference also comes in. The science of case-law being wholly conventional, we might, if we chose, absolutely limit the field of observation to reported cases, as it now is practically limited with trifling exceptions, or even to the authorised Law Reports, without any loss to the scientific character of our work': 'The science of case-law' in *Jurisprudence and Legal Essays*, selected by A. L. Goodhart (London, 1961), p. 174. For a broad critique of this view, see A. W. B. Simpson, *Leading Cases in the Common Law* (Oxford, 1995).

[6] In the most recent work considering the writ's English history, 159 reports of 143 cases are cited from the three centuries before 1789: R. J. Sharpe, *The Law of Habeas Corpus*, 2nd edn (Oxford, 1989). The principal American work cites seventy-two reports of fifty-nine cases from the same period: W. F. Duker, *A Constitutional History of Habeas Corpus* (Westport: CT, 1980). Earlier scholars worked with far fewer cases: e.g. R. C. Hurd, *A Treatise on the Right of Personal Liberty, and on the Writ of Habeas Corpus and the Practice Connected with It*, 2nd edn (Albany: NY, 1876), pp. 75–91, and W. S. Church, *A Treatise on the Writ of Habeas Corpus*, 2nd edn (San Francisco, CA, 1893), pp. 4–16. An important exception is the unpublished treatise of Frederick Solly-Flood, who studied the King's Bench controlment rolls. The manuscript is in the library of the Royal Historical Society, London.

Four conceptual foundations of habeas corpus

Before going further, I must stipulate four conceptual premises of habeas corpus that appear when viewed from within thousands of cases found in the court's archive.

Firstly, habeas corpus is a writ of the prerogative, not a writ of liberty.[7] The writ's history has generally been written from the assumption that because it has come to provide a means by which we might protect modern liberal norms concerning individual rights, we must seek the writ's origins in ideas about liberty that resemble or foretell our own. Americans in particular have wanted this kind of history, in which habeas corpus is a synecdoche for modern liberal ideals. But that habeas protected what was always called 'the liberty of the subject' goes straight to the heart of the writ's conceptual origins: in subjecthood, not the modern autonomous self. Once we see the writ's genesis in mutual obligations binding subject to sovereign, we can understand why it packed enormous legal force. That this was a prerogative writ does not simply provide a neat category in which we can group habeas with certiorari, mandamus, and other judicial devices; it is the key to understanding this legal force.[8] In the years around 1600, especially in the years 1604–6, court files allow us to watch the justices of Queen's and King's Bench perform a rhetorical capture of the most critical kind: taking for their own use the greatest power of all, the king's. This would give to habeas corpus the capacity to protect ideas about liberty and the modern self as they developed in later epochs and largely outside of the law.[9]

Secondly, taking control of the prerogative in this way gave the judges an instrument of such force and flexibility that we may rightly call it equitable, though many might have blanched at using that label given the personal and institutional competition between common law and equity in the early seventeenth century. This should not surprise us, given that one of the writ's chief functions was to monitor the conciliar courts and other courts of equity and, in so doing, to restrict, if not seize, their jurisdiction. But there was more here than the poaching of purview;

---

[7] On the prerogative in habeas corpus, see Halliday, *Habeas Corpus*, ch. 3.

[8] On the prerogative writs, see S. A. de Smith, 'The prerogative writs' (1951–53) 11 *C.L.J.* 40–56.

[9] On pre-liberal notions of liberty in and around habeas litigation, see Halliday, *Habeas Corpus*, ch. 6.

there was imitation of equitable practice, as the judges of King's Bench used habeas to speak to matters well beyond the status of prisoners and as they did so by means often in apparent violation of their own rules.[10] Furthermore, given the conceptual proximity of habeas corpus to judicial instruments like mandamus and *quo warranto*, we must see that habeas was much less concerned with what we might like to call the rights of the prisoner than with the wrongs of the jailer. Like *quo warranto* or mandamus, habeas was for inspecting the use of royal franchises: in this case, the franchises of jailers and the courts or officers who wrote their orders. The writ was concerned to protect the relationship between king and subject by ensuring that subjects' bodies were held by the king's officers in accordance with law. By appreciating that the writ's focus was on jailers, not on prisoners, we can see how this would ultimately widen the writ's ambit rather than narrow it.[11]

Thirdly, the relationship of King's Bench and the writ of habeas corpus to Parliament and to statute was ambivalent. The writ's history has often been told in statutory terms, especially by Americans, who followed Blackstone in celebrating the Habeas Corpus Act of 1679 as 'that second Magna Carta'.[12] Since much authority to imprison was given by statute to officers commissioned by the king – Justices of the Peace, Special Commissioners, and after 1689, the Privy Council – we should see statute as typically posing problems to be solved in habeas jurisprudence. Using habeas, King's Bench carefully policed the bounds of statutes, sometimes pulling them in. We can see this in the tendency of the court to bail or discharge those seemingly imprisoned in strict accordance with statutes concerned with bastard-bearing or alehouse-keeping in the seventeenth century. In the eighteenth century, we can watch the use of statutes defining the bounds of impressment inspected in much the same way. Nonetheless, King's Bench always recognised that Parliament was the greater court, and only Parliament's imprisonment orders, not the Privy Council's, would remain above question by habeas corpus. We can thus appreciate all the more the irony of every statute after 1689 that suspended bail in cases of treason – what we usually call the suspension of habeas corpus – as such statutes returned

---

[10] This is apparent, for instance, in the judges' violation of ostensible evidentiary rules limiting them to matter found in the writ's return. Halliday, *Habeas Corpus*, pp. 108–16; more generally on the writ's equitable character, see pp. 87–93.

[11] On this franchise view and the prerogative writs, see Halliday, *Habeas Corpus*, pp. 41–4, 74–84, and 184–7.

[12] 1 *Commentaries* 133.

to the Privy Council the very powers that had been taken from it by Parliaments in 1628 and 1641.[13]

We might, like Blackstone, try to compensate for this statutory embarrassment – and that's what many MPs thought Suspension Acts were – by pointing to the glories of the Habeas Corpus Act of 1679. But a close look at thousands of writs granted before 1679 shows that the procedural requirements detailed in that Act had long been accomplished in the work of the judges themselves.[14] That judges did not need that Act in order to innovate in the use of the writ is suggested by the formulaic note on the back of John Golding's writ, showing that it had been granted by the judges at common law rather than according to the terms of the Habeas Corpus Act. The common law writ, not the statutory one, would provide the principal site for major innovations in habeas corpus across the eighteenth century.

Fourthly, we see in the writ's operation the concept of subjecthood taken to its outer limits. For subjecthood relied on the idea of the king's protection. All who came within his protection were his subjects.[15] This helps to explain why allegations of foreign status, even enemy alien status, were almost never discussed in early-modern habeas cases and did not bar use of the writ. When we appreciate that it was royal authority that empowered the judges, we can see how a habeas jurisprudence focused more on the wrongs of jailers acting by the king's franchise than on the rights of prisoners had the surprising effect of making the writ widely available to those who were not the king's 'natural subjects', but who were nonetheless under his protection as what Sir Matthew Hale called 'local subjects'.[16] The force of the prerogative and the concern with franchises explain how the writ would go well beyond England and cover much more than the English. It explains how the writ would go to North America, where it would be used in many colonies without any explicit grant; and how later, at the same time that the writ was taken from Americans by the suspension statutes of 1777

---

[13] On suspension, see P. D. Halliday and G. E. White, 'The suspension clause: English text, imperial contexts, and American implications' (2008) 94 *Va. L. Rev.* 613–28. On the transposition of constraints on habeas corpus from Privy Council to Parliament over the seventeenth century, see Halliday, *Habeas Corpus*, ch. 7.

[14] e.g. it has long been said that one could not get a writ of habeas corpus during the court's vacations before 1679. On vacation usage, see Halliday, *Habeas Corpus*, pp. 54–8 and 239–40.

[15] As Sir Matthew Hale put it, 'Every person that comes within the king's dominions owes a local subjection and allegiance to the king, for he hath here the privilege of protection': D. E. C. Yale (ed.), *Sir Matthew Hale's The Prerogatives of the King*, Selden Society, vol. 92 (London, 1976), p. 56.

[16] *Ibid.*, p. 54.

and following, the writ would be extended to natives of Bengal, a part of the world where the 1765 Treaty of Allahabad had not made anything like a full British sovereignty.[17]

With these conceptual premises in mind, let us turn to examine a few of the patterns we can see if we aggregate information from many writs.

The survey

If we make a thorough search in the archives of the Crown side of King's Bench, counting all writs used every fourth year from 1502 to 1798, inclusive, we find evidence concerning 2,757 users of the writ. In all, 11,000 prisoners – and probably something more than that – used the writ from 1500 to 1800. One more number: 53 per cent. This was the likelihood that one would be bailed or discharged when using habeas corpus. Sharp deviations from such an average, correlated to variations in the wrongs alleged, the type of official who ordered imprisonment or many other variables can help us identify moments needing closer scrutiny. Across three centuries, we can closely track judicial practices, and by correlating outcomes to other variables such as the wrong alleged against each prisoner, we can use habeas as a barometer of popular anxieties, of official responses to those anxieties and of the court's oversight of those who imprisoned or detained others.

Wrongs

Let us begin with large numbers over the long view (Figure 1). Multiplying by four the totals derived from our quadrennial survey, we can estimate total habeas corpus activity. Setting aside the prominent spike in the middle of the sixteenth century, explained by just two writs of early 1554 used to move ninety-seven of Sir Thomas Wyatt's partners in rebellion to trial and their doom (an important reminder that habeas was not always sued by the prisoner), we can identify three distinctive periods.[18] The first peak, in the decades around 1600 to 1630, we might call the era in which habeas was made great, or by an easier title, the age of Popham and Fleming. The second peak, at century's end, we might label the age of Holt. The final peak

---

[17] For more on the vastness of subjecthood and on the writ's movement to America and India, see Halliday, *Habeas Corpus*, pp. 69–72, 201–8 and 281–99, and Halliday and White, 'Suspension clause', pp. 644–83.

[18] See the writ for Walter Rydwyn *et al.*, TNA KB 145/12/1 (7 Feb. 1554) and KB 29/187/20d.; and the writ for Philip Robynson *et al.*, KB 29/187/20d.

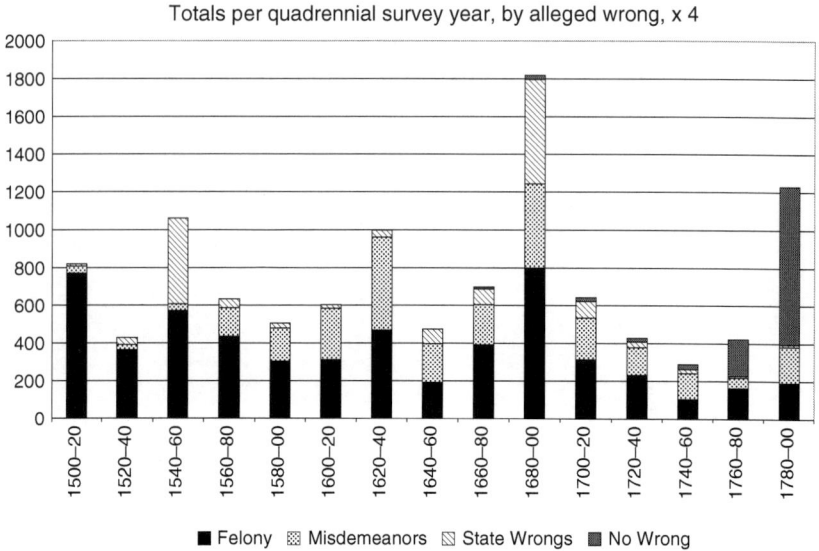

Figure 1 Projected totals of habeas corpus use, 1500–1800. (Totals per quadrennial survey year, by alleged wrong, x 4.)

from the late 1750s to the late 1780s we can call the age of Mansfield. I name these peaks for judges not only in recognition of the theme of this book, but to suggest that there may be more than simple correlation between periods of interesting activity and the tenure of certain justices.

Looking closely, we can see that each peak displays a different underlying geology. By placing the writs into four bands of alleged wrong, plus that ever-maddening category of the unknowable,[19] we can see that a different layer pushes each peak upward. Peaks of total usage mark periods of transition in the writ's purposes and possibilities. In the sixteenth century, habeas corpus was a device overwhelmingly concerned with moving around bodies in aid of felony process. But beginning in the last two decades of Elizabeth's reign, and especially from 1592 to 1613, when Sir John Popham and Sir Thomas Fleming presided in King's Bench, we can see a pronounced increase in habeas use to inspect imprisonment for non-felony wrongs, from alehouse violations to whoremongering. Looking at the stratigraphy in

---

[19] This includes a tiny group of writs returned with no wrong named, and a larger one of writs damaged or for which there is otherwise incomplete information.

the bars charting the period 1580 to 1680, we might think of this as the century of misdemeanours.

The peak at century's end is made overwhelmingly of results from the 1690s, the decade with the heaviest recorded use of habeas corpus. This is also the decade with the heaviest use of habeas corpus to inspect imprisonment orders made by the Privy Council and the decade with the heaviest use for prisoners confined on allegations of wrongs against the state: treason, sedition or 'treasonable practices'. The beginning of Michaelmas 1689 and the end of Michaelmas 1690 bound the most intensive period of habeas use before 1800. The start of Michaelmas 1689 is significant: it marked the end of the first statutory suspension of habeas corpus. Much can and should be said about parliamentary suspension of the writ.[20] For now, we should observe that during these fourteen months after the first suspension, King's Bench handled 251 cases on habeas corpus, 147 of which concerned wrongs against the state. Despite persistent fears of rebellion and invasion among beneficiaries of the Revolution of 1688 such as Sir John Holt CJ and his fellows on the bench, these same justices bailed or discharged 80 per cent of those who had been imprisoned for fear that they posed a danger to the new regime of William and Mary.[21]

The results of 1689–90 were not isolated. Writ usage remained vigorous throughout the war years of the decades following.[22] The use of habeas corpus for a 'prisoner at war', like John Golding, was hardly an oddity, nor was the result surprising once placed against a backdrop of hundreds of other cases available to us in the recorda files.[23]

The third peak appears late in the eighteenth century. Again, we see not only increased usage beginning before 1760 and culminating in the 1780s, coinciding with Lord Mansfield's leadership in King's Bench. We see a pronounced change in the purposes served by habeas corpus. We have arrived at the age of no wrongs. Since the 1670s, and increasingly across the eighteenth century, habeas corpus was used to adjudicate family custody contests. None of these cases concerned detentions

---

[20] Halliday, *Habeas Corpus*, pp. 247–56.

[21] Of the 147 habeas cases concerning state wrongs found in this period, results for 14 are unknown. Percentages are thus for 133 cases. Twenty-six were remanded, fifty-one bailed, and fifty-six discharged. Writs for 1689 and 1690 are in TNA KB 11/14 and KB 16/1/1, with court orders in KB 21/23.

[22] Release rates for the entirety of Holt's chief justiceship (to 1710) ran at 82 per cent.

[23] 381 cases are in the survey years for Holt's period in King's Bench, giving us a projected total of approximately 1,524 habeas cases for 1689–1710.

behind which stood even the least hint of legal wrong. We might say then that habeas corpus in this period had begun more clearly to be used to adjudicate claims of right. Quite true, though these rights claims were not premised on ideas about one's condition as a human being according to nature, nor as an Englishman according to English law. They were premised on ideas about status: of husband and wife, of parent and child. Such cases were numerically insignificant but conceptually very significant, widening as they did ideas about what constituted proper constraint of one person by another and about the purposes to which habeas corpus might be put in considering this issue.[24]

The same cannot be said for naval impressment cases, which were both numerically and conceptually significant. Their use had everything to do with the expansion of the state that followed and drove the expansion of empire.[25] The Seven Years' War and the American Revolution, when habeas use to question naval impressment rose sharply, were fundamentally imperial wars. Foreign crewmen used the writ with particular success as alien status provided the basis on which Portuguese, Spanish or Scandinavian sailors picked up in Caribbean ports might escape such servitude.[26] In all, nearly 1,000 unfortunate seamen probably used habeas corpus this way from 1760 to 1800. King's Bench during Mansfield's years on the court sent home many a royal sailor: 94 per cent of impressed habeas users were ordered discharged.[27]

---

[24] Halliday, *Habeas Corpus*, pp. 121–33.

[25] From 1750 to 1800, twenty-three cases concerning family custody disputes, lunacy or apprenticeship indentures appear in the quadrennial survey years, giving us an average of just over one such case per year. Given a total of 405 cases for which the reason for detention is known (of a total of 459 cases, 1750–1800), custody disputes constitute 5.7 per cent of the whole for this period. By comparison, we find 236 impressment cases, or 58 per cent.

[26] e.g. see the writ for two Scandinavian sailors impressed at Port Royal, in Jamaica. TNA ADM 1/1787 (unfoliated), 10 Oct. 1760. See also the case of Peter Fretus and Joseph Silvy, both Portuguese subjects impressed at Port Royal. The Admiralty solicitor recommended that they be discharged in reply to their writ of habeas corpus. TNA ADM 1/3686 (unfoliated), 29 May 1798.

[27] 239 sailors' writs may be found in the court files for the quadrennial survey years, yielding a projected total of 956. Given the state of the evidence, this is certainly an undercount. Results survive in only thirty-six cases (15 per cent). Contrary to usual practice, most impressment writs do not have judicial results written in the margin of the writ or return, nor is there an indication in the rulebooks. We can only speculate – in part based on the frequent recommendation of the Admiralty's solicitor that the Admiralty not fight one writ after another – that King's Bench and the Admiralty

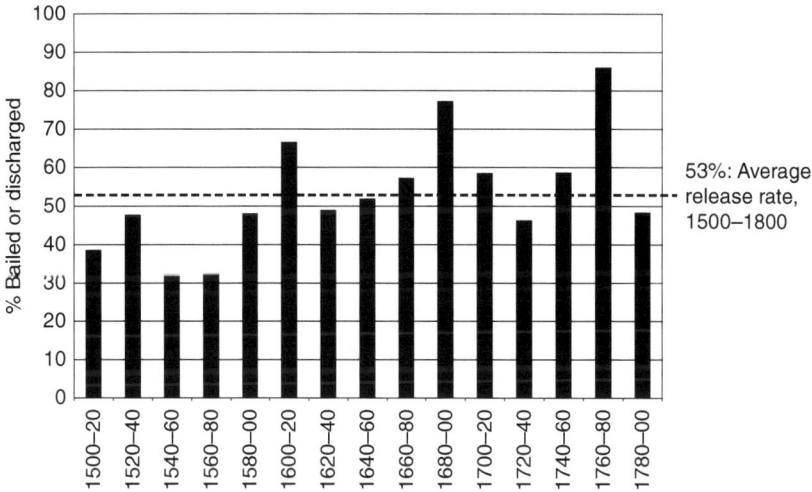

Figure 2 Release rates when using habeas corpus. Those released shown as a percentage of all cases where the result is known.

Release rates

From these extraordinary release rates for impressed sailors, let us turn to release rates for prisoners more generally (Figure 2). Immediately, we notice three spikes that overlap almost perfectly with the spikes in usage, spikes rising well above the average release rate of 53 per cent across three centuries. If, as we have seen, periods of sharply increased usage were marked by important changes in the writ's purposes, then putting the writ to new uses, or using it in large quantities, correlate closely with increased success for prisoners. If we dig a little deeper into these numbers – for instance, if we aggregate by chief justice rather than in groupings of two decades each – we can see more clearly what was going on in these apparently pivotal periods: individual justices made a difference.

worked out an accommodation by which the Admiralty simply released such sailors rather than returning their bodies with all these writs. The tone in many of the letters by Samuel Seddon, the Admiralty's solicitor during the Seven Years' War, is one of resignation as he repeatedly advised that sailors be discharged to save costs in fighting the writs. See e.g. TNA ADM 1/3678, ff. 4, 30, 32, 205 and 281. A letter of James Dyson suggests that if a sailor was discharged, it would obviate the need for a return: ADM 1/ 3680, ff. 428–9 (26 Sep. 1778). For more on impressment, see K. Costello, 'Habeas corpus and military and naval impressment, 1756–1816' (2008) 29 *J. Legal Hist.* 215–51.

Release rates could change abruptly from one chief justice to the next: for instance, when Holt was succeeded by Sir Thomas Parker in 1710, when Mansfield was followed by Sir Lloyd Kenyon in the 1780s, or when Sir Edward Coke succeeded Fleming in 1613.[28] The numbers show us powerful correlations; turning to other sources can help us think about causation. In Holt's case, his readiness, which we can see in the reports, to hear evidence well beyond that provided in the return to the writ suggests a temperament that explains the high rate of release in the decades to each side of 1700. In Mansfield's case, we can find in the affidavit files plenty of signs of his unusual willingness to entertain suitors at home, receiving supplicants there who provided on oath the information that would justify issuing the writ.

The difference a judge makes

In Coke's case, what needs explaining is not a rise in release rates, but a decrease made all the more impressive by the famed associations of Coke with this writ (Figure 3). Release rates under Coke (36 per cent) were well below average (53 per cent). Compare this to his predecessor and his successors. Under Fleming, chief justice from 1607 to 1613, release rates ran at an astonishingly high 78 per cent.[29] Coke's successors also outdid the oracle of the law in their use of the writ of liberty: release rates under Sir Henry Montagu and Sir James Ley CJJ during the decade after Coke's removal from the bench in late 1616 ran at just over two-thirds of all prisoners using the writ.[30] If we look more closely at other aspects of habeas activity, we see that the line charting release rates does not curve alone, but is paralleled by others tracing usages that reflect the writ's availability and utility to prisoners.

By charting activity across five periods – groupings of chief justices[31] – we can zero in on what made the years around 1600 special, and then consider what made for the apparent retreat under Coke.

---

[28] Halliday, *Habeas Corpus*, pp. 331–3.

[29] Actually, in the only survey year falling within the period of Fleming's chief justiceship (1610), 95 per cent were released. In order to correct for any imbalance produced by a small sample size, we can look beyond 1610 to examine all writs for 1607 to 1613 for which we have results information (seventy-seven). This shows that 78 per cent (sixty) were discharged or bailed.

[30] The rate under Montagu was 69 per cent, under Ley 70 per cent.

[31] First, considering together all chief justices from 1500 to the departure from Queen's Bench of Sir Edward Saunders at the beginning of 1559; the second, treating the period

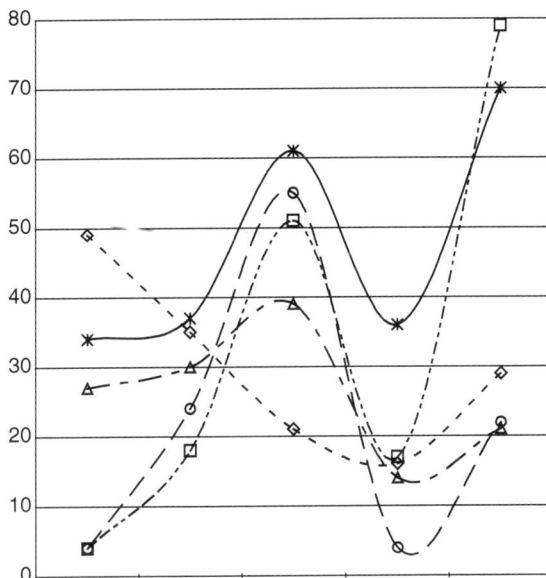

	Fyneux to Saunders, 1500–1558	Catlin to Wray, 1559–1592	Popham to Fleming, 1592–T1613	Coke, M 1613–1616	Montagu to Ley, 1617–1625
--◻-- % Return Immediately	4	18	51	17	79
—△— % Issued in Vacation	27	30	39	14	21
—○— % Return to Chambers	4	24	55	4	22
—✳— % Bailed or Discharged	34	37	61	36	70
--◇-- % Returns with Wrong or Jailing Authority Unspecified	49	35	21	16	29
Total Prisoners Using Writ	577	208	179	130	100

Figure 3   Changing usages on habeas corpus, 1500–1625.

Firstly, consider return speed. Increasingly, rather than name a specific date, writs demanded their return 'immediately after receipt'.[32] Each writ contained in it a statement about when it should be returned: when

1559 through 1592, when Sir Robert Catlin and then Sir Christopher Wray presided; the third, when Popham and Fleming served, from 1592 through Trinity term 1613; the fourth, the brief period when Coke sat as chief justice; and finally, from the end of 1616 to the beginning of 1625, when Montagu and Ley presided (see Table 1 below). For the tenure dates of chief justices, see J. Sainty, *The Judges of England, 1272–1990* (London, 1993), p. 10.

[32] William Style, writing in 1670, thought that King's Bench would not grant writs returnable immediately, 'for though the law doth favor liberty, yet it allows convenient time for doing of things'. But the recorda files in the 1660s show dozens of writs so

the body and the cause of imprisonment should be brought into court. Initially, nearly all writs named a specific date, anywhere from one to over one hundred days in the future. Over time, more writs simply demanded their return 'immediately'. There was a marked increase in this practice under Popham and Fleming.[33] Little evidence survives to tell us what 'immediately' meant to the justices or their clerks. But by comparing issuance and return dates for writs with a specified date for return to those marked 'immediately after receipt', we find that the new usage produced a clear increase in speed of use.[34]

Secondly, the use of writs during the court's lengthy vacations between terms presents a similar picture of a court expanding the writ's utility by making it more readily available all year round. This is indicated by the jump in vacation writs after 1592, followed by a sharp retreat under Coke.

Thirdly, and more marked, was the increase in the use of writs returnable to a single justice in chambers. From only a negligible use of chamber returns before 1558, we see a jump to nearly one-quarter of writs returnable to chambers after 1558; after 1592 their use more than doubled again. This was good news for prisoners given the dramatically

granted. This helps explain the modifying statement that followed: 'But it is in the discretion of the court to do it': *The Practical Register, Or the Accomplish'd Attorney: Consisting of Rules, Orders, and the most Principal Observations Concerning the Practice of the Common Law* . . . (London, 1670), p. 234.

[33] From 8 per cent of writs with such a designation in the period prior to 1591, to 51 per cent in the years 1592 to 1613. In London and Middlesex, 'immediately' appears to have meant that returns should be made the day the writ issued or the day following. For a later statement to this effect, see Anon., *Rules and Orders for the Court of the Upper Bench at Westminster Made and Published by the Judges of the Said Court, in the Terme of St. Michael, In the yeare 1654* (London, 1655), p. 14; Halliday, *Habeas Corpus*, pp. 53–4 and 240.

[34] Examining sixty writs from 1550, 1570, and 1590 for which we have both the issuance date and a specific return date (excluding those tested on the last day of term, which date was often fictionalised for writs granted in vacation), we find that writs to London or Middlesex appointed on average four days for making the return. For writs to the rest of the country, twenty-eight days were allowed, on average. There was a very high degree of variation. Turning to writs marked 'immediately', we find no firm rule about the meaning of 'immediately', even for prisoners held in or near the capital. But for prisoners held in London or Middlesex, return times on writs ordered returnable 'immediately' were generally one or two days, clearly faster than before. Returns always took longer for one held in the provinces, though here, too, return times on writs marked 'immediately' were faster than those marked with a specific date. Measuring the days between issuance and return for writs with a named return date is simple since both dates were entered on the writ. Doing so for writs marked 'immediately' is more difficult since the return date must be found from other evidence. This is only possible after 1589, when the rulebooks (KB 21), from which we can sometimes learn when a writ was returned, commence.

higher rate (79 per cent) at which prisoners were bailed or discharged by a single justice in chambers than by the full court.[35]

As we look at these lines, we see remarkably similar curves traced through Coke's years on the bench. But did he shape this statistical valley?

The simple answer is yes. We can point to a few signs of his imprint on these numbers. Consider the vacation writs curve: it is probably Coke's pronouncement in the *Institutes* saying that habeas did not properly issue from King's Bench in vacation that explains why later justices were unsure about their authority to use the writ out of term.[36] In keeping with his later words on this score, vacation activity fell while Coke was chief justice. On all three markers we have used here to chart ease of writ use, Coke seems to have made it harder for prisoners to use the writ.

One of the reasons for this may lie on the curve tracing the number of writs returned without naming either the alleged wrong or the jailing officer. One clear pattern from the mid-sixteenth century through to the early seventeenth is a steady decline in such non-specific returns. Under Coke, such returns dwindled further. One reason was the marked increase in orders to amend returns we can find in the rulebooks in 1615. Orders to amend had first appeared in habeas proceedings about twenty years earlier.[37] But such orders were rare: the justices apparently preferred to take returns as they received them and, if found deficient, to order the prisoner's release rather than to ask the jailer for a second, more full answer to the writ.[38] This pattern changed dramatically as

---

[35] Halliday, *Habeas Corpus*, pp. 53–5.

[36] Coke writes of Chancery: 'if a man be wrongfully imprisoned in the vacation, the Lord Chancellor may grant a habeas corpus and do him justice according to law, where neither the King's Bench nor Common Pleas can grant that writ but in the term time': 4 *Institutes* 81. This was not published until 1644, but Coke's actions on the bench seem to prefigure his pronouncement about vacation usage.

[37] From the beginning, such orders often took a nisi form: that the jailer amend his return or be fined for failure to do so. The first such order went to the mayor and aldermen of London, whose powers to imprison were a frequent source of conflict, for an unnamed prisoner in Easter 1595. TNA KB 21/1/94.

[38] Halliday, *Habeas Corpus*, pp. 106–7. When the judges did issue orders to amend returns, more often than not these concerned returns that challenged the court's purview of the returning officer – a return, then, that usually defied the authority of King's Bench – rather than one that included some, but not enough, information about the prisoner and the charges against him. Thus Queen's and King's Bench fought battles to receive more respectful returns from the University of Cambridge, the Council in the Marches of Wales, and the corporation of Berwick-upon-Tweed. The court prevailed in each

Coke's court asked one jailer after another to make a better return. Perhaps the chief justice's concern was not to let people out of prison more readily, but to ensure that he received the fullest possible answer to his requests for information from jailers. In other words, perhaps his principal interest in using habeas corpus was the jailer, not the prisoner.[39]

By ordering returns amended, Coke's court taught the officers of other tribunals how to answer the court's commands and thereby how to retain hold of their prisoners. This is illustrated by the eleven prisoners whose writs the judges considered in a June 1615 conference held in Coke's chambers in Serjeants' Inn. All had been jailed by command of the Chancery, the Privy Council, or the High Commission. The story of one of these prisoners, Richard Glanvill – jeweller and cheat, imprisoned by the Chancellor – is well known.[40] The court had ordered that the return to his writ and the returns for these ten others should be amended. To make a complex story very short, the bulk of the judges' discussion focused on the fullness of these amended returns. Glanvill and one other prisoner were bailed, the returns to their writs striking for their lack of specificity.[41] But the other nine prisoners were remanded after Coke's

---

instance. TNA KB 21/2/17v and 19 (Cambridge, 1598), and 87 (Berwick, 1601); and KB 21/3/24, 28, and 39v (Council in the Marches, 1604).

[39] Consider an example. We do not know what was wrong with the first return made by the sheriff of Leicestershire to the writ for George Herd and Agnes Wallyn in Easter 1615, but the court asked the sheriff to amend it. This second return explained fully their arrest on a writ of *excommunicato capiendo* for their failure to receive the Eucharist according to the rites of the Church of England, a sign of their probable Catholicism. We might reasonably surmise that the court simply did not want to release them, but instead wanted to ensure they had good legal ground for holding them. By ordering an amended return, perhaps by giving some instruction about what language it should contain, the court gave the sheriff a second chance to produce just this result: the return came back, was found good, and they were remanded. TNA KB 145/14/13 (13 Feb. 1615), and KB 21/5a/10v.

[40] J. H. Baker, 'The common lawyers and the Chancery: 1616' in *The Legal Profession and the Common Law: Historical essays* (London, 1986), pp. 205–29.

[41] The return to the third writ for Glanvill stated simply that he had been committed by the command of the Chancellor, with no further details. The return for Michael Apsley explained only his commitment for contempt of Chancery, with nothing further to explain of what his contempt consisted: ugly words, defiance of a Chancery order, or worse, non-performance of a Chancery decree: TNA KB 145/14/13 (16 Jun. 1615); KB 29/259/68 and 69d.; and KB 21/5a/28v. Apsley had used the writ earlier, apparently without effect, as no result survives, despite more than one order to amend the return. The return stated simply that he had been jailed by order of Chancery: TNA KB 145/14/12 and KB 21/5/48 and KB 21/5a/7, 9v, 10v, 13v, 14, 17, and 19v. We might be tempted to say that the court found the returns insufficient for their vagueness and that this led to

court showed their jailers how to make a more full return. Throughout
the numerous printed and manuscript reports of these cases, it is Coke's
voice we hear most often declaring the sufficiency of each return and
explaining the factors that made it so, thereby bounding his own court's
ambit on habeas corpus.[42]

Table 1

Chief Justices	Fyneux to Saunders 1500–58	Catlin + Wray 1559–92	Popham + Fleming 1592–1613	Coke 1613–16*	Montagu + Ley 1617–25
% Return Immediately	4	18	51	17	79
% Issued in Vacation	27	30	39	14	21
% Return to Chambers	4	24	55	4	22
% Bailed or Discharged	34	37	61	36	70
% Returns with Wrong or Jailing Authority not Specified	49	35	21	16	29
Total # Writs Studied	577	208	179	130	100

*To produce the most reliable results, all writs for the period when Coke presided
in King's Bench have been studied since only one survey year (1614) falls within
this period. Information for the other four periods comes from the survey years.

their release. This is suggested in the reports for Glanvill and Apsley: 1 Rolle 218–19, 81
E.R. 445, and Bod., MS Rawl. C.382, f. 71.

[42] As Coke explained, a return containing all the elements found in the return to Henry
Rosewell's writ was good as it 'comprehend[ed] the effect of the [Chancery] decree',
non-performance of which had been the reason for Rosewell's imprisonment: 1 Rolle
219, 81 E.R. 445. A full report of the discussion in Rosewell is in Bod., MS Rawl. C.382, f.
56v–57v. Rosewell was remanded: TNA KB 145/14/13 (15 Jun. 1615); KB 29/259/79d.;
and KB 21/5a/23v, 25, 27, 28v, and *passim*. Similarly, the court ordered the initial return
for William Allen amended. He was then remanded on a second return that noted his
detention for contempt of Chancery's decree. Though that return named the Chancery
case concerned, it gave no other specifics of the decree: TNA KB 145/14/13 (16 Jun.
1615); KB 29/259/73; and KB 1/5a/6v, 12, 12v, 15, 17v, 19v, 23v, 25, 27 and 28v; Moore
KB 840, 72 E.R. 940. Sir Samuel Saltonstall likewise had a return to his writ saying he had
given a contempt to Chancery, without further explanation of the contempt: TNA KB
145/14/13 (19 Jun. 1615); KB 29/259/71; and KB 21/5a/27 and 28v. Saltonstall had also

We have, in the end, returned to the reports and other traditional sources for habeas history. But we have done so only after working in the court's archive to identify the serious questions we must answer and to provide the many contexts for understanding the answers we might find there. If it is with judges and judging that we are concerned, such an approach suggests that we must attend to what judges did before we can hope to make sense of what they said. Only then can we appreciate the enormous shaping influence judges had on the use of this greatest of writs. And only then can we understand how they took the prerogative to their own use, enabling them to inspect the behaviour of all other courts and officers. Only then can we see how they crafted a writ that could wander the globe, following those lesser courts and officers wherever they claimed to act in the king's name. That judges like Holt made this a great writ was a lesson learned by John Golding as well as anyone. We don't know the legal reasoning that informed that decision. But we do know that an Irish captain, sailing under the French king's commission, defending an erstwhile English king, had made effective use of this great writ. That we know this story certainly matters. How we know it matters, too. After all, there are 11,000 more.

used habeas earlier in the year, only to be remanded on a return that was the same in substance as the later return to his later writ: KB 145/14/12 (8 Feburary 1615); KB 21/5/48; and KB 21/5a/7, 9v, 10v, 13v, 14v, and 17v. But Saltonstall's returns contained a wrinkle not found in the others, noting that he had also been jailed on the order of the Privy Council. Reports of the discussion of his writ all focus not on the part of his return noting his confinement by Chancery for contempt, but on this conciliar command. No wrong was specified in the Council's return, only that he had been jailed by their command. The justices, led by Coke, ordered remand on this return: 1 Rolle 219, 81 E.R. 444–5 and LI MS Maynard 22, f. 117. Bod., MS Rawl. C.382, f. 71v. As Coke put it earlier in the same discussions, 'if a man is committed by the warrant of the privy council and no cause is expressed in the warrant no court may bail him nor examine the cause': *Ibid.*, f. 56v.

14

Some difficulties of colonial judging: The Bahamas 1886–93

MARTIN J. WIENER

Judgeships in the British Empire were different from judgeships in England. English and Scottish High Court judges, removable only by parliamentary impeachment, served in practice for life. Colonial judges, on the other hand, were appointed at the pleasure of the Crown, and could be removed by their colony's governor, if the Colonial Office approved. Even if this was rarely done, the sword of removal always hung over their heads, and sometimes (as we will see) indeed fell. Executive officials, at home and in the colonies, saw this lack of complete security for judges as appropriate to the more Baconian role they were expected to fill, as arms of a more authoritative, if not authoritarian, government of distant dependencies. What was wanted were men who could co-operate, and not contend, with colonial governors. Yet this was not always what happened. Despite holding their positions as other colonial officials did, colonial judges, as part of a separate arm of government with a long tradition of independence at home, had the potential to clash with the executive arm – if governors looked for Bacons, sometimes they got Cokes, starting with Robert Thorpe J in Upper Canada in the first decade of the1800s and Forbes CJ in New South Wales in the 1820s and 1830s.[1] Nor were they as easily removable in practice as they were in principle. As Lord Kimberley, who headed at various times the Colonial Office and the India Office, privately noted in 1884, 'no class of man is more difficult to deal with than a wrong-headed Indian or colonial judge. The public always thinks that any rebuke of a Judge means interference with his judicial independence although his proceedings may be anything

---

[1] See J. McLaren, '"The Judicial office … bowing to no power but the supremacy of the law': Judges and the rule of law in colonial Australia and Canada, 1788–1840' (2003) 7 *Aust. J. Legal Hist.* 177–92.

but judicial.'[2] Tensions with judges are a thread running through the papers of many colonial officials. To take just one: Sir Frederick Lugard, when governor of Hong Kong in 1907, wrote a friend that 'the Chief Justice [Sir Francis Piggott] is like all Chief Justices, I [hadn't] been here a week before I got letters about "ignoring the position and dignity of the Bench" and so on, and since then he has shot me in a series of letters raking up every conceivable grievance'.[3]

Their relations with local officials below the level of governor and with important non-officials were not necessarily easier; like governors, judges were centripedal actors in the empire. Like governors, judges were moved frequently from colony to colony, their loyalty fixed on the empire as a whole, and the more-or-less uniform imperial criminal law. As John Lonsdale has pointed out, 'they circled the world on promotion within one legal service; their precedents were imperial. Unfamiliarity with local ruling culture was deemed to be a strength, a shield of impartial judgment that relied not on "some one who knew the people and their ways" but on evidence proven in court.' Not that judges were always oppositional; Lonsdale went on to note that 'a desire to fit in with local culture could also create . . . a nervous complaisance with local prejudice'.[4] Judges could irritate governors or locals by being confrontational, or they could annoy Whitehall by falling in with local interests, and on occasion they could manage to do both over the period of an appointment. The official historian of the Colonial Office reflected in 1937 that a judge 'may be at loggerheads with the governor and his council, or may be so oppressed with a sense of the ill-treatment of one class that he becomes too biased the other way, does something wrong and thus has to be removed, or he may try to curry favour with the planter class, or he may simply prove unfit for the post'.[5] Most important for this chapter, however, was the significant number of judges who sought to follow British norms of equal justice in situations of colonial inequality, and by so doing provoked serious confrontations with local non-official whites. In these ongoing clashes, the late nineteenth century,

[2] Letter to Lord Ripon, Viceroy of India, 24 Oct. 1884, quoted in J. Powell (ed.), *Liberal by Principle: The politics of John Wodehouse, First Earl of Kimberley* (London, 1996), p. 173.

[3] From the Lugard MSS, quoted in P. Wesley-Smith, entry on Piggott in the *Oxford Dictionary of National Biography* (Oxford, 2004). Piggott may not have been popular with the governor, but he seems to have been well liked by the Hong Kong bar.

[4] J. Lonsdale, 'Kenyatta's trials: Breaking and making an African nationalist' in P. Coss (ed.), *The Moral World of the Law* (Oxford, 2000), p. 200.

[5] H. L. Hall, *The Colonial Office* (London, 1937), p. 136.

when Whitehall's interest in interfering in local affairs was at a low ebb, saw perhaps the nadir of judicial power. Again and again in this era, justices were defeated by hostile governors or local white interests.[6] This chapter examines one revealing case – the Bahamas– in which local interests triumphed over the efforts of several successive judicial officials to uphold what they saw as the 'rule of law'.

It was not always easy to fill colonial judgeships. Less secure, and also carrying a lower salary, judicial posts in the empire were much less prestigious than the small number of judgeships at home. The imperial government depended on the ambitions of British barristers, and the excess supply of them during most of the nineteenth century.[7] There was no formal examination to take, as existed after 1860 for the Indian Civil Service, and appointment depended upon patronage. Lawyers in the colonies themselves were more eager for judgeships, but the Colonial Office much preferred Britons, to prevent the growth of localism, favouritism and corruption. Sometimes, however, it was forced to accept local candidates – relatives or protégés of powerful persons there – but it tried throughout our period to limit their number. While British candidates helped the Colonial Office hold local interests in check, they could also fall victim to such interests, as the imperial government carried out an ongoing balancing act to hold a widespread and diverse empire together. Such was the case in the Bahamas.

Before our era of long-distance holidays, the Bahamas, one of the first British colonies, was an unpromising backwater of the empire – a collection of not very fertile islands off the coast of Florida. In the 1880s the colony had a population of barely 70,000, of whom less than 5,000 were white, the rest descended from African slaves; its economy was stagnant. There was no racial distinction in law, but the elite of merchants and landowners was almost purely white, and social life assumed a hierarchy of colour. A significant body of generally lighter-skinned 'coloured' people made up together with some whites a middling class below the white elite; some coloureds were lawyers, businessmen or small farmers, and the Assembly had a small number of coloured members. The vast majority of blacks were labourers or sharecroppers. The few British officials and expatriates in the islands tended to be Anglican, while most white Bahamians were Methodist, reproducing a

---

[6] For more on this ongoing empire-wide conflict, see M. J. Wiener, *An Empire on Trial: Race, violence and justice under British rule 1870–1935* (Cambridge, 2009).

[7] See Hall, *The Colonial Office*. We lack a general study of the colonial judiciary.

class divide common in England.[8] These officials and expatriates tended to look down upon Bahamian-born whites, even those with money, as not really gentlemen, all the more as few native whites could be sure, after generations in a multi-racial society, of the 'purity' of their blood. There was also much reference, when British were among themselves, to the origins of the colony in piracy. Such condescension only strengthened the solidarity of white Creoles and their distaste for paying salaries of officials sent from overseas to fill positions that Bahamians, they agreed, should be holding.

The politics of the Bahamas, which like Bermuda held a charter of partial self-government, were frozen in the eighteenth century, with property qualifications for the franchise (raised in 1882), plural voting, open balloting and both bribery and intimidation accepted. In the 1840s the Crown had established a nominated Legislative Council (as it did elsewhere in the West Indies), with the ultimate goal of replacing the elected Assembly. Yet while in many colonies the Legislative Council, dominated by the governor and his appointees, became the key organ of government, here the opposite happened: this Council fell under the sway of the leaders of the Assembly, itself 'little less than a family gathering of Nassau whites, nearly all of whom are related to each other, either by blood or marriage'.[9] Their leaders also came to sit on, and dominate, the governor's Executive Council. After the middle of the nineteenth century, the colony was virtually ruled by a caucus of white merchants and landowners known as the 'Bay Street Boys' (for the main street of the capital, Nassau, where their offices were located). They or their relatives filled most of the posts of government.

In 1880 this caucus suffered a double blow, when the newly elected Liberal imperial government ended a long-standing subsidy, and a Canadian barrister, Sir Henry Austin, was appointed as chief justice, a post hitherto usually filled by Bahamians. The position was to remain out of Bahamian hands until 1897, and these years were to see the most serious challenge to Bay Street until the run-up to Independence many years later. By the end of the nineteenth century, two successive chief justices had been sent packing, and the Colonial Office ceased to concern itself with the rule of law in the Bahamas. In his first years Austin did little to endanger Bay Street interests. His downfall was initiated by a

---

[8] Not surprisingly, one of the few allies the beleaguered judicial officials were to possess was the Anglican Archdeacon in Nassau.

[9] L. D. Powles, *The Land of the Pink Pearl, or, Recollections of Life in the Bahamas* (London, 1888), p. 41.

murder trial, the second within two years that involved young men from the same elite family. In December 1886, Charles Sands had murdered a black policeman, and was almost lynched in response by an angry black mob. He was prosecuted by the Attorney-General, his uncle by marriage, found insane (though his former teacher, uncalled by the prosecution, did not think him so), and sent to confinement in Jamaica. Two years later another Sands boy, Frank, was involved in the killing of a black fisherman, Shadrach Gay. Sands and several drunken friends had set upon Gay to avenge a supposed insult. By this time, Austin CJ had become alienated from the Bay Street establishment. He had expressed his doubts when the local Savings Bank had failed, about whether improper behaviour by its managers was being hushed up. Following that, in a ship salvage case, he had been privately told that his salary, paid by the legislature, would be increased if he ruled in favour of Bay Street against the New York insurers; he refused the offer, and ruled for the insurers.[10] From this point on, Bay Street was looking for a way to end his tenure. The tensions on both sides came to a head during the legal proceedings following upon Shadrach Gay's death.

Confronted with another nephew involved in a killing, Attorney-General Malcolm, a leading member of Bay Street, found a way out: as soon as the coroner's jury returned a murder finding against five men, he instructed the presiding magistrate, also a relative of his (and thus also of Sands) by marriage, to separate the case into two proceedings: all the assailants (including Frank Sands) except the one who had delivered the fatal knife-thrust, were charged only with 'affray', a misdemeanour, while this one alone was charged with murder. Moreover, the affray trial was held first, and in it Malcolm, conducting the prosecution, took care to keep witnesses from saying anything that linked the fight to its fatal outcome. This crafty handling of Gay's killing produced a judicial explosion. In charging the jury in the affray trial, Austin made clear his belief that even the incomplete evidence heard was sufficient to support a charge not of affray but a more serious one of aiding and abetting in the murder (particularly as there was evidence that Sands had handed the knife to the man charged with the murder). Ignoring this, the jury acquitted the prisoners, an outcome that enabled them to serve as defence witnesses the following week in the murder trial. There Malcolm began his

[10] 'Lucile' case, late Feb. 1889 (see Austin's account in his privately published pamphlet, *Ten Years Chief Justice of the Bahamas, 1880–1890* (copy in the National Archives: CO 23/235, file 163)).

opening of the case by attempting to vindicate his course of action in the previous trial, citing various legal authorities. Austin let him go on in this vein, and then at the close of the trial unwisely replied, prefacing his charge to the jury with a lengthy disquisition on the duties of the Attorney-General and arguing, citing a long series of rulings on the subject of accessories, that the men who were tried for affray should have been in the dock in this trial. The jury found the accused guilty of manslaughter only, a verdict the judge deplored. He then exercised his discretion to pronounce the maximum possible penalty, penal servitude for life (ensuring his unpopularity with the white population).

Austin's enemies (which included the venal governor, Ambrose Shea, formerly a Newfoundland businessman with influential friends) saw their opportunity to dispose of him,[11] for he had already irreparably damaged his standing with the Colonial Office through an incident the year before. In July 1888, a black prisoner, Matthew Taylor, upon being convicted of burglary, had attacked the chief justice with a stick seized from a table in the courtroom. Aiming at the judge's head, he hit only his arm raised in defence; however, he kept trying and had to be pulled away, not before drawing blood. A week later, still seething, Austin summarily sentenced him for contempt of court to thirty lashes and life imprisonment. Governor Shea immediately queried the Colonial Office about this sentence; there it was called 'of course utterly illegal'; one official noted that 'the Judge seems to think he may inflict any punishment for contempt of court – it is fortunate that he did not sentence the man to be hung'. The sentence was annulled. Moreover, the governor was told to inform Austin that 'should any similar grave miscarriage occur again it may have very serious consequences for the Chief Justice'.[12] Bay Street made sure its friends in England were informed, and several questions was raised in the House of Commons by Radical members objecting to the use of flogging for contempt of court and to the excesses of this colonial chief justice.[13]

---

[11] Shea was not a typical colonial governor. He had gone into politics from a business career and had become the Speaker of the Newfoundland Legislative Assembly. Representing the colony on various diplomatic missions seems to have given him an interest in colonial government in a warmer clime. There is evidence that Shea was rewarded for his solicitude for their interests by the leaders of the Assembly in very generous grants for 'travel expenses' on his trips to Canada and the United States, and perhaps in less noticeable ways as well.

[12] CO 23/230, files 93 and 94.

[13] Ibid. The Times, 16 Mar. 1889, headed its description of the parliamentary questions by Radical members Fowler and Pickersgill 'Flogging in the Bahamas'.

Knowing that the chief justice was on probation in Whitehall, Attorney-General Malcolm did not let his 'rebuke' in the murder trial rest, but demanded a retraction of what he called the slanderous charge that he had suppressed evidence. Shea backed him up, asking Austin to support his 'charges' or publicly withdraw them. Austin equivocated, and Shea sent the matter to Whitehall, making sure to emphasise the judge's increasing deafness and irascibility with age. The Colonial Office responded that both men had acted unwisely, but also (to the governor's chagrin) that 'it may be necessary to hold an inquiry' into 'the most serious feature in this case' – the allegation that relevant facts that were known to the Attorney-General were suppressed.[14] To prevent this, Shea convened a court of his own, by having a bill rushed through the Assembly allowing him to administer oaths and issue summons to appear before the governor and Executive Council. This body (which Austin called a 'totally incompetent body to decide a question of law') then took evidence for several days, including from a protesting Austin and witnesses called by him. While this inquiry was being held, Austin was being privately urged to back down and come to an arrangement with the governor; he refused.[15] Austin later recalled an anonymous letter placed under his door the night before the enquiry closed – 'I believe it was written by Judge Camplejohn (the Coroner) – one of the parties interested'. It said, "Take advice of one who knows, who feels for you, who condemns in a great measure the course you have adopted, ask a private interview with the Governor, without loss of time. He is a good man, be prepared to make some concession. You are lost if you go on. Malcolm may get *hurt* – but you ruined.' 'On the same day', Austin recounted, 'Thompson [the magistrate in the case] called at my house ... He had never called upon me in ten years. He said he came from Government House; that he came to see me in a friendly way – to ask me to withdraw the case against Mr. Malcolm ... "You know the Governor's influence at the Colonial Office. You will be ruined."'[16]

Pressure apparently was applied on others as well; a witness called by the chief justice, Charles A. Demerett, recounted his experiences in the affray trial: 'I was *interrupted* and *checked* by the Attorney General several times in giving my evidence. He said, "I don't want this," "I don't want that," when I was examined, when I answered. I wanted to tell more ... After the evidence at the Police Court I was threatened by Tom Sands, one of the

[14] Knutsford to Shea, 27 Mar. 1889, CO 23/231, file 38.   [15] *The Freeman*, 7 May 1889.
[16] Austin, *Ten Years Chief Justice of the Bahamas*, CO 23/235, file 163.

brothers of the defendant, Frank Sands ... Tom Sands called out, "You white son of a bitch, if you give evidence against my brother, you will have your guts cut out." W. R. Kemp heard this; he also told me not to go forward as my life had been threatened by one of the Sands. The elder brother Sands said he would do anything for me he could [if I didn't testify].'[17] These interchanges were not entered in the minutes of the proceedings.

Despite some striking evidence supporting Austin's position (one witness in the audience during the affray trial observed that 'if I had been a stranger in Court I should have thought the Attorney General was DEFENDING INSTEAD OF PROSECUTING'), it concluded (not surprisingly) that the chief justice had misconducted himself, and was 'deserving of the severest censure'.[18] A one-sidedly edited version of the proceedings was sent to the Colonial Office, and Shea himself left for England to personally lobby for Austin's removal.

After hearing in person from Shea, the Colonial Office threw its support behind the governor. Lord Knutsford, the Secretary of State, gave him a letter to take back to the colony declaring that 'after what has occurred in this case, and in the case of Taylor, [the chief justice's] further continuance in the office which he holds has become very undesirable in the public interest'. Seizing upon Austin's growing deafness, he suggested that the Assembly might be willing to grant the chief justice a pension if he retired on grounds of infirmity.[19] Faced with the alternative of being dismissed without a pension, Austin surrendered, accepting the Assembly's pension and going home in 1890 to Montreal to detail his grievances in a pamphlet. He was not without local supporters, and upon his retirement he was presented with a memorial signed by 32 ministers of religion, and another signed by over 600 Nassau citizens, praising his career and regretting his retirement. The two chief newspapers in the colony, however, refused to print these memorials, instead writing editorials heaping scorn upon the departing judge. At the Colonial Office, he was remembered as 'a hopeless incompetent judge'.[20]

One might have expected Austin's successor to be more cautious, but, quite the contrary, Sir Roger Yelverton, an English barrister, immediately

---

[17] *Ibid.*   [18] *Ibid.*   [19] Knutsford to Shea, 30 Sep. 1889, CO 23/231/ff. 486–7.

[20] Wingfield minute, 24 Oct. 1892, regarding Austin's request for a review of his case, CO 23/235/163. Austin's 1892 pamphlet was not appreciated at the Colonial Office; Wingfield remarked in 1895 that he 'did not improve his case by public violent pamphlets attacking Sir Angus Shea and the Imperial Government': minute, 19 Aug. 1895, CO 23/242.

began reducing a backlog of cases by establishing more frequent sittings, and seeking other ways to make the legal system in the colony work more effectively.[21] This did not make him liked on Bay Street, for whom the system already worked quite effectively. Yelverton's actions were making it feasible for poorer persons – even sharecroppers – to bring suits against the wealthy, and he became quite popular among the 'common people'. The most serious step he took in defiance of the elite was a ruling in a shipwreck case heard in Admiralty Court in January 1892. A steamer wrecked upon one of the Out-Islands had been, in Yelverton's judgment, 'swamped upon by some of the natives dishonestly'. His ruling against them and for the foreign shipowners – and, even more, his subsequent action appointing deputy marshals throughout the Out-Islands responsible to Admiralty Court for the proper conduct of 'so-called salvors' within their districts – 'put an end to such conduct', he later observed with satisfaction, at the expense of local businessmen, who had made a good deal of money out of looting wrecked ships. Yelverton was increasingly planting himself as a barrier between government business and private interests, and in the process arousing ever-greater dislike among the powerful. The proverbial last straw was his blocking, soon after the shipwreck case, the leader of the Assembly, R. H. Sawyer, from using government agents to advance his land claims against a group of coloured and black small proprietors in the Out-Islands.[22] Immediately after that, the Bahamas papers began to attack him, and at the same time stories detailing his arrogance and abuse of his authority began to appear in the English press.

The hostilities came to a head at the beginning of May when the colony's leading paper published an anonymous letter making fun of Yelverton. The chief justice demanded the editor reveal the author of what he considered defamatory and seditious writing. The editor, Alfred Moseley, closely related to the leaders of the Assembly, refused, and Yelverton ordered him jailed for contempt of court. Again a judge had overreached himself. Governor Shea immediately telegraphed the Colonial Office, asking their permission to use his delegated prerogative powers to free Moseley. He obtained assent and released Moseley, over

---

[21] *In the Matter of the Release by the Governor of The Bahamas of Alfred E. Moseley. Notes by the Chief Justice of the Colony* (London, 1892), p. 22 (written by Yelverton and sent by him to Privy Council, received 15 Dec. 1892; copy in CO 23/236).

[22] See affidavits regarding this matter in *In the Matter of . . . Moseley. Notes by the Chief Justice.*

the protests of the chief justice, less than two days after his committal; Bay Street put on a public demonstration (with free food and drink ensuring a large turnout) to celebrate his release. Moseley, speaking to loud cheers at the demonstration, declared that 'victory had been secured for the freedom of the press and the people'. Governor Shea then wrote the Colonial Office to complain about Yelverton, noting that among other things he had come to see himself as 'protector of the rights of the coloured population', an unneeded role that could only end badly. 'The race question', Shea warned, 'is pregnant with trouble and, if urged into activity, the issues would be calamitous.'[23]

Yelverton also wrote the Colonial Office, and Edward Wingfield, chief official in charge of the West Indies, concluded that although the governor was justified in releasing Moseley, 'I am afraid it is not unlikely to be true that Sir Angus Shea is too much influenced by the white natives.' Since neither party was ready to back down, the only thing to do was to submit the Moseley issue (in which the Colonial Office had already backed up Shea) to the Judicial Committee of the Privy Council.[24] A hearing was set for December, and this time it was the chief justice who travelled to England. Austin, inspired by this controversy to press for a reconsideration of his own treatment, gave Yelverton a supporting letter for the Colonial Office and Privy Council. 'I think', Austin concluded in it, 'the only thing to do is to make it a *Crown* colony again!'[25] A friend from the Bahamas urged Yelverton to seek support from among all the colonial judges; it was ultimately an issue that threatened the independence of them all as 'recent events in Trinidad' have shown. 'Don't be beaten', he concluded.[26] Yelverton certainly gave it his best, listing in his pamphlet and in letters to the Colonial Office all the misdeeds that had taken place in recent years as fruit of a rotten tree. The treatment of Gay's murder was typical: 'the system', he wrote, 'which ... allowed of the indecent spectacle of the Attorney General of the Colony prosecuting his wife's nephew for a minor offence when a man's body had been fatally ripped open by a knife possibly wielded by Sands, is corrupt to the core'.[27]

---

[23] Shea to Knutsford, 9 Jun. and 20 Jun. 1892, CO 23/234/362–70.

[24] Wingfield minute, 6 Jul. 1892, CO 23/234/255–257.

[25] Austin to Yelverton, 12 Aug. 1892, included in pamphlet sent to Privy Council; copy in CO 23/236.

[26] Anon. to Yelverton, 20 Jul. 1892, included in pamphlet sent to Privy Council, *ibid.* He was alluding to a commission that, after complaints from local landowners, had recently investigated and censured judges there.

[27] Yelverton to Secretary of State, 28 Nov. 1892, CO 23/236.

Yelverton's contempt for the 'corrupt' government of the colony was coloured by a good deal of class (and race) snobbery: the piratical and otherwise dubious origins of the island's elite was a theme in his private correspondence; as his friend Archdeacon Wakefield complained to him, the colony was run by 'the offspring of blackguard whites'. In an article published in the English press Yelverton sneeringly described Malcolm as a 'half-caste'. Austin, writing supportingly to Yelverton that year, recalled how 'Malcolm had the audacity once to tell me he was one of the Malcolms of Scotland! I know him to be a son of a bastard in Nassau, and that "Drimmie"[28] (which always amused me) is his mother's name, an Ethiopian he had *shut* up in his own house. When I was there, she never showed.' A frequent topic among Englishmen in the West Indies was the laughable aristocratic airs put on by 'old families' when their origins were rarely free from illicit interracial liaisons, and here Austin, Yelverton and Wakefield were typical.[29]

He published his charges as a pamphlet, and wrote a long letter on the case to the *Pall Mall Gazette*. Bay Street joined in the fray, and a pamphlet and press articles critical of Yelverton also appeared in England. Yelverton declared to the Privy Council that in addition to himself two other chief justices – not only Austin but also Burnside CJ of Ceylon, who had formerly been Attorney-General of the Bahamas – were 'prepared to testify before your Lordships, or before any Royal Commission, that the Government of the Bahamas has been and is corrupt' and that 'it is only by the firm and thoroughly fair administration of justice by Englishmen unrelated to the native families that the present most unsatisfactory state of things can be remedied'.[30] However, the Privy Council turned down the offer as beyond the scope of its remit, and confined its attention to the specific issue of Moseley's jailing and release. Its attitude was indicated in the course of the hearing by unfriendly remarks to Yelverton about the near-libellous remarks he had published about various public officials in the colony. After a month it issued a decision that not only did the governor have the undoubted authority to release Moseley (as the Colonial Office had ruled), but that his refusal to reveal the author of the objectionable letter did

---

[28] This was Malcolm's middle name.

[29] Austin to Yelverton, 12 Aug. 1892, included in pamphlet sent to Privy Council; copy in CO 23/236.

[30] Yelverton to Privy Council, with pamphlet, CO 23/236. 'The Bay Street gang', Burnside wrote to Yelverton 'have driven every honest man out of the place, and they'll drive you out too, unless you can persuade Downing Street that the judges of the colonies are not outlaws': *In the Matter of . . . Moseley. Notes by the Chief Justice*.

not constitute contempt of court, and thus the chief justice had erred in the first place.[31]

With Yelverton thus rebuffed and humiliated, Shea now moved to obtain his dismissal, arguing that his wholesale attacks on local men had made it impossible for him to serve impartially. The Colonial Office was receptive to this argument, for it saw his denunciations as bringing the government itself into discredit. Such 'casting [of] wholesale aspersions' only served to raise questions among officials about his own discretion; as one clerk observed, 'Mr. Yelverton's genealogical trees (which he has watered with so much ink) require pruning.'[32] As soon as the Privy Council decision was announced, the Legislative Council and House of Assembly passed a joint resolution against Yelverton's return, arguing that 'public confidence' in him had been destroyed.

However, Yelverton did not go quietly, particularly since, as he and Austin had hoped, while the conflict over his imprisonment of Moseley had raged, Gladstone had returned to office. Yelverton wrote to the new Liberal Colonial Secretary, Lord Ripon, reiterating his request for an official investigation, and simultaneously had an MP friend put down a question calling for a full enquiry into his charges concerning the administration of the colony. Shea turned back this second threat of an enquiry by calling on his political ace in the hole, no one less than the rising power in the Conservative Party, Joseph Chamberlain. He had met Chamberlain in Montreal in the summer of 1890, and the two former businessmen had hit it off. Shea had given him, Chamberlain wrote to his wife, 'a romantic account of the resurrection of his colony . . . due to the discovery . . . that a weed peculiar to the place would give the best quality fibre for hemp'.[33] This was just when Chamberlain was beginning to turn towards what was to be the focus of the rest of his political life, the economic development of the empire, and he was in a receptive state for Shea's pitch – receptive personally as well, for his family finances were pinching, and he was on the lookout for new investment opportunities. Shea urged him to get in on the ground floor by growing the 'weed', sisal, in the Bahamas. A few months later, Chamberlain's personal finances became seriously squeezed by a crash of Argentine securities, and he turned to Shea's offer. Eager no doubt to have Chamberlain in his debt,

---

[31] *The Times*, 3 Feb. 1893, p. 15 (the hearing had been held on 15–16 Dec. 1892).

[32] H. W. Just, minute 25 Jan. 1893, CO 23/236.

[33] Joseph to Mary Chamberlain, 27 Sep. 1890, quoted in P. Marsh, *Joseph Chamberlain: Entrepreneur in politics* (New Haven, 1994), p. 324.

Shea arranged to sell him government land at a special price and spend government money building a wharf to serve it. Chamberlain bought 10,000 acres on Andros in 1891 and put his younger son Neville in charge. While Shea's battle with Yelverton was going on, Neville was in the Bahamas, sending his father the views of his fellow landowners. The investment proved a mistake; by 1897 Chamberlain had to liquidate at a heavy loss.[34] However, Shea's political investment in the future Colonial Secretary paid off handsomely. With Shea's position in danger in 1893, Chamberlain stepped forward to stop Yelverton. He first wrote to Charles Buxton, the Liberal Parliamentary Under-Secretary at the Colonial Office, passing on the aspersions on the character of the chief justice which Neville and Governor Shea had forwarded to him, and accusing him of trying to stir up racial animosity in a colony where the races had 'for the last twenty years at least lived in perfect harmony'.[35] When the question was put in the House of Commons a few days later, he intervened with a biting speech. He cited the refusal of the Privy Council to entertain Yelverton's charges:

> Lord Herschell would not permit the Chief Justice's notes to remain on record in the Judicial Committee of the Privy Council, on the ground that it was impossible to allow that Court to be made the vehicle for disseminating the scandalous allegations against a great number of persons in the colony which they contained, and I myself will now take my part in preventing the Committee of the House of Commons from being used for the same purpose.

Claiming direct knowledge from 'a relative' there, he praised the work of Governor Shea in reviving a moribund economy, and denounced the malicious efforts of a vindictive man to besmirch his name. Chamberlain then went on to do what he could to besmirch Yelverton, portraying him as an eccentric and egomaniacal figure, obsessively spreading 'disgraceful calumnies and insinuations' against seemingly everyone holding any authority in the Bahamas. 'The Bahamas', he declared, 'has been most unfortunate in its Chief Justices. They were appointed by this country, and I wonder what genius of discord presided over their appointment. The late Chief Justice had got into hot water over a particular case of murder, and was retired upon a pension which the colony still paid'. Yet the next appointment was even worse: 'Mr. Yelverton', he observed,

---

[34] D. Dilks, *Neville Chamberlain*, I: *1869–1929* (Cambridge, 1984), pp. 71–2.
[35] Chamberlain to Buxton, 3 Sep. 1893, CO 23/236.

'swaggered about as Chief Justice', obsessed with his high position. When a harmless letter appeared in a local paper 'in which his conduct was criticized in a humorous manner', he reacted in a monarchical fashion, setting off the sequence of events that led to the present situation. Even after being rebuked by the Judicial Committee of the Privy Council, he continued having 'calumnies' against the governor published in the press, and now sought to involve the House of Commons in his destructive efforts. Dismissing the notion of an enquiry, Chamberlain asked the House 'whether the Chief Justice, after having provoked, insulted, and libeled the inhabitants of the colony, can be allowed to return to it in an official capacity'. He sat down to strong applause from the benches behind him.[36]

The man who had been called 'the best debater in the House' thus killed the possibility of an enquiry.[37] A defensive government spokesman accepted that 'there was a considerable abuse of judicial power in some of their colonies' and that 'the Chief Justices had an undue idea of their powers'. Yelverton's fate was now sealed. The Colonial Office was aware, as one official minuted, that 'the islands are no doubt as bad as he says'; nonetheless, 'by his own rashness or want of discretion . . . he has made them too hot to hold him'.[38] The Colonial Office now asked the Privy Council to decide whether Yelverton should be removed from his position. At the hearing of its Judicial Committee, Yelverton vainly raised the general issue of the protection of judicial independence in the empire, while the judges did little to hide their exasperation with his behaviour. 'How could you', asked Lord Coleridge, 'write such a letter as [the one published in the *Pall Mall Gazette*, which accused the governor and other officials of corruption and perversion of justice] and expect to be sent back to the Bahamas afterwards?'[39] When the hearing ended, and it was clear what the Committee's formal answer would be, he was asked for his resignation, under threat of being dismissed; he unwillingly complied, and a new chief justice was immediately appointed, even before the Privy Council issued its ruling.[40] When that came, it was, as

---

[36] *The Times*, 9 Sep. 1893, p. 8.

[37] By the seasoned parliamentary correspondent Henry Lucey, quoted in Marsh, *Joseph Chamberlain*, p. 308.

[38] H. W. Just, minute, Oct. 1893, and R. W. [?], minute, 1 Nov. 1893, CO 23/236.

[39] *The Times*, 7 Dec. 1893, p. 5.

[40] He went out making it clear that he had not jumped but been pushed, and warning that 'the independence of the Judges in the smaller colonies is seriously endangered by the present attitude of the Colonial Office towards them': Letter, *The Times*, 1 Jan. 1894, p. 12.

expected, an endorsement of the appropriateness, if he had not resigned, of his dismissal.[41]

In the space of a half-decade, under both Conservative and Liberal governments, two chief justices had been got rid of. In the aftermath their friend, the Archdeacon of Nassau, bleakly wondered whether 'it is quite impossible to rule an English Colony on upright principles', while the colonial white elite and its friends in England congratulated themselves that they had turned back 'judicial tyranny'.[42] Bay Street was not again to be challenged for more than a half-century. To their surprise, Her Majesty's chief judicial officers discovered that in the Bahamas 'the rule of law' was not under their control.

[41] 7 Mar. 1894, CO 23/240.
[42] Wakefield to Yelverton, in pamphlet, CO 23/236; the 'Bay Street' view was presented regularly in the pages of the *Nassau Guardian*.

15

Australia's early High Court, the fourth Commonwealth Attorney-General and the 'Strike of 1905'

SUSAN PRIEST[*]

It seems fitting to commence this curious and quintessentially Australian narrative concerning the country's early High Court, between the months of July 1904 and August 1905,[1] with a glimpse at the late Josiah Henry Symon. Described by an 'international visitor'[2] to South Australia at the turn of the twentieth century as 'the most considerable person in Adelaide from an intellectual standpoint',[3] it is perhaps of little surprise that he was regarded as an individual who 'invited description'.[4] 'Over six feet in height'[5] and endowed with a rather formidable and willowy appearance, he possessed a stern and grim expression that could be foiled with looks of merriment and gentleness.[6] An individual in his late fifties, he was 'recognized as one of the most brilliant men in Federal Parliament'.[7]

Symon's extensive collection of personal papers tell us he was of Scottish origin,[8] a rural landowner,[9] a successful winemaker and was considered one

---

[*] The author wishes to express appreciation to Ms Rosemary Nicholson, the Deputy Librarian of the High Court of Australia. The author also accepts full responsibility for the analysis, conclusions and any errors contained in the ensuing pages.

[1] See also W. G. McMinn, 'The High Court imbroglio and the fall of the Reid–Mclean government' (1978) 64 *Journal of the Royal Australian Historical Society* 14–31; S. Priest, 'Strike of 1905' in T. Blackshield *et al.* (eds.), *The Oxford Companion to the High Court of Australia* (Oxford, 2001), pp. 650–1 and D. I. Wright, 'Sir Josiah Symon, federation and the High Court' (1978) 64 *Journal of the Royal Australian Historical Society* 73–86.

[2] Wright, 'Sir Josiah Symon, federation and the High Court', p. 73.   [3] *Ibid.*

[4] H. Campbell Jones, 'Sir Josiah Symon – a sketch', *Today*, 1 May 1934, p. 13.   [5] *Ibid.*

[6] *Ibid.*   [7] The *Sydney Morning Herald*, 19 Aug. 1904, p. 5.

[8] See generally the National Library of Australia (NLA), The Symon Papers MS 1736.

[9] The State Library of South Australia (SLSA) PRG 249 refers to Symon's home, 'Manoah', as being large and impressive and set in the Adelaide Hills on approximately 43 acres.

of Australia's early scholarly authorities on the works of Shakespeare.[10] Matching his political finesse with the skills of an exceptional lawyer,[11] Josiah Symon was also an individual passionate about Australia becoming a federated nation. So much so that in 1886, he declined a safe conservative seat in the British House of Commons to dedicate himself to Australia's federal cause,[12] particularly with regards to the development of the judicial branch of the Constitution.[13] His contribution to Australian legal history turned out to be both significant and unexpected.

In August 1904, Josiah Symon became the fourth Commonwealth Attorney-General in Australia's first coalition government, the Reid–McLean Ministry,[14] and, upon taking the position entered into what has since been regarded as a bitter, escalating and ultimately public confrontation with Australia's original High Court.[15] This incident culminated in May 1905, when the High Court adjourned proceedings and went on 'strike'[16] due to continued uncertainty concerning the travelling expenses, accommodation costs and the provision of staff to run the Court. It was an event that remains exceptional in the High Court's history, and an event the circumstances of which made a marked contribution towards shaping both the independence of the judiciary and the future operation of the Court.

When Symon took office, the Australian High Court had been in operation for less than a year, sitting for the first time in Melbourne on 6 October 1903, only months after the enactment of the Commonwealth Judiciary Act of 1903. The Court consisted of three original members whose choice for a position on the bench was not as obvious as it may have

---

[10] See J. H. Symon, *Shakespeare at Home* (Adelaide, 1905), and *Shakespeare the Englishman* (Adelaide, 1924).

[11] Symon's legal skills were so esteemed that the dignified title of jurist was deemed to be more appropriate. See [Author Unknown], 'Eminent Federalists Senator Sir Josiah H. Symon KC KCMG', *United Australia*, 20 Jan. 1902, p. 12.

[12] D. I. Wright, 'Symon, Sir Josiah Henry (1846–1934)' in J. Richie (ed.), *Australian Dictionary of Biography*, XII: *1891–1939* (Melbourne, 1990), p. 156.

[13] Symon was a South Australian member of the Australasian Federal Convention in 1897–8 and chaired its judiciary committee. See *ibid.*

[14] So called because it was the first federal coalition, comprising the two non-Labor parties of Australia's tripartite Parliament in the House of Representatives consisting of a shared partnership headed by George Reid and supported by his Free Traders with a group of Liberal Protectionists led by Allan McLean.

[15] G. Souter, *Lion and Kangaroo: The initiation of Australia* (Melbourne, 2000), pp. 110–14.

[16] The use of the term 'strike' to describe the High Court adjourning proceedings in May 1905 was penned by Josiah Symon in a letter to Prime Minister George Reid on 22 May 1905. See the Symon Papers NLA MS 1736/11/591. For further discussion about judicial strikes in other countries see G. Winterton, *Judicial Remuneration in Australia* (Melbourne, 1995), pp. 1–2.

initially seemed.[17] As John M. Williams indicates, 'the list of potential candidates, especially given the intimacy that many had with the drafting of the Constitution, was long',[18] and even when the choice of judges was finally announced, the composition of the Court was not without its critics.[19] Samuel Walker Griffith, a former Premier and Chief Justice of Queensland,[20] whose outstanding command of the law was seen as 'the most powerful guarantee of the High Court's success',[21] was appointed as Chief Justice along with senior puisne Justice Edmund Barton, Australia's former first Prime Minister,[22] and puisne Justice Richard O'Connor, the government leader in the Senate during Barton's ministry,[23] who was thought to be 'liberal-minded [and] brought to the Bench "sound commonsense"'. [24]

All three members of the High Court and Attorney-General Symon, had been involved tirelessly, though by no means harmoniously,[25] throughout the Constitutional Convention Debates of the 1890s in shaping line by line the bill that would eventually become Australia's Constitution. Their decade-long struggle for the federation of the Australian colonies came to its successful conclusion when, on 1 January 1901, 'An Act to Constitute the Commonwealth of Australia'[26] brought into being a new nation.

The structure of Australia's Constitution reflects that of the Constitution of the United States.[27] It vests, through Chapters I, II and III respectively, the legislative,[28] executive[29] and judicial powers[30] of the Commonwealth in

---

[17] J. M. Williams, *One Hundred Years of the High Court*, the Trevor Reese Memorial Lecture (London, 2003), p. 10.

[18] *Ibid.* See also, B. Galligan, *Politics of the High Court* (Brisbane, 1987), 78–9.

[19] Prime Minister Reid reportedly denounced the appointment of Barton, *ibid.*, p. 12, and Symon was highly critical of the appointment of both Griffith and Barton. See 'What Quiz thinks' [date and author unknown] in the Symon Papers NLA MS 1736/3/14, at p. 20.

[20] R. B. Joyce, *Sir Samuel Griffith* (Brisbane, 1984).

[21] J. M. Bennett, *Keystone of the Federal Arch* (Canberra, 1980), p. 21.

[22] G. Bolton, *Edmund Barton* (St. Leonards, NSW, 2000), chs. 13 and 14.

[23] M. Rutledge, 'O'Connor, Richard Edward' in Blackshield, *Oxford Companion to the High Court of Australia*, pp. 509–11.

[24] *Ibid.*, p. 510.

[25] Symon was greatly offended by Griffith's criticism of the judiciary clauses drafted when he chaired the judiciary committee in 1897–8. See particularly J. M. Williams, *The Australian Constitution: A documentary history* (Melbourne, 2005), pp. 614–15.

[26] The Commonwealth of Australia Constitution Act 1900.

[27] See art I, s. 1; art II, s. 1; art II, s. 1.

[28] Chap. I vests legislative power in the Parliament; s. 1.

[29] Chap. II vests executive power in the queen; s. 61.

[30] Chap. III of the Australian Constitution, 'The Judicature', under s. 71 vests the judicial power of the Commonwealth in the High Court and in 'such other federal courts as the Parliament creates'.

three different institutions of government so as to protect against 'the accumulation of all powers ... in the same hands'.[31] Nonetheless, in the Australian context, the framers of the Constitution also adopted the British Westminster principles of responsible government and, in so doing, diminished to some extent, the strict separation between the legislative and executive powers.[32] In contrast, what does remain clear is that as early as 1909, in *Huddart, Parker & Co. Pty Ltd* v. *Moorehead*,[33] the strong emphasis on the strict separation of judicial personnel and functions from the other powers within the Commonwealth was upheld by the original members of the Australian High Court[34] – a position perhaps best explained by the necessity that the judicial power of the Commonwealth was regarded as the 'bulwark of the Constitution against encroachment whether by the legislature or the executive'.[35] This was a constitutional position, however,[36] which, in guaranteeing the independence of Australia's original High Court judges as 'judicial nation builders ... piecing together their colonial inheritance with the aspirations of the new Commonwealth',[37] would ultimately take on a new significance in a way the justices were completely unprepared for.

Other concepts relating to Australia's judicature entertained by Josiah Symon at the time of federation would also prove to be contentious: that the original High Court be the final Court of Appeal[38] and also that it be

---

[31] J. Madison, *The Spirit of the Laws* (1748) in H. Irving, 'Advisory opinions, the rule of law and the separation of powers' (2004) 4 *Macquarie L.J.* 121.

[32] The separation between these powers is not strictly maintained in the Australian Constitution as, according to s. 64, members of the executive must also be members of Parliament.

[33] 8 C.L.R. 330 at 335.

[34] See later examples such as *Attorney-General (Cth.)* v. *R, Ex p. Boilermakers' Society of Australia* (1957) 95 C.L.R. 529 at 540; *Polyukhovich* v. *Commonwealth* (1991) 172 C.L.R. 501 at 684–5 and *Wilson* v. *Minister for Aboriginal and Torres Strait Islander Affairs* (1996) 189 C.L.R. 1 at 11. Also, former High Court Justice M. Gaudron, 'Some reflections on the Boilermakers case' (1995) *J.I.R.* 308.

[35] *Attorney-General (Cth.)* v. *R; Ex p. Boilermakers' Society of Australia* at 540.

[36] See the Australian Constitution s. 72(ii)–(iii) for affording further protection to the independence of the Judiciary with regards to security of tenure and remuneration. Also Winterton, *Judicial Remuneration in Australia*, pp. 2–10. At pp. 37–9 Winterton indicates that in Australia in 1907, when basic wage figures became available for the first time, a High Court judge's salary was more than twenty-seven times the basic wage. The original Judiciary Act 1903 (Cth.) s. 47 provided that the Chief Justice be paid 'Three thousand five hundred pounds a year,' and the other Justices, 'Three thousand pounds a year'.

[37] Williams, *One Hundred Years of the High Court*, p. 2.

[38] Symon held to this position throughout the 1890s and perhaps even earlier. Appeals to the Privy Council were finally abolished with the implementation of the Australia Acts (1986 (U.K.) and 1986 (Cth), at s. 11 respectively). See T. Blackshield and G. Williams,

created with a permanent seat like the United States Supreme Court.[39]
His arguments against Privy Council appeals had been met with particular
resistance from Samuel Griffith in 1900,[40] and the Court's practice of undertaking sittings in various states had been facilitated by section 12 Judiciary
Act 1903 (Cth).[41] It can also be added that Symon had been one of the many
candidates considered, but not chosen for a place on Australia's first High
Court,[42] and instead, upon becoming the fourth Commonwealth Attorney-
General, found himself as the head of a department that had already started
to scrutinise the cost of running the newly formed High Court. [43]

By 1904, with high expectations of the new High Court's role, the
potential for conflict over the Court's place in the new polity was
mounting. A combination of intense personal differences between individuals, now appointed to the apex of Australian politics and law,
together with strong and contending ideals concerning the judicial
function of the new Court, were sufficient to provide the impetus for
what would become an escalating, protracted battle between the executive and the judiciary. The dispute was monitored closely by the
Australian press[44] and important enough for some members of the
public to write poetry about the disagreement to their local newspapers.[45]

The surviving archival material reveals that the feud was fought out
largely through reams of correspondence including telegrams,[46] preserved
in original handwritten form or typeset, and most of it later published as
part of a parliamentary enquiry.[47] Particularly striking are the voluminous
telegrams and eloquent, often lengthy letters passing between Symon and
Griffith CJ. According to one commentator, they were, on Symon's part,

Australian Constitutional Law and Theory, 4th edn (Annandale, NSW, 2006), pp. 168, 600.

[39] The Symon Papers NLA MS 1736/11/457–8.
[40] Williams, The Australian Constitution: A documentary history, ch. 34.
[41] s. 12 Judiciary Act states that 'Sittings of the High Court shall be held … as may be required at the principal seat of the Court and at each place at which there is a District registry.'
[42] The Bulletin, 1 Oct. 1903, p. 5.
[43] The Symon Papers contain copies of the correspondence between the former Attorney-General H. B. Higgins and the High Court in this regard. See the Symon Papers NLA MS 1736/11/720 and 11/849.
[44] The details of the incident can be found in most of Australia's major newspapers between Aug. 1904 and as late as Oct. 1905.
[45] See 'Argument in the High Court' in the Evening Journal, 29 Mar. 1905, p. 1 and 'The passing show' by Oriel, in the Argus, 25 Mar. 1905, p. 5.
[46] The Symon Papers NLA MS 1736 Series 11.
[47] The Symon Papers NLA MS 1736/11/720–35 and 11/849–68. For ease of referencing it is these series of papers that have been most frequently cited throughout this chapter.

written with fiendish ingenuity and sinister powers[48] while to another, were 'marked on both sides by suppressed fury, and deadly icy courtesy'.[49]

Shortly after Josiah became the Attorney-General, he assumed the additional position which he highly valued, as 'the leader for the government in the Senate'.[50] It was at this time that he 'found a pile of papers of considerable magnitude entitled "High Court expenditure and travelling expenses"'.[51] These documents in his own words were 'literally a legacy from the previous Government'.[52]

The discovery of this correspondence demonstrates that Symon cannot solely be blamed for the tumultuous events of 1904–5.[53] It was his predecessor, Henry Bourne Higgins on behalf of the Watson government, who had commenced an investigation into the accumulating travelling expenses of the Court with a stated desire to 'make other arrangements'.[54] On taking office on 18 August 1904, Josiah gave careful consideration to this already-initiated inquiry. However, due to the subsequent pressure of parliamentary business associated with the new government, including combating a vote of no confidence in the new coalition two weeks after Parliament began sitting,[55] Symon 'was unable at once to go into the matter fully'[56] and no instant action was taken.

Towards the end of 1904, Griffith CJ wrote to Prime Minister George Reid, following up on an earlier 'conversation',[57] indicating with some reluctance his intention to move from his home in Brisbane in Queensland and take up permanent residence in Sydney, New South Wales. The other Justices of the Court already lived in Sydney and this was perhaps one way his travelling expenses could be reduced.[58] He also requested that his chambers in Sydney be furnished to accommodate his law library[59] and exhorted the

---

[48] J. A. La Nauze, *Alfred Deakin: A biography*, 2 vols. (Sydney, 1976), II, p. 383.

[49] Souter, *Lion and Kangaroo*, p. 110.

[50] *The Parliamentary Debates of the Senate*, 24 Aug. 1904, p. 4284, Josiah Symon, Senator.

[51] *Ibid.*, 28 Nov. 1905, p. 5835, Josiah Symon, Senator.   [52] *Ibid.*

[53] The Symon Papers NLA MS 1736/11/461.   [54] *Ibid.*, p. 849.

[55] *The Parliamentary Debates of the Senate*, 15 Sep. 1904, p. 4683, Josiah Symon, Senator. Reid ultimately survived the no-confidence motion with a majority of two. See *The Parliamentary Debates of the House of Representatives*, 13 Oct. 1904, p. 5577.

[56] The Symon Papers NLA MS 1736/11/461.

[57] *Ibid.*, p. 721. The letter is dated 12 Nov. 1904.

[58] See *The Parliamentary Debates of the Senate*, 28 Nov. 1905, p. 5837, Josiah Symon, Senator, where Symon claimed that from Oct. 1903 until Jun. 30 1904 Griffith drew travelling allowances of £591.2s.7d, Barton £263.0s.1d and O'Connor £352.11s.4d.

[59] *Ibid.*

Prime Minister seriously to consider making Sydney the 'Principal Seat of the Court',[60] on the understanding that all three Justices would continue to live there as permanent residents.

When Griffith's requests were brought to the attention of the Attorney-General, in a letter dated 2 December 1904,[61] it was Josiah Symon's prompt and blunt response[62] that turned any mere formalities into what one observer described as a verbal 'declaration of war'.[63] Symon reminded Griffith of the Court's earlier and unsuccessful attempts to negotiate with the previous Attorney-General, Higgins, to secure satisfactory travel finances, particularly for its associates.[64] He indicated that 'the travelling expenses accrued by the Bench in less than a year had attained a magnitude which . . . both inside and outside Parliament, has occasioned remark and evoked sharp criticism . . . and I feel sure I shall not look in vain to the Justices of the High Court to assist in securing a substantial reduction in those expenses'.[65] He appealed to the Justices to consider his views about the need for greater financial efficiency and immediately targeted the 'avoidable'[66] expenditure associated with the ambulatory nature of the Court as one way of controlling the costs currently imposed upon the Commonwealth.[67] Reflecting his personal sentiments expressed at the earlier Convention debates, he emphasised that the High Court as a Circuit Court was unnecessary and that 'the High Court *qua* Full Court ought not, unless under very exceptional circumstances, to incur any travelling expenses'.[68] He also insisted that the proper seat of the Court was Melbourne, because it was also the seat of the Commonwealth government. He then went on and proposed that, from the beginning of January 1905, all travelling expenses were to be reduced. The starting point of computation would no longer be the judges' places of residence but from the principal seat of the Court, that each Justice would receive no more that a maximum of 'three guineas'[69] a day for this purpose, and that these costs would also include those of his associates.[70]

---

[60] The Symon Papers NLA MS 1736/11/146–146a and 11/721. The Judiciary Act 1903 (Cth.) under s. 10 had created the principal seat of the High Court to be at the seat of government. At the time of the dispute this was Melbourne, Victoria.

[61] *Ibid.*, pp. 849–50.   [62] *Ibid.*, pp. 850–1. The letter is dated 23 Dec. 1904.

[63] Souter, *Lion and Kangaroo*, p. 111.

[64] The Symon Papers NLA MS 1736/11/850. The letter is dated 23 Dec. 1904.   [65] *Ibid.*

[66] *Ibid.*   [67] *Ibid.*   [68] *Ibid.*

[69] *Ibid.* Symon indicated that at this stage in the dispute, it was '*carte blanche* in regard to the sum which might be certified'. See *The Parliamentary Debates of the Senate*, 28 Nov. 1905, p. 5836.

[70] The Symon Papers NLA MS 1736/11/850.

The request by the Chief Justice for shelving to accommodate his law library in his Sydney Chambers was subsequently deferred.[71]

In an immediate response on behalf of the Court, Griffith made it clear that he would become a formidable opponent.[72] He was of a 'cold, clear, collected and acidulated'[73] personality as much as Symon was 'quarrel-some'[74] and leapt to the defence of the Court's independence suggesting that the High Court as a Court of Appeal and sitting in the state capitals was a practice that had been 'adopted after full consideration and with warm concurrence of the Federal Government'.[75] Further, as far as the Chief Justice was concerned, the practice of an ambulatory Court had also 'received the approval of public opinion throughout the Commonwealth'[76] and he felt justified in assuming that these arrange-ments, which could only be altered by 'Rule of Court or Statute',[77] 'would not be disturbed'.[78]

During the early part of 1905, in letters throughout January and February,[79] Symon emphasised the necessity of reducing the 'burden-some expenditure of the High Court'.[80] His correspondence became increasingly personal and combative. In an attempt to justify his position on the matter he wrote: 'it would not be in the interests of the Court itself, or of the people of Australia if the Attorney-General of the day did not maintain a rigorous control over its non-judicial action and its expendi-ture so far as it comes within the cognisance of this Department and the sphere of the executive. I intend to do my duty in this respect.'[81]

Prime Minister Reid, well aware of the mounting quarrel through dis-cussions with the judges and his Attorney-General on separate occasions,[82] as well as engaging in personal correspondence with the latter,[83] intervened and offered a compromise. He suggested that the circuit system ought to be simplified so that New South Wales and Queensland appeals would be heard in Sydney and all other appeals 'at the principal seat of the Court in Melbourne'.[84] The Justices appear to have made no formal response to this

---

[71] *Ibid.*, p. 851. The letter is dated 13 Jan. 1905.
[72] *Ibid.*, pp. 850–1. The letter is dated 27 Dec. 1904.
[73] A. Deakin, *And Be One People: Alfred Deakin's federal story* (Melbourne, 1995), p. 12.
[74] R. R. Garran, *Prosper the Commonwealth* (Sydney, 1958), p. 157.
[75] The Symon Papers NLA MS 1736/11/850.   [76] *Ibid.*, p. 851.   [77] *Ibid.*   [78] *Ibid.*
[79] *Ibid.*, pp. 723–33.   [80] *Ibid.*, p. 852. The letter to the court is dated 31 Jan. 1905.
[81] *Ibid.*   [82] *Ibid.*, p. 461.
[83] Reid and Symon also wrote to each other on 1 Jan. 1905 and 7 Jan. 1905 respectively. See *ibid.*, pp. 163–5.
[84] McMinn, 'The High Court imbroglio', p. 17.

suggestion[85] and opposition from the states and the legal profession to the possibility of curtailing the practice of circuits soon began to emerge in the newspapers.[86]

The correspondence between the Attorney-General and the High Court continued and perhaps if Reid's compromise had been offered earlier it may well have been accepted.[87] However, Griffith had threatened to 'take an early opportunity'[88] to provide the public with an explanation of the absence of his library from Sydney. Symon remained unmoved by any threats, believing with equal resolve that his policy was correct.[89]

In a long, detailed and 'angry'[90] letter,[91] towards the end of February, the Attorney-General reminded the Justices of the 'excessive' sum of £2,285 that the Court's first fifteen months of sittings had cost the Commonwealth and iterated his previous position that, as a 'trustee for the public in relation to High Court expenditure',[92] he had every intention of continuing with his economic measures in order to 'prevent its recurrence'.[93] Symon went on to say that he regretted the attitude of antagonism and unwillingness the Justices had adopted in the matter of circuits, and again emphasised that it was 'circuits which gave occasion for swollen travelling expenses'.[94] He was indignant and unable to understand how the Chief Justice could doubt that 'Parliament, rightly following the Constitution [had] never contemplated circuits of any sort'.[95]

In early March 1905, responding defiantly to Symon's unrelenting 'arguments',[96] the Justices left for circuit in Hobart. On their return the Justices promptly sent another letter to the Attorney-General. It urged the view that his cost-cutting measures were an improper interference with judicial independence.[97] A week earlier, they had indicated in pointed terms that the tone Symon adopted was 'unusual in official correspondence',[98] that a 'more careful perusal of our letters would have enabled you to avoid some

---

[85] Nothing remains in the archives to indicate there was a formal response sent to Reid in this regard. See especially the Symon Papers NLA MS 1736/11/849–59.

[86] See as examples, *The Age*, 15 Mar. 1905 (for complaints in Sydney) and *The Advertiser*, 20 Mar. 1905 (for a report about the protest by the Queensland Bar). The newspaper clippings can be found in the Symon Papers NLA MS 1736/3/14 at pp. 57 and 68 respectively.

[87] McMinn, 'The High Court imbroglio', p. 17.

[88] The Symon Papers NLA MS 1736/11/725. The letter is dated 21 Jan. 1905.

[89] *Ibid.*, pp. 186–92.   [90] McMinn, 'The High Court imbroglio', p. 20.

[91] The Symon Papers NLA MS 1736/11/854–6. The letter is dated 22 Feb. 1905.

[92] *Ibid.*, p. 854   [93] *Ibid.*   [94] *Ibid.*   [95] *Ibid.*   [96] *Ibid.*, p. 856.

[97] *Ibid.*, p. 857. The letter is dated 8 Mar. 1905.

[98] *Ibid.*, pp. 733–4. The letter is dated 1 Mar. 1905.

errors into which you have fallen'[99] and they found his constant intrusion 'intolerable'.[100] The Attorney-General, who perhaps would have been 'wiser to restrain himself',[101] chose instead to do otherwise.

Reflecting on the series of remarkable events that had unfolded so far, former Prime Minister Alfred Deakin had written privately to the Chief Justice saying, 'I cannot tell you how [Symon's] letters shocked me ... Still at *any cost to yourselves*, to your sentiments of honour and dignity, for the sake of the Commonwealth and the High Court *this correspondence ought to be destroyed*.'[102]

Despite the conflict, the High Court continued sitting. Griffith wrote to Symon to inform him that the Full Court intended to go to Brisbane and asked for a courtroom to be placed at the High Court's disposal.[103] In a calculated attempt to escalate the dispute, Symon refused.[104] Furthermore, literally with one long sweep of a pen, in the same letter, Symon opened up more areas of bitter contention.[105] He notified Griffith that travelling costs would be limited to the provision of one associate and one tipstaff, rather than the customary three associates and three tipstaves.[106] This has since been regarded as rather a deft move because both Griffith and Barton had sons for associates.[107]

Finally, the archives also tell us that the number of telephones in the chambers of all Justices and their associates in Sydney was reduced from five to one, and payment for telephones in the private residences of the Justices would be discontinued.[108] Moreover, Symon refused reimbursement for the cost of any additional travelling expenses incurred by the Justices outside the standard use of their government-issued railway passes.[109] He also requested that detailed information be supplied to him about all the current costs associated with running the Court.[110]

According to R. B. Joyce, a contemporary commentator, this letter proved to be the last straw.[111] The Court swiftly moved to bring the details of the

---

[99] *Ibid.*   [100] *Ibid.*   [101] McMinn, The High Court imbroglio', p. 19.
[102] La Nauze, *Alfred Deakin*, II, p. 384.   [103] The Symon Papers NLA MS 1736/11/858.
[104] *Ibid.*, p. 858. The letter is dated 26 Apr. 1905.   [105] *Ibid.*
[106] *Ibid.* The suggested changes to High Court personnel came in part from correspondence Symon received from the registry of the United States Supreme Court dated 13 May 1905, *ibid.*, pp. 693–704.
[107] McMinn, 'The High Court imbroglio', p. 20.
[108] The Symon Papers NLA MS 1736/11/858.
[109] Members of Parliament were also given government-issued railway passes but were unable to claim any further travelling allowances. See *The Parliamentary Debates of the Senate*, 28 Nov. 1905, p. 5839, Josiah Symon, Senator.
[110] *Ibid.*   [111] Joyce, *Sir Samuel Griffith*, p. 264.

crisis to public attention. O'Connor J was due to hear a case in Melbourne on 1 May 1905, but the Justices had met in Sydney on the preceding Saturday and decided to suspend the sitting. The decision made newspaper headlines around the country.[112]

On hearing about the adjournment, Symon, in a state of high agitation, sent an urgent telegram to O'Connor: 'I shall, therefore, be obliged if you will state to me the reason for the adjournment of the Court, and also whether you propose to proceed with the trials next Tuesday ... forgive my pointing out the importance of an immediate reply'.[113] Griffith's response on behalf of the Court was short and to the point. He defended the High Court's action as a necessary defence of judicial independence. 'We cannot recognise your right to demand the reasons for any judicial action taken by the Court, except such request as may be made by any litigant in open Court.'[114]

Symon, in a frustrated response, is reported to have scribbled on a scrap of paper: 'How can any Ct. because of disagreement as to Hotel expenses go on strike? ... no wharflabourers union do such thing.'[115]

Days before the dispute ended however, Griffith had the final say. 'When we accepted our offices we did so with an assurance that the Executive Government of the Commonwealth, not reduced to writing, but carried into effect by executive Action, that the Government would provide such facilities for the maintenance of the dignity of our office, and the efficient discharge of our duties as are usual in Australia ...'[116]

On 5 July 1905, as suddenly as the dispute had begun, it was over. Prime Minister George Reid resigned. The lack of support for his coalition party in Parliament had meant he was unable to withstand a challenge from the Opposition with regards to the threat his proposed legislative reform would have for the future of protective tariffs in Australia.[117]

---

[112] The *Argus* referred to the court's action as 'High Court friction', 24 May 1905, p. 7. The *Sydney Morning Herald* called it both a 'High Court deadlock', 24 May 1905, p. 8 and a 'High Court difficulty' on 10 Jun. 1905, p. 11.

[113] The Symon Papers NLA MS 1736/11/859.   [114] *Ibid.*

[115] Joyce, *Sir Samuel Griffith*, p. 265.

[116] The Symon Papers NLA MS 1736/11/864. The letter is dated 22 Jun. 1905. There is an indication that after Reid's resignation as Prime Minister, Symon continued to write to Griffith as if he still had 'departmental authority'. See McMinn, 'The High Court imbroglio', p. 28.

[117] For more details, particularly about the political complexities associated with Reid's defeat see the 'Professional speech of Mr Alfred Deakin, MP to his constituents, at the Alfred Hall, Ballarat, 24 June 1905' (publisher unknown).

Alfred Deakin was sworn in as Australia's Prime Minister for the second time, and Sir Isaac Isaacs as the new Attorney-General. Isaacs wrote to Griffith less than a week later and, in correspondence throughout July and August,[118] the government was able to offer a 'satisfactory and permanent solution of the matters agitated'.[119]

The Court would continue its practice of sitting in each state capital 'as may be required',[120] the government would have full confidence in 'their Honours' wisdom'[121] with regards to travelling expenses, the numbers of associates and tipstaves would not be reduced and the 'trivial matter'[122] of shelving was attended to. The affair had ended.

Griffith was delighted. 'On behalf of my learned colleagues and myself I have pleasure in saying that we concur in the opinion of the Government that the conclusions set out in your letter constitute a satisfactory, and, as we trust, a permanent solution of the matters in question.'[123]

In an undated memorandum prepared for Cabinet,[124] Symon provided a brief insight into the reasons for his actions. He felt it had been 'incumbent upon me ... as well as in discharge of my duty as Minister as the head of the [Attorney-General's] Department to strictly scrutinize the High Court expenditure and to devise if necessary, plans for its reduction'.[125] Yet, ironically at no time in undertaking his duties did he see his actions as interfering with the judiciary. On the contrary, at a later date he explained to the Senate that in his view the 'High Court in its judicial capacity, is above all executive interference and executive criticism, as it ought to be; but in regard to its administrative position ... it is just as much subject to the control of the Executive and ought to be so, as any other department in the Public Service'.[126] Significantly, Symon in defeat also admitted that he had 'been proud to discharge'[127] his duties as leader for the government in the Senate, but tellingly with regard to his duties as the Attorney-General he remained silent.

Now, over a century later, the same question is posed as that of a letter to the editor of the *Sydney Morning Herald* on 13 June 1905.[128] Can it be

---

[118] The Symon Papers NLA MS 1736/11/867–8. The letters are dated 12 Jul., 16 and 22 Aug. 1905.

[119] *Ibid.*, p. 868. The letter is dated 22 Aug. 1905.   [120] *Ibid.*   [121] *Ibid.*   [122] *Ibid.*

[123] *Ibid.*, p. 869. The letter is dated 23 Aug. 1905.   [124] *Ibid.*, pp. 456–73.

[125] *Ibid*, p. 457.

[126] *The Parliamentary Papers of the Senate*, 28 Nov. 1905, p. 5836, Josiah Symon, Senator.

[127] *Ibid.*, 5 Jul. 1905, p. 134, Josiah Symon Senator.

[128] The Symon Papers MS 1736/3/14 at p. 116.

said that 'too much has been made of too little?' in considering this bitter conflict over expenses?

Certainly, Symon's political and personal embarrassment as Australia's fourth Commonwealth Attorney-General quashed any aspirations he may have had for a future place on the High Court bench.[129] Yet, for all the turbulence he had caused, both for the executive and the judiciary, his actions were not without support.[130] Even so, Josiah Symon left a positive legacy, as demonstrated by the plaudits that opened this narrative. He was remarkable not just for his contribution to the development of Australia's early legal profession but also for his early dedication to the federal cause. Importantly during his brief time as the Attorney-General, Symon was instrumental in giving life to the Commonwealth Conciliation and Arbitration Act,[131] where the regulation of industrial disputes had proved to be the downfall of earlier Australian governments.[132]

What of the conduct of the original High Court Justices? Griffith's resolve to protect the judicial independence of the Court laid down an important marker in the development of the Commonwealth of Australia as a new polity. His actions between August 1904 and July 1905 consolidated the pattern of the Court's sitting practice that, in a modified form, remains to this day as an important symbol of the parity of the states within the Commonwealth.[133] Perhaps it is for these reasons that a recent Justice of the High Court describes the circumstances of the 'Strike' as 'events whose importance should not be underestimated'.[134] Perhaps too, there is something uniquely Australian that so important a principle as judicial independence should emerge and be guaranteed in such a curious manner.

This Antipodean story of judicial assertion took place just over a century after the great John Marshall CJ established the judicial supremacy and

---

[129] La Nauze, *Alfred Deakin*, II, p. 416.

[130] See as examples *The WA Record*, 25 Mar. 1905; *The Advertiser*, 7 Apr. 1905; *The Sydney Morning Herald*, 13 Jun. 1905. The newspaper clippings can all be found in the Symon Papers NLA MS 1736/3/14 at pp. 80, 81 and 116 respectively. See also *The Parliamentary Debates of the Senate*, 28 Nov. 1905, p. 5848, Senator T. Givens (Queensland).

[131] See *The Parliamentary Debates of the Senate*, 19 Oct. 1904, pp. 5710–32 for Josiah Symon's second reading of the bill in the Senate.

[132] G. Sawer, *Australian Federal Politics and Law*, 2 vols. (Melbourne, 1956) I (1901–1929), chs. 3 and 4 and R. McMullin, *So Monstrous a Travesty* (Melbourne, 2004), chs. 4 and 6.

[133] G. Del Villar and T. Simpson, 'Circuit system' in Blackshield, *Oxford Companion to the High Court of Australia*, pp. 96–7.

[134] The Hon. Justice Ian Callinan, 'Griffith as the Chief Justice of the High Court of Australia' in M. White QC and A. Rahemtula (eds.), *Sir Samuel Griffith: The law and the Constitution* (Pyrmont, NSW, 2002), p. 13.

independence of his Supreme Court in the new United States in the seminal case of *Marbury* v. *Madison* (1803).[135] By risking their careers and reputations through a judicial 'strike', Australia's first High Court Justices, Samuel Griffith CJ and the puisne Justices, Edmund Barton and Richard O'Connor, validated their own Court's claim to supremacy in a newly emerging polity, and we remain, to this day, the beneficiaries of their courage.

---

[135] 1 Cranch 137 (2 Law Ed. 60), 5 U.S. 137 (1803).

16

Judges and judging in colonial New Zealand: Where did native title fit in?

DAVID V. WILLIAMS

Five judges

This chapter looks at contributions of five judges in New Zealand between 1847 and 1914 regarding the law on native title to land. William Martin, the first chief justice of the Colony of New Zealand, presided over the Supreme Court of New Zealand.[1] He served in that role from 1841 to 1857. In a private capacity, after early retirement for health reasons, he made further contributions to the law and politics of the colony until he returned to England in 1874.[2] The first puisne judge of the Supreme Court was H. S. Chapman. He was a judge in New Zealand from 1843 to 1852, and again from 1864 to 1875. During the intervening years between his two periods as a New Zealand judge, he engaged in government service in the Colony of Van Diemen's Land (now Tasmania) and then turned to politics, academia and journalism in the Colony of Victoria.[3] C. W. Richmond was a settler politician holding office in various ministries, including a term as Native Minister, prior to appointment to the bench. He sat in the Supreme Court and Court of Appeal

---

[1] The Supreme Court was established in New Zealand by the Supreme Court Ordinance 1841. As in most Australasian colonies, the Supreme Court was the first-instance superior court. Appeals lay to the Court of Appeal, after it was established in 1863, and to the Judicial Committee of the Privy Council in London. This first-instance Supreme Court was renamed the High Court in 1980. Confusingly, the final appellate court for New Zealand since 2004, following the abolition of appeals to the Privy Council, is called the Supreme Court: Supreme Court Act 2003.

[2] G. P. Barton, 'Martin, William 1807?–1880, judge, writer' in *Dictionary of New Zealand Biography*, www.dnzb.govt.nz (updated 22 Jun. 2007); G. Lennard, *Sir William Martin: The life of the first Chief Justice of New Zealand* (Christchurch, 1961).

[3] D. G. Edwards, 'Chapman, Henry Samuel 1803–1881, journalist, lawyer, newspaper proprietor and editor, judge, philologist' in *Dictionary of New Zealand Biography*; P. Spiller, *The Chapman Legal Family* (Wellington, 1992).

from 1861 to 1895.[4] James Prendergast, after many years as Attorney-General, was appointed the third chief justice of New Zealand. His was the first judicial appointment made not by the Colonial Office, but on the advice of a responsible ministry of colonial politicians. He served as chief justice from 1875 to 1899.[5] His successor was a former premier and Liberal Party leader, Robert Stout, who presided over the superior courts for another long judicial stint. Stout was chief justice from 1899 to 1926.[6]

Common law doctrine of aboriginal title

All five judges made significant contributions to the reception and development of English law in New Zealand. My focus is on one important feature of their judicial work that had a special colonial context – decisions concerning Maori customary rights to land in the colony, and the lawful mechanisms for the extinguishment of those rights (if any). Legal relations between indigenous peoples and the state in territories colonised by Great Britain comprise an area of law that is now spoken of as the common law doctrine of aboriginal title.[7] The leading case on this doctrine, cited in many Commonwealth jurisdictions, is the 1921 Privy Council opinion in *Amodu Tijani v. The Secretary, Southern Nigeria*.[8] In the late twentieth and early twenty-first centuries the recognition of aboriginal title in this leading case was developed by courts in Canada, Australia, New Zealand and South Africa into a significant body of case

---

[4] K. Sinclair, 'Richmond, Christopher William 1821–1895, lawyer, politician, judge' in *Dictionary of New Zealand Biography*; S. D. Carpenter, 'History, law and land: The languages of native policy in New Zealand's General Assembly, 1858–62', unpub. MA thesis, Massey University (Albany, 2008), chs. 1 and 3.

[5] J. Bassett and J. G. H. Hannan, 'Prendergast, James 1826–1921, lawyer, judge' in *Dictionary of New Zealand Biography*; G. Morris, 'James Prendergast and the New Zealand Parliament: Issues in the Legislative Council during the 1860s' (2005) 3 *New Zealand Journal of Public and International Law* 177; G. Morris, 'James Prendergast and the Treaty of Waitangi: Judicial attitudes to the Treaty during the latter half of the nineteenth century' (2004) 35 *V.U.W.L.R.* 117.

[6] D. Hamer, 'Stout, Robert 1844–1930, lawyer, politician, premier, chief justice, university chancellor' in *Dictionary of New Zealand Biography*; D. A. Hamer, 'The law and the prophet: A political biography of Sir Robert Stout, 1844–1930', unpub. MA thesis, University of Auckland (Auckland, 1960); W. H. Dunn and I. L. M. Richardson, *Sir Robert Stout* (Wellington, 1961).

[7] P. G. McHugh, *Aboriginal Societies and the Common Law: A history of sovereignty, status, and self-determination* (Oxford, 2004).

[8] *Amodu Tijani v. The Secretary, Southern Nigeria* [1921] 2 A.C. 399 (P.C.) [*Tijani*]. See also *Oyekan v. Adele* [1957] 2 All E.R. 785 (P.C.).

law. A number of these cases have made a considerable impact on contemporary law and politics in those nations as relationships between settler populations and indigenous peoples have been reassessed in the light of human rights and indigenous rights norms.[9]

Despite the name given to it, this is not a doctrine sourced in the common law of England. That it is called a common law doctrine obscures its origins in European international law, United States Supreme Court reasoning and British Colonial Office imperial policy. It is easy to assume – incorrectly in my view – that the doctrine has been part of New Zealand law since the reception of English common law in 1840.[10]

A golden thread of reasoning

The notion that the doctrine of aboriginal title has always formed part of New Zealand law is described by Mark Hickford as 'a golden thread of reasoning about native title independently actionable at common law in the courts'.[11] The most notable of the academic writers identified by Hickford who have taken this line are Paul McHugh (though only in his early career writings),[12] F. M. (Jock) Brookfield and John William Tate. A recent addition to their ranks is Jim Evans.[13] The golden-thread line of

---

[9] Canada: *Calder* v. *Attorney-General of British Columbia* (1973) 34 D.L.R. (3d) 145 (S.C. C.); *Delgamuukw* v. *British Columbia* [1997] 3 S.C.R. 1010 (S.C.C.); Australia: *Mabo* v. *Queensland (No 2)* (1992) 175 C.L.R. 1 (H.C.A.): *Wik* v. *Queensland* (1996) 187 C.L.R. 1 (H.C.A.); New Zealand: *Te Weehi* v. *Regional Fisheries Officer* [1986] 1 N.Z.L.R. 680 (H.C.); *Attorney-General* v. *Ngati Apa* [2003] 3 N.Z.L.R. 643 (C.A.) [*Ngati Apa*]; South Africa: *Alexkor Ltd* v. *Richtersfeld Community* (2004) 5 S.A. 460 (S.A.C.C.).

[10] The English Laws Act 1858 declared 14 Jan. 1840 to be the reception date for English law. That reception date is maintained in current law by the Imperial Laws Application Act 1988.

[11] M. Hickford, 'John Salmond and native title in New Zealand: Developing a Crown theory on the Treaty of Waitangi, 1910–1920' (2007) 38 *V.U.W.L.R.* 853, 873 at n. 93. Hickford there cites P. G. McHugh, 'Aboriginal title in New Zealand courts' (1984) 2 *Canterbury L. Rev.* 235, 245–51; F. M. Brookfield, *Waitangi and Indigenous Rights: Revolution, law and legitimation*, rev. edn (Auckland, 2006), pp. 128–9; J. W. Tate '*Hohepa Wi Neera*: Native title and the Privy Council challenge' (2004) 35 *V.U.W.L.R.* 73, 103 at n. 107.

[12] Hickford notes that McHugh altered his approach to New Zealand legal history principally due to the methodological influence of J. G. A. Pocock. For McHugh's own take on his Pocockian turn, see P. G. McHugh, 'A history of the modern jurisprudence of aboriginal rights' in D. Dyzenhaus *et al.* (eds.), *A Simple Common Lawyer: Essays in honour of Michael Taggart* (Oxford, 2009), pp. 209, 221–3.

[13] J. Evans, 'Reflections on *Nireaha Tamaki* v. *Baker*' (2007) 2 *Te Tai Haruru: Journal of Maori Legal Writing* 101.

reasoning, which Hickford considers ahistorical in its methodology, suggests that:

- New Zealand courts fully recognised native title at common law early in colonial history in the *Symonds* case in 1847.[14]
- The 1877 judgment of Prendergast CJ in *Parata* wrongly denied the existence of native title in colonial law.[15]
- The Privy Council at the turn of the twentieth century in *Tamaki* (1901) rejected this 'notorious' judgment.[16] Lord Davey thought it was 'rather late in the day' to argue that 'there is no customary law of the Maoris of which courts of law can take cognizance'.[17]
- The approach of New Zealand judges to native title issues was again criticised by the Privy Council in *Wallis* (1903).[18]
- Regrettably, since *Parata* had not been formally overruled, colonial judges felt at liberty to continue to follow it in cases such as *Neera*.[19] They also lambasted the Privy Council's reasoning on native title in the course of a public protest against the *Wallis* reversal of the Court of Appeal.[20]
- Sections 84–7 of the Native Land Act 1909 stipulated that any claims by Maori that their customary title rights had not been properly extinguished prior to the issue of a Crown grant or a Native Land Court order were non-justiciable in the ordinary courts. Bolstered by this statutory incorporation, *Parata* continued to distort New Zealand common law reasoning and statutory interpretation for more than a century. An example was the 1912 *Korokai* decision of the Court of Appeal. The court did overrule Crown objections and did permit Maori applicants to pursue a claim in the Native Land Court for a

---

[14] *Regina* v. *Symonds* [1847] *New Zealand Gazette* 63; enclosure in despatch no. 33, Grey to Earl Grey, 5 Jul. 1847 in *British Parliamentary Papers, Colonies New Zealand* (Shannon, 1969), VI, p. 64; later included in *New Zealand Privy Council Cases, 1840–1932* (Wellington, 1938), pp. 387 *et seq.* (S.C.) [*Symonds*].

[15] *Wi Parata* v. *Bishop of Wellington* (1877) 3 N.Z. Jur. (N.S.) S.C. 72 [*Parata*]. I do not follow the norm of referring to this as the *Wi Parata* case. Wi is a diminutive of the plaintiff's Christian name Wiremu – akin to Will or Bill in English usage.

[16] The *Parata* judgment is routinely described as 'notorious' in modern writings. An early example is P. G. McHugh, 'Case and comment: Aboriginal title returns to the New Zealand courts' [1987] *N.Z.L.J.* 39, 41.

[17] *Nireaha Tamaki* v. *Baker* [1901] A.C. 561, 577 (P.C.) [*Tamaki*].

[18] *Wallis* v. *Solicitor-General* [1903] A.C. 173 [*Wallis*].

[19] *Hohepa Wi Neera* v. *Bishop of Wellington* (1902) 21 N.Z.L.R. 655 (C.A.) [*Neera*].

[20] 'Protest of the Bench and Bar' in (1903) *New Zealand Privy Council Cases, 1840–1932* (Wellington, 1938), p. 730.

title to lake-bed land. This result was reached, however, not by the court recognising the existence of unextinguished aboriginal title rights, but by an interpretation of provisions in the Native Land Act on the jurisdiction of the Native Land Court.[21]

- A new dawn finally arrived in 1986. Williamson J in the High Court distinguished earlier precedents. He found that an aboriginal right to collect seafood continued to exist, and was enforceable by a court, regardless of the extinguishment long ago of native title over the lands adjacent to the fishery.[22]

- The *Parata* decision was clearly inconsistent with the tenor of dicta and judgments in many cases on 'the principles of the Treaty of Waitangi' decided from 1987 onwards.[23] *Parata* came to be dismissed as an 'infamous' nineteenth-century decision.[24]

- *Parata* was finally and comprehensively discredited by the judgments in *Ngati Apa* (2003). The Court of Appeal embraced the doctrine of aboriginal title and held that it had been part of New Zealand common law since the original reception of English law.

The *Ngati Apa* decision

In *Ngati Apa*, a unanimous decision by a bench of five Court of Appeal judges reversed a High Court decision in favour of unqualified Crown ownership of foreshore and seabed lands. The appellate court noted the apparently clear wording of a number of Acts of Parliament asserting that foreshore and seabed lands were vested in Crown ownership. The judges held, nevertheless, that the statutory wording was insufficient to extinguish aboriginal rights (if evidence could be produced to the Maori Land Court that such rights continued to be exercised). Aboriginal title rights could be extinguished only by precise statutory words that explicitly extinguished those rights. The leading judgment of Elias CJ stated:

> The approach adopted in the judgment under appeal in starting with the expectations of the settlers based on English common law and in

---

[21] *Tamihana Korokai* v. *Solicitor-General* (1912) 32 N.Z.L.R. 321 (C.A.) [*Korokai*].

[22] *Te Weehi* v. *Regional Fisheries Officer* [1986] 1 N.Z.L.R. 682 (H.C.). In arriving at this outcome the judge explicitly adopted the reasoning propounded in the early writings of Paul McHugh.

[23] *New Zealand Maori Council* v. *Attorney-General* [1987] 1 N.Z.L.R. 641 (C.A.); Te Puni Kokiri, *He Tirohanga o Kawa ki te Tiriti o Waitangi: A guide to the principles of the Treaty of Waitangi* (Wellington, 2001).

[24] See, though: Morris, 'James Prendergast and the Treaty of Waitangi'.

expressing a preference for 'full and absolute dominion' in the Crown pending Crown grant (para 7 above) is also the approach of *Wi Parata*. Similarly, the reliance by Turner J [in *Re the Ninety-Mile Beach*] upon English common law presumptions relating to ownership of the foreshore and seabed (an argument in substance rerun by the respondents in relation to seabed in the present appeal) is misplaced. The common law as received in New Zealand was modified by recognised Maori customary property interests. If any such custom is shown to give interests in foreshore and seabed, there is no room for a contrary presumption derived from English common law. The common law of New Zealand is different.[25]

In reaching this result the Court of Appeal overruled a prior Court of Appeal decision: *Re Ninety-Mile Beach*.[26] That case, decided in 1963, had cited *Parata* without disapproval:

> I agree with Keith and Anderson JJ and Tipping J that *Re the Ninety-Mile Beach* was wrong in law and should not be followed. *Re the Ninety-Mile Beach* followed the discredited authority of *Wi Parata* v. *Bishop of Wellington* (1877) 3 NZ Jur (NS) SC 72, which was rejected by the Privy Council in *Nireaha Tamaki* v. *Baker* [1901] AC 561. This is not a modern revision, based on developing insights since 1963. The reasoning the Court applied in *Re the Ninety-Mile Beach* was contrary to other and higher authority

The higher authority invoked was from the empire's final appellate body, the Privy Council in 1921:

> That the common law recognised pre-existing property after a change in sovereignty was affirmed by the Privy Council in *Amodu Tijani* v. *Secretary, Southern Nigeria* at pp 407–408:
>> 'A mere change in sovereignty is not to be presumed as meant to disturb rights of private owners; and the general terms of a cession are prima facie to be construed accordingly. The introduction of the system of Crown grants which was made subsequently must be regarded as having been brought about mainly, if not exclusively, for conveyancing purposes, and not with a view to altering substantive titles already existing.'[27]

There were other 'higher authority' rulings that might have been discussed. A number of Privy Council opinions on appeals from Canada,

---

[25] *Ngati Apa* at [86] (Elias CJ).

[26] *In re Ninety Mile Beach* [1963] N.Z.L.R. 461 (C.A.); R. Boast, '*In re Ninety Mile Beach* revisited: The Native Land Court and the foreshore in New Zealand legal history' (1993) 23 *V.U.W.L.R.* 145; R. Boast, *Foreshore and Seabed* (Wellington, 2005).

[27] *Ngati Apa* at [13] (Elias CJ).

Australia and Southern Rhodesia prior to *Tijani* in 1921 were adverse (explicitly or implicitly) to the recognition and/or enforceability of native title rights in imperial and colonial courts.[28] These cases, however, were not cited in *Ngati Apa* and are overlooked by adherents to the golden-thread version of reasoning on the doctrine of aboriginal title.

Serious legal mistakes about native title

A 2007 article by Jim Evans deserves scrutiny. It is focused on *Tamaki* – the advice of the Privy Council in 1901 on appeal from New Zealand. According to Evans, the judgments of Martin CJ and Chapman J in *Symonds* in 1847 'stated clearly that native title was a right under the common law'.[29] On the other hand, the judgment in *Parata* 'finding that native title is a right only under the *jus gentium*' was 'an aberrant judgment'; *Parata* 'misunderstood' *Symonds*; it was 'unsound' and it 'was unprincipled and wrong'.[30] Stout CJ in *Neera* was in error when he 'agreed that the law on native title stated in *Wi Parata* was still valid'.[31] In the 1903 'Protest of Bench and Bar' Stout 'misunderstood the basis of the Privy Council decision' in *Tamaki*.[32] Later, in 1912, Stout was wrong again in *Korokai*. The chief justice incorrectly 'treated native title as having only a statutory basis'.[33]

For Evans it is abundantly clear that native title was always more than a moral and political right derived from international law (*jus gentium*). It 'was a right under the common law existing from the foundation of the colony' in 1840.[34] It existed independently of any incorporation of native title recognition into legislation. Unfortunately, Evans admits, the Privy Council opinion in *Tamaki* was obscure and 'if not read with great care could be interpreted as holding that *Wi Parata* was right to the extent that it held no native title existed without statutory authority'. The *Parata* judgment was 'always wrong' but 'for eighty-five years after the

---

[28] *St. Catherines Milling & Lumber Co* v. *The Queen* (1888) 14 App. Cas. 46 (P.C.); *Cooper* v. *Stuart* (1889) 14 App. Cas. 286 (P.C.); *Ontario Mining Co.* v. *Seybold* [1903] A.C. 73 (P.C.); *Re Southern Rhodesia* [1919] A.C. 211 (P.C.).

[29] Evans, 'Reflections', p. 116.

[30] *Ibid.*, pp. 120, 128, 129. Evans attributes the judgment to Prendergast CJ only, but it was a joint judgment of the court.

[31] *Ibid.*, p. 103.

[32] 'Protest of the Bench and Bar', pp. 730, 732; Evans, 'Reflections', p. 122. The protest was against the reasoning and advice of the Privy Council in *Wallis*.

[33] Evans, 'Reflections', p. 122.   [34] *Ibid.*, p. 104.

decision in *Nireaha Tamaki*, New Zealand courts, its administrators, and its politicians continued to deal with issues of native title on the basis of a serious legal mistake'.[35]

How, I ask, can Evans be so sure that his is the correct view of New Zealand law? In what way were the decisions of Prendergast, Richmond and Stout 'wrong'? The answer he gives is that the enforceability of native title in common law was upheld by the Privy Council's 1921 *Tijani* opinion and it was correctly applied in New Zealand by the Court of Appeal in the 2003 *Ngati Apa* case. Any other view of the law on native title is a serious legal mistake.

Ngati Apa is indeed a modern revision

The burden of this chapter is to argue, contrary to Brookfield, Tate and Evans, that the *Ngati Apa* reasoning is indeed new law. I am aware of the chief justice's insistence that her judgment, and that of her colleagues on the bench, was 'not a modern revision'. With respect, I disagree. The work of scholars in the 1980s, especially McHugh and Brookfield, and reliance on their work by counsel enabled modern judges to reinterpret and re-fashion the old law found in the judgments of colonial judges delivered between 1847 and 1912. Below I discuss the older judgments and seek to clarify the actual understandings of the judges in the context of their own times. In doing so, I do not mean to discount the value of forensic reinterpretations of history in litigation. For more than a decade I worked outside academia as an independent consultant briefed to advocate for Maori claimants bringing historical claims to the Waitangi Tribunal.[36] I have written a great deal of advocacy history.[37] Also, I happen to believe (again, from an advocacy for Maori rights point of view) that the new law in *Ngati Apa* was a distinct and welcome advance on the old law and I was among those who objected vigorously

---

[35] *Ibid.*, pp. 128–9.

[36] The Waitangi Tribunal is a permanent commission of inquiry established by the Treaty of Waitangi Act 1975. Since an Amendment Act in 1985 it has had jurisdiction to inquire and report to the government on historical claims by Maori against the Crown.

[37] In addition to six substantial (but unpublished) commissioned reports filed with the Waitangi Tribunal between 1998 and 2007, see D. V. Williams, '*Te Kooti tango whenua*': *The Native Land Court 1864–1909* (Wellington, 1999); D. V. Williams, *Crown Policy Affecting Maori Knowledge Systems and Cultural Practices* (Wellington, 2001); D. V. Williams, *Matauranga Maori and Taonga* (Wellington, 2001).

when the *Ngati Apa* outcome was set aside by an Act of Parliament.[38] What I wish to challenge in this chapter is the notion that the old law was aberrant and always wrong.

The dimension of time and legal norms

I think that the difference between my approach and that of Brookfield, Tate and Evans is a disagreement about the dimension of time in the norms of the common law. In linguistics, a synchronic analysis is one which views linguistic phenomena only at one point in time, usually the present, and usually without reference to their historical context. This may be distinguished from a diachronic analysis, which regards a phenomenon such as the language of the law in terms of developments through time. Brookfield, in particular, adopts a synchronic point of view. He then sharply criticises my unwillingness to accept his views on correct legal reasoning.[39] The problem is that common law lawyers tend to write about the law solely from the point of view of how law is now understood. Many of them find it very difficult to accept that law laid down by judges in the past was thought by those judges to be the correct and appropriate law for their 'present', even though in our contemporary 'present' judges have come to different conclusions.

This leads many historians to express impatience with the presentism of legal reasoning, and sometimes to ridicule it. A good New Zealand example of the former is Bill Oliver's critique of history as written by judges in the Waitangi Tribunal's reports. He attacked the ahistorical methodology of the tribunal's reports and their reliance on counterfactual assumptions to criticise Crown policy, acts and omissions. The tribunal's common law style of history, he said, provided a 'retrospective reconstruction' of a 'millennialist' history that has 'a utopian character' with 'elements of the religion of the oppressed and the promise of delivery from bondage to a promised land'.[40] An example of ridicule is J. P. Reid's comment that the 'way lawyers think about history is an eccentricity foisted on them by their professional training' which 'may

---

[38] Foreshore and Seabed Act 2004; D. V. Williams, '*Wi Parata* is dead, long live *Wi Parata*' in C. Charters and A. Erueti (eds.), *Maori Property Rights and the Foreshore and Seabed: The last frontier* (Wellington, 2007), p. 31.

[39] F. M. Brookfield, '*Ngati Apa*, legal history and judicial method' [2009] *N.Z.L.J.* 134.

[40] W. H. Oliver, 'The future behind us: The Waitangi Tribunal's retrospective Utopia' in A. Sharp and P. McHugh (eds.), *Histories, Power and Loss* (Wellington, 2001), pp. 13, 26–7; W. H. Oliver, *Looking for the Phoenix: A memoir* (Wellington, 2002), pp. 154–70.

amuse historians who stumble over lawyering anachronisms' even though it is not a matter of controversy among lawyers. He goes on to claim that:

> Even today, a lawyer trained in the common law methodology thinks that a judge who rules on a question in litigation is stating the law as it has always been. If the judge reverses a previous decision and states a new rule in its place, lawyers are aware that the law has changed, but the new rule is thought of by lawyers less as being new than as having always been *potentially* the law on that particular matter. What to a historian is now the "old" rule, to the lawyer is the 'erroneous' rule. A long line of precedents that has been overruled is not, to the lawyer, the former law it would be to the historian, but incorrect law, discarded law, or not law at all.[41]

It might be noted, in response to Reid, that historians are not a monolithic group and their work is not immune to the charge of present-mindedness. Blair Worden, commenting on the historical-mindedness approach of the Cambridge historians J. G. A. Pocock and Quentin Skinner, agrees that historians do need to reconstruct the assumptions and vocabularies of the past. He agrees with the commitment to the study of values we no longer endorse and questions we no longer ask. But Skinner also suggests that by recovering 'lost' ideas historians can supply practical alternatives to current political values. At that point, Worden asks:

> Are not the historical particularities of past ideas impediments to their present usefulness? If we wish to use those ideas, do we need to strip them (if that is possible) of their historical encumbrances and revise or adapt them to meet our own circumstances? And if so, were not those unhistorically-minded critics who believed that past texts should be 'appropriated and put to work', so as to answer 'general questions of society and politics at the present time', in a position at least as strong as that of their successors?[42]

Neither are lawyers a monolithic group with a shared understanding of presentism and with clear answers to Worden's questions. Reid is quite wrong to assume that presentist perspectives, and acceptance of the retrospective element involved in judicial development of the common

---

[41] J. P. Reid, 'The jurisprudence of liberty' in E. Sandoz (ed.), *The Roots of Liberty: Magna Carta, ancient constitution, and the Anglo-American tradition of rule of law* (Columbia, MO, 1993), p. 203; 2nd edn (Indianapolis, IN, 2008), p. 204.

[42] B. Worden, 'Factory of the revolution', Review of Q. Skinner, *Liberty before Liberalism* (Cambridge, 1997) (1998) 20 *London Review of Books* 14.

law, are not matters of controversy among lawyers. Legal theorists worry about such issues a great deal. An excellent opportunity arose for debate on these issues when the House of Lords decided *Kleinwort Benson* v. *Lincoln City Council* in 1999.[43] In that case it was decided by a 3–2 majority, overruling a number of prior cases, that the law of restitution for payments mistakenly made applied to mistakes of law as well as to mistakes of fact. It was accepted by the majority that this development of the law would have a retrospective effect in relation not only to the parties to the litigation but also to anyone else the facts of whose case arose before the new decision. Lord Browne-Wilkinson in dissent attacked the declaratory theory of the common law:

> The theoretical position has been that judges do not make or change law: they discover and declare the law which is throughout the same. According to this theory, when an earlier decision is overruled the law is not changed; its true nature is disclosed, having existed in that form all along. This theoretical position is, as Lord Reid said in the article 'The Judge as Law Maker' (1972–1973) 12 J.S.P.T.L. (N.S.) 22, a fairy tale in which no one any longer believes. The whole of the common law is judge made and only by judicial change is the common law kept relevant in a changing world. But whilst the underlying myth has been rejected, its progeny – the retrospective effect of a change made by judicial decision – remains.[44]

Lord Goff's leading judgment for the majority, however, explicitly adopted a reinterpreted version of the declaratory theory of judicial decisions:

> Occasionally, a judicial development of the law will be of a more radical nature, constituting a departure, even a major departure, from what has previously been considered to be established principle, and leading to a realignment of subsidiary principles within that branch of the law. . . . It is into this category that the present case falls; but it must nevertheless be seen as a development of the law, and treated as such. . . . The historical theory of judicial decision . . . was indeed a fiction . . . [but] when the judges state what the law is, their decisions do, in the sense I have described, have a retrospective effect. I must confess that I cannot imagine how a common law system, or indeed any legal system, can operate otherwise if the law is be applied equally to all and yet be capable of organic change. [45]

---

[43] *Kleinwort Benson* v. *Lincoln City Council* [1999] 2 A.C. 349 [*Kleinwort Benson*]. See L. D. Smith, 'Restitution for mistakes of law' [1999] *R.L.R.* 148; P. Birks, 'Mistakes of law' (2000) 53 *C.L.P.* 205.

[44] *Kleinwort Benson*, 358.   [45] *Ibid.*, 378–9.

If golden-thread writers on the doctrine of aboriginal title in New Zealand do not fully embrace what Lord Reid called the fairy-tale view of the common law, they certainly tend in that direction. The appeal of the declaratory theory of the common law, or some modified version of it, is plain. I think that Richard Tur identifies the crux of the matter:[46]

> That there is a Rubicon hereabouts to cross is jurisprudentially controversial in that theorists and practitioners remain divided as to whether the judicial role is ever legitimately creative (or legislative) rather than exclusively declaratory (or adjudicative).

A viewpoint that Lord Goff and the *Kleinwort Benson* majority, Elias CJ and her brethren in *Ngati Apa*, and the golden-thread scholars Brookfield, Tate and Evans appear to hold in common is a concern to minimise the perception that judges are legislators. Lord Goff's modern version of the declaratory theory of the common law allows for the common law to develop but rejects the accusation that judges have legislated when they overrule previous decisions. As Tur writes, some may wish rule-of-law and separation-of-powers stories to be embedded in the law so that 'it is always improper even for a court of last resort to act legislatively'. Others:

> ... may wish to bring different moral or political commitments to the law which would permit (and perhaps celebrate) strongly legislative judicial departures from long-standing legal standards or 'ancient heresies' if justice is best served thereby, on the basis perhaps that the judicial duty of fidelity to 'law' is to law and justice rather than to law alone. [47]

I would place myself on the side of the Rubicon that celebrates creative development of the common law in fidelity to law and justice. Even so, I think it behoves a legal historian to look at the old law on native title in New Zealand in its own terms and in light of the historical context of its own time. I turn therefore to the five colonial judges who are my focus, and the decisions they made between 1847 and 1912, without the presentist lens that their now discarded judgments were incorrect law, or not law at all at the time.

---

[46] R. H. S. Tur, 'Time and law' (2002) 22 *O.J.L.S.* 463, 464.

[47] *Ibid.*, 465. The words 'ancient heresies' are from Lord Hoffman in *Kleinwort Benson*, 401. The irony of the *Kleinwort Benson* case is that the majority overruled prior cases and propounded significant changes in the law of restitution, yet disclaimed acting legislatively. The minority thought all forms of the declaratory theory to be fairy tales and that only by judicial change is the common law kept relevant in a changing world – yet refused to adjudicate legislatively.

The old law as developed between 1847 and 1912

The main planks of the old law on native title, developed in New Zealand in cases decided between 1847 and 1912, include propositions I would summarise as follows:

- British imperial policy in 1840 accepted that on the erection of a new colony, in a territory not previously subject to rule by a civilised European power, the reception of English law accommodated the ongoing exercise by native peoples of usufructuary (use-rights) and possessory rights over occupied lands until extinguished by the Crown.
- *Jus gentium* as expounded in European treatises and commentaries ought to be observed in relations between civilised peoples and other peoples.
- *Jus gentium* was not enforceable in the courts of a common law jurisdiction unless it had been explicitly incorporated by statute into domestic law.
- Stipulations contained in treaties – including treaties between a European power and a native people – were not enforceable in the domestic courts unless the terms of the treaty had been explicitly incorporated by statute into domestic law.
- On 'discovery' by a European explorer, followed by occupation by settlers from that nation, the entire territory of a new colony and its native inhabitants were deemed to be conquered and to be subject to the laws and prerogative powers of the colonising power and its colonial administrations.
- In the British Empire the Crown held a monopoly right, often termed the right of pre-emption, to enter into deeds of cession acquiring land from native peoples and extinguishing native title – with or without a prior cession of whatever sovereignty they might possess from native peoples to the Crown.
- The Crown assumed a duty as supreme protector of aborigines to secure native peoples against any infringement of their right of occupancy, and generally to act as their protector in any dealings they might have with European settlers.
- By the application of Norman feudal notions of the Crown's underlying title to all land in its domains – known now as the radical title of the Crown – the Crown was the sole source of authority to issue freehold titles or other tenures to land.

- All customary native land was, by operation of law from the very inception of a colony, vested in the Crown. By statute, individual Maori (under the Native Lands Acts from 1862 onwards) became entitled to have their customary title to land (including potentially the beds of lakes) investigated by the Native Land Court and then transformed into a species of freehold title.

- Native title in itself was not entitled to legal recognition and if 'pure Maori title' was invoked by litigants in the superior courts, the judges would treat such issues as non-justiciable and would refuse to inquire into the matter.

- The superior courts would also treat as non-justiciable any claims based on the Treaty of Waitangi and would characterise such claims as merely moral or political claims to be attended to by the executive government – which would be the sole arbiter of its own justice.

- Many Ordinances and Acts, from the Land Claims Ordinance 1841 onwards (including the Native Land Acts), did selectively incorporate certain elements of the Treaty of Waitangi into domestic law. The courts interpreted those statutes in accordance with the ordinary canons for statutory interpretation.

- Prerogative acts of the Crown and, in particular, the issuing of Crown grants to land would not be inquired into by superior courts. Unless there was an error on the face of a grant (for which the writ of *scire facias* might be relevant), the judges would never question nor go behind a Crown grant to ascertain whether or not native customary title (if any) had been fully or properly extinguished.

What did *Symonds* decide?

Many planks of the old law are laid down in *Symonds*. The policy of the newly appointed governor, George Grey, was to seek curial confirmation of the government's view that the pre-emption waiver certificates issued by Governor Fitzroy, Grey's recalled predecessor, were null and void.[48] The claimant in this contrived litigation, seeking confirmation of the validity of his pre-emption waiver certificate, was McIntosh. The land McIntosh had purchased from Maori was granted in 1847 to Symonds, a

---

[48] Fitzroy, he of *HMS Beagle* and Darwinian fame, was relieved of his commission as governor in 1845 and recalled, in large part because influential New Zealand Company lobbyists for settler interests perceived that he had mishandled land policy and native affairs: I. Wards, 'Fitzroy, Robert 1805–1865: Naval officer, hydrographer, colonial governor, meteorologist' in *Dictionary of New Zealand Biography*.

minor official in Grey's government. Symonds made no payment to Maori for the land. He made no payment to the governor either.

The parties to the litigation and the judges all assumed, but without any inquiry into the actual facts of the matter, that the native title of the Maori 'vendors' was fully extinguished by McIntosh's 'purchase' under the waiver certificate.[49] One might have thought that, in proceedings concerning the monopoly right of the Crown to purchase land from natives, any unlawful private transaction between a settler and Maori would be null and void for all purposes. If pre-emption waiver certificates issued between 1843 and 1845 were unlawful then legal logic might dictate that native title had not been lawfully extinguished. No such argument was put to the court. Grey's governmental policy was to promote the acquisition of land from Maori as rapidly as possible and thus to provide for the land needs of incoming British settlers. Waiver certificate holders sought judicial confirmation of their title to the land they had purchased. The colonial administration sought affirmation of its monopoly over land dealings with Maori. None of the participants in the litigation desired an inquiry into extinguishment of native title. The question of law devised by the Attorney-General, Swainson, was whether the private purchaser under a waiver certificate acquired a title that colonial law would recognise and enforce when a Crown grant to the same piece of land had been issued to someone else.[50] The Supreme Court decided the holder of the Crown grant held an unimpeachable title to the land. Crown pre-emption won the day in court.

Symonds is now viewed as the origin and source of the modern doctrine of aboriginal title in New Zealand common law. Invariably it is one passage from the judgment of Chapman J that is quoted and emphasised. It reads:

> Whatever may be the opinion of jurists as to the strength or weakness of the Native title, whatsoever may have been the past vague notions of the Natives of this country, whatever may be their present clearer and still growing conception of their dominion over land, it cannot be too solemnly asserted that it is entitled to be respected, that it cannot be

---

[49] The Fitzroy pre-emption waiver regulations and how transactions were conducted under those regulations are now the subject of detailed analysis in *Agreement in Principle for the Settlement of the Historical Claims of Ngati Whatua o Orakei*, 9 Jun. 2006, Attachment B: Agreed Historical Account, section 3, 'Ngati Whatua and Governor Fitzroy: The Pre-emption Waivers 1843–1845', pp. 15–18. See www.ots.govt.nz;%20www.nz01.2day.terabyte.co.nz/ots/DocumentLibrary/NgatiWhatuaoOrakeiAIP.pdf.

[50] Swainson to Grey, 21 Apr. 1847 in *British Parliamentary Papers*, VI, p. 35.

extinguished (at least in times of peace) otherwise than by the free consent of the Native occupiers. [51]

The authorities cited for this proposition were drawn from American case law – in particular, three United States Supreme Court judgments known as 'the Marshall trilogy' or 'the Cherokee Indian cases'. John Marshall, the fourth (and to date the longest serving) chief justice of the United States presided in all three cases: *Johnson* v. *M'Intosh* (1823),[52] *Cherokee Nation* v. *State of Georgia* (1831),[53] and *Worcester* v. *State of Georgia* (1832).[54] For a distillation of this case law, the New Zealand colonial judges referred to commentaries by two distinguished American jurists, Story and Kent.[55] Kent, in particular, was relied upon. In his third to fifth editions published between 1836 and 1844, Kent wrote:

> In discussing the rights and consequences attached by the international law of Europe to prior discovery, it was stated in *Johnson* v. *M'Intosh*, as an historical fact, that on the discovery of this continent by the nations of Europe, the discovery was considered to have given to the government by whose subjects or authority it was made, a title to the country, and the sole right of acquiring the soil from the natives, as against all other European powers. Each nation claimed the right to regulate for itself, in exclusion of all others, the relation which was to subsist between the discoverer and the Indians. That relation necessarily impaired to a considerable degree, the rights of the original inhabitants, and an ascendancy was asserted in consequence of the superior genius of the Europeans, founded on civilization and Christianity, and of the superiority in the

---

[51] *Symonds*, 390. Chapman J. refers, at 388, to the principles governing intercourse between civilised nations and aboriginal natives in colonial courts and 'Courts of such of the United States of America as have adopted the common law of England'. These principles are derived from 'higher principles', charters and treaties. This passage does not as such identify the common law of England as a source of the principles.

[52] *Johnson and Graham's Lessee* v. *William M'Intosh*, 21 U.S. 543 (1823) [*Johnson* v. *M'Intosh*].

[53] *The Cherokee Nation* v. *The State of Georgia*, 30 U.S. 1 (1831) [*Cherokee Nation*].

[54] *Samuel A. Worcester, Plaintiff in Error* v. *The State of Georgia*, 31 U.S. 515 (1832).

[55] The editions of Story and Kent available to Chapman J and Martin CJ in New Zealand were probably J. Story, *Commentaries on the Constitution of the United States* (Cambridge, MA, 1833), ch. 1, §§ 6–8; and J. Kent, *Commentaries on American Law*, 3rd edn (New York, 1836), III, part VI, lec. LI [51]. Kent's lecture 51 appears in exactly or near identical terms in later editions of Kent that may have been available in New Zealand by 1847: 4th edn (New York, 1840) and possibly 5th edn ('Printed for the Author'; New York, 1844). (Similar material, but prior to the completion of the Marshall trilogy of cases, was numbered lecture 50 in the earlier editions of Kent.) The judges in *Symonds* and in *Parata* did not specify the edition of Kent from which they were quoting.

means and in the art of war. The European nations which respectively
established colonies in America, assumed the ultimate dominion to
themselves, and claimed the exclusive right to grant a title to the soil,
subject only to the Indian right of occupancy. The natives were admitted
to be the rightful occupants of the soil, with a legal[56] as well as just claim
to retain possession of it, and to use it according to their discretion,
though not to dispose of their soil at their own will, except to the
government claiming the right of preemption. [57]

Kent in his own lifetime was well aware of the discrepancy between the
views of his text and the practice of United States administrations. Thus
his text (as cited in the 1847 decision of *Symonds* and unchanged
through three editions) includes this comment:

> The government of the United States, since the period of our independ-
> ence, has pursued a steady system of pacific, just and paternal policy
> towards the Indians within their wide spread territories. It has never
> insisted upon any other claim to the Indian lands, than the right of
> preemption, upon fair terms; [58]

In the 1836 edition, however, Kent adds a note:

> This was the case down to the year 1829. But under the administration of
> President Jackson, the policy and course of conduct of the government of
> the United States ... has essentially changed. ... The President [in
> 1832] ... declared his conviction 'the destiny of the Indians within the
> settled portion of the United States depends on their entire and speedy
> migration to the west of the Mississippi' ... [and in 1835 he insisted that
> the removal policy] 'ought to be persisted in till the object is
> accomplished' ... [because] 'All preceding experiments for the improve-
> ment of the Indians have failed. They cannot live in contact with a
> civilized community and prosper.' [59]

Worse was to follow, and a new addition by Kent to that footnote
appeared in the 1840 edition (though without any amendment to the,
by now, wildly inaccurate pre-1829 text on the 'pacific, just and paternal
policy' of the United States government):

---

[56] Adherents to the golden-thread approach to modern aboriginal title doctrine might
understand this word 'legal' to be referring to a 'common law' right. It is to be noted,
however, that Kent's passage is specifically concerned with 'the international law of
Europe' as expounded in *Johnson* v. *M'Intosh*.

[57] Kent, *Commentaries*, 3rd edn (1836), III, pp. 378–9. The quotation is identical in the
1840 and 1844 editions, though a line or two of the pagination on pp. 378–9 differs from
one edition to another.

[58] *Ibid.*, p. 397.   [59] Kent, *Commentaries*, 4th edn (1840), III, pp. 399–400.

> Since the preceding part of this note was written, and in 1838, those Indians have finally been expelled, by military force from the southern states, and transported across the Mississippi. President Van Buren ... held that a mixed occupancy of the same territory by the white and the red man was incompatible with the safety and happiness of either, and that their removal was dictated by necessity.[60]

No quotations from Kent's footnotes on American law in practice appear in the *Symonds* judgments, only the older roseate text.

The Marshall trilogy of cases bestowed power on the federal government rather than on the state of Georgia to deal with 'Indians'. That might have been thought a potentially useful outcome for the Cherokee nation at first. The Georgians were hell-bent on taking over Cherokee lands for settlers as rapidly as possible. They sought to do this by the passage of state laws, without bothering to negotiate with the Cherokee themselves. However, the federal government did not use the powers ascribed to it by the Supreme Court to protect Cherokee land rights. On the contrary, as Kent noted, Presidents Jackson and Van Buren 'negotiated' removal treaties and Congress passed laws in 1830 and 1832 to implement a transcontinental evictions policy. The federal government legally imposed forcible segregation of 'the white and the red man'.

The practical outcome of the Cherokee nation court cases contradicted the law's pretensions of respect for the rights of native occupiers of land. There was a loss of life of genocidal proportions, and abject suffering for the survivors, during the 'trail of tears' removal of the Cherokee nation from Georgia to beyond the Mississippi and into what is now Oklahoma.[61]

Was *Symonds* a praiseworthy decision?

Why then did selective quotations from the Marshall trilogy of cases, and selective references to Kent and Story, appeal to the colonial judges in *Symonds* in 1847? Why did Chapman J rely on American case law, based on the dogma of discovery and deemed conquest, to justify his view of Crown pre-emption and his view of aboriginal title occupancy rights?

---

[60] Kent, *Commentaries*, 3rd edn (1836), III, pp. 398–9.
[61] See R. A. Williams Jr, *Like a Loaded Weapon: The Rehnquist court, Indian rights, and the legal history of racism in America* (Minneapolis, MN, 2005); R. A. Williams Jr, *The American Indian in Western Legal Thought: The discourses of conquest* (Oxford, 1990); R. J. Miller, *Native America, Discovered and Conquered: Thomas Jefferson, Lewis and Clark, and manifest destiny* (Lincoln, NE, 2008).

Why were these rights taken to be subordinated rights – always subject to extinguishment at the discretion of a colonial government on the issuance of a Crown grant? Part of the explanation must be that, immediately prior to his appointment to the New Zealand bench, Chapman had been a paid advocate – and a zealous one at that – for the New Zealand Company.

The Company sought to promote the systematic colonisation of New Zealand by British settlers in the 1840s. The lands proposed for the Company's settlements were the subject of some transactions in 1839 between Company agents and a small number of Maori. According to Company claims, the transactions conveyed to it ownership and possession of more than one-third of the entire colony's land area. In seeking Crown recognition of these hastily negotiated transactions, the Company conducted a fierce lobbying effort directed at the British government, its Colonial Office officials, and members of Parliament.[62] Chapman fulfilled a number of roles during the Company's lobbying efforts to restrict the areas to be reserved for Maori within the Company's claim area. Hickford has noted that as an anonymous journalist in 1840 Chapman wrote that 'the New Zealanders do not require an enormous breadth of land, for they are, and always have been cultivators'.[63] As proprietor-editor from 1840 of the *New Zealand Journal*, published fortnightly for the next three years and subsidised by the Company, he vigorously promoted the systematic colonisation of New Zealand.[64] In the fifth issue of that journal in 1840, Chapman praised Kent as the 'American Blackstone'.[65] In 1843, after his appointment to be the first puisne judge in the Supreme Court, he published *The New Zealand Portfolio*. Chapman made his position on the New Zealand Company's land claims abundantly clear:

> No body of colonists ever had larger claims upon the sympathies of their fellow countrymen at home than the first settlers under the Company, – none a better title to the fostering aid of the government. It was a bold

---

[62] See P. Burns, *Fatal Success: A history of the New Zealand Company* (Auckland, 1989); P. Temple, *A Sort of Conscience: The Wakefields* (Auckland, 2003); P. Adams, *Fatal Necessity: British intervention in New Zealand 1830–1847* (Auckland, 1977).

[63] (H. S. Chapman), 'New Zealand' (1840) 9 *Dublin Rev.* 188 – as cited in M. Hickford, '"Decidedly the most interesting savages on the globe": An approach to the intellectual history of Maori property rights, 1837–53' (2006) 27 *Hist. Pol. Thought* 122, 143.

[64] Edwards, 'Chapman, Henry Samuel'.

[65] (H. S. Chapman), 'The English, the French, and the New Zealanders' (4 Apr. 1840) 5 *The New Zealand Journal* 1 – as cited in Hickford, 'Maori property rights, 1837–53', p. 145.

adventure theirs, to trust themselves, with no better protection than the proud consciousness of their own good intentions, among a set of untamed savages, inhabiting a part of New Zealand scarcely known to Europeans, and where their favourable reception by the denizens of the soil, was at that time extremely problematical. [66]

Judges in office do not always act on views they may have expressed prior to sitting on the bench. Nevertheless, Chapman's enthusiasm, prior to his appointment, for a restrictive approach to aboriginal title based on American precedents is fully consistent with the views he expressed in *Symonds*.

The reasons for Martin's acceptance of the American case law are less easy to ascertain. The chief justice was a Cambridge University Fellow in classics and mathematics whilst a student in Lincoln's Inn. He did not resign his fellowship until 1838, and had worked on equity conveyancing in a chancery chambers for less than three years when he was appointed chief justice of New Zealand. Martin's legal training and limited professional experience on appointment early in 1841 gave him little preparation for his future role. His interest in New Zealand was clearly related to his close friendship with the newly appointed bishop of New Zealand, George Augustus Selwyn. Selwyn was another Cambridge man, and one with whom he was to share a lifelong enthusiasm for the propagation of the Gospel of Christ. Martin was a humanitarian. He hoped Maori would play a significant role in the life of the new colony.[67] In the *Symonds* proceedings, however, it seems that Martin relied a great deal on Chapman's draft judgment and on the American materials that Chapman supplied to him.[68] Certainly his judgment reads pretty much like an echo of that written by Chapman.

Not all lawyers and imperial policy-makers in the 1840s shared Chapman's enthusiasms for American law, as Hickford's research has shown. James Stephen, the long-serving and highly influential permanent under-secretary at the Colonial Office, was scathing in his dismissal of American case law. His unflattering portrayal of the Marshall decision in *Johnson v. M'Intosh* (and of the role of international law jurists in general) should be noted by modern advocates for the doctrine of aboriginal title:

---

[66] H. S. Chapman, *The New Zealand Portfolio; Embracing a Series of Papers on Subjects of Importance to the Colonists* (London, 1843), p. iv.

[67] Barton, 'Martin, William'.

[68] Hickford, 'Maori property rights, 1837–53', p. 149 quoting from Chapman to Chapman senior, 15 Jun. 1847, f. 437, qMs-0419, ATL.

> Whatever may be the ground occupied by international jurists they never forget the policy and interests of their own Country. Their business is to give rapacity and injustice, the most decorous veil which legal ingenuity can weave. Vattel, in the interests of Holland, laid down the principle of open fisheries. Mr Marshall, great as he was, was still an American, and adjudicated against the rights of the Indians. ... [T]he decision of the Supreme Court of the United States, though it may be very good American law, is not the law we recognize and act upon in the American continent. [69]

Stephen was not blinded by fine language concerning the rights of Indians in the Marshall decisions. He looked at the reality of the law in practice, and in his view the Marshall adjudications were 'against the rights of the Indians'. He was not alone in the 1840s. In 1845 the British government, led by Sir Robert Peel, faced a vote of no confidence in the House of Commons that focused on the New Zealand question. One member of the House supporting the government was Sir Howard Douglas. He attacked the views of the 1844 House of Commons Select Committee, chaired by Viscount Howick. That committee received New Zealand Company submissions that the Treaty was a 'praiseworthy device for amusing and pacifying savages for the moment'.[70] It reported that 'It would have been much better if no formal treaty whatever had been made' and recommended to the House a resolution: 'That the conclusion of the Treaty of Waitangi ... was part of a series of injudicious proceedings.' It also found in favour of a fundamental principle of colonial law that native rights to the ownership of land should be admitted only when arising from occupation.[71] Douglas declaimed:[72]

---

[69] Stephen to Vernon Smith, 28 Jul. [1840], ff. 343–343a, CO 209/4, NA (ANZ) as cited in Hickford, 'Maori property rights, 1837–53', p. 152. I assume that Stephen actually intended to refer to Hugo Grotius, the Dutch advocate of open seas. Grotius wrote *Mare Liberum* (On the Freedom of the Seas) (1609) which was indeed highly conducive to Dutch maritime interests then challenging trade monopolies claimed by other European nations. The opinions of Emerich de Vattel, the Swiss philosopher of international law who wrote *Le Droit des gens* (The Law of Nations) (1758), were referred to a great deal in mid nineteenth-century debates on British colonial policy, but seem not quite apposite to Stephen's remarks quoted above.

[70] 'Report from the Select Committee on New Zealand together with the Minutes of Evidence, Appendix, and Index' in *British Parliamentary Papers*, II, Appendix no. 2, 'Land Claims', Somes to Stanley, 24 Jan. 1843, p. 30.

[71] *Ibid.*, pp. v–vi, xii (2nd Resolution).

[72] *A Corrected Report of the Debate in the House of Commons on the 17th, 18th, and 19th of June 1845 on the State of New Zealand and the Case of the New Zealand Company* (London, 18 June 1845), p. 124 – as cited in Hickford, 'Maori property rights, 1837–53', p. 159.

> I suspect I know the origin of this new fundamental principle of colonial law. It comes, I think, from the land in which the Black Man is a slave, and the Red Men of the forest are driven and hunted from their lands, as the Seminole and other Indians have been, according to certain adjudications that Indians have no property to the soil of their respective territories than that of mere occupancy.

Looking at British policy and imperial law from an 1845 point of view, it appears that those with a broader view of Maori rights, and with a deeper commitment to the Treaty of Waitangi, rejected the American approach to native title rights. Those who argued for a narrow view of Maori occupation rights, and expressed little or no commitment to the Treaty of Waitangi, favoured the application in New Zealand of the doctrines espoused by Marshall CJ and the United States Supreme Court.

Earl Grey's waste land doctrines, 1846

By 1847 the political tides had turned in Britain. Peel's Tory administration, which Douglas had defended in June 1845, was finally defeated a year later. Lord Stanley as Colonial Secretary had firmly repudiated the New Zealand Company position against the Treaty of Waitangi. He had instructed George Grey, when he appointed him to replace Fitzroy, that 'You will scrupulously fulfil the conditions of the Treaty of Waitangi.'[73] He was now out of office. To the delight of the New Zealand Company, and also (as noted below) of Chapman J, the incoming Whig administration appointed none other than Viscount Howick, now the third Earl Grey, to be the Colonial Secretary. Earl Grey's new set of Royal Instructions to the colonial governor in December 1846, replacing those of Lord Stanley, were a matter of huge controversy. His adoption of Thomas Arnold's views on waste lands, and on the very limited nature of Maori property rights, were published in the colony in 1847. He entirely dissented from certain views that had been influential in moulding former British policy:

> The opinion assumed . . . by a large class of writers on this and kindred subjects is, that the aboriginal inhabitants of any Country are the proprietors of every part of its soil of which they have been accustomed to make any use, or to which they have been accustomed to assert any title. This claim is represented as sacred, however ignorant such natives may be of the arts or of the habits of civilized life, however small the number of

---

[73] Stanley to Grey, 13 Jun. 1845 in *British Parliamentary Papers*, V, p. 230.

their tribes, however unsettled their abodes, and however imperfect or occasional the uses they make of the land.[74]

Earl Grey dissented from that opinion and sought the rapidest possible assertion of Crown control over waste and unappropriated lands that were not actually occupied or cultivated by Maori.

In the bitter controversy over these instructions that erupted shortly after the *Symonds* judgments were delivered, Chapman and Martin took very different positions. Chapman wrote privately with delight that the 'principles [Earl Grey] lays down in relation to the native title to the land are precisely what I have asserted'.[75] Martin was much less circumspect and expressed a diametrically opposed viewpoint. He authored a stinging criticism of Earl Grey's Instructions in a pamphlet published by Bishop Selwyn. This was circulated both in the colony and at home.[76] Selwyn and other missionaries, including Octavius Hadfield at Otaki, well knew that Maori customary usages and knowledge systems extended to the whole of the country. They knew that Maori would not countenance a policy that restricted their cognisable property rights to land 'occupied' and 'laboured on' in accordance with the precepts of John Locke and Thomas Arnold favoured by Earl Grey. Their view on the scope of Maori claims was consistent with a letter by Te Wherowhero of Waikato (later the first Maori king) to the queen to protest against talk of taking away the land of natives without cause.[77]

Despite their very different approaches to Earl Grey's waste lands doctrine, however, I think that Chapman and Martin would have remained in agreement in the *Symonds* case even if it had been argued after news of the despatch reached the colony. This is because, as mentioned above, the voluntary extinguishment of native title was assumed in that case without the need for evidence on the point. The judges in *Symonds* did not have to grapple with the difficult question of whether Maori customary rights were legal entitlements enforceable in the ordinary courts if Maori came to court claiming that their native title

---

[74] Earl Grey to Grey, 23 Dec. 1846 in *British Parliamentary Papers*, V, pp. 523–5; D. V. Williams, 'Maori social identification and colonial extinguishments of customary rights in New Zealand' (2007) 13 *Social Identities* 735, 737–9.

[75] Hickford, 'Maori property rights, 1837–53', pp. 161–2 quoting from Chapman to Chapman Sr, 15 Jun. 1847, ff. 437–8, qMs-0419, ATL.

[76] (W. Martin), *England and the New Zealanders. Part I. Remarks upon a Despatch from the Right Hon. Earl Grey to Governor Grey dated Dec. 23 1846* (Auckland, 1847).

[77] Te Wherowhero and others to the Queen, 8 Nov. 1847, enclosure in Grey to Earl Grey, 13 Nov. 1847 in *British Parliamentary Papers*, VI, p. 16.

had not been properly extinguished. They did not have to consider whether native title rights were more than the political and moral rights affirmed in British imperial policy. They did not have to consider whether native title rights might prevail in the face of a Crown assertion that those rights had been extinguished.

Martin (in retirement) in 1863 adopted a view consistent with the old law as summarised above. He was opposed to government proposals, later enacted as the New Zealand Settlements Act 1863, to confiscate land from all Maori in entire districts where some Maori were in 'rebellion'. Yet even as he wrote with passion to uphold Maori customary rights, he acknowledged the non-enforceability of those rights in courts:

> The case stands thus: no native can in any way enforce any right of ownership or occupation of land, held by the native tenure in the courts of the Colony. [78]

Despite his modern reputation as a 'socially liberal humanitarian',[79] Martin's position on aboriginal title in 1847 and in 1863 was not significantly different to that of Prendergast and Richmond in the *Parata* judgment to which I will turn shortly.

A solitary reference to 'the common law of England'

A comment is necessary on the only explicit suggestion in the case law from 1840 to 1912, apart from the ambiguous comment in *Symonds* mentioned above,[80] that the common law in itself might be a source of aboriginal title. In the post-1986 golden-thread view of aboriginal title, judges and scholars invariably evoke two pre-*Tijani* judicial pronouncements: first, the solicitous comment by Chapman J in *Symonds*; secondly,

---

[78] Martin to Fox, 16 Nov. 1863, 'Observations on the proposal to take native lands under an Act of the Assembly', CO 209/178, f. 163 (35), National Archives, Kew, London, as quoted in M. Hickford, 'Strands from the afterlife of confiscation: Property rights, constitutional histories and the political incorporation of Maori, 1910s–1940s' in R. Hill and R. Boast (eds.), *Raupatu: The confiscation of Maori land* (Wellington, 2009), p. 176. Martin's comment is in line with the later refusal by the Supreme Court to provide any remedy for native tenure land owners who brought an action against a trespasser harvesting timber from their land: *Mangakahia* v. *The New Zealand Timber Company* (1881) 2 N.Z.L.R. 345 (S.C.).

[79] G. Morris, 'Salmond's Bench: The New Zealand Supreme Court judiciary 1920–1924' (2007) 38 *V.U.W.L.R.* 813, 816.

[80] See n. 51, above.

this quotation from the *Lundon and Whitaker* judgment of Arney CJ in 1872:

> The Crown is bound, both by the common law of England and its own solemn engagements, to a full recognition of Native proprietary right.[81]

This explicit reference to 'the common law of England' is not explained in any way in the remainder of the judgment. Its inclusion there is at odds with other reported judgments, and known unreported judgments, of colonial courts and the Privy Council from 1847 to 1912. Martin CJ in *Symonds* wrote of 'the general law of England, or rather of the British colonial empire'. He cited Kent on American law and the Land Claims Ordinance 1841.[82] In no pre-1986 case other than *Lundon and Whitaker* does a court mention 'the common law of England' in taking cognisance of aboriginal rights or Treaty of Waitangi rights. In no other case is judicial enforcement of those putative rights ever contemplated unless a statute has explicitly incorporated them into imperial or New Zealand colonial law.

The court in *Lundon and Whitaker* had to deal with orders of the Native Land Court under the Native Lands Act 1865, certificates of title issued pursuant to that Act, and the validity of leases of the land in question in the light of the Crown Grants Act 1866 and Crown Grants Amendment Act 1867. All of the reasoning that led to the decision in the case concerned the interpretation of New Zealand statutes that in various ways took cognisance of Maori customary rights, extinguished them, and transmuted them into various forms of statutory entitlements. The entire proceedings of the Court of Appeal in this case arose from an unusual jurisdiction specifically created by the Lundon and Whitaker Claims Act 1871. First Johnston J sat as a commissioner appointed under the Act. His report inquired whether the claimants had a legal or equitable right existing in them prior to the passing of the Act. It focused entirely on 'the policy and provisions adopted by the Legislature with regard to the alienation of lands by aboriginal natives'. It noted that the Treaty of Waitangi 'has been assumed by the Imperial Parliament and the Legislature of the Colony as the basis of the policy and legislation of both respecting the aboriginal inhabitants of New Zealand'. The commissioner insisted that his task was not to pronounce an opinion on 'the

---

[81] *In re the Lundon and Whitaker Claims Act 1871* (1872) 2 N.Z.C.A. 41 (C.A.), 49 [*Lundon and Whitaker*].

[82] *Symonds* in *British Parliamentary Papers*, VI, pp. 64, 68.

political or moral propriety' of the legislature's conduct. His report then reviewed 'the current of legislation' and discussed 'the policy and intention which it manifests'.[83] Johnston J found against the claimants. Then, as provided by the special Act, there was an appeal by way of a case stated to the Court of Appeal. Arney CJ presided in a court that included Johnston J himself, along with Gresson, Richmond and Chapman JJ. This full bench unanimously agreed with the commissioner's report and findings. 'The question of right or wrong in such a case', stated the court, 'is one of State policy, and not a matter of law.'[84]

In speaking of the Crown's 'solemn engagements', Arney CJ was undoubtedly referring to the Treaty of Waitangi which had been explicitly invoked by Johnston J. What the chief justice meant by 'the common law of England' he did not explain. The phrase does not appear in the commissioner's report. It does not appear to be remotely relevant to the decision in the case on the interpretation of various statutes. As between Evans's view that the statement was part of the *ratio decidendi* of the 1872 case, and Hickford's careful debunking of that proposition, I have no hesitation in siding with Hickford.[85]

Parata follows *Symonds*

The judges in *Symonds* and in *Lundon and Whitaker* did not have to deal with the native title of Maori litigants. They did not have to consider what New Zealand colonial law's response should be to a claim lodged by a Maori litigant that native title had never been extinguished over land that was the subject of a Crown grant to another party. The judges in *Parata* did have to confront this issue. The plaintiff asserted that a Crown grant to the bishop of New Zealand in 1850 comprising some 500 acres of land at Porirua (near Wellington) was a fraud upon the tribe who had donated the land for a school that had never been built. The native title to the land, it was alleged, had not been lawfully extinguished.

Prendergast and Richmond were both English-trained barristers. They both had considerable political and legal experience of dealing with native rights issues in the tumultuous years before, during and after the period of colonial warfare from 1860 to 1872. Unlike Martin,

[83] A. J. Johnston, Commissioner, 15 Apr. 1872, 'The commissioner's decision' [1872] *A.J.H.R.*, G-6, 6–7.

[84] *Lundon and Whitaker*, 12.

[85] Hickford, 'John Salmond and native title', pp. 873–4, n. 93.

neither of these judges were known to have taken an interest in the values, customs and cultural knowledge systems of Maori. They were judges appointed not by the Colonial Office (as Martin and Chapman were), but by the governor on the advice of responsible ministers in the settler administration. One might reasonably expect that their thinking would be close to the mainstream of thinking in colonial society. The dominant motif of the period was the policy of racial amalgamation.[86] Maori were expected (if they were to avoid extinction) to amalgamate by learning and adopting British norms of civilisation. Native communism had to be replaced as rapidly as possible with individualised property rights. How, then, might mainstream judges respond to an assertion that a Crown grant to support the education of Maori to be civilised Christians should be set aside in favour of restoring tribal customary rights? That is the essence of the action brought by Wiremu Parata Te Kakakura, a chief of the Ngati Toa tribe at Porirua. He himself was a well-educated Christian who had been an elected member of the House of Representatives and also a member of the Executive Council.[87]

The Supreme Court judges responded, as one might expect of common law judges, by drawing on case law precedents. In particular they focused on the 1847 *Symonds* precedent, and on the American case law discussed in that case. Although they did not agree with the reasoning of the *Symonds* judges in all respects, their decision to uphold a Crown grant according to its tenor, and to frustrate any attempt to go behind a Crown grant and examine the validity of pre-grant transactions, was firmly based on the *Symonds* precedent. Where the *Parata* judges differed from Chapman J in *Symonds* was over dicta on the standing of native Indians to bring a suit to vindicate their property rights. Chapman J clearly misread *Cherokee Nation* v. *State of Georgia* on that point. In that case the Cherokee were recognised, though not as a nation. The Supreme Court described the Cherokee as a 'domestic dependent nation'. They were under the protection of the federal government, but this recognition did not give them a right of suit in federal courts. Marshall CJ wrote:

> If it be true that the Cherokee Nation have rights, this is not the tribunal in which those rights are to be asserted. If it be true that wrongs have been

---

[86] A. Ward, *A Show of Justice: Racial 'amalgamation' in nineteenth century New Zealand* (Auckland, 1974).

[87] H. Solomon, 'Parata, Wiremu Te Kakakura, ? –1906: Ngati Toa and Te Ati Awa leader, farmer, politician' in *Dictionary of New Zealand Biography*.

inflicted, and that still greater are to be apprehended, this is not the tribunal which can redress the past or prevent the future. [88]

The *Parata* judgment was more accurate than Chapman J on this aspect of American law. It also cited *Johnson* v. *M'Intosh* as authority against the proposition 'that a Crown grant could be impeached in an American Court'.[89] In that case Marshall CJ wrote:

> An absolute title to lands cannot exist, at the same time, in different persons, or in different governments. An absolute title must be an exclusive title, or at least a title which excludes all others not compatible with it. All our institutions recognise the absolute title of the crown, subject only to the Indian right of occupancy, and recognise the absolute title of the crown to extinguish that right. This is incompatible with an absolute and complete title in the Indians. [90]

Applying this *Johnson* v. *M'Intosh* reasoning, there was no factual basis for Ngati Toa to claim a continuing right of occupancy in the Crown-granted land at Porirua. On the contrary, the plaintiffs' complaint was that the land had been leased out to settlers to provide income to the Church of England, and that no school had been established for the benefit of the tribe as contemplated by the chiefs when possession of the land was given over to the church in 1848. The judges refused, therefore, to consider whether the customary entitlements of Ngati Toa had been properly and lawfully extinguished prior to the governor's 1850 grant to the bishop of New Zealand. Richmond J in his vigorous questioning of the plaintiff's counsel expressed incredulity that Maori title should ever revive once a Crown grant had been issued:[91]

> What an unheard of thing it is that a Maori tribe should come in again by the Maori title, in consequence of the expiry of a trust contained in a Crown grant.

The only possible basis for enforceable native rights would be the provision of an Act of Parliament. This required the judges to consider s. 3 Native Rights Act 1865 which bestowed a jurisdiction on the Supreme Court 'touching the title to land held under Maori custom and usage'. The judges sought to avoid potential questioning of Crown titles, a 'most alarming consequence', by asserting:

---

[88] *Cherokee Nation* v. *State of Georgia*, 30 U.S. 1, 17. None of the nineteenth-century New Zealand judges discussed the applicability or otherwise of the 'domestic dependent nation' concept to Maori tribes.

[89] *Parata*, 80.   [90] *Johnson* v. *M'Intosh*, 588.   [91] *Parata*, 75.

> The Act speaks further on of the 'Ancient Custom and Usage of the Maori people', as if some such body of customary law did in reality exist. But a phrase in a statute cannot call what is non-existent into being. [92]

This particular contention of Prendergast and Richmond certainly did put these judges out on a limb – even in the historical context of the law in their own times. Parliamentary sovereignty as a doctrine required and requires judges to interpret the words of a statute and to give them meaning. Judges in a common law jurisdiction are not supposed to declare a phrase in a statute meaningless. It is not surprising, therefore, that it was on this point that the *Parata* reasoning was criticised by the Privy Council in the *Tamaki* opinion:

> [It] was said in the case of *Wi Parata* v. *Bishop of Wellington*, which was followed by the Court of Appeal in this case, that there is no customary law of the Maoris of which the Courts of law can take cognizance. Their Lordships think that this argument goes too far, and that it is rather late in the day for such an argument to be addressed to a New Zealand Court. It does not seem possible to get rid of the express words of ss. 3 and 4 of the Native Rights Act, 1865. [93]

The Privy Council viewed the Land Claims Ordinance 1841 and the Native Rights Act 1865 as explicit recognitions of Maori custom for the purposes of those statutes. It was statutory provisions – not the Treaty of Waitangi, not international law and not common law – 'of which Courts of law can take cognizance'.

Apart from that criticism of a (non-crucial) aspect of its reasoning, the *Parata* decision stood as good law throughout the period from 1877 to 1912 and beyond. In language drawn from Kent, from the Marshall trilogy and from *Symonds*, Prendergast and Richmond agreed that there were obligations imposed by the *ius gentium* on colonial governments. They had a duty to act 'as supreme protector of aborigines, of securing them against any infringement of their right of occupancy'. This duty was equated in later cases with the notion of the Crown as *parens patriae* being under a solemn obligation to protect the rights of native owners of the soil.[94] The protective principle in *Parata* is virtually always overlooked nowadays, although it was cited in support of Maori

---

[92] *Ibid.*, 79.   [93] *Tamaki*, 577.
[94] *Solicitor-General* v. *Bishop of Wellington* (1901) 19 N.Z.L.R. 665, 686 (C.A.) [Williams J.]

claimants to the Sim Royal Commission on confiscated lands in 1927.[95] The important point for the *Parata* judges, though, was that it is not for the Supreme Court to enforce the government's protective duty to aborigines. In carrying out that duty 'the supreme executive Government must acquit itself, as best it may, of the obligation to respect native proprietary rights, and of necessity must be the sole arbiter of its own justice'.[96] Political and moral matters were none of the court's business.

Parata is followed and applied in New Zealand colonial law

The most crucial feature of the *Parata* decision, as cited and applied in subsequent litigation involving Maori challenges to Crown assertions that native title had been extinguished, was that political and moral matters were none of the courts' business. The precise legal basis for this *Parata* doctrine of non-interference by the colonial courts in relations between Maori and the Crown has been the subject of critical comment. The judgment maintained that Maori tribes were on the same footing as foreigners whose rights were secured by treaty stipulations. Citing two cases concerning the East India Company and Indian states, the judges wrote:

> Transactions with the natives for the cession of their title to the Crown are thus to be regarded as acts of State, and therefore are not examinable by any court. [97]

McHugh, Brookfield and others have commented on the oddness of reasoning that Maori were British subjects of the Crown and yet foreigners, or non-subjects in a protectorate, at one and the same time. McHugh pointed out that it had long been established in English law that the Crown could not rely on 'act of state' in relation to subjects, though he also noted that the *Parata* reasoning was consistent with nineteenth-century policy and practice of Sir John Robinson in Upper Canada.[98] Whether or not 'act of state' was an appropriate doctrinal peg to hang their argument on, however, there can be no doubt that judges then and now do find public-policy reasons for declaring certain issues to be non-justiciable in the courts.

[95] Smith K.C. to the Sim Royal Commission on Confiscated Lands, 1927, Opening submissions on the Waitara confiscations: Hickford, 'Strands from the afterlife of confiscation', p. 29, citing 'Mr Smith's argument on section 1 as to enquiry No 1', undated, CL179/2, f. 1, ANZ.

[96] *Parata*, 78.   [97] *Ibid.*, 79.

[98] P. G. McHugh, 'Tales of constitutional origin and crown sovereignty in New Zealand' (2002) 51 *U.T.L.J.* 69, 77–8.

In contemporary New Zealand common law there are a number of leading cases in which the judges have pointedly refused to interfere in Crown negotiations with Maori concerning the Treaty of Waitangi, statutory or common law rights and proposed legislative changes to Maori rights.[99] In any case, the key point, and the one that later colonial judgments endorsed, was the view of Prendergast CJ and Richmond J that 'the supreme executive Government must acquit itself, as best it may, of the obligation to respect native proprietary rights, and of necessity must be the sole arbiter of its own justice'.

Both judges played leading roles in the later cases. Richmond J wrote the judgment for a full bench of the Court of Appeal (including Prendergast CJ) in 1894 in *Tamaki* v. *Baker*.[100] This litigation was one of a significant number of late nineteenth- and early twentieth-century attempts by Maori litigants to challenge titles to land that had been acquired, they said, without proper extinguishment of pre-existing Maori customary rights.[101] Richmond J expressly reaffirmed his own reasoning in *Parata* with his short-shrift rejection of the argument that the courts had jurisdiction to consider such matters. 'The plaintiff comes here', he wrote, 'on a pure Maori title, and the case is within the direct authority of *Wi Parata* v. *Bishop of Wellington*.' He went on:

> The Crown is under a solemn engagement to observe strict justice in the matter [of native territorial rights], but of necessity it must be left to the conscience of the Crown to determine what is justice. The security of all titles in the country depends on the maintenance of this principle.[102]

The Privy Council reversed the Court of Appeal's judgment in 1901 on the basis that Nireaha Tamaki might have statutorily protected rights under the Native Rights Act 1865. However, their Lordships advice also declared explicitly that they had 'no reason to doubt the correctness' of the conclusions arrived at by the *Parata* judges, as 'the issue of a Crown

---

[99] *Te Runanga o Wharekauri Rekohu* v. *Attorney-General* [1993] 2 N.Z.L.R. 301 (C.A.); *NZ Maori Council* v. *Attorney-General* [2007] N.Z.C.A. 269 (C.A.). In these cases, concerning the Sealords commercial fisheries settlement in 1993 and a proposed Te Arawa historic treaty claims settlement in 2007 respectively, very differently constituted Court of Appeal benches refused to entertain claims by non-signing Maori groups that their customary entitlements had been disregarded in the negotiation by the Crown of those settlement deals.

[100] *Nireaha Tamaki* v. *Baker* (1894) 12 N.Z.L.R. 483 (C.A.) (*Tamaki*, C.A.).

[101] See also *Timu Kerehi* v. *Duff* (1902) 21 N.Z.L.R. 416 discussed in Williams, 'Maori social identification', pp. 743–6.

[102] *Tamaki*, C.A., 488.

grant implies a declaration by the Crown that Native Title has been extinguished'.[103] As to the facts of the *Tamaki* case, the colonial legislature made triply sure that Tamaki obtained no remedy, despite his successful appeal to the Privy Council.[104]

Stout CJ continues the *Parata* orthodoxy

The handover in 1899 from the long-serving Prendergast CJ to the similarly long-serving Stout CJ did not herald a change in view within the colonial judiciary on the issues being discussed in this chapter. The main planks of the old law on the extinguishment of Maori native title rights were reaffirmed. Native title or Treaty of Waitangi rights were always refused recognition unless a litigant could point to a provision in a statute; extinguishment of those rights was a matter for the Crown, not for the courts. This was made abundantly clear by Stout CJ in the 1903 Protest of Bench and Bar against the *Wallis* advice of the Privy Council:

> It is an incorrect phrase to use to speak of the Treaty as a law. The terms of the Treaty were no doubt binding on the conscience of the Crown. The Courts of the Colony, however, had no jurisdiction or power to give effect to any Treaty obligations. These must be fulfilled by the Crown. All lands of the Colony belonged to the Crown, and it was for the Crown under Letters Patent to grant to the parties to the Treaty such lands as the Crown had agreed to grant. The root of title being in the Crown, the Court could not recognize Native title. This has been ever held to be the law in New Zealand . . .[105]

The chief justice then cited *Symonds* and *Parata* as precedents for his proposition, and he noted that the Privy Council in *Tamaki* did not overrule this view. He and his Court of Appeal colleagues had taken exactly the same position in the 1902 re-run of the *Parata* litigation in *Neera*. In that case Stout CJ wrote:

---

[103] *Ibid.*, 383–4.

[104] First, the Privy Council result in relation to the block of land in issue was specifically reversed by The Native Land Claims Adjustment and Laws Amendment Act 1901, s. 27; secondly, the Land Title Protection Act 1901 in s. 2 declared more generally that no Native Land Court order that had subsisted for over ten years could be called into question in any court; thirdly, ongoing litigation initiated by the ever-persistent Nireaha Tamaki was 'discontinued' and further proceedings by him or on his behalf in relation to this land were permanently barred by s. 4 Maori Land Claims and Adjustment and Laws Amendment Act 1904.

[105] 'Protest of the Bench and Bar', p. 732.

> It does not, however, seem to me necessary to inquire how far the
> decision in *Tamaki* v. *Baker* ... has set aside the law and procedure of
> the Supreme Court in dealing with the claims of Maoris to land the titles
> of which have not been ascertained by the Native Land Courts ... The
> important point in that decision bearing on this case seems to me to be
> that it declares that *Wi Parata* v. *The Bishop of Wellington* was rightly
> decided, though it disapproves of certain dicta in the judgment. It is
> affirmed [in *Tamaki*] that the Supreme Court has no jurisdiction to annul
> the grant for matters not appearing on its face, and that 'the issue of a
> Crown grant implies a declaration by the Crown that the Native title has
> been extinguished'. In my opinion, this Court should follow the decision
> in *Wi Parata* v. *The Bishop of Wellington* ... and, following it, an answer
> adverse to the plaintiff ... must be entered. [106]

Some scholars, most particularly Tate, affect to find a development away
from the old law in the 1912 *Korokai* Court of Appeal decision. This case
concerned native title to the bed of Lake Rotorua. Tate describes this
decision as 'Healing the Imperial Breach'. Stout implemented a 'subtle
strategy', Tate asserts, 'attempting to elide some of the Court's past
differences with the Privy Council, albeit somewhat unsuccessfully, in
an attempt to minimize the break of some nine years before'.[107] I can find
no evidence of a 'subtle strategy'. It is true that the judges did on this
occasion decide in favour of Maori litigants. It is true that this decision
was in many respects not at all to the liking of John Salmond, the
Solicitor-General who prepared and presented the Crown's submission
that native title could not exist in a lake-bed area.[108] It is true that some
of the barbed and stinging criticism of the Privy Council to be found in
the 1903 Protest and the *Neera* judgment are not evident in Stout's 1912
reasoning. Nevertheless, Stout CJ and his brethren refused to issue a
declaration that Te Arawa tribes held native title rights over the lake-bed.
Rather, they decided that the Native Land Court, under powers statutorily granted to it in the Native Land Act 1909, had jurisdiction to
inquire into such matters. Despite what Tate calls Stout's 'more concil-
iatory line' on the Treaty of Waitangi as a moral source of Maori rights,
the chief justice did not abandon the *Parata* orthodoxy:[109]

> The decision of *Wi Parata* v. *The Bishop of Wellington* does not derogate
> from that position. It only emphasized the decision in *Reg.* v. *Symonds*

[106] *Neera*, p. 667.
[107] J. W. Tate, '*Tamihana Korokai* and native title: Healing the imperial breach' (2005) 13
    Waikato L. Rev. 108, 109.
[108] Hickford, 'John Salmond and native title', pp. 862–70.   [109] *Korokai*, 344.

that the Supreme Court could take no cognizance of treaty rights not embodied in a statute, and that Native customary title was a kind of tenure that the Court could not deal with. In the case of *Nireaha Tamaki v. Baker* the Judicial Committee of the Privy Council recognized, however, that the Natives had rights under our statute law to their customary lands.

As a matter of fact, the existence or otherwise of native title in the Rotorua lake-bed was never ascertained in the Native Land Court.[110] The Crown preferred to negotiate an out-of-court settlement with Maori on the basis of political expediency and moral suasion, and then to enact legislation rather than run the risk of losing a case in the Land Court.[111]

Conclusion

It has been my contention in this chapter that the polarity perceived between the *Symonds* and the *Parata* judgments by adherents to the golden-thread line of reasoning on aboriginal title is a false dichotomy. Both those cases were leading cases in the old colonial law. There is no example in the colonial era of an ordinary court recognising and enforcing unextinguished native title unless a legislature has granted the court that power. In the understandings of colonial judges and the Privy Council prior to 1921, there was no such thing as the common law doctrine of aboriginal title.

[110] Hickford, 'John Salmond and native title', pp. 921–3.
[111] Native Land Amendment and Native Land Claims Adjustment Act 1922, s. 27.

INDEX

Printed in Great Britain
by Amazon